Persuasion

CURRENT COMMUNICATION
AN ADVANCED TEXT SERIES

Series Editor

Jesse G. Delia *University of Illinois*

VOLUMES IN THE SERIES

James A. Anderson and Timothy P. Meyer
Mediated Communication
A SOCIAL ACTION PERSPECTIVE

Daniel J. O'Keefe
Persuasion
THEORY AND RESEARCH

FORTHCOMING VOLUME

Victoria O'Donnell
Analyzing Media
MAKING MEANINGS OUT OF MEDIA

CURRENT COMMUNICATION is a series of advanced texts spanning the full range of the communication curriculum and including all the core areas of the field. Each volume in the series is a substantive, lucidly written book appropriate for use in advanced undergraduate and beginning graduate-level courses. All the volumes survey current theories and concepts, research and critical literatures, and scholarly methods, but each does this within a distinctive and original framework that makes the material accessible to students while enhancing and shaping understanding of its area for professionals.

Persuasion
Theory and Research

Daniel J. O'Keefe

SAGE PUBLICATIONS
The International Professional Publishers
Newbury Park   London   New Delhi

Copyright © 1990 by Sage Publications, Inc.

For information address:

SAGE Publications, Inc.
2111 West Hillcrest Drive
Newbury Park, California 91320

SAGE Publications Ltd.
28 Banner Street
London EC1Y 8QE
England

SAGE Publications India Pvt. Ltd.
M-32 Market
Greater Kailash I
New Delhi 110 048 India

Printed in the United States of America

Library of Congress Cataloging-in-Publication Data

O'Keefe, Daniel J., 1950-
    Persuasion : theory and research / by Daniel J. O'Keefe.
       p.   cm. -- (Current communication, an advanced text series ;
  v. 2)
    Includes bibliographical references.
    ISBN 0-8039-3368-1
    1. Persuasion (Psychology) I. Title II. Series.
  BF637.P4054   1990
  153.8'52--dc20   90-30772
                                           CIP

FIRST PRINTING, 1990

Contents

Preface

THIS PREFACE IS INTENDED to provide a general framing of this book, and is particularly directed to those who already have some familiarity with the subject matter. Such readers will be able to tell at a glance that this book is in many ways quite conventional (in the general plan of the work, the topics taken up, and so forth). There are a few departures from the standard list of topics, primarily through omissions occasioned largely by space considerations, and some of these might merit a few words. About behavioristic views of attitude (e.g., attitude conditioning processes such as discussed by Staats & Staats, 1958): Although from time to time one sees efforts at reviving such views (e.g., J. K. Burgoon, Burgoon, Miller, & Sunnafrank, 1981; McSweeney & Bierley, 1984), there are good conceptual (e.g., Chomsky, 1959) and empirical (e.g., Allen & Janiszewski, 1989; Brewer, 1974, esp. pp. 21-22) reasons for thinking such efforts to have poor prospects. About the Yale school (e.g., Hovland, Janis, & Kelley, 1953): As pointed out some time ago by C. A. Kiesler, Collins, and Miller (1969, pp. 103-104), the Yale school offered not so much a distinctive theoretical approach as an extensive and far-ranging research program. Thus one will see Yale-school research mentioned throughout the book, but not gathered together under some theoretical housing. About balance theory (e.g., Heider, 1946, 1958) and congruity theory (e.g., Osgood & Tannenbaum, 1955; for a subsequent version, see Bostrom, 1982) — that is, consistency theories other than cognitive dissonance theory: These now seem to be largely of historical interest so far as the study of persuasion is concerned, and to have made relatively little in the way of distinctive enduring contributions to persuasion studies (as opposed to, e.g., social judgment theory — of much the same vintage, but with arguably greater long-term yield). About functional approaches to attitude (e.g., Katz, 1960): Twenty years ago, such views faced

7

some rather serious conceptual and methodological obstacles (see C. A. Kiesler et al., 1969, pp. 302-330), but recently—particularly stimulated by work by Herek (1986, 1987) and DeBono (1987; Snyder & DeBono, 1989)—some progress has been made, especially in the assessment of attitude function (for a nice discussion of which, see Shavitt, 1989). Regrettably, as pointed out by Katz (1989, p. xiv), empirical work in this area has for the most part not yet made the links to social-influence processes that one might desire, and hence these views are not discussed here (several relevant papers appear in Pratkanis, Breckler, & Greenwald, 1989). Students of persuasion may continue to hope that functional theories of attitude will yield fruits that go beyond the insights contributed by expectancy-value formulations of functional ideas (e.g., Belch & Belch, 1987; Lutz, 1981)—beyond, for example, the insight that the same attitude in two persons might be underwritten by very different sorts of beliefs.

Knowledgeable readers will notice these and other omissions—and over-simplifications, bypassed subtleties, elided details, and such. Because this book is pitched at roughly the level of a graduate-undergraduate course, it is likely to be defective both by having sections that are too shallow or general for some and by having segments that are too detailed or technical for others; perhaps one should be satisfied if complaints are not too badly maldistributed across these two categories.

But this aims to be a rather conservative treatment of the persuasion litera-ture, in the sense of being a treatment that seeks to exemplify prudence with respect to generalization. This conservatism is occasioned by two considera-tions. The first is a recognition of the limitations of research evidence based on a few persuasive messages, a matter addressed in Chapter 7. Here I will only point out the curiosity that generalizations about persuasive message effects— generalizations intended to be general across both persons and messages—have commonly been offered on the basis of data from scores or hundreds of human respondents but from only one or two messages. One who is willing to entertain seriously the possibility that the same manipulation may have different effects in different messages should, with such data in hand, be rather cautious.

The second consideration is a recognition of the shortcomings of the usual ways of interpreting and integrating research findings in the persuasion litera-ture. To illuminate the relevant point, consider the following hypothetical puzzle:

> Suppose there have been two studies of the effect on persuasive outcomes of having a concluding metaphor (versus having an ordinary conclusion that does not contain a metaphor) in one's message, but with inconsistent results. In study A, conclusion type made a statistically significant difference (such that greater effectiveness is associated with the metaphor conclusion), but study B failed to replicate this result.
>
> In study A, the participants were female high school students who read a written communication arguing that most people need from 7 to 9 hours of sleep each night. The message was attributed to a professor at the Harvard Medical School; the communicator's identification, including a photograph of the professor (an attractive, youthful-looking male), was provided on a cover sheet immediately

preceding the message. The effect of conclusion type on persuasive outcome was significant, $t(60) = 2.35$, $p < .05$: Messages with a concluding metaphor were significantly more effective than messages with an ordinary (nonmetaphorical) conclusion.

In study B, the participants were male college undergraduates, who listened to an audio message that used a male voice. The message advocated substantial tuition increases (of roughly 50-60%) at the students' university, and presented five arguments to show the necessity of such increases. The communicator was described as a senior at the university, majoring in education. Though the means were ordered as in study A, conclusion type did not significantly affect persuasive outcome, $t(21) = 1.39$, ns.

Why the inconsistency (the failure to replicate)?

The ordinary inclination of many persuasion researchers, I think, would be to entertain possible explanatory stories based on such differences as the receivers' sex ("Females are more influenced by the presence of a metaphorical conclusion than are males"), or the medium ("Metaphorical conclusions make more difference in written messages than in oral messages"), or the advocated position ("Metaphorical conclusions are helpful in proattitudinal messages, but not in counterattitudinal ones"), and so on. Readers with such impulses may well be disappointed or surprised by some of this book's contents and omissions, because for this hypothetical example those sorts of explanatory stories are misplaced. Not only is the direction of effect identical in study A and study B (each finds that the concluding-metaphor message is more effective), but also the *size* of the advantage enjoyed by the concluding-metaphor message is the same in the two studies (expressed as d, the effect size is .61). The difference in the level of statistical significance achieved is a function of the difference in sample size, not any difference in effect size.

Obviously, misunderstandings of statistical significance can lead to misunderstandings of research findings — and when the customary way of assessing the influence of a factor on persuasive outcomes is by tallying up and sorting out the statistically significant and statistically nonsignificant findings, much confusion is possible. We are not yet in a position to do full justice to the issues engaged by the extensive research literature in persuasion, given the current paucity of — and uncertainties and difficulties in doing — relevant, careful, reflective research reviews. Still, consumers of that literature (whether they be naive or sophisticated about matters statistical) are surely due something better than they have usually received.

Of course, one cannot hope to survey the range of work covered here without errors, oversights, and unclarities. These have been reduced by the advice and assistance this project has received from a number of quarters. Students in my persuasion classes at Michigan and Illinois have helped make my lectures — and so this book — clearer than otherwise might have been the case. For helpful commentary on the manuscript, I am grateful to Sally Jackson, David Swanson, Jesse Delia, and particularly to Greg Shepherd. And I thank Barbara O'Keefe both for useful commentary and for life support.

Part I

Introduction

This introductory section provides some general background information bearing on the study of persuasive communication. The concept of persuasion, the concept of attitude, and various attitude measurement procedures are discussed.

1

Persuasion and
the Concept of Attitude

THIS BOOK SURVEYS social scientific theory and research concerning persuasive communication. The relevant work, as will become apparent, is scattered across the academic landscape — in communication, psychology, advertising, marketing, political science, law, and so on. Although the breadth and depth of this literature are such as to rule out a completely comprehensive and detailed treatment, the main lines of work are at least sketched here.

This introductory chapter begins, naturally enough, with a discussion of the concept of persuasion. But because social scientific treatments of persuasion have closely linked persuasion and attitude change, the concept of attitude is discussed as well, and some common attitude assessment procedures are described.

THE CONCEPT OF PERSUASION

ABOUT DEFINITIONS

A common way to clarify a concept is to provide a definition of it, for a definition specifies some set of instances to which the concept applies. A definition of "persuasion" can illuminate the concept of persuasion by specifying some delimited set of cases that are to be labeled "persuasion." So, for instance, a definition of persuasion that characterizes persuasion as "human communication designed to influence others by modifying their beliefs, values, or attitudes" (Simons, 1976, p. 21) implicitly identifies certain instances of communication as "persuasion" (while excluding other cases from the category of "persuasion").

But definitions can be troublesome things, precisely because they commonly are treated as providing sharp-edged distinctions, as somehow drawing sharp lines (between what is and is not persuasion, in the case of definitions of persuasion). And what is troublesome about such sharp lines is that, no matter where they're drawn, it is possible to sustain objections to their location. Thus one definition might be deemed unsatisfactory because it is too broad (that is, it includes cases that it shouldn't), while another is deemed unsatisfactory because it is too narrow (it excludes instances that it should include).

FUZZY EDGES AND PARADIGM CASES

Why are definitions almost inevitably open to criticism, no matter where the definitional lines are drawn? Because most concepts have fuzzy edges, gray areas in which application of the concept is arguable. For any concept, there are some cases that virtually everyone agrees *are* cases of the concept (few would deny that a chair is an instance of the category "furniture") and there are some cases that virtually everyone agrees *are not* cases of the concept (a pencil is not an instance of furniture) — but there are also some cases that fall in a gray area and can give rise to disagreements (Is a television set a piece of furniture? Or perhaps is it an appliance?). And no matter how the line is drawn, some objection is possible. If you define furniture so as to include televisions, those who believe televisions are not furniture will object; if your definition of furniture excludes televisions, those who believe televisions are furniture will object.

So, for example, if one defines "persuasion" in such a way as to distinguish cases of "persuasion" from cases of "manipulation" by requiring that in genuine instances of persuasion the persuader "acts in good faith" (as do Burnell & Reeve, 1984), then some will object that the definition is too narrow; after all, such a definition almost certainly excludes at least some instances of advertising. But including "manipulation" as an instance of "persuasion" will meet objections from those who think it important to exclude instances of sheer "manipulation" from the definition of persuasion.

Happily, it is possible to clarify a concept without having to be committed to a sharp-edged definition of the concept (and thus without having to settle such border disputes). Such clarification can be obtained by focusing on the shared features of paradigm cases of the concept. Paradigm cases of a concept are the sorts of instances that nearly everyone would agree are instances of the concept in question; they are straightforward, uncontroversial examples. By identifying the common features of paradigm cases, one can get a sense of the concept's ordinary central application, without having to draw sharp-edged definitional lines.

THE COMMON FEATURES
OF PARADIGM CASES OF PERSUASION

Consider, then: What is ordinarily involved when we say that someone (a persuader) has persuaded someone else (a persuadee)? In such straightforward applications of the concept of persuasion, what sorts of shared features can be observed? (For an alternative to the following analysis, see Simons, 1986.)

First, when we say that one person persuaded another, we ordinarily identify a successful attempt to influence. That is, the notion of *success* is embedded in the concept of persuasion. Notice, for instance, that it doesn't make sense to say, "I persuaded him but failed." One can say, "I *tried* to persuade him, but failed," but to say simply "I persuaded him" is to imply a successful attempt to influence.[1]

Recognition that persuasion is connected to the notion of success leads directly to the next two features of paradigm cases of persuasion: the presence of some criterion or goal, and the existence of some correlative intent to reach that goal. To speak of "success" is to imply some standard of success, some goal, some criterion (one cannot, for instance, win a race if there is no finish line). And in the case of persuasion, the usual implication drawn from the invocation of the concept is that the persuader had some intention of achieving the persuasive goal. For example, if I say, "I persuaded Sally to vote for Jones," you are likely to infer that I intended to obtain that effect. For just that reason it is entirely understandable that someone might say, "I accidentally persuaded Mary to vote for Brown" precisely in the circumstance in which the speaker does not want a hearer to draw the usual inference of intent; absent such mention of accident, the ordinary inference will be that the suasion was purposeful.

A fourth feature shared by paradigm cases of persuasion is some measure of freedom (free will, free choice, voluntary action) on the persuadee's part. Consider, for example, a circumstance in which a person is knocked unconscious by a robber, who then takes the victim's money; one would not (except humorously) say that the victim had been "persuaded" to give the money. By contrast, being induced by a television ad to make a donation freely to public television is pretty obviously an instance of "persuasion."

Notice that when the persuadee's freedom is minimized or questionable, it becomes correspondingly questionable whether "persuasion" is genuinely involved; one no longer has a straightforward exemplary case of persuasion. Suppose a robber threatens to shoot the victim if the money is not forthcoming, and the victim complies: Is this an instance of persuasion? We need not settle this question here; settling this question would require some sharp line that distinguishes persuasion and nonpersuasion (and that sharp line is not something sought here). It is enough to notice that such cases are borderline instances of persuasion, precisely because the persuadee's freedom is not so clear-cut as in paradigm instances.

Fifth, paradigm cases of persuasion are ones in which the effects are achieved through communication (and perhaps especially through the medium of language). That is, persuasion is something achieved through one person communicating with another. My physically lifting you and throwing you off the roof of a building is something quite different from my talking you into jumping off the same roof; the latter might possibly be a case of persuasion (depending on the circumstances, exactly what I've said to you, and so on), but the former is certainly not. And what distinguishes these two instances is that communication is involved in the latter case, but not in the former.

Finally, paradigm cases of persuasion involve a change in the mental state of the persuadee (principally as a precursor to a change in behavior). Some ordinary instances of persuasion may be described as involving *only* a change in mental state (as in "I persuaded Joe that the United States should refuse to recognize the authority of the World Court"). But even when behavioral change is involved (as in "I persuaded Charlie to take piano lessons"), there is ordinarily presumed to be some underlying change in mental state that gave rise to the behavioral change; in learning that Charlie was persuaded to take piano lessons, we might plausibly presume (depending on the circumstances) any number of appropriate underlying changes in mental state (Charlie came to believe that his piano skills were poor, that his skills could be improved by taking lessons, or whatever). Thus even where a persuader's eventual aim is to influence what people *do* (to influence, say, how people vote, or what products they buy), at least in paradigm cases of persuasion that aim is ordinarily seen to be accomplished by changing what people *think* (for instance, what people think of the political candidate, or of the product). That is, persuasion is ordinarily conceived of as involving influencing others by influencing their mental states (rather than by somehow influencing their conduct directly).

In persuasion theory and research, the relevant mental state has most commonly been characterized as an *attitude* (and thus the concept of attitude receives direct discussion later in this chapter). Indeed, some have claimed that "persuasion inherently has attitude change as its goal" (Beisecker & Parson, 1972, p. 5). Even where a persuader's ultimate goal is the modification of another's behavior, that goal is typically seen to be achieved through a process of attitude change—the presumption being that attitudes are "precursors of behavior" (A. R. Cohen, 1964, p. 138), that "attitude change is a principal determinant of behavioral change" (Beisecker & Parson, 1972, p. 5). The preoccupation of persuasion researchers with attitude has not gone unchallenged (e.g., Jaccard, 1981; Larson & Sanders, 1975; G. R. Miller, 1980), but attitude remains central to most investigators' treatments of persuasion.

A DEFINITION AFTER ALL?

These shared features of exemplary cases of persuasion can be strung together into something that looks like a definition of persuasion: a successful intentional effort at influencing another's mental state through communication in a circumstance in which the persuadee has some measure of freedom. But it should be apparent that constructing such a definition would not eliminate the fuzzy edges of the concept of persuasion. Such a definition leaves it open to dispute just how much "success" is required, just how "intentional" the effort must be, and so on.

Hence by recognizing these shared features of paradigm cases of persuasion, one can get a sense of the central core of the concept of persuasion, but one need not draw sharp definitional boundaries around that concept. Indeed, these paradigm-case features permit one to see clearly just how it is that definitional disputes can arise — for instance, disputes over the issue of just how much, and what sorts, of freedom the persuadee must have before an instance qualifies as an instance of "persuasion." It is also easy to see that there can be no very satisfactory definitive solution to these disputes, given the fuzzy edges that the concept of persuasion naturally has. Definitions of persuasion can serve useful functions, but a clear sense of the concept of persuasion can be had without resorting to a hard-edged definition.

THE CONCEPT OF ATTITUDE

As mentioned above, the mental state that has been seen (in theory and research) to be most centrally implicated in persuasion is that of attitude. The concept of attitude has a long history (see Fleming, 1967). Early uses of the term referred to posture or physical arrangement (as in someone's being in "the attitude of prayer"), uses that can be seen today in descriptions of dance or airplane orientation. Gradually, however, attitudes came to be seen as "orientations of mind" rather than of body, as internal states that exerted influence on overt behavior.

Perhaps it was inevitable, thus, that in the early part of the twentieth century, the emerging field of social psychology should have seized upon the concept of attitude as an important one. "Attitude" offered to social psychologists a distinctive psychological mechanism for understanding and explaining individual variation in social conduct, and indeed by 1935 Allport could declare attitude to be *the* central concept in social psychology. Understandably, then, it has been within social psychology that the greatest amount of conceptual attention has been given to attitude.

This extensive conceptual attention has not, however, produced any easy consensus on a definition or conception of attitude. The astonishing range of diverse views will not be canvassed here, as there are a number of extant discussions of the varieties of attitude definition and of the issues surrounding that task (e.g., Audi, 1972; Greenwald, 1968; McGuire, 1969, 1985; G. R. Miller, Burgoon, & Burgoon, 1984); one may see something of the variety of available views by examining Audi (1974), Bagozzi (1978), Bagozzi, Tybout, Craig, and Sternthal (1979), Breckler (1984), Lalljee, Brown, and Ginsburg (1984), and Maze (1973).

If there is a predominant treatment of attitudes, however, it is the view that an attitude is a person's general evaluation of an object (where "object" is understood in a broad sense, as encompassing persons, events, products, policies, institutions, and so on). The notion of an attitude as an evaluative judgment of (reaction to) an object is a common theme in definitions of attitude, and (as made clear by Fishbein & Ajzen, 1975, pp. 59-89) is also implicit in traditional attitude assessment techniques.

Beyond the broad idea that an attitude is an evaluation of an object, there are three other points of apparent consensus concerning the concept of attitude. One is that, overwhelmingly, attitudes are learned (as opposed to being innate); attitudes represent a residue of experience. It may be that humans enter life with some preestablished evaluative judgments, but overwhelmingly attitudes are taken to be a function of the sorts of experiences a person has (and thus with changing experiences, a person's attitudes may change). Second, attitudes are taken to be relatively enduring. That is, an attitude is something different from a mood, from a temporary emotional state. To say that attitudes are enduring is not to say that they cannot change, of course; indeed, precisely because attitudes are learned, they are susceptible to change. Third, attitudes are taken to influence conduct. Attitudes, that is to say, are not mental entities that float about unconnected to action. Rather, attitudes exert an influence on behavior. This influence may not be simple or direct—an attitude will not *guarantee* that a person will act in some specified fashion, but instead will simply predispose the person to act in some ways rather than in others—but attitudes are presumed to play some role in action.

ATTITUDE MEASUREMENT TECHNIQUES

If persuasion is conceived of as fundamentally involving attitude change, then the systematic study of persuasion requires means of assessing persons' attitudes: Without procedures for measuring attitudes, one cannot tell (for example) whether a given persuasive effort has induced any attitude change.

As it happens, the assessment of attitudes is itself a substantial research area. A great many different attitude measurement techniques have been proposed, and there is a large literature relevant to the use of attitude measures in specific circumstances such as public opinion polling and survey research. The intention here is to give a brief treatment of some exemplary attitude measurement techniques; more detailed information can be obtained from articles in the anthologies of Fishbein (1967c) and Summers (1970) and from the reviews of Dawes and Smith (1985) and W. A. Scott (1969).

Attitude assessment procedures can be usefully distinguished by the degree of directness with which they assess the respondent's evaluation of the attitude object. Some techniques obtain an evaluative judgment quite directly; others do so in somewhat more roundabout ways.

DIRECT TECHNIQUES

Direct attitude measurement techniques are ones that directly ask the respondent for an evaluative judgment of the attitude object. There are two commonly employed direct assessment procedures: semantic differential evaluative scales and single-item attitude questions.

SEMANTIC DIFFERENTIAL EVALUATIVE SCALES One popular means of directly assessing attitude is to employ the evaluative scales from the semantic differential scale of Osgood, Suci, and Tannenbaum (1957). In this procedure, respondents rate the attitude object on a number of (typically) 7-point bipolar scales that are end anchored by evaluative adjective pairs (such as good-bad or desirable-undesirable). For example, a measure of attitude toward the United Nations might be presented as follows.

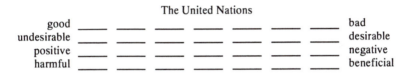

The accompanying instructions ask the respondent to place a check mark at the point on the scale that best represents the respondent's judgment. The investigator can straightforwardly assign numerical values to the scale points (say, +3 for the extreme positive point, through 0 for the midpoint, to –3 for the extreme negative end) and then sum each person's responses so as to obtain an indication of the person's attitude toward (general evaluative judgment of) the object.

SINGLE-ITEM ATTITUDE MEASURES Another direct means of assessing attitude is simply to have the respondent complete a single questionnaire item that asks for the relevant judgment. For example:

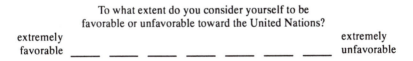

There are, of course, various ways of wording the question and of anchoring the scale (e.g., "In general, how much do you like the United Nations?" with end anchors "very much" and "not at all"), and it is possible to vary the number of scale points, but the basic procedure is the same.

This is an understandably attractive technique for circumstances such as public-opinion polling. The attitude assessment can be undertaken orally (as in telephone surveys or face-to-face interviewing); the question is typically straightforward and easily comprehended by the respondent; the question can be asked (and answered) in a short time.

The central drawback of single-item assessments of attitude is potentially weak reliability. That is, a person's response to a single attitude question may not be as dependable an indicator of attitude as the person's response to three or four items all getting at roughly the same thing.

FEATURES OF DIRECT TECHNIQUES Direct attitude measurement techniques obviously offer the advantage of being simple and straightforward, easy to administer, and so forth. Another advantage of these techniques is that they are relatively easy to construct. For instance, a public-opinion survey of attitudes toward possible presidential candidates can easily accommodate some new possible candidate: The surveyor simply asks the standard question but inserts the name of the new candidate. And general evaluative scales from the semantic differential can obviously be used for rating all sorts of different attitude objects (consumer products, political candidates, government policies, and so on); to assess attitudes toward Crest toothpaste rather than toward the United Nations, one simply makes the appropriate substitution above the rating scales. (However, this may be a false economy: for arguments emphasizing the importance of customizing semantic differential evaluative scales for each different attitude object, see Fishbein & Ajzen, 1975, pp. 77-78.)

One salient disadvantage of these direct techniques is that, because they are so direct, they yield an estimate *only* of the respondent's attitude. Of course, this is not a drawback if all the researcher wants to know is the respondent's attitude. But very often investigators will want other information as well (about, for example, beliefs that might lie behind the attitude), and in such circumstances direct attitude assessment techniques will need to be supplemented or replaced by other procedures.

QUASI-DIRECT TECHNIQUES

Quasi-direct attitude measurement techniques assess attitude not by directly eliciting an evaluative judgment of the attitude object, but by eliciting information that is obviously attitude-relevant and that offers a straightforward basis for attitude assessment. For example, paired-comparison procedures and ranking techniques (see, e.g., Hughes, 1971, pp. 103-105) do not ask directly for an evaluation of any single attitude object, but ask for comparative judgments of several objects: In a paired-comparison technique, the respondent is asked a series of questions about the relative evaluation of each of a number of pairs of objects (e.g., "Which candidate do you prefer, Archer or Barker? Archer or Cooper? Barker or Cooper?"), and in a ranking procedure, the respondent ranks a set of attitude objects (e.g., "Rank order these various leisure activities, from your most favorite to your least favorite"). The obtained responses obviously permit an investigator to draw some conclusions about the respondent's evaluation of a given object. Similarly, the "attitude pie" technique (Lull & Cappella, 1981) does not ask directly for an overall evaluation, but instead asks respondents to indicate separately (by dividing a circle into "slices") the degree of their positive, negative, and noncommittal sentiments about the attitude object; the investigator then combines these reports into an overall measure of attitude.

The two most common and well-known quasi-direct attitude measurement procedures, however, are those devised by Louis Thurstone and by Rensis

Likert. In these procedures, the respondent's attitude is inferred from judgments of (or reactions to) statements that are rather obviously attitude-relevant. The attitude assessment instrument, then, consists of a number of statements to which the respondent reacts (say, by agreeing or disagreeing with each statement), and the respondent's attitude is inferred from the pattern of responses.

Obviously, however, if a researcher is going to gauge respondents' attitudes by examining their reactions to a set of statements, not just *any* statements will do; for example, one is not likely to learn much about attitudes toward the United Nations by assessing respondents' agreement with a statement such as "Baseball is a better game than football." Thus the task faced in constructing a Thurstone or Likert attitude scale is the task of selecting items (statements) that appear to serve as suitable indicators of attitude. One may start with a large pool of statements that might possibly be included on a final attitude instrument, but the problem is to somehow winnow that pool down. Thurstone and Likert proposed different methods for doing so, with corresponding differences in the nature of their attitude scales.

THURSTONE ATTITUDE SCALES The idea that one might obtain information about a person's attitude by examining his or her reactions to attitude-relevant statements was the basis for one of the earliest attitude assessment procedures, that developed by L. L. Thurstone (1931; Thurstone & Chave, 1929). What follows is a brief and abstracted description of Thurstone's procedures (for details, see Green, 1954).

The investigator begins by assembling a pool of a hundred or so possible items, opinion statements that may indicate something about a person's attitude toward the object under investigation. For example, if the topic of investigation concerns attitudes toward the First Federal Bank, the initial pool might include statements such as these: "This bank is reliable"; "This bank is inefficient"; "I would prefer not to do business with this bank"; "This bank is old-fashioned"; "This bank has unfriendly personnel"; "This bank is trustworthy"; and "This bank is not dynamic."

Then a hundred or so people are asked to serve as "judges" of these items. The judges are asked to indicate the degree of favorableness or unfavorableness toward the attitude object that would be implied by agreement with each item. Concretely, the judges are asked to sort the items into 11 categories, equally spaced along the evaluative dimension; category 1 is to contain statements indicating the most extreme negative attitude toward the object, category 11 is for statements indicating the most extreme positive attitude toward the object, category 6 is for statements that indicate a neutral attitude, and so on.

Items on which the judges disagree widely are discarded. Thurstone's procedure is aimed at identifying statements such that one can dependably tell something about a person's attitude from whether they agree with a given statement; hence if a statement is not consistently seen (by the judges) as indicating a given attitude, the statement is a poor candidate for inclusion in the final attitude scale. For instance, the item "This bank is old-fashioned" as a possible item for assessing attitude toward a given bank might engender such disagreement; some judges might think agreement with this item indicated a positive attitude (where "old-fashioned" was taken to indicate solidity, reliability, and the like) whereas other judges might think agreement would indicate a negative attitude (where "old-fashioned" was taken to mean stodgy, behind the times, and so forth). If this item were to appear in the final attitude scale, one would not be able to make sound inferences about the attitude of a respondent who agreed with the statement; hence the item is discarded.

The final attitude scale is composed of approximately 20 items selected from among those still remaining in the pool. The investigator computes the average scale value for each of the remaining items (that is, the average across the judges' ratings), and then selects 20 or so items such that they are equally spaced along the evaluative dimension. Thus, for instance, an investigator might ideally try to obtain items with scale values of 1.0, 1.5, 2.0, 2.5, . . . 10.0, 10.5, and 11.0.

When this attitude scale is administered, respondents are instructed to check all the items with which they agree. A respondent's attitude score consists of the average scale value of the items that are endorsed. A respondent who agreed with items that had scale values of 9.3, 10.0, and 10.7 would have an attitude score of 10.0 (a strongly positive attitude, reflecting the respondent's agreement with three highly positive items).

Two possible problems with Thurstone's method of attitude scale construction have been noted. The first is that the attitudes of the judges may influence their placement of items along the evaluative dimension, thus biasing the scale; the empirical evidence, however, suggests that any changes in scale values are likely to be small (see M. Sherif & Hovland, 1961), and in any event the judges should be representative of the population to be studied. The other potential difficulty is that judges may not clearly understand the task they are asked to perform (Romer, 1983), but careful instructions may minimize this problem.

LIKERT ATTITUDE SCALES The attitude measurement technique developed by Likert (1932), like Thurstone's technique, draws inferences about a respondent's attitude from his or her agreement or disagreement with attitude-relevant statements. Thus, as in the case of Thurstone scales, constructing a Likert attitude scale begins with assembling a large number of attitude-relevant statements as an initial pool from which the scale items will be selected. But Likert's procedure differs from Thurstone's in the manner of selecting items from the pool and in the sort of response that respondents are asked to give. The following is a brief description of Likert's procedures (for details, see Likert, 1932, or Green, 1954).

The investigator begins by discarding any neutral or ambiguous statements from the initial item pool. He or she then has test respondents react to each of the remaining statements. These test respondents are asked to indicate the extent of their agreement or disagreement with each item, commonly on a 5-point scale. For example:

This bank is reliable

strongly   strongly
agree _____ _____ _____ _____ _____ disagree

Each response is then scored from 1 to 5, with 5 representing the most favorable response; in the example above, the "strongly agree" pole would be scored as 5 and the "strongly disagree" pole scored as 1 (note, however, that if the item had been worded "This bank is unreliable," then the scoring would be reversed, with "strongly agree" scored as 1). An overall attitude score can then be computed for each test respondent; if there are 100 items in the initial pool, overall attitude scores could range from 100 (the most negative attitude possible) to 500 (the most positive attitude).

An item analysis is then undertaken, in which responses to each item are correlated with the overall attitude score. The 20 or 25 items with the highest correlations are then selected for the final attitude scale. The selected items are presumably the best indicators of attitude, because they are the items most strongly associated with (most predictive of) the overall attitude score.

On the final attitude scale, the selected items are presented as in the test research, with 5-point scales assessing the respondent's agreement with the item; overall attitude is estimated by the total across the items.

FEATURES OF QUASI-DIRECT TECHNIQUES There is a good deal of variation in quasi-direct attitude assessment techniques, but, as a rule, these procedures provide more information than do direct attitude measurement techniques. For example, when a Thurstone or Likert scale has been employed, a researcher can see what specific items were especially likely to be endorsed by respondents with particular attitudes; an investigator who finds that, for instance, those with unfavorable attitudes toward the bank very often agreed with the statement "This bank has unfriendly personnel" may well have learned about a possible cause of those negative attitudes. Similarly, ranking techniques can give information about a large number of attitudes and so provide insight about comparative evaluations; the "attitude pie" technique offers the possibility of distinguishing respondents with neutral attitudes from those who are indifferent; and so on. Precisely because quasi-direct procedures involve acquiring attitude-relevant information (rather than direct attitude assessments), these procedures offer information not available with direct measurement techniques.

But this additional information is obtained at a cost. Thurstone and Likert attitude scales have to be constructed anew for each different attitude object; obviously one can't use the First Federal Bank attitude scale to assess attitudes toward Greg's Golf Shop or Randy's Record Store, or even toward City Savings and Loan. (Indeed, the substantial effort needed to obtain a sound Thurstone or Likert scale is often a deterrent to the use of such techniques.) And procedures such as paired-comparison ratings, ranking tasks, and the attitude pie technique may take more time to administer than would direct attitude measures.

INDIRECT TECHNIQUES

Indirect attitude measurement techniques assess attitude not by directly eliciting an evaluation of the attitude object, or even by eliciting information obviously relevant to such an overall evaluation, but instead by some more roundabout (indirect) means. Quite a few different indirect techniques have appeared in the literature; useful reviews include Dawes and Smith (1985) and Kidder and Campbell (1970). Three examples of indirect attitude assessment procedures are discussed here: physiological indices, information tests, and the lost-letter technique.

PHYSIOLOGICAL INDICES One group of indirect attitude measurement techniques relies on physiological indices as potential indicators of attitude. These have included measures of pupil dilation and contraction, galvanic skin response (a measure of the electrical resistance of the skin), heart rate, respiration rate, and perspiration rate. Each different physiological index has spawned a body of research bearing on the utility of that index as a possible indicator of attitude, and different substantive issues arise in those various lines of research. Nevertheless, there is a general conclusion that seems appropriately drawn about the physiological indices mentioned above: These indices may assess general arousal, but do not measure attitude (Mueller, 1970; Woodmansee, 1970; compare Tognacci & Cook, 1975). Specifically, the evidence suggests that at best these indices can indicate something about a respondent's degree of arousal or anxiety, but they cannot distinguish the direction of the associated affect (cannot distinguish positive arousal from negative arousal); and of course this inability to distinguish positive from negative affect makes these indices unsuitable as measures of attitude. However, there has recently been some work suggesting that an index of facial EMG (electromyographic) activity — the contractions of the major muscles in the face — holds some promise as a physiological attitude measure (e.g., Cacioppo, Petty, Losch, & Kim, 1986; for a general discussion, see Cacioppo, Petty, & Geen, 1989).

INFORMATION TESTS Another class of indirect attitude assessment procedures is known as "information tests." These tests are based on the idea that persons' attitudes can influence their factual judgments, and hence by examining a respondent's judgments about factual matters one can learn something about the respondent's attitude.

Hammond's (1948) error-choice attitude measurement technique is an example of such an information test. In this procedure, respondents are presented with a number of multiple-choice questions concerning matters of fact, with two answers available for each question — but both answers are actually incorrect. The respondent is forced into choosing a wrong answer (hence the label "error-choice"), with the respondent's attitude being inferred from the nature of the wrong answer chosen. For example, Hammond's assessment of labor-management attitudes included an item like this one: "Financial reports show that out of every business dollar, (a) 16 cents is profit, (b) 3 cents is profit," with the true figure midway between those given. The assumption (which

Hammond showed to be sound) was that persons with pro-management attitudes would likely underestimate profits, while those with pro-labor attitudes would probably give an overestimate.

Other "information test" ways of assessing attitude can be seen as variations on this basic procedure (see Kidder & Campbell, 1970, pp. 351-358). One can provide more than two erroneous choices (to assess the respondent's degree of error); one can include items where the truth is indeterminate, but force respondents to choose between two extreme answers; one can ask open-ended questions ("What percentage of business dollar volume is profit?"); and so forth. Whatever particular form an "information test" attitude measure takes, however, the critical question is whether the items on the instrument are in fact diagnostic of attitude — that is, whether in fact persons' attitudes are being reflected in their answers to the items. One cannot justifiably assume that answers to a given question will be influenced by attitude; instead, validating evidence needs to be acquired in the course of constructing the attitude measure.

LOST-LETTER TECHNIQUE The lost-letter technique (Milgram, Mann, & Harter, 1965) is an indirect means of assessing attitudes in a community. Briefly, the technique involves addressing a large number of envelopes to two (fictitious) organizations that appear to have opposing views on the attitude topic. If the topic is abortion, for instance, the researcher addresses half the envelopes to an organization whose name clearly indicates that the organization is pro-life; the other half of the envelopes are addressed to an organization that is clearly pro-choice. These envelopes are stamped and then randomly scattered in the community. A person who comes upon an envelope will presumably treat it as a "lost letter" that was supposed to be mailed. The question is whether the finder will mail the letter, and the presumption is that finders will not be willing to mail letters to organizations opposing their views, but will mail letters to organizations whose attitudes are in line with their own. All the mailed envelopes, of course, come to the researcher, who tallies the number of pro-life and pro-choice letters received. If, for instance, many more pro-choice letters are received than pro-life letters, the conclusion will be that, in the community studied, pro-choice attitudes predominate. (For examples and discussion of this technique, see Bolton, 1974; Hines, 1980; Shotland, Berger, & Forsythe, 1970.)

A common problem with this technique, as noted by Dawes and Smith (1985, p. 544), is that the return rate tends to be closer to a 50-50 split than more direct attitude measures (such as public-opinion surveys in the community) would suggest; it may be that some people mail the letters no matter what their own opinions are, and others don't mail the letters no matter what their opinions are, thus tending to minimize the impact of those persons whose letter mailing is influenced by their attitudes.

FEATURES OF INDIRECT TECHNIQUES Indirect attitude assessment techniques are a varied lot: Some involve paper-and-pencil questionnaires (as in the error-choice technique), but others do not; some can be used to assess the attitude of particular individuals, but others (such as the lost-letter technique) cannot; some can be employed effectively only in a laboratory setting (the physiological techniques, for instance, require appropriate equipment), but others are equally at home in laboratory or field settings.

What these techniques have in common, of course, is that they are indirect. Their indirectness naturally suggests the most appropriate circumstances for use: indirect attitude assessment techniques are likely to be most attractive in circumstances in which one fears respondents may, for whatever reason, distort their true attitudes. In most research on persuasion, however, these circumstances are rather uncommon (respondents are assured anonymity, message topics are generally not unusually sensitive ones, and so on) and, consequently, indirect attitude measures are rarely employed.

SUMMARY

As this brief survey suggests, a variety of different attitude measurement techniques are available. The overwhelmingly most frequently used attitude measurement procedures are direct or quasi-direct techniques; reliability and validity are more readily established for attitude measures based on these techniques than for measures derived from indirect procedures. And direct procedures are often preferred over quasi-direct techniques because of the effort required for constructing Thurstone or Likert scales. But which specific attitude assessment procedure an investigator employs in a given instance will depend on the particulars of the situation. Depending on what the researcher wants to find out, the amount of time available to prepare the attitude questionnaire, the amount of time available to question respondents, the sensitivity of the attitude topic, and so forth, different techniques will recommend themselves.

CONCLUSION

This introductory chapter has elucidated the concepts of persuasion and attitude and has described some common attitude assessment procedures. In the following sections, extant social scientific theory and research about persuasion is reviewed. Part II discusses several theoretical perspectives that have been prominent in the explanation of persuasive effects. Part III surveys research on various factors influencing persuasive effects. Part IV reviews research concerning how and why persons produce persuasive messages.

NOTE

1. For those familiar with the distinctions among locutionary, illocutionary, and perlocutionary speech acts (Searle, 1969): This point can also be expressed by saying that to persuade is a perlocutionary act, whereas (for example) to urge is an illocutionary act.

Part II

Theoretical Approaches to Persuasive Effects

In the five chapters that follow, five different theoretical approaches to understanding persuasive effects are surveyed. Two of these (social judgment theory, discussed in Chapter 2, and the elaboration likelihood model, discussed in Chapter 6) are viewpoints distinctively focused on persuasive communication. The other approaches (information-integration models of attitude, in Chapter 3; cognitive dissonance theory, in Chapter 4; and the theory of reasoned action, in Chapter 5), though not directly theories of persuasion, nevertheless are viewpoints that have enjoyed prominence in the study of persuasion. In good measure this is a consequence of persuasion's having been conceptualized as fundamentally involving attitude change, for the approaches surveyed in Chapters 3, 4, and 5 either are or grew out of theories of attitude. All the views considered here, however, have stimulated relatively extensive research and have reasonably well-considered applications to persuasion and social influence processes.

2

Social Judgment Theory

SOCIAL JUDGMENT THEORY is a theoretical perspective most closely associ-
ated with Muzafer Sherif, Carolyn Sherif, and their associates, particularly Carl
Hovland and Roger Nebergall (C. W. Sherif, Sherif, & Nebergall, 1965; M.
Sherif & Hovland, 1961; for a classic review, see C. A. Kiesler, Collins, &
Miller, 1969, pp. 238-301; for additional discussions, see Granberg, 1982; C.
W. Sherif, 1980). The central tenet of social judgment theory is that attitude
change is mediated by judgmental processes and effects. More specifically, the
claim is that the effect of a persuasive communication depends upon the way in
which the receiver evaluates the position it advocates. Thus persuasion is seen

as a two-step process in which initially the receiver assesses the position advocated by the message, and attitude change occurs after that judgment (with the amount and direction of change dependent upon that judgment). As the receiver's assessment of the position being forwarded by the communication varies, different persuasive effects will occur.

The plausibility of this general approach should be apparent. It surely seems likely that our reaction to a particular persuasive communication will depend (at least in part) on what we think of (how favorable we are toward) the point of view it advocates. But this suggests that, in order to understand a receiver's reaction to a message on a given issue, it is important to understand how the receiver assesses the various positions on that issue (that is, the various stands that a message might advocate). Hence the next section discusses the nature of persons' judgments of the alternative positions on an issue. A subsequent section discusses receivers' reactions to persuasive messages. A concluding section explores some criticisms of social judgment theory.

JUDGMENTS OF
ALTERNATIVE POSITIONS ON AN ISSUE

On any given persuasive issue, there are likely to be a number of different positions or points of view available. Consider, for example, some different possible stands on an issue such as abortion: One might think that all abortion should be illegal, or that a legal abortion should be permitted only if childbirth would bring about the woman's death, or that a legal abortion should be permitted only during the first three months of pregnancy, or that a woman should be permitted to have a legal abortion whenever she requests it (and of course these don't exhaust the possibilities). A person is likely to have varying assessments of these different positions—a person will likely find some of the positions acceptable, some of the positions objectionable, and some neither particularly acceptable nor unacceptable. Since, from a social judgment theory point of view, the person's reaction to a persuasive communication on this topic will depend on the person's judgment of the position the message advocates, it is important to be able to assess persons' judgments of the various possible positions. The assessment procedure offered by social judgment theory is known as the Ordered Alternatives questionnaire.

THE ORDERED ALTERNATIVES QUESTIONNAIRE

An Ordered Alternatives questionnaire provides the respondent with a set of statements, each representing a different point of view on the issue being studied. These statements are chosen so as to represent the range of positions on the issue (from the extreme view on one side to the extreme view on the other), and are arranged in order (from one extreme to the other)—hence the name "Ordered Alternatives." (Commonly, 9 or 11 statements are used, but what is important is that all the prevailing views on the issue are somehow represented in rank order.) For example, the following Ordered Alternatives questionnaire was developed for research on a presidential election campaign (M. Sherif & Hovland, 1961, pp. 136-137; for other examples, see Hovland, Harvey, & Sherif, 1957; C. W. Sherif, 1980).

_____ (A) The election of the Republican presidential and vice presidential candidates in November is absolutely essential from all angles in the country's interests.

_____ (B) On the whole the interests of the country will be served best by the election of the Republican candidates for president and vice president in the coming election.

_____ (C) It seems that the country's interests would be better served if the presidential and vice presidential candidates of the Republican party are elected this November.

_____ (D) Although it is hard to decide, it is probable that the country's interests may be better served if the Republican presidential and vice presidential candidates are elected in November.

_____ (E) From the point of view of the country's interests, it is hard to decide whether it is preferable to vote for the presidential and vice presidential candidates of the Republican party or the Democratic party in November.

_____ (F) Although it is hard to decide, it is probable that the country's interests may be better served if the Democratic presidential and vice presidential candidates are elected in November.

_____ (G) It seems that the country's interests would be better served if the presidential and vice presidential candidates of the Democratic party are elected this November.

_____ (H) On the whole the interests of the country will be served best by the election of the Democratic candidates for president and vice president in the coming election.

_____ (I) The election of the Democratic presidential and vice presidential candidates in November is absolutely essential from all angles in the country's interests.

In completing this questionnaire, the respondent is asked initially to indicate the one statement that he or she finds most acceptable (say, by putting ++ in the corresponding blank). The respondent is then asked to indicate the other statements that are acceptable to the respondent (+), the one statement that is most objectionable to the respondent (XX), and the other statements that are unacceptable (X). The respondent need not mark every statement as either acceptable or unacceptable; that is, some of the positions can be neither accepted nor rejected by the respondent. (For a discussion of procedural details, see Granberg & Steele, 1974.)

These responses are taken to define the respondent's judgmental latitudes on that issue. The range of positions that the respondent finds acceptable is said to form the respondent's *latitude of acceptance*, the positions that the respondent finds unacceptable constitute the *latitude of rejection*, and the *latitude of noncommitment* is formed by the positions that the respondent neither accepts nor rejects.

Obviously, the structure of these judgmental latitudes may vary from person to person. In fact, two respondents might have the same "most acceptable" position, but have very different latitudes of acceptance, rejection, and non-commitment. For example, suppose that on the presidential election issue Carol and Mary both find statement B most acceptable — their own most preferred position is that, on the whole, the interests of the country will be served best by the election of the Republicans. Mary finds statements A, C, D, and E also acceptable, is noncommittal toward F, G, and H, and rejects only the extreme Democratic statement I; Carol, on the other hand, thinks that A is the only other acceptable statement, is noncommittal regarding C and D, and rejects E, F, G, H, and I. Mary thus has a larger latitude of acceptance than Carol (Mary finds five of the statements acceptable, whereas Carol finds only two so), a larger latitude of noncommitment (three statements as opposed to two), and a smaller latitude of rejection (only one statement is objectionable to Mary, whereas five are to Carol). Notice (to jump ahead for a moment) that even though Carol and Mary have the same most preferred position, they would likely react quite differently to a persuasive communication advocating position E: Mary finds that to be an acceptable position on the issue, but Carol finds it objectionable.

Thus, from the point of view of social judgment theory, a person's stand on an issue must be seen as involving something more than simply the person's most preferred position. Only understanding the person's judgment of the various alternative positions — only understanding the person's latitudes of acceptance, rejection, and noncommitment — will permit one to understand the individual's reactions to persuasive messages on that issue.

Social judgment theory proposes that there is a systematic source of variation in the structure of these judgmental latitudes: ego-involvement. As the respondent's level of ego-involvement with the issue varies, so will the structure of the judgmental latitudes. Before discussing the nature of this relationship, however, some attention to the concept of ego-involvement is required.

THE CONCEPT OF EGO-INVOLVEMENT

The concept of ego-involvement has been variously described in social judgment theory, and hence there is room for some uncertainty about just what "ego-involvement" comes to (for discussion, see Wilmot, 1971a). However, very broadly speaking, what is meant by "ego-involvement" is in some ways akin to what one might colloquially mean in referring to someone's being "involved with an issue." Thus a person might be said to be ego-involved when the issue has personal significance to the individual, when the person's stand on the issue is central to his or her sense of self (hence "ego-involvement"), when the issue is important to the person, when the person intensely holds a given position, when the person is strongly committed to the position, and so on.

Two additional clarifications may be helpful. First, ego-involvement is issue-specific (see C. W. Sherif, 1980, pp. 37-40). A person might be highly involved in one issue (say, abortion) but not at all involved in another (such as environmental protection). That is to say, ego-involvement is not a personality characteristic such that persons who are highly involved on one issue will also be highly involved on most other issues; instead, involvement is topic-specific, in the sense that it can vary from issue to issue.

Second, ego-involvement and extremity of most preferred position are distinct concepts (see C. W. Sherif, 1980, p. 36). That is, to be ego-involved in an issue is not the same thing as holding an extreme position on the issue. For example, one might take an extreme stand on an issue without being highly ego-involved (e.g., I might hold an extreme position on the issue of controlling the federal deficit, even though I'm not especially ego-involved in that stand). And one can be highly ego-involved in a middle-of-the-road position ("I'm strongly committed to this moderate position, my sense of self is connected to my holding this moderate view," and so on). Thus involvement and position extremity are conceptually different.

Social judgment theory does suggest that ego-involvement and position extremity will be *empirically* related, such that those with more extreme positions on an issue will tend to be more ego-involved in that issue; indeed, M. Sherif and Hovland (1961, pp. 138-140) report research evidence supporting such an empirical relationship. But this empirical relationship should not obscure the conceptual difference between involvement and position extremity. Even though those with extreme positions may tend to be more involved than are those with moderate positions, it is quite possible for persons holding moderate positions to be highly involved (and equally possible for persons with extreme positions to be relatively uninvolved); hence it is important to recognize the conceptual distinction between position extremity and involvement.

EGO-INVOLVEMENT AND THE LATITUDES

Social judgment theory suggests that one's level of ego-involvement on an issue will influence the structure of one's judgmental latitudes on that issue. Specifically, the claim is that as one's level of ego-involvement increases, the size of the latitude of rejection will also increase (and the sizes of the latitudes of rejection and noncommitment will decrease). Hence highly involved persons are expected to have a relatively large latitude of rejection and relatively small latitudes of acceptance and noncommitment. The more involved person thus will find comparatively few stands on the issue to be acceptable, and won't be neutral (noncommittal) toward very many stands, and will find a comparatively large number of positions to be objectionable.

Obviously, in order to gather evidence bearing on this claim, one needs to have a procedure for assessing ego-involvement. A number of different measurement procedures have been proposed; two of these are discussed in the next section. (Of course, one also needs a procedure for assessing the sizes of the various latitudes; the Ordered Alternatives questionnaire provides such a procedure.)

MEASURES OF EGO-INVOLVEMENT

Several different techniques have been devised for assessing the degree of ego-involvement a person has in a given issue. Two particular measures have commonly been employed, and can serve as useful examples.

SIZE OF THE ORDERED-ALTERNATIVES LATITUDE OF REJECTION As a preliminary way of studying the relationship of ego-involvement to the structures of the judgmental latitudes, the individuals studied were often persons whose involvement levels could be presumed on the basis of their group memberships.[1] One example is provided by Hovland, Harvey, and Sherif's (1957) study of the topic of prohibition in Oklahoma (at a time when that state still had prohibition laws). Some of the participants were recruited from Women's Christian Temperance Union groups, Salvation Army workers, and the like, the presumption being that these persons would be highly involved in the topic. For comparison, other participants were obtained from unselected samples (e.g., undergraduate students). Participants completed an Ordered Alternatives questionnaire, from which the structure of the latitudes could be obtained.

In studies such as these, persons in the presumably higher-involvement groups had larger latitudes of rejection than did presumably less involved participants (for a general review of such work, see C. W. Sherif et al., 1965). On the basis of such results, the size of the latitude of rejection on the Ordered Alternatives questionnaire has been recommended as a measure of ego-involvement (e.g., Granberg, 1982, p. 313; C. W. Sherif et al., 1965, p. 234): The larger one's latitude of rejection, the greater one's degree of involvement.

Of course, as the latitude of rejection increases in size, the combined size of the latitudes of acceptance and noncommitment must necessarily decrease. It appears that it is primarily the latitude of noncommitment that shrinks — that is, with an increase in the size of the latitude of rejection, there is a decrease in the size of the latitude of noncommitment, and little change in the size of the latitude of acceptance (for a review, see C. W. Sherif et al., 1965). This regularity has sometimes led to the suggestion that the size of the latitude of noncommitment can serve as an index of involvement (e.g., C. W. Sherif et al., 1965, p. 234), but the size of the latitude of rejection is the far more frequently studied index.

OWN-CATEGORIES PROCEDURE A second measure of ego-involvement was derived from what is called the "own-categories" procedure. Participants are provided with a large number of statements (60 or more) on the topic of interest, and are asked to sort these statements into however many categories they think necessary to represent the range of positions on the issue. They are told to sort the items such that those in a given category seem to reflect the same basic viewpoint on the topic, and so hang together as a category. (For procedural details, see C. W. Sherif et al., 1965, pp. 92-126.) What is of central interest here is the *number* of categories created by a respondent.[2] As in the studies of the Ordered Alternatives questionnaire, results were compared from selected and unselected respondents whose involvement levels could be presumed on independent grounds.

Systematic differences were observed in the number of categories employed. Those participants who were presumably highly involved created fewer categories than did low-involvement participants. Such results suggested the use of the own-categories procedure as an index of ego-involvement: The fewer categories created, the greater the degree of ego-involvement (e.g., C. W. Sherif et al., 1965, p. 126).

This result can seem to be counterintuitive, but it makes good sense from the perspective of social judgment theory — particularly against the backdrop of assimilation and contrast effects (to be discussed shortly). With increasing involvement, increased perceptual distortion is thought to be likely. When involvement is exceptionally high, the individual's thinking takes on an absolutist, black-or-white quality; in such a case, only two categories might be thought to be necessary by the respondent ("Here are the few statements representing the right point of view — the one I hold — and here are all the wrongheaded ones"). Thus it is that social judgment theory expects that greater involvement will mean fewer categories created in the own-categories procedure.[3]

As is probably apparent, the own-categories procedure is rather cumbersome for large-scale administration, especially compared to an Ordered Alternatives questionnaire. Not surprisingly, of these two means of assessing ego-involvement, the more frequently used index has been the size of the latitude of rejection on the Ordered Alternatives questionnaire.

REACTIONS TO COMMUNICATIONS

Social judgment theory holds that a receiver's reaction to a given persuasive communication will depend centrally on how he or she assesses the point of view it is advocating. This implies that, in reacting to a persuasive message, the receiver must initially come to decide just what position the message is forwarding. Social judgment theory suggests that, in reaching this judgment (about what position is being advocated), the receiver may be subject to perceptual distortions termed "assimilation and contrast effects."

ASSIMILATION AND CONTRAST EFFECTS

Assimilation and contrast effects are perceptual effects concerning the judgment of what position is being advocated by a persuasive message. An assimilation effect is said to occur when the receiver perceives the message as advocating a position closer to his or her own position than it actually does; that is, an assimilation effect involves the receiver minimizing the difference between the message's position and the receiver's position. A contrast effect is said to occur when the receiver perceives the message as advocating a position further away from (more discrepant from) his or her own position than it actually does; thus a contrast effect involves the receiver's exaggerating the difference between the message's position and the receiver's position.[4]

Social judgment theory offers a rule of thumb concerning the occurrence of assimilation and contrast effects (see C. W. Sherif et al., 1965, p. 129). Broadly speaking, a communication advocating a position that falls in the receiver's latitude of acceptance is likely to be assimilated (perceived as even closer to the receiver's own view), and a communication advocating a position in the latitude of rejection will probably be contrasted (perceived as even more discrepant from the receiver's view). In the latitude of noncommitment, it appears that one might find either assimilation or contrast effects; social judgment theory does not clearly identify the point at which assimilation effects stop and contrast effects begin, but this point seems likely to occur somewhere in the latitude of noncommitment but close to the latitude of rejection (see C. A. Kiesler et al., 1969, p. 247).

Notice, thus, that the perceived position of a persuasive communication may be different for persons with differing stands on the issue. An illustration of this phenomenon was offered by M. Sherif and Hovland (1961, p. 151), who constructed a message concerning a presidential election. The communication briefly listed the claims of the two major parties on various campaign issues, but did not take sides or draw clear conclusions; that is, the message represented something like position E—the middle position—on the Ordered Alternatives questionnaire presented above. When pro-Republican respondents were asked what position the message advocated, they characterized it as being slightly pro-Democratic; pro-Democratic respondents, on the other hand, saw the message as being slightly pro-Republican. Both groups of respondents thus exhibited a contrast effect, exaggerating the difference between the message and their own stand on the issue. (For other research illustrating assimilation and contrast effects, see Atkins, Deaux, & Bieri, 1967; Hurwitz, 1986; Manis, 1960; C. W. Sherif et al., 1965, pp. 149-163.)

Assimilation and contrast effects appear to be magnified by ego-involvement. That is, there is a greater degree of perceptual distortion (regarding what position a message is advocating) as the receiver's degree of involvement increases (C. W. Sherif, Kelly, Rodgers, Sarup, & Tittler, 1973; C. W. Sherif et al., 1965, p. 159). However, it appears that assimilation and contrast effects are minimized by messages that make clear what position is being advocated. That is, only relatively ambiguous communications are subject to assimilation and contrast effects (see Granberg & Campbell, 1977; C. W. Sherif et al., 1965, p. 153; M. Sherif & Hovland, 1961, p. 153). When a persuader makes clear just what view is being forwarded, assimilation and contrast effects are minimized.

ATTITUDE CHANGE EFFECTS

Whether receivers will change their attitudes following reception of a persuasive communication is said by social judgment theory to depend on what position the message is perceived to be advocating—that is, the perceived location of the communication with respect to the latitudes of acceptance, rejection, and noncommitment. The basic principle offered by social judgment theory is this: A communication that is perceived to advocate a position that falls in the latitude of acceptance or the latitude of noncommitment will produce attitude change in the advocated direction (that is, in the direction sought by the message), but a communication that is perceived to advocate a position that falls in the latitude of rejection will produce no attitude change, or perhaps "boomerang" attitude change (that is, change in the direction *opposite* that advocated by the message).

Several investigations have reported findings consistent with this general principle. For example, more favorable attitude change is produced when the message is perceived to fall within the latitude of acceptance than when it falls outside it (Atkins et al., 1967; Eagly & Telaak, 1972). And less favorable attitude change has been found as the size of the latitude of rejection (or involvement) increases (Eagly & Telaak, 1972; C. W. Sherif et al., 1973).[5]

This general principle has important implications for the question of the effects of discrepancy (between the message's position and the receiver's position) on attitude change. A persuader might advocate a position very discrepant from (very different from) the receiver's own view, thus asking for a great deal of attitude change; or a persuader might advocate a position only slightly discrepant from the receiver's, so seeking only a small amount of change. But what degree of discrepancy between the message's position and the receiver's position will produce the greatest amount of favorable attitude change?

Social judgment theory suggests that with increasing discrepancy, more favorable attitude change will occur—up to a point, namely, the latitude of rejection; but beyond that point, increasing discrepancy will produce less favorable reactions (indeed, may produce boomerang attitude change). Thus the general relationship between discrepancy and attitude change is suggested to be something like an inverted-U-shaped curve, and indeed (as discussed in more detail in Chapter 9) the available research evidence is consistent with that suggestion (e.g., Aronson, Turner, & Carlsmith, 1963; Whittaker, 1965).[6]

But social judgment theory also points to the importance of the receiver's level of ego-involvement as an influence on the effects of discrepancy on attitude change. As receivers become increasingly involved in an issue, their latitudes of rejection presumably grow larger. Thus for low-involvement receivers, a persuader might be able to advocate a very discrepant viewpoint without entering the (small) latitude of rejection; but for high-involvement receivers, a very discrepant message will almost certainly fall into the (large) latitude of rejection. Thus, with any one influence attempt, a persuader facing a highly involved receiver may be able to advocate safely only a small change; obtaining substantial change from the highly involved receiver may require a series of small steps over time. By contrast, considerable attitude change might be obtained from the low-involvement receiver rather rapidly, through advocating a highly discrepant (but not too discrepant) position (as suggested by Harvey & Rutherford, 1958).

It should be kept in mind, however, that (from the point of view of social judgment theory) it is not discrepancy per se that is the relevant factor, but the perceived location of the communication relative to the receiver's judgmental latitudes. Consider, for example, a receiver whose most acceptable position on the A-to-I Ordered Alternatives questionnaire was position D; positions A, B, and C formed the rest of the latitude of acceptance; position E was the latitude of noncommitment; and positions F, G, H, and I formed the latitude of rejection. A message perceived to advocate position A would be more discrepant (from the receiver's most preferred position) than a message perceived to advocate position F—yet the first message, despite being more discrepant, would be expected to elicit a more favorable reaction than the second. Thus, for social judgment theory, any effects of discrepancy on attitude change are simply indirect reflections of the role played by the judgmental latitudes—and correspondingly the inverted-U curve (relating discrepancy to attitude change) is only a crude and general guide to what persuasive effects may be expected in a given circumstance.

ASSIMILATION AND CONTRAST EFFECTS RECONSIDERED

The reader may have noticed that the attitude-change principles discussed in the preceding section refer to what position the message is *perceived* to be advocating. It thus becomes important to reconsider the role of assimilation and contrast effects in persuasion, since these influence the perceived position of a message. The crucial point to be noticed is this: Assimilation and contrast effects reduce the effectiveness of persuasive communications.

THE IMPACT OF ASSIMILATION AND CONTRAST EFFECTS ON PERSUASION

Consider first the case of a contrast effect. If a message that advocates a position in the receiver's latitude of rejection—and so is already unlikely to yield much favorable attitude change—is perceived as advocating a position even *more* discrepant from the receiver's view, then the chances for favorable change diminish even more (and indeed the chances for boomerang attitude change increase). Obviously, then, contrast effects will impair the effectiveness of persuasive messages.

But assimilation effects also reduce persuasive effectiveness. When an assimilation effect occurs, the perceived discrepancy between the message's stand and the receiver's position is reduced—and hence the communicator is seen as asking for less change than he or she actually seeks. So consider the case of a message that advocates a position in the latitude of acceptance or the latitude of noncommitment; with increasing perceived discrepancy, the chances of favorable attitude change presumably increase. But an assimilation effect will *reduce* the perceived discrepancy between the message's view and the receiver's position, and so will *reduce* the amount of attitude change obtained. Indeed, in the extreme case of complete assimilation, receivers may think that the message is simply saying what they already believe—and hence receivers don't change their attitudes at all. Thus it is that assimilation effects, like contrast effects, reduce the effectiveness of persuasive communications.

How might persuaders minimize assimilation and contrast effects? By being clear about their position on the persuasive issue at hand. As discussed previously, only relatively ambiguous communications (that is, messages that aren't clear about their stand on the persuasive issue) are subject to assimilation and contrast effects. Thus social judgment theory emphasizes for persuaders the importance of making clear one's position on an issue.

AMBIGUITY IN POLITICAL CAMPAIGNS One might think that the prevalence (and apparent success) of ambiguity in political campaigns suggests that something is amiss (with social judgment theory, if not with the political campaign process). After all, if ambiguity reduces persuasive effectiveness, why is it that successful political campaigners so frequently seem to be ambiguous about their stands on the issues?

It is crucial to keep in mind the persuasive aims of the political campaign. Ordinarily, the candidate is *not* trying to persuade audiences to favor this or that approach to the matter of gun control or abortion or arms control (or any other "campaign issue"); rather, the persuasive aim of the campaign is to get people to vote for the candidate. That is, candidates are trying to convince voters on the question of who to vote for — and candidates are *never* ambiguous about their stand on that issue (the true persuasive issue of the campaign). Thus on the topic on which candidates seek persuasion (namely, who to vote for), candidates do not take unclear positions.

Candidates do adopt ambiguous positions on the "campaign issues" of environmental protection, gun control, and so forth. If a candidate were trying to persuade voters that "the right approach to the issue of gun control is thus-and-so," then being ambiguous about his or her position on gun control would reduce the chances of successful persuasion on that topic. Such ambiguity would encourage assimilation and contrast effects, thereby impairing the candidate's chances of changing anyone's mind about gun control.

But, ordinarily, candidates don't seek to persuade voters about the wisdom of some particular policy on a given campaign issue. Usually, the candidate hopes to encourage voters to believe that the candidate's view on a given issue is the same as the voter's view. That is to say, candidates hope that, with respect to campaign issues (such as abortion or arms control), voters will assimilate the candidate's views (overestimate the degree of similarity between the candidate's views and their own).

Social judgment theory, of course, straightforwardly suggests how such an effect might be obtained. Suppose — as seems plausible — that for most voters, the positions around the middle of the scale on a given campaign issue (arms control, environmental protection, or whatever) commonly fall in the latitude of noncommitment or the latitude of acceptance; for a small number of voters (e.g., those with extreme views and high ego-involvement on that topic), such positions might fall in the latitude of rejection, but most of the electorate feels noncommittal toward (if not accepting of) such views. In such a circumstance, if the message suggests some sort of vaguely moderate position on the issue, without being very clear about exactly what position is being defended, then the conditions are ripe for an assimilation effect regarding the candidate's stand on that topic. (For research concerning assimilation and contrast effects in political campaigns, see J. A. Anderson & Avery, 1978; Brent & Granberg, 1982; Granberg, 1982; Granberg & Jenks, 1977; Granberg, Kasmer, & Nanneman, 1988; Judd, Kenny, & Krosnick, 1983; M. King, 1978.)

CRITICAL ASSESSMENT

Social judgment theory obviously offers a number of concepts and principles useful for illuminating persuasive effects. But several problems in social judgment theory and research have become apparent.

THE CONFOUNDING OF INVOLVEMENT
WITH OTHER VARIABLES

One weakness in much social judgment research stems from the use of participants from preexisting groups thought to differ in involvement (e.g., in the research on the prohibition topic, using members of the Women's Christian Temperance Union to represent high-involvement subjects). This research procedure has created ambiguities in interpreting results, because the procedure has confounded involvement with a number of other variables.

Two variables are said to be "confounded" in a research design when they are associated in such a way as to make it impossible to disentangle their separate effects. In the case of much social judgment theory research, the persons selected to serve as high-involvement participants differed from the low-involvement participants not just in involvement, but in other ways as well. For example, the high-involvement participants had more extreme attitudes than the low-involvement participants (e.g., M. Sherif & Hovland, 1961, pp. 134-135). In such a circumstance, when the high-involvement group displays a larger latitude of rejection than the low-involvement group, one cannot unambiguously attribute the difference to involvement (as social judgment theory might propose). The difference in latitude size might instead be due to position extremity.

From a social judgment theory point of view, the apparent empirical association between involvement and position extremity (higher involvement being associated with more extreme positions) complicates the research process. One might well expect that, on the whole, higher involvement, more extreme attitudes, and larger latitudes of rejection would go hand in hand. But involvement and position extremity are treated as distinct concepts by social judgment theory, and so it is important for theoretical purposes to be able to distinguish the effects of involvement from the effects of position extremity. Social judgment theory claims that larger latitudes of rejection are the result of heightened ego-involvement, not the result of extreme positions per se (e.g., C. W. Sherif et al., 1965, p. 233); hence it is particularly unfortunate that the research designs confounded involvement and position extremity.

In fact, the groups used in much social judgment research differed not only in involvement and position extremity, but in age, educational level, and so on.

As a result, one cannot confidently explain observed differences (e.g., in the size of the latitude of rejection, or in the number of categories used in the own-categories procedure) as being the result simply of involvement; one of the other factors, or some combination of other factors, might have been responsible for the observed effects. Hence much of the research evidence bearing on social judgment theory is not as strong as one might want; these various confoundings complicate the task of drawing clear conclusions from the research evidence. (For a more general discussion of this problem with social judgment research, see C. A. Kiesler et al., 1969, pp. 254-257.)

THE CONCEPT OF INVOLVEMENT

Ego-involvement is not a carefully defined idea. The notion of ego-involvement seems to involve a variety of conflated concepts — the person's stand on the issue being central to the person's sense of self, the issue's importance to the person, the issue's relevance to the person, the degree of commitment the person has to the position, the degree of intensity with which the position is held, and so on (for a useful discussion, see Wilmot, 1971a).

But these are distinguishable concepts. For instance, I can think an issue is important without my stand on that issue being central to my self-concept (e.g., I think the issue of controlling the federal deficit is important, but my sense of identity isn't connected to my stand on this matter). I can hold a given belief intensely, even though the issue isn't very important to me (e.g., my belief that the earth is round). An issue may not be personally relevant to me (e.g., abortion), but I could nonetheless be strongly committed to a position on that issue, and my stand on that issue could be important to my sense of self. I can hold a belief strongly (say, about the superiority of a given basketball team) even though that belief isn't central to my self-concept.

The general point is that the notion of involvement contains a number of distinct concepts that have been run together in an unsatisfactory manner. It is possible to distinguish (conceptually, if not empirically) commitment to a position, importance of the issue, personal relevance of the issue, and so forth, and hence a clear understanding of the roles these play in persuasion will require separate treatment of each. (For examples of efforts at clarifying one or another aspect of involvement, see Greenwald & Leavitt, 1985; Park & Mittal, 1985; Zaichkowsky, 1985.)

THE MEASURES OF INVOLVEMENT

Several worrisome findings have been reported concerning the common measures of ego-involvement: the size of the latitude of rejection in the Ordered Alternatives questionnaire and the number of categories created in the own-categories procedure. No one of these findings is especially damaging by itself, but taken together they indicate some cause for concern.

For example, Wilmot (1971b) examined the association between the size of the Ordered Alternatives latitude of rejection and the number of categories used in the own-categories procedure. One would expect a substantial negative correlation between these measures (persons with larger latitudes of rejection should use fewer categories), but the observed correlation (.03) was not significantly different from zero. Wilmot also found that these measures were not substantially correlated with respondents' ratings of how important the topic was to society, how important the topic was to them personally, or how committed they were to their most acceptable position: The correlations ranged from −.03 to .08 (for related results, see R. A. Clark & Stewart, 1971).

R. A. Clark and Stewart (1971) examined the average size of the Ordered Alternatives latitude of rejection on a number of different issues. Social judgment theory would expect that issues with relatively large latitudes of rejection would be ones that are relatively ego-involving for the respondents, whereas issues with relatively small latitudes of rejection would presumably be comparatively uninvolving. But Clark and Stewart found that, for college undergraduate respondents, the average latitude of rejection was larger for the issue of the quality of Walter Cronkite as a newscaster than for the issue of the harms and benefits of drug use; the average latitude of rejection was nearly identical for the question of the desirability of ice cream as a dessert and the issue of the extent to which grades accurately reflect class achievement. Results such as these obviously cast some doubt on the viability of the Ordered Alternatives latitude of rejection as an index of ego-involvement. (For additional relevant work concerning indices of ego-involvement, see Hartley, 1967, pp. 99-100; Makdah & Diab, 1976; Markley, 1971.)

Some related difficulties (concerning measures of ego-involvement) have arisen in the context of the claim that ego-involvement is issue-specific. In studying this claim, researchers have obtained ego-involvement indices from respondents concerning a number of different topics, examining the extent to which persons are consistent (across issues) in their apparent levels of involvement. Significant cross-topic consistencies have been observed by several investigators using a variety of involvement measures, including the Ordered Alternatives latitude of rejection and the number of categories created in the own-categories procedure (e.g., R. A. Clark & Stewart, 1971; Glixman, 1965; McCroskey & Burgoon, 1974; see also F. A. Powell, 1966; compare Eagly & Telaak, 1972).

At least some of these findings of cross-issue consistency can be accommodated by social judgment theory. As C. W. Sherif (1980, p. 38) has pointed out, social judgment theory acknowledges that when topics are closely related in some fashion (e.g., where the issues all concern some fundamental ideological dimension relevant for the respondent), then the level of involvement on one of the issues will likely be similar to the level of involvement on the other issues. Thus in studies where the topics are related, a finding of cross-topic consistency is not damaging to social judgment theory. This analysis can be used to explain some of the reported cases of cross-topic consistency, namely, ones where the topics are related (e.g., McCroskey & Burgoon, 1974), but it cannot easily explain other cases in which the topics are apparently not related (e.g., R. A. Clark & Stewart, 1971).

Taken at face value, then, the finding of significant cross-topic consistency (among unrelated topics) suggests two possible conclusions. One is that these "measures of ego-involvement" are *not* really assessing ego-involvement; after all, ego-involvement is topic-specific, and whatever these measures are assessing isn't topic-specific. The other possible conclusion is that social judgment theory is wrong to claim that ego-involvement is issue-specific; this conclusion presumes that these measures *are* assessing ego-involvement, and hence the finding that the measures exhibit significant cross-topic consistency means that involvement levels are similarly associated across topics. Of course, one can't draw both conclusions — but either one reflects unfavorably on social judgment theory and research.

In short, there are good empirical grounds for concern about the adequacy and meaning of the common measures of ego-involvement.[7] This is perhaps to be expected, given the lack of clarity surrounding the concept of ego-involvement; one cannot hope to have a very satisfactory assessment procedure for a vague and indistinct concept. In any case, the empirical evidence suggests that the various indices of ego-involvement ought not be employed unreflectively.

CONCLUSION

In some ways social judgment theory is obviously too simplified to serve as a complete account of persuasive effects. Notice, for example, that from a social judgment theory point of view, the only features of the message that are relevant to its impact are (a) the position it advocates and (b) the clarity with which it identifies its position. It doesn't matter whether the message contains sound arguments and good evidence, or specious reasoning and poor evidence; it doesn't matter just what contents the message contains, or how the message material is organized. Everything turns simply on what position the message is seen to defend. And surely this is an incomplete account of what underlies persuasive message effects.

But a theory can be useful even when incomplete. Social judgment theory does draw one's attention to important facets of the process of persuasion: the relevance of assimilation and contrast effects, the possibility that two persons with the same most acceptable position on an issue might nonetheless have very different assessments of the alternative stands on the issue, the importance of considering variations in receiver involvement in the topic, and so forth. Despite some obvious weaknesses, then, one may surely credit social judgment theory with some positive contributions.

NOTES

1. In fact, as C. A. Kiesler et al. (1969, p. 244) point out, the anchoring of attitudes in reference groups is emphasized in some social judgment theory conceptualizations of involvement, and consequently this was an attractive research procedure for social judgment studies.

2. Of subsidiary interest is the *distribution* of statements across categories: High- and low-involvement participants often differ in their use of their created categories, with high-involvement participants tending to use some categories disproportionately (C. W. Sherif et al., 1965, p. 239).

3. The own-categories procedure can also be used to obtain measures of the judgmental latitudes (by asking the respondent to indicate the most acceptable category, other acceptable categories, and so forth, and then examining the proportion of statements falling into the various latitudes), but there is more research evidence concerning number of categories created than concerning the comparative sizes of the judgmental latitudes thus assessed, and hence attention here is focused on the use of the number of categories created as an index of ego involvement.

4. Assimilation and contrast effects (more broadly defined than here) are familiar psychophysical phenomena. If you've been lifting 25-pound boxes all day, a 40-pound box will feel even heavier than 40 pounds (contrast effect), but a 27-pound box will probably feel much like all the others (assimilation effect). The psychophysical principle involved is that when a stimulus (the 40-pound box) is distant from one's judgmental anchor (the 25-pound boxes), a contrast effect is likely; but when the stimulus is close to the anchor, an assimilation effect is likely. Indeed, social judgment theory was explicitly represented as an attempt to generalize psychophysical judgmental principles and findings to the realm of social judgment, with the person's own stand on the issue serving as the judgmental anchor (see M. Sherif & Hovland, 1961).

5. However (as discussed in Chapter 6), there have been several reported cases in which increased involvement has been associated with increased persuasiveness of counterattitudinal messages (e.g., Petty & Cacioppo, 1979b), findings that would seem not easily reconciled with social judgment theory (but see Chapter 6, note 9, for further discussion).

6. For any individual receiver, the relation of discrepancy and attitude change is presumably not expected to be an inverted-U curve, but something rather more like half of such a curve: increasing attitude change up to the latitude of rejection, but with a sharp drop-off (not a gentle decline) at that point. But when data are averaged across many respondents, one expects (because of small individual variations, inevitable measurement error, and so on) to obtain something more like the inverted-U-shaped curve discussed in the text.

7. Though not discussed here, less frequently employed measures of ego-involvement — particularly ones based on Diab's (1965, p. 312) suggested procedure — appear to have similar problems; see L. Powell (1976) and Wilmot (1971b).

3

Information-Integration Models of Attitude

THIS CHAPTER DISCUSSES information-integration approaches to the analysis of attitude and attitude change. The central theme of these approaches is that one's attitude toward an object is a function of the way in which one integrates (combines) the information one has about the object. There are a number of variants of this general approach, with the variations deriving primarily from differences in the way in which information is seen to be integrated. One particular information-integration approach, Fishbein's summative model of attitude, has enjoyed special prominence among students of persuasion and social influence, and hence is the focus of the chapter's attention. (This chapter discusses Fishbein's initial attitude model. Fishbein's subsequent general model of behavior and intention — the theory of reasoned action — is discussed in Chapter 5.)

FISHBEIN'S SUMMATIVE MODEL OF ATTITUDE

THE MODEL

Martin Fishbein's (1967a, 1967b) summative model of attitude is based on the claim that one's attitude toward an object is a function of one's *salient beliefs* about the object. For any given attitude object, a person may have a large number of beliefs about the object. But at any given time, only some of these are likely to be salient (prominent) — and it is those that are claimed to determine the person's attitude. In, say, a public-opinion or marketing questionnaire, one might elicit the respondent's salient beliefs (e.g., about a product or a political candidate) by asking him or her to list the characteristics, qualities, and attributes of the object. (For procedural details concerning the identification of salient beliefs, see Ajzen & Fishbein, 1980, pp. 68-71; Fishbein & Ajzen, 1975, pp. 218-219.)

In particular, the model holds that one's attitude toward an object is a function of belief strength (that is, the strength with which one holds one's salient beliefs about the object) and belief evaluation (the evaluation one has of these beliefs). Specifically, the relation of belief strength and evaluation to attitude is said to be described by the following formula.

$$A_O = \Sigma b_i e_i$$

where A_O is the attitude toward the object, b_i is the strength of a given belief, and e_i is the evaluation of a given belief. The sigma (Σ) indicates that one sums across the products of the belief-strength and evaluation ratings for each belief; that is, one multiplies each belief evaluation by the strength with which that belief is held, and then sums those products to arrive at an estimate of the overall attitude toward the object. If there are five salient beliefs about the object, then, the attitude estimate is given by $b_1 e_1 + b_2 e_2 + b_3 e_3 + b_4 e_4 + b_5 e_5$.

The procedures for assessing the elements of this model are well established (see, e.g., Fishbein & Raven, 1962). One's attitude toward the object (A_O) can be obtained by familiar attitude-measurement techniques. The evaluation of a given belief (e_i) is assessed through semantic differential evaluative scales, such as good-bad, desirable-undesirable, and favorable-unfavorable. The strength with which a given belief is held (b_i) can be assessed through scales such as likely-unlikely, probable-improbable, and true-false.

As an example: Suppose that a preliminary survey had indicated that the most salient beliefs held about Senator Smith by his constituents were that the senator supports defense cuts, is helpful to constituents, is respected in the Senate, and is unethical. One might assess the strength with which the first of these beliefs was held by respondents through items such as the following:

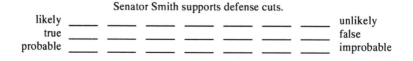

Senator Smith supports defense cuts.

likely	___	___	___	___	___	___	___	unlikely
true	___	___	___	___	___	___	___	false
probable	___	___	___	___	___	___	___	improbable

And the evaluation of that belief can be assessed with items such as the following:

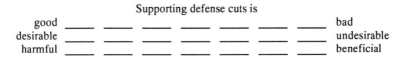

Supporting defense cuts is

good	_____ _____ _____ _____ _____ _____ _____	bad
desirable	_____ _____ _____ _____ _____ _____ _____	undesirable
harmful	_____ _____ _____ _____ _____ _____ _____	beneficial

Suppose (to simplify matters) that, for each belief, belief strength and evaluation were assessed by a single scale (perhaps "likely-unlikely" for belief strength, "good-bad" for evaluation) scored from +3 ("likely" or "good") to –3 ("unlikely" or "bad"). A particular respondent might have the following pattern of responses.

	b_i	e_i	$b_i e_i$
supports defense cuts	+3	–2	–6
helpful to constituents	–3	+3	–9
respected in the Senate	+2	+1	+2
unethical	–2	–3	± 6
			$-7 = \Sigma b_i e_i$

That is to say, this particular respondent believes it is quite likely that the senator supports defense cuts (belief strength of +3), and supporting defense cuts is seen as a moderately negative characteristic (evaluation of –2); the respondent thinks it very unlikely that the senator is helpful to constituents (helpfulness to constituents being thought to be a very good quality); the respondent thinks it moderately likely that Smith is respected in the Senate, and that's a slightly positive characteristic; and the respondent thinks it rather unlikely that Smith possesses the highly negative characteristic of being unethical.

Since (in this example) each belief-strength score (b_i) can range from –3 to +3 and each evaluation score (e_i) can range from –3 to +3, each product ($b_i e_i$) can range from –9 to +9, and hence the total (across the four beliefs in this example) can range from –36 to +36. A person who thought that the qualities of supporting defense cuts, being helpful to constituents, and being respected in the Senate were all very positive characteristics (evaluations of +3 in each case) and who thought it very likely that the senator possessed each of these qualities (belief strength of +3 for each), and who also thought it quite unlikely (–3 belief strength) that the senator possessed the strongly negative (–3 evaluation) characteristic of being unethical would have a total ($\Sigma b_i e_i$) of +36, indicating an extremely positive attitude toward the senator — as befits such a set of beliefs. By comparison, the hypothetical respondent with a total of –7 might be said to have a slightly negative attitude toward Senator Smith.

Perhaps it is apparent how this general approach could be used for other attitude objects (with different salient beliefs, of course). In consumer marketing, for example, the attitude object of interest is a product or brand, and the salient beliefs typically concern the attributes of the product or brand ("tastes great," "less filling," and so on). Thus, for instance, the underlying bases of consumers' attitudes toward a given brand of toothpaste might be investigated by examining the belief strength and evaluation associated with consumers' salient beliefs about that brand's attributes: whitening power, taste, ability to prevent cavities, cost, ability to freshen breath, and so forth.

Or, as another example of application, persons' attitudes toward public policy proposals can be studied; here the salient beliefs might well include beliefs about the consequences of adoption of the policy. Consider, for instance, some possible cognitive bases of attitudes toward capital punishment. Does capital punishment deter crime (belief strength), and how good an outcome is that (belief evaluation)? Is capital punishment inhumane, and how negatively valued is that? Is capital punishment applied inequitably, and how disadvantageous is that? And so forth. Two persons with opposed attitudes on this issue might value crime deterrence equally — that is, have the same evaluation of that attribute — but disagree about whether capital punishment has that attribute (has the consequence of deterring crime). Or two people with opposed attitudes might agree that capital punishment has the characteristic of satisfying the desire for vengeance, but differ in the evaluation of that characteristic.

COMMENTARY ON THE MODEL

GENERAL RESEARCH EVIDENCE A number of investigations have examined the correlation between a measure of the respondent's attitude toward the object (A_O) and the predicted attitude based on Fishbein's summative formula ($\Sigma b_i e_i$). Reasonably strong positive correlations have commonly been found, ranging roughly from .55 to .80 with a variety of attitude objects including public policy proposals (e.g., Infante, 1971, 1973; Peay, 1980), political candidates (e.g., M. H. Davis & Runge, 1981; Holbrook & Hulbert, 1975), and consumer products (e.g., Holbrook, 1977; Nakanishi & Bettman, 1974). That is to say, attitude appears often to be reasonably well predicted by this model.

ATTRIBUTE IMPORTANCE AND RELEVANCE Several investigations have explored the potential role of attribute importance or relevance in predicting attitude. Fishbein's model, it will be noticed, uses only belief strength and evaluation to predict attitude; some researchers have thought that the predictability of attitude might be improved by adding the importance or relevance of the attribute as a third variable (with belief strength and evaluation). That is, in addition to assessing belief strength and belief evaluation, one also obtains measures of the relevance or importance of each belief to the respondent; then some three-component formula, such as $\Sigma b_i e_i I_i$ (where I_i refers to the importance of the attribute), is used to predict attitude.[1]

But the research evidence suggests that adding relevance or importance to Fishbein's formula does not improve the predictability of attitude (e.g., L. R. Anderson, 1970; Hackman & Anderson, 1968; Holbrook & Hulbert, 1975). In understanding this result, it may be helpful to consider the possibility that the attributes judged more important or relevant may also have more extreme evaluations; that is, the assessment of belief evaluation (e_i) may already involve indirect assessment of relevance and importance (e.g., Holbrook & Hulbert, 1975). Moreover, if an investigator selects only salient attributes as the basis for attitude prediction, then it is likely that all the attributes assessed are comparatively relevant and important ones — and hence adding importance or relevance ratings would not be expected to improve the prediction of attitude. In any event, there appears to be little reason to suppose that the predictability of attitude from Fishbein's original formula ($\Sigma b_i e_i$) can be improved by adding a belief-importance or belief-relevance component.

THE ROLE OF BELIEF-STRENGTH SCORES There has been some clarification of the role played by belief-strength scores in the prediction of attitude. This clarification has come from research comparing Σe_i (that is, the simple sum of the belief evaluations) with $\Sigma b_i e_i$ (Fishbein's formula) as predictors of attitude. The relative success of these two formulas varies, depending upon the way in which the list of salient beliefs is prepared.

The most common way of preparing the list of salient beliefs (in research on this attitude model) is by eliciting beliefs from a test sample, identifying the most frequently mentioned beliefs, and using these on the questionnaire. In this procedure, a *standardized* belief list is composed (i.e., every respondent receives the same standard set of beliefs). An alternative procedure is to elicit the salient beliefs from each respondent individually, and so have each respondent provide belief-strength and evaluation ratings for his or her own unique set of salient beliefs; that is, an *individualized* belief list can be constructed for each respondent.

The research evidence indicates that, when individualized belief lists are used, Σe_i and $\Sigma b_i e_i$ are equally good predictors of attitude; adding belief-strength scores to the formula does not improve the predictability of attitude. With standardized belief lists, however, $\Sigma b_i e_i$ is a better predictor than is Σe_i. That is to say, belief-strength scores significantly improve the predictability of attitude only when standardized (as opposed to individualized) belief lists are used (Cronen & Conville, 1975; Delia, Crockett, Press, & O'Keefe, 1975).

Upon reflection, of course, this result makes good sense. With individualized belief lists, the respondent has just indicated that he or she thinks the object possesses the attribute; that is, only beliefs that the respondent already holds are rated for belief strength. By contrast, with standardized belief lists, belief-strength scores serve to distinguish those beliefs the respondent holds from those the respondent does not hold.

What this suggests is that the apparent contribution of belief-strength scores to the prediction of attitude is "an artifact of the employment of standard belief lists" (Cronen & Conville, 1975, p. 48), not an indication of the role of belief strength in the cognitive states underlying attitude. If variations in belief strength genuinely made a difference to attitude, then one would expect that with individualized belief lists, $\Sigma b_i e_i$ would be a better predictor of attitude than would Σe_i — but it isn't. Belief-strength scores do make a contribution to the prediction of attitude when standardized belief lists are used — not because belief strength actually influences attitude, but because the use of standardized belief lists creates a predictive role for belief-strength scores (namely, the role of differentiating those beliefs the respondent holds from those the respondent doesn't).

To put the point somewhat differently: These results suggest that — insofar as the underlying bases of attitude are concerned — we may more usefully think of persons' beliefs about an object as being rather more categorical ("I think the object has the attribute," "I don't think the object has the attribute," or "I'm not sure") than continuous ("I think that the probability that the object possesses the attribute is thus-and-so"). The belief-strength scales give the appearance of some continuous gradation of belief probability, but these scales make a contribution to attitude prediction only because standardized belief lists are used. When individualized belief lists are used, belief-strength scores are unhelpful in predicting attitude because in each case the individual thinks the object has the attribute — and it is that simple categorical judgment (not variations in the reported degree of probabilistic association) that is important in determining the individual's attitude.[2]

This clarification of the role of belief-strength scores provides a basis for understanding the occasional finding that Σb_i is as good a predictor of attitude as $\Sigma b_i e_i$. It might be thought that this finding indicates the substantive influence of belief strength on attitude and perhaps suggests some basis for wondering whether belief evaluations actually affect attitude (see, e.g., Lutz & Bettman, 1977). But one should expect this empirical result when all three of the following conditions obtain: (a) Standardized belief lists are used, (b) there is little variability in respondents' evaluation of each belief (that is, there's substantial agreement among respondents on the evaluation of a given belief), and (c) all the beliefs in the standardized list are of the same valence (that is, all are positively evaluated or all are negatively evaluated). In this circumstance, including belief evaluation in the formula isn't likely to add much to the predictability of attitude (given the lack of variability in evaluations, including belief evaluation amounts to multiplying each belief-strength score by a fixed value); but including belief-strength scores would contribute to attitude predictability (because the use of a standardized belief list means that one needs to be able to distinguish the beliefs the respondent holds from those the respondent does not). And indeed, when $\Sigma b_i e_i$ has been found to be no better a predictor of attitude than Σb_i, these conditions appear to have obtained (see Mazis, Ahtola, & Klippel, 1975, Experiments 2 and 3; Nakanishi & Bettman, 1974). Thus the finding that sometimes Σb_i is as good a predictor of attitude as is $\Sigma b_i e_i$ reflects not some genuine influence of belief strength on attitude, but the same artifactual role for belief-strength scores as described above.

SCORING PROCEDURES There has been a fair amount of discussion in the literature concerning how the belief-strength and belief-evaluation scales should be scored (e.g., Ajzen & Fishbein, 1980, p. 71; Bagozzi, 1984; Bettman, Capon, & Lutz, 1975; Fishbein & Ajzen, 1975, pp. 82-86; Steinfatt, 1977). The two most common ways of scoring a 7-point scale, for example, are from −3 to +3 ("bipolar" scoring) and from 1 to 7 ("unipolar" scoring); thus, with belief-strength and belief-evaluation scales, one might score both scales −3 to +3, or score both scales 1 to 7, or score one scale −3 to +3 and the other 1 to 7. But these different scoring procedures can yield different correlations of $\Sigma b_i e_i$ with attitude, and hence a question has arisen concerning which scoring procedures are preferable.

There is much confused discussion on this matter. One important source of confusion is the conflation of two distinct questions: (a) What scoring procedure maximizes the predictability of attitude? (b) What scoring procedure accurately models the cognitive processes underlying attitude? It has become easy to confuse the two questions, because models of the underlying cognitive processes are usually assessed by their success in predicting attitude. To see the unhappy consequences of this confusion, consider the status of an argument such as this: Belief-strength scales should not be scored in a bipolar fashion such as −3 to +3, because it's not psychologically meaningful for attitude objects to be negatively associated with attributes; instead, belief-strength scales should be scored in a unipolar way (from 1 to 7, or from 0 to 6). To justify a particular scoring procedure, this argument appeals to considerations of what will make for a plausible picture of the underlying psychological processes (suggesting that a particular scoring procedure implies an implausible model). (For examples of such arguments, see Bagozzi, 1984; Ryan & Bonfield, 1975.)

But this argument carries weight only if one is seeking to model the underlying processes. If all one wants to do is maximize the predictability of attitude from responses to standardized belief lists (as, for example, many marketers want), then one should choose whatever scoring procedures maximize attitude predictability; arguments that one or another scoring procedure represents an implausible picture of the underlying psychological processes can be dismissed as irrelevant, since the interest isn't in modeling those processes, but only in maximizing attitude predictability. As it happens, what evidence there is appears to suggest that often, but not always, the predictability of attitude from standardized lists is greatest when both the belief-evaluation scales and belief-strength scales are scored in a bipolar fashion, such as from −3 to +3 (Bettman et al., 1975; Holbrook, 1977; Lutz, 1976; compare Hewstone & Young, 1988).

If, on the other hand, one wants a picture of the cognitive underpinnings of attitude, then the issue of scoring procedures might well be premature. After all, the question of how to score the belief-strength scales so as to model accurately the underlying psychological processes assumes that belief strength actually does influence attitude — but, as discussed previously, there is research evidence that casts doubt on that assumption. The evidence suggests that $\Sigma b_i e_i$ may not be a very satisfactory model of the underlying cognitive processes (since, with individualized belief lists, Σe_i is just as good a predictor of attitude as is

$\Sigma b_i e_i$). Obviously, if belief strength doesn't influence attitude, then questions of which scoring procedures accurately model the influence of belief strength on attitude are misplaced.

PERSUASIVE STRATEGY IMPLICATIONS

Since, on this view, one's attitude is taken to be a function of the belief strength and evaluation of one's salient beliefs about the object, attitude change will involve changing these putative bases of attitude. The model thus suggests a number of ways in which attitude might be changed.

ALTERNATIVE PERSUASIVE STRATEGIES For example, in attempting to induce a favorable attitude toward a given attitude object (e.g., Senator Smith), one might attempt to lead the receiver to add a new salient positive belief about the object ("You might not have realized it, but Senator Smith was a war hero"). A second possibility is to attempt to increase the favorability of an existing positive belief ("Senator Smith is, as you know, respected in the Senate, but you may not realize just how desirable that is: It means Senator Smith can be more effective in passing legislation to help our state"). Third, a persuader might attempt to increase the belief strength (likelihood) of an existing positive belief ("You already know it's true that Senator Smith has worked hard for the people of this state — but you don't know just how true that is . . . "). Fourth, one might try to decrease the unfavorability of an existing negative belief ("Sure, Senator Smith was only an average student — but then again, being an average student isn't so bad"). Fifth, one might attempt to decrease the belief strength (likelihood) associated with an existing negative belief ("It's simply not true that Senator Smith accepted kickbacks"). Finally, attitude could be changed without adding any new beliefs and without changing the belief strength or evaluation of any existing beliefs, but simply by shuffling the current beliefs around in such a way that a different set of beliefs is salient; that is, changing the relative saliency of currently held beliefs can presumably influence attitudes ("Have you forgotten that five years ago Senator Smith helped keep XYZ Industries from moving out of state?"). Obviously, these are not mutually exclusive possibilities; a persuader might well offer arguments designed to implement all these different strategies.

ASSESSMENT OF THE ALTERNATIVE STRATEGIES There is scant evidence bearing on the relative effectiveness of these different strategies (see, e.g., Infante, 1975; Stutman & Newell, 1984). There is, however, some very general evidence indicating covariation between attitude change and change in the underlying bases of attitude. That is to say, changes in belief strength and evaluation (or $\Sigma b_i e_i$) have been found to be accompanied by corresponding changes in attitude (e.g., Carlson, 1956; DiVesta & Merwin, 1960; Infante, 1972; Lutz, 1975a, 1975b; Peay, 1980), suggesting that (as the model indicates) attitude change can be influenced by changes in belief strength and evaluation.

However, the apparently artifactual role of belief-strength scores in the model suggests the implausibility of certain strategies that the model might recommend. Consider a persuader who is trying to induce a favorable attitude toward Belch Beer. Suppose that a particular respondent has the salient belief that Belch Beer tastes good, and on 7-point scales (scored -3 to $+3$) indicates that this attribute is highly desirable ($+3$ for belief evaluation) and that it is moderately likely ($+2$ for belief strength) that Belch Beer tastes good. Fishbein's attitude model would suggest that this respondent's attitude could be made more positive by influencing the belief-strength rating for this attribute — specifically, by getting the respondent to believe that it is very likely that Belch Beer tastes good ($+3$ for belief strength).

But (as discussed earlier) belief strength does not appear to influence attitude; the contribution of belief-strength scores to attitude prediction is an artifact of the use of standardized belief lists. This evidence thus suggests that, so long as a person already has the relevant categorical judgment in place, trying to influence the *degree* of association between the object and the attribute won't influence attitude. If our hypothetical respondent already believes that Belch Beer tastes good, there appears to be little point in seeking changes in the exact degree of the respondent's subjective probability judgment that Belch Beer tastes good.

Of course, if our respondent thinks Belch Beer *doesn't* taste good, then in seeking to induce a positive attitude toward the beer, a persuader may well want to influence that belief by attempting to induce the belief that Belch does taste good. But this will be a matter of changing the relevant categorical judgment (from "Belch Beer doesn't taste good" to "Belch Beer does taste good"), and needn't be approached as though there is some psychologically-real probabilistic degree of perceived association between object and attribute.

ADVERTISING AND THE SUFFICIENCY OF THE MODEL It is easy enough to see how consumer advertising might be approached from this perspective. The advertiser's task is to get the consumer to believe that the product has various attributes thought desirable by the consumer (and, correlatively, to avoid having the consumer believe that the product has seriously undesirable attributes). That is, advertising presumably attempts to influence the consumer's beliefs about the product's attributes or characteristics, thereby influencing the consumer's attitude toward the product. But the question has arisen whether product attribute beliefs are in fact the only mediator of advertising's effects on attitudes. The matter at issue is whether advertising might influence product attitudes in ways other than by influencing product attribute beliefs — which is to say, in ways other than represented in Fishbein's model of attitude. Expressed somewhat differently, the question is one of the sufficiency of $\Sigma b_i e_i$ to predict attitude: might some additional factor, beyond beliefs about the product (that is, beyond $\Sigma b_i e_i$), contribute to the prediction of attitude?

There is now evidence to suggest that, at least under some circumstances, the influence of advertising on receivers' attitudes toward a given brand or product comes about not only through receivers' beliefs about the product's characteristics, but also through the receivers' evaluation of the advertisement itself (the receivers' "attitude-toward-the-ad"). As receivers have more favorable evaluations of the advertising, they come to have more favorable attitudes toward the product being advertised. And this effect occurs over and above the advertising's effects on product beliefs; that is, attitude-toward-the-ad and $\Sigma b_i e_i$ jointly have been found to be more successful in predicting attitude than has $\Sigma b_i e_i$ alone (Gardner, 1985; Mitchell, 1986; Mitchell & Olson, 1981; for related findings, see Lutz, MacKenzie, & Belch, 1983; MacKenzie, Lutz, & Belch, 1986).

However, this role for attitude-toward-the-ad is apparently minimized as product familiarity increases (see D. S. Cox & Locander, 1987; Machleit & Wilson, 1988; for related results, see Muehling & Laczniak, 1988). Thus how much receivers like the ad can influence product liking for unfamiliar products or brands, but will have little influence with familiar products or brands (toward which the consumer presumably has more firmly established attitudes). These findings are consistent with other research suggesting that the predictability of attitude from Fishbein's formula improves as the respondents' familiarity with the attitude object increases (M. H. Davis & Runge, 1981; Dover & Olson, 1977; Milord & Perry, 1976; J. C. Olson & Dover, 1978).

IDENTIFYING FOCI FOR APPEALS   Finally, it should be noted that Fishbein's attitude model may be useful in identifying likely foci for persuasive appeals. This facet of the model is particularly apparent when considering mass-persuasion contexts. Suppose, for example, that one was undertaking a persuasive campaign concerning the construction of nuclear power plants, and had undertaken a survey assessing the beliefs of those favoring and those opposing such plants, with survey results that included the following findings (with these means having a possible range of +3 to −3).

| | b_i | | e_i | |
nuclear power attributes	*pro-NP*	*anti-NP*	*pro-NP*	*anti-NP*
prevents a future energy crisis	+2.8	−2.5	+2.7	+2.7
increases risk of nuclear accident	−2.4	+2.9	−2.8	−2.6
creates waste disposal problems	+2.2	+2.3	−1.3	−2.8
leads to higher energy costs	+1.9	+2.0	−2.5	−2.4

These results suggest that (among these hypothetical respondents) those who favor and oppose nuclear power equally value the attribute of preventing an energy crisis (mean belief evaluations of 2.7 in each group), but those favoring nuclear power think this outcome much more likely (mean belief-strength rating of 2.8) than do those opposing nuclear power (mean belief-strength rating of −2.5). Both groups of respondents negatively evaluate any increased risk of a nuclear accident, but only those opposed to nuclear power think this outcome very likely. Both groups think nuclear power will create waste disposal problems, but those opposed to nuclear power think this a much more undesirable outcome than do those favoring nuclear power. And everybody thinks nuclear power is reasonably likely to lead to the negatively evaluated consequence of higher energy costs.

It is probably apparent how one can pretty quickly identify the most likely avenues for persuasive efforts in this circumstance — and how one can also identify probable blind alleys. For instance, suppose one's campaign is aimed at inducing favorable attitudes toward nuclear power (and so aimed at persuading those who are anti-nuclear power). There wouldn't be much point in constructing messages aimed at showing just how desirable it would be to prevent a future energy crisis — because even those respondents opposed to nuclear power already believe that such an outcome is quite desirable. With respect to the attribute of "preventing a future energy crisis," what these opponents of nuclear power need to be persuaded of is not whether such an outcome is desirable, but rather whether nuclear power will produce such a result. By contrast, the campaign's messages concerning potential waste disposal problems might well focus profitably on receivers' evaluations of such problems (rather than trying to instill the belief that such problems will occur).

SUMMARY

Fishbein's summative model of attitude obviously offers some straightforward recommendations to persuaders (to attend to the receiver's salient beliefs, to focus the message on altering belief strength and belief evaluation in appropriate ways, and so on). Notice, however, that the model emphasizes message content as central to persuasive effects, and does not speak directly to the roles played by such factors as communicator credibility, message organization, and receiver personality traits. From the model's point of view, all such factors influence message-induced attitude change only indirectly — indirectly in the sense that their influence is felt only through whatever effects they might have on belief strength and evaluation.

Unhappily, there is little research evidence that directly supports this claim. Indeed, as discussed previously, there is some evidence that, at least under some circumstances, such "external" factors as the receiver's attitude-toward-the-ad can be found to have effects on attitude that are not mediated by belief strength and belief evaluation. The empirical evidence thus offers tantalizing hints that perhaps this attitude model best describes the underpinnings of only some (not all) attitudes — specifically, relatively well-defined, stable, internally coherent attitudes.[3]

ALTERNATIVE INFORMATION-INTEGRATION MODELS

OTHER EXPECTANCY-VALUE MODELS

Fishbein's summative model of attitude is sometimes referred to as an "expectancy-value" model of attitude. An expectancy-value (EV) model of attitude represents attitude as a function of the products of (a) the value of a given attribute (e.g., the attribute's desirability) and (b) the expectation that the object has the attribute (e.g., belief strength). Fishbein's is only one version of an EV model, however. This basic EV idea has been formulated in various ways (e.g., Peak, 1955; Rosenberg, 1956). For example, in "adequacy-importance" versions of this approach, one assesses the respondent's judgment of (a) the importance of a given quality or characteristic and (b) the object's adequacy with regard to that characteristic (see, e.g., Sheth & Talarzyk, 1972). (For recent general discussions of EV models of attitude, see Bagozzi, 1984, 1985; Eagly & Chaiken, 1984, pp. 316-321).

For a time there was in some quarters no little confusion about the relation- ships among these various expressions of the general expectancy-value idea; in some cases, all the different EV models seem to have been treated as though they were identical models (for a lucid treatment of this matter, see J. B. Cohen, Fishbein, & Ahtola, 1972). It has now become plain that, despite some very general similarities in overall approach, there are important differences among these various models (and so, for instance, evidence concerning one EV model ought not be presumed to be relevant to the assessment of another EV model). Of all the various expectancy-value models of attitude, Fishbein's is the most studied, appears to have been the most successful empirically, and indeed is the standard against which alternative expectancy-value models have commonly been tested (e.g., Bettman et al., 1975; Holbrook & Hulbert, 1975).

ANDERSON'S AVERAGING MODEL

THE WEIGHTED-AVERAGING MODEL There is another well-studied infor- mation-integration model, one not based so directly on expectancy-value ideas: Norman Anderson's weighted-averaging model (see, e.g., N. H. Anderson, 1971, 1981b).[4] Anderson's model represents attitude as a function of the weight (w) and scale value (s) of each piece of information (belief) about the object. The scale value represents the degree of favorability of the information (akin to e_i in Fishbein's model); the weight represents the relative impact of each piece of information on the attitude (e.g., the importance or relevance of the informa- tion). The model embodies the idea that when new information is received, the resulting attitude will be a function of both the prior attitude and the new information. Specifically, the weighted-averaging model of attitude can be expressed as follows:

$$A_O = \frac{w_0 s_0 + \Sigma w_i s_i}{w_0 + \Sigma w_i}$$

In this equation, A_O represents the attitude toward the object, w_0 and s_0 represent the weight and scale value of the original attitude, and w_i and s_i represent the weight and scale value of each new piece of information.

ADDING VERSUS AVERAGING The existence of different models of infor- mation integration has naturally given rise to research aimed at comparing these models. A common research setting for the comparison of adding and averaging models involves the study of attitude formation (so that the scale value for the initial attitude is neutral, thus simplifying matters). A context found attractive by many researchers is that of personality impression formation, in which information about some stimulus person is presented (usually in the form of personality traits ascribed to that person); following the presentation of this information, the respondent's attitude toward the stimulus person is assessed. The evaluation of each individual personality trait is ordinarily obtained prior to the presentation of the combination of traits, thereby permitting predictions about how a given combination of traits will be evaluated. The further simplifying assumption is sometimes made that each piece of presented information receives equal belief strength (b_i, for Fishbein's model) or weight (w_i, for Anderson's model).

Some version of this format constitutes a common forum in which adding and averaging models of information integration have been compared. This research, however, has not provided compelling evidence to prefer one model over the other (for a useful general discussion of much of this research literature, see Wyer, 1974, pp. 263-306). There are several reasons for this inconclusive state of research.

First, the two models often make equivalent predictions (say, when the number of beliefs is constant). Imagine, for example, that in an impression-formation task, respondents are presented with trait information about two different persons: The information about person A consists of four traits, each evaluated moderately positively (so the set consists of traits rated +2, +2, +2, and +2, on some +3/−3 scale), and the information about person B consists of four highly positive traits (+3, +3, +3, +3). The adding model predicts that respondents will have a more favorable attitude toward B (the sum of the evaluations is +12) than toward A (the sum of the evaluations being +8); but the averaging model makes the same prediction, that B (whose traits average 3.00) will be liked better than A (whose traits average 2.00).

Second, in cases where the two models make different predictions, the research evidence is not conclusive: Sometimes the results have appeared to support an averaging model, sometimes an adding model. On the one hand, for example, there is research evidence suggesting that the evaluation based on several pieces of equally favorable information is more extreme than the evaluation of any one such piece of information (e.g., Fishbein & Hunter, 1964); this finding appears to favor an adding model. So, for instance, if stimulus person A is described as having three moderately positive traits (+2, +2, +2), and stimulus person B is described as having two moderately positive traits (+2, +2), stimulus person A will be better liked (which is what an adding model predicts, whereas an averaging model predicts A and B will be evaluated equally positively).[5]

On the other hand, there is also evidence indicating that evaluations based on a combination of extreme and moderate information are less extreme than evaluations based on the extreme information alone (e.g., N. H. Anderson, 1965); such evidence suggests the superiority of an averaging model. For instance, suppose stimulus person A is described by two extremely positive traits and one slightly positive trait (+3, +3, +1), and stimulus person B is described by only the two extremely positive characteristics (+3, +3); stimulus person B is typically better liked (which is what an averaging model predicts, whereas an adding model predicts that A will be better liked than B).

Finally, much of the research comparing adding and averaging models appears to require questionable assumptions about information-integration processes. At least some tests, for example, assume that the various pieces of information have equal weights; but obviously this assumption will not always be sound. Commonly, the out-of-context evaluation of a piece of information is assumed to be the same as the evaluation of that information when combined with other pieces of information; but there is evidence indicating that this assumption is not sound (e.g., Delia, 1976a).[6] And often respondents' attitudes are taken to be strictly a function of the presented information, without considering the ways in which respondents might make inferences that go beyond the information given; but a failure to consider such inferential beliefs can obviously make for misleading conclusions. The general point is this: The implausibility of assumptions such as these should make one wary about the degree to which extant research evidence can provide a basis for firm conclusions about the relative superiority of adding and averaging models of information integration.

Indeed, the difficulties in obtaining evidence yielding satisfactory comparisons of these models, the apparent evidence indicating no general superiority of one over the other, the very real possibility that neither model provides an entirely satisfactory account of information-integration processes — considerations such as these recommend the conclusion that there is not likely to be any very simple general resolution of this matter (see, e.g., Wyer, 1974, pp. 305-306; Yamagishi & Hill, 1981).

An inability to display any decisive general superiority of one model over the other is in some ways unfortunate, as adding and averaging models can yield very different recommendations to persuaders. Suppose, for example, that voters have a generally favorable attitude toward some policy issue (e.g., gun control) that appears as a referendum ballot item. The organizers of the campaign favoring that policy discover some new advantage to the proposed policy. Naturally enough, they undertake an advertising campaign to publicize this new positive attribute of the policy, hoping to make voters' attitudes even more favorable toward their position.

The initiation of this new campaign rests implicitly on an adding model of how this new information will be integrated: Adding a new positive belief about an object should make attitudes toward that object more favorable. But an averaging model will predict that, at least under some circumstances, the addition of this new positive attribute will make attitudes toward the policy *less* favorable than they had been — and hence would suggest that this new advertising campaign is ill advised. For example, suppose that the existing favorable attitudes toward the policy were based on four beliefs (pieces of information) evaluated +3, +3, +3, and +2, while the new belief (the new attribute) is evaluated +2 (and, to simplify matters, assume equal weights for each attribute). The mean of the initial four attributes is 2.75, but the mean of the set of five attributes is 2.60 (that is, adding the new attribute lowers the mean evaluation). But in the absence of good evidence about just what sort of information-integration model might best describe what will occur in a circumstance such as this, one can hardly give persuaders firm recommendations.[7]

CONCLUSION

The general idea that the information one has about an object influences one's attitude toward that object is in some ways fundamental to the concept of persuasion. After all, persuasion might plausibly be seen to turn on the notion that attitudes can be influenced through the presentation of information. Hence it is not surprising that information-integration models of attitude have received such attention from students of persuasion. But there is probably no single simple rule by which persons integrate the information available to them about an object so as to yield an overall attitude toward the object — and there is as yet no clear picture of when different information-integration principles might come into play.

NOTES

1. Though not discussed here, the difficulties in assessing belief importance should not be underestimated; see Jaccard, Brinberg, and Ackerman (1986) and Jaccard and Sheng (1984).

2. Notably, the failure of belief-strength scores to contribute to attitude prediction with individualized belief lists is apparently not due to a lack of variability in belief-strength scores; see Delia et al. (1975, p. 16).

3. Cast in terms of the elaboration likelihood model (Chapter 6), perhaps the attitudes under discussion are those formed through relatively central (as opposed to peripheral) routes.

4. Actually, Anderson offers a much broader theory — called "information integration theory" — than is described here (see, e.g., N. H. Anderson, 1981a). The general notion is that there are many different information-integration principles that persons employ, with the weighted-averaging principle being only one of these. But the weighted-averaging principle is the one most studied, and there is not yet any good account of the conditions under which one or another principle will be employed; consequently the averaging model is the focus of attention here. Eagly and Chaiken (1984, pp. 321-331) provide a useful discussion both of Anderson's general theory and of the weighted-averaging model.

5. However, it is possible for this finding to be reconciled with an averaging model, by assuming that an initially neutral attitude is integrated with the presented information (N. H. Anderson, 1965). In this example, if one includes another information item with a scale value of zero (to represent this initial neutral attitude), then the mean for stimulus person A would be 1.5, and the mean of B would be 1.33 (i.e., A would be predicted to be better liked).

6. Notice that the possibility of shifting evaluations of information (depending on the information context) makes it very difficult to place heavy reliance on research findings based on methods not attuned to this possibility. Consider, for example: The evidence indicating that evaluations based on a combination of extreme and moderate information are less extreme than evaluations based on the extreme information alone — evidence putatively supporting the superiority of an averaging model — looks rather less compelling when one remembers that such evidence commonly presumes the stability of information evaluation.

7. One ought not think that the research evidence discussed earlier—concerning the effects of combining extreme and moderate information—proves that the averaging model's prediction will be accurate in this circumstance. As discussed in the preceding note, once it is acknowledged that the evaluations of attributes may shift depending on the particular combination of attributes, such conclusions appear to go beyond the evidence available.

4

Cognitive Dissonance Theory

A NUMBER OF DIFFERENT attitude theories have been based on the idea of "cognitive consistency"—the idea that persons seek to maximize the internal psychological consistency of their cognitions (beliefs, attitudes, and so on). Cognitive inconsistency is taken to be an uncomfortable state, and hence persons are seen as striving to avoid it (or, failing that, seeking to get rid of it). Heider's (1946, 1958) balance theory was perhaps the earliest effort at developing such a consistency theory (for a review of some relevant research, see Crockett, 1982). Osgood and Tannenbaum's (1955) congruity theory represented another variety of consistency theory (for a later version of congruity theory, see Bostrom, 1982; for a review of some relevant research, see Wyer, 1974, pp. 151-185).

But of all the efforts at articulating the general notion of cognitive consistency, the most influential and productive has been Leon Festinger's (1957) cognitive dissonance theory. This chapter offers first a sketch of the general outlines of dissonance theory, and then a discussion of several areas of research application.

GENERAL THEORETICAL SKETCH

ELEMENTS AND RELATIONS

Cognitive dissonance theory is concerned with the relations among cognitive elements (also called "cognitions"). An element is any belief, opinion, attitude, or piece of knowledge about anything — about other persons, objects, issues, oneself, and so on.

There are three possible relations that might hold between any two cognitive elements. They might be *irrelevant* to each other, that is, have nothing to do with each other. My belief that university tuition will increase next year and my favorable opinion of Swiss chocolate are presumably irrelevant to each other. Two cognitive elements might be *consonant* (consistent) with each other; that is, they might hang together, form a package. My belief that golf is a noble game and my liking to play golf are presumably consonant cognitions.

Finally, two cognitive elements might be *dissonant* (inconsistent) with each other. The careful specification of a dissonant relation is this: Two elements are said to be in a dissonant relation if the opposite of one element follows from the other. Thus (to use Festinger's classic example) my cognition that I smoke and my cognition that smoking causes cancer are dissonant with each other; from my knowing that smoking causes cancer, it follows that I shouldn't smoke — but I do.[1]

DISSONANCE

When two cognitions are in a dissonant relation, the person with those two cognitions is said to have dissonance, or to experience dissonance, or to be in a state of dissonance. Dissonance is taken to be an aversive motivational state; persons will want to avoid experiencing dissonance, and if they do encounter dissonance they will attempt to reduce it.

Dissonance may vary in magnitude: One might have a lot of dissonance, a little, or a moderate amount. As the magnitude of dissonance varies, so will the pressure to reduce it; with increasing dissonance, there will be increasing pressure to reduce it. With small amounts of dissonance, there may be little or no motivational pressure.

FACTORS INFLUENCING THE MAGNITUDE OF DISSONANCE

Expressed most broadly, the magnitude of dissonance experienced will be a function of two factors. One is the relative proportions of consonant and dissonant elements. Thus far, dissonance has been discussed as a simple two-element affair, but usually what is involved is actually two *clusters* of elements. Thus a smoker may believe, on the one hand, that smoking reduces his anxiety, makes him appear sophisticated, and tastes good, and on the other hand also believe that smoking causes cancer and is expensive. There are here two clusters of cognitions, one of elements consonant with smoking (reduces anxiety and so on) and one of dissonant elements (expensive and so on). Just how much dissonance this smoker experiences will depend on the relative size of these two clusters. As the proportion of consonant elements (to the total number of elements) increases, less and less dissonance will be experienced; but as the cluster of dissonant elements grows (compared to the size of the consonant cluster), the amount of dissonance will increase.

The second factor that influences the degree of dissonance is the importance of the elements or issue. The greater importance this smoker assigns to the expense and cancer-causing aspects of smoking, the greater the dissonance he will feel; correspondingly, the greater importance the smoker assigns to anxiety reduction and the maintenance of a sophisticated appearance, the less dissonance he will feel. Or if the entire question of smoking is devalued in importance, less dissonance will be felt.

MEANS OF REDUCING DISSONANCE

There are two broad means of reducing dissonance, corresponding to the two factors influencing the magnitude of dissonance. The first way to reduce dissonance is by changing the relative proportions of consonant and dissonant elements. This can be accomplished in several ways. One can add new consonant cognitions; the smoker, for instance, might come to believe that smoking prevents colds — a new consonant cognition added to the consonant cluster. Or one can change or delete existing dissonant cognitions; the smoker might persuade himself that, say, smoking doesn't really cause cancer.

The other way to reduce dissonance is by altering the importance of the issue or the elements involved. The smoker could reduce dissonance by deciding that the expense of smoking isn't that important to him (devaluing the importance of that dissonant cognition), or might come to think that reducing his anxiety is a very important outcome to him (increasing the importance of a consonant cognition), or might decide that the whole question of smoking just isn't that important.

SOME RESEARCH APPLICATIONS

Cognitive dissonance theory has produced a great deal of empirical work (for a general review, see Wicklund & Brehm, 1976). In the study of persuasive communication, there are three specific research areas of interest: decision making, selective exposure to information, and forced compliance.

DECISION MAKING

One interesting application of dissonance theory comes in the area of decision making (or choice making). Dissonance is said to be a postdecisional phenomenon; that is, dissonance arises after a decision or choice has been made. When facing a decision (in the simplest case, a choice between two alternatives), one is said to experience conflict. But after making the choice, one will almost inevitably experience at least some dissonance, and thus will be faced with the task of dissonance reduction. So the general sequence is (a) conflict, (b) decision, (c) dissonance, and (d) dissonance reduction.

CONFLICT Virtually every decision a person makes is likely to involve at least some conflict. It is rare that an individual faces a choice between one perfectly positive option and one absolutely negative alternative. Usually, the choice is between two (or more) alternatives that are neither perfectly good nor perfectly bad — and hence there is at least some conflict, because the choice is not without some trade-offs. Just how much conflict is experienced by a person facing a decision will depend (at least in part) on the initial evaluation of the alternatives. When (to take the simplest two-option case) the two alternatives are initially evaluated quite similarly, the decision maker will experience considerable conflict; two nearly equally attractive options make for a difficult choice.

This conflict stage is the juncture at which persuasive efforts are most obviously relevant. Ordinarily, persuasive efforts are aimed at regulating (either increasing or decreasing) the amount of conflict experienced by decision makers. If one's friend is inclined toward seeing the new Clint Eastwood film rather than the new Woody Allen movie, one can attempt to undermine that preference and so increase the friend's conflict (by saying things aimed at getting the friend to have a less positive evaluation of the Eastwood film, and by saying things aimed at producing a more positive evaluation of the Allen movie), or one can attempt to persuade the friend to follow that inclination and so reduce the friend's conflict (by saying things aimed at enhancing the evaluation of the already-preferred Eastwood film, and by saying things aimed at reducing further the evaluation of the Allen movie).

Of course, a persuader might attempt to regulate a decision maker's conflict by trying to alter the evaluation of only *one* (not both) of the alternatives; I might try to get you to have a more positive attitude toward my preferred position on the persuasive issue, even though I don't attack the opposing point of view. But — perhaps not surprisingly — a review of the research evidence (Jackson & Allen, 1987) suggests that "one-sided" persuasive communications (which only make arguments supporting the persuader's position) are generally not as effective as "two-sided" messages (which additionally undertake to refute arguments favoring the opposing side). This evidence (also discussed in Chapter 9) suggests that, as a rule, persuaders are most likely to regulate successfully the conflict experienced by the persuadee if they attempt to influence the evaluation not only of their preferred alternative, but of other options as well.

In any case, by regulating the degree of conflict experienced, the persuader can presumably make it more likely that the persuadee will choose the option desired by the persuader. But after the persuadee has made a choice (whether the one wanted by the persuader or not), he or she will almost inevitably face at least some dissonance — and, as will be seen, the processes attendant to the occurrence of dissonance have important implications for persuasion.

DECISION AND DISSONANCE The reason that at least some dissonance is probably inevitable after a decision is that, in virtually every decision, there are at least some aspects of the situation that are dissonant with one's choice. Somewhat more specifically, there are likely to be some undesirable aspects to the chosen alternative and some desirable aspects to the unchosen alternatives; each of these is dissonant with the choice made, and hence at least some dissonance is likely to be created.

Consider, for example, a person's choosing where to eat lunch. Al's Fresco Restaurant offers good food and a pleasant atmosphere, but is some distance away and usually has slow service. The Bistro Cafe has so-so food, and the atmosphere isn't much, but it's nearby and has quick service. No matter which restaurant one chooses, there will be some things dissonant with one's choice. In choosing the Bistro, for instance, one will face certain undesirable aspects of the chosen alternative (e.g., the poor atmosphere) and certain desirable aspects of the unchosen alternative (e.g., the good food one could have had at Al's).

FACTORS INFLUENCING THE DEGREE OF DISSONANCE The amount of dissonance one faces following a choice is taken to depend most centrally on two factors. One is the similarity of the initial evaluations: The closer the initial evaluations of the alternatives, the greater the dissonance. Thus a choice between two nearly equally attractive sweaters is likely to evoke more dissonance than a choice between one fairly attractive and one fairly unattractive sweater. The other factor is the relative importance of the decision, with more important decisions predicted to yield more dissonance. A choice about what to eat for dinner this evening is likely to provoke less dissonance than a choice of what career to pursue.

Notice that these two factors represent merely particularized versions of the general factors influencing the degree of dissonance experienced: the relative proportions of consonant and dissonant elements (since where the two alternatives are evaluated quite similarly, the proportions of consonant and dissonant elements will presumably approach 50-50) and the importance of the issue or elements (here represented as the importance of the decision).

DISSONANCE REDUCTION One convenient way in which a decision maker can reduce the dissonance felt following a choice is by reevaluating the alternatives. By evaluating the chosen alternative *more* positively than one did before, and by evaluating the unchosen alternative *less* positively than before, the amount of dissonance felt can be reduced. Since this process of re-rating the alternatives will result in the alternatives being less similarly evaluated than they were prior to the decision, this effect is sometimes described as the postdecisional "spreading" of alternatives ("spreading" in the sense that the alternatives are spread further apart along the evaluative dimension than they had been). If (as dissonance theory predicts) persons experience dissonance following decisions, then one should find dissonance reduction in the form of this postdecisional spreading of the alternatives; and one should find greater spreading (i.e., greater dissonance reduction) in circumstances in which dissonance is presumably greater.

In simplified form, the typical experimental arrangement in dissonance-based studies of choice making is one in which respondents initially give evaluations of a number of objects or alternatives, and are then faced with making a choice between two of these. After making the choice, respondents are then asked to reevaluate the alternatives, with these rankings inspected for evidence of dissonance reduction through postdecisional spreading of alternatives.

In general, the research evidence appears to indicate that one does often find the predicted changes in evaluations following decisions (e.g., Brehm, 1956; White & Gerard, 1981); the evidence is not quite so strong that the magnitude of dissonance reduction is greater when the conditions for heightened dissonance are present (as when the two alternatives are initially rated quite closely, or the decision is quite important), for conflicting findings have been reported, especially for the effects of decisional importance (for discussion, see Converse & Cooper, 1979).

The general finding of postdecisional spreading in the evaluations of the alternatives suggests that decision-maker satisfaction will (in the words of Wicklund & Brehm, 1976, p. 289) "take care of itself." Since persons are likely to value more positively that which they have freely chosen, if one can induce persons to choose a given alternative, they will be likely to value more positively that alternative just because they've chosen it. For example, if one can induce persons to buy one's product, they'll likely have a more positive attitude toward the product just as a consequence of having chosen to buy it. Of course, this does not mean that every purchaser is guaranteed to end up being a satisfied customer; it still may happen that (say) a new-car buyer decides that the car purchased is a "lemon," and so returns it to the dealer. Nevertheless, there are forces at work that incline persons to be happier with whatever they've chosen, just because they've chosen it.

Persuaders might infer from this that once a persuadee has been induced to decide the way the persuader wants, the persuader's job is done; after all, having made the choice, the persuadee is likely to become more satisfied with it through the ordinary processes of dissonance reduction. This inference is quite unsound, however; persuaders who reason in this fashion may find their persuasive efforts failing in the end, in part because of the occurrence of "regret."

REGRET Though not anticipated in Festinger's (1957) original treatment of decision making, the phenomenon of "regret" has emerged as an important aspect of postdecisional cognitive processes (see Festinger, 1964). What appears to happen is that after the decision has been made, but before the dissonance has been reduced (through postdecisional spreading of alternatives), the alternatives are temporarily evaluated *more similarly* (that is, rated closer together) than they were initially. Then, following this "regret" phase (during which dissonance presumably increases), the person moves on to the matter of dissonance reduction, with the evaluations of the alternatives spreading further apart (see Festinger & Walster, 1964; Walster, 1964).

One plausible account of this "regret" phenomenon is that, having made the choice, the decision maker now faces the task of dissonance reduction. Quite naturally the decision maker's attention focuses on those cognitions that are dissonant with his or her choice — on undesirable aspects of the chosen option, and on desirable aspects of the unchosen option, perhaps in the hope of eventually being able to minimize each. As the decision maker focuses on undesirable aspects of the chosen alternative, that alternative may seem (at least temporarily) less attractive than it had before; and focusing on desirable aspects of the unchosen option may make that option seem (at least temporarily) more attractive than it had before; and with the chosen alternative becoming rated less favorably, and the unchosen alternative becoming rated more favorably, the two alternatives naturally become evaluated more similarly than they had been.

In fact, during this "regret" phase, it is even possible that the initial evaluations become reversed, so that the initially unchosen alternative becomes rated more favorably than the chosen option. In such a circumstance, the decision maker may back out of the original choice. This sort of outcome becomes more likely when the two alternatives are initially evaluated rather similarly, since in such a circumstance comparatively small swings in absolute evaluations can make for reversals in the relative evaluations of the alternatives.

There is a moral here for persuaders, and it concerns the importance of follow-up persuasive efforts. It can be too easy for a persuader to assume that the job is done when the persuadee has been induced to choose in the way the persuader wants; but the possibility of regret, and particularly the possibility of the decision maker's mind changing, should make the persuader realize that simply inducing the initial decision may not be enough.

A fitting example is provided by Donnelly and Ivancevich's (1970) study of automobile buying. In purchases of automobiles from a dealer, there is ordinarily some time that elapses between the buyer's agreeing to buy the car and the actual delivery of the car to him or her. It sometimes happens that during this interval, the would-be purchaser changes his or her mind, and backs out of the decision to buy the car. (There are likely any number of reasons this happens, but it should be easy enough to imagine that at least some of the time something like the regret phenomenon is at work.) In Donnelly and Ivancevich's investigation, during the interval between decision and delivery, some automobile purchasers received two follow-up telephone calls from the seller; the calls emphasized the desirable aspects of the automobile that had been chosen, reassured the purchaser of the wisdom of the decision, and (one might say) encouraged the purchaser to move past the regret phase and into the stage of dissonance reduction. Other purchasers received no such call. Significantly fewer of the purchasers receiving the follow-up calls backed out of their decisions than did those not receiving the call (the back-out rate was cut in half), underlining the potential importance of follow-up persuasive efforts.

SELECTIVE EXPOSURE TO INFORMATION

A second area of dissonance theory research that is relevant to persuasion concerns persons' propensities to expose themselves selectively to information. In what follows, the dissonance-theoretic analysis of information exposure is presented, and then the relevant research is reviewed and discussed.

THE DISSONANCE THEORY ANALYSIS If dissonance is an aversive motivational state, then naturally persons will want to do what they can to avoid dissonance-arousing situations, and will prefer instead to be in circumstances that do not arouse dissonance (or even that increase the consonance of their cognitions). This general idea finds specific expression in the form of dissonance theory's "selective exposure" hypothesis. Broadly put, this hypothesis has it that persons will prefer to be exposed to information that is supportive of (consonant with) their current beliefs rather than to nonsupportive information (which presumably could arouse dissonance).

At one point in the study of the effects of mass communication, this selective exposure hypothesis was especially attractive to researchers. Early in the study of mass communication's effects, it was commonly presumed that the mass media had significant and far-reaching impacts on the audience's attitudes and beliefs. But in fact it proved rather difficult to find convincing evidence of the supposedly powerful effects of mass communication. As a result, the focal question for researchers became not, Why and how does mass communication have these powerful effects? but, instead, Why *doesn't* mass communication have the tremendously powerful and obvious effects we expected it to have? (For discussion of these developments, see Blumler & Gurevitch, 1982; DeFleur & Ball-Rokeach, 1982.)[2]

Against this backdrop, the attractiveness of the selective exposure hypothesis should be plain. If persons generally expose themselves only to media sources that confirm or reinforce their prior beliefs (and, correlatively, avoid exposure to nonsupportive or inconsistent information), then the powerful effects of the mass media would naturally be blunted: Media messages would only be preaching to the converted (at least on topics on which persons already had well-established attitudes).

More generally, of course, the selective exposure hypothesis suggests that persuaders (through the mass media or otherwise) may need to be concerned about getting receivers to attend to their messages. If, as dissonance theory suggests, there is a predisposition to avoid nonsupportive information, then persuaders may face the task of somehow overcoming that obstacle so that their communications can have a chance to persuade.

THE RESEARCH EVIDENCE In the typical experimental research paradigm for the investigation of selective exposure, respondents' attitudes on a given issue are assessed. Then respondents are given the choice of seeing (reading, hearing) one of several different communications on the issue. These communications are described in such a way as to make clear what position on the issue is advocated by each, and both supportive and nonsupportive messages are included. The respondent is then asked to select one of the messages. Support for the selective exposure hypothesis consists of respondents' preferring to see supportive rather than nonsupportive communications.

For some time it proved quite difficult to detect any consistent selective exposure principle at work in persons' informational preferences. Indeed, several reviews in the 1960s concluded that there was little or no evidence to support the selective exposure hypothesis (Freedman & Sears, 1965a; Sears & Freedman, 1967); there did not seem to be any general preference for supportive information such as had been expected from dissonance theory. Other observers, however, argued that much of the experimental work failed to control for possible confounding factors and so never offered a realistic chance for the detection of a preference for supportive information (for discussions of some problems with early research on selective exposure, see Rhine, 1967; Wicklund & Brehm, 1976).

Subsequent research that attempted to avoid the weaknesses of earlier studies was able to detect a preference for supportive information (e.g., Cotton & Hieser, 1980; J. M. Olson & Zanna, 1979). Thus at present the research on selective exposure seems to suggest that there is in fact some preference for supportive information — but this research has also pointed up a number of *other* (often competing) influences on information exposure (for useful reviews, see Cotton, 1985; Frey, 1986).

OTHER INFLUENCES ON EXPOSURE One such additional influence on information exposure appears to be the perceived utility of the information, with persons preferring information with greater perceived utility. Consider, for example, an investigation by Rosen (1961), in which undergraduates initially chose to take either a multiple-choice exam or an essay exam. The students were then asked for their preferences among reading several articles, some supporting the decision and some obviously nonsupportive. For instance, for a student who chose the multiple-choice exam, the nonsupportive articles were described as arguing that students who prefer multiple-choice tests would actually be likely to do better on essay exams. Contrary to the selective exposure hypothesis — but not surprisingly — most of the students preferred articles advocating a change from the type of exam they had chosen. Obviously, in this study, the nonsupportive communication offered information that might be of substantial usefulness to the students, and the perceived utility of the information could well have outweighed any preference for supportive information.

Surely another influence on information exposure is sheer curiosity. An investigation by Freedman (1965) had respondents listen to a tape recording of an interview in which the interviewee came off as either exceptionally well suited or exceptionally poorly suited to the position being sought. Respondents were asked to indicate their own judgment of the applicant's suitability for the position; as one might expect, these judgments were heavily influenced by which of the two versions of the interview was heard. Respondents were then given the opportunity of reading either a supportive or a nonsupportive communication; for instance, a respondent who heard the poorly suited applicant's interview, and who realized the applicant was poorly suited for the position, could read either a communication confirming that judgment or a communication asserting that the applicant was well qualified. Respondents did not exhibit a general preference for supportive information, and in fact overwhelmingly preferred to see the contradictory evaluation. One plausible explanation for this result is that often the respondents were simply curious about the basis for the opposing judgment ("How could *anybody* think that guy was qualified? I want to see that evaluation!").

What might be called "fairness norms" may also play a role in information exposure. In certain social settings, there is an emphasis on obtaining the greatest amount of information possible, on being fair to all sides, on being open-minded until all the evidence is in. One such setting is the trial. In Sears's (1965) study, participants received brief synopses of a murder case, and then rendered a judgment about the guilt of the defendant. They were subsequently offered a chance of seeing either confirming or disconfirming information (e.g., for a mock juror who thought the defendant was guilty, disconfirming information would consist of information indicating that the defendant was actually innocent). Participants showed a general preference for nonsupportive information, perhaps because the trial setting was one that made salient the norms of fairness and openness to evidence.

SUMMARY All told, there may be some (slight) preference for supportive information, as expected by dissonance theory. However, this preference is only one of many (often competing) influences on information exposure, and hence this preference may be overridden by other considerations. This general conclusion — based largely on experimental laboratory investigations — is consistent with the results of field research concerning information exposure. As a rule, investigations of selectivity in exposure to mass communications have typically turned up little evidence of strong selective exposure effects (e.g., Bertrand, 1979; Chaffee & Miyo, 1983; Swanson, 1976). Hence even if there is some general preference for supportive over nonsupportive information, the existence of other competing preferences may mean that in practice the effects of a preference for supportive material will often be washed out.

Even so, persuaders who hope to encourage attention to their messages will want to be attentive to the factors influencing information exposure, as these may suggest avenues by which such attention can be sought. In this connection, the American political scene in the summer of 1984 offered an instructive example of an attempt to influence information exposure. The Democratic presidential candidate nominating convention occurred first, and it had some potentially interesting aspects about it; although Walter Mondale was surely going to be the party's presidential nominee, there was some uncertainty about the stance that Gary Hart might adopt and about the role that Jesse Jackson might play, and there was additionally the attraction of a female vice presidential nominee (Geraldine Ferraro). Consequently, the Democratic convention held some appeal for television viewers, which presumably would be all to the good for the Democrats: The networks would televise the convention as part of their news coverage, thus providing a good deal of free air time for the Democratic party. The subsequent Republican convention, by contrast, was to be pretty much a pro forma affair; the nominees (Ronald Reagan and George Bush) were all settled, there was no great uncertainty about the course of events in the convention, and hence there might be little reason for anyone to watch. After the Democratic hurly-burly, but before the Republican convention, the Republican party placed advertisements aimed at getting the public to watch its convention. A central theme in these ads (which featured Barry Goldwater) was (in effect) the message that "it's your *duty*, your *responsibility*, to watch the Republican convention — to give a fair hearing to the Republicans." Obviously enough, the use of this theme represents an instance of the invocation of fairness norms in an attempt to influence information exposure.

FORCED COMPLIANCE

Perhaps the greatest amount of dissonance-theory-inspired research concerns what is commonly called "forced compliance." Forced compliance is said to occur when an individual is induced to act in a way discrepant with his or her beliefs and attitudes. Since in fact force need not be involved, the label *"forced compliance"* is rather misleading; *"induced* compliance" might be a more accurately descriptive term. But "forced compliance" is the phrase that is overwhelmingly used in the research literature, and hence it is the phrase used here.

One special case of forced compliance is counterattitudinal advocacy, which is said to occur when a person is led to advocate some viewpoint opposed to his or her own position. Most of the research on forced compliance concerns counterattitudinal advocacy, because that circumstance has proved a convenient focus for study.[3]

INCENTIVE AND DISSONANCE IN FORCED COMPLIANCE Obviously, forced-compliance situations have the potential to arouse dissonance; after all, a person is acting in a way discrepant with his or her beliefs. But what determines just how much dissonance a person will feel?

Dissonance theory suggests that the amount of dissonance experienced in a forced-compliance situation will depend centrally on the amount of *incentive* offered to the person to engage in the discrepant action. Any incentive offered for performing the counterattitudinal action (for example, some promised reward or threatened punishment) is consistent with engaging in the action — that is, is consonant with engaging in the action. Thus someone who performs a counterattitudinal action with very large incentives for doing so will experience relatively little dissonance.

To use Festinger's (1957) example: Suppose you're offered a million dollars to state publicly that you like reading comic books (assume, for the purpose of the example, that you find this offer believable and that you don't like reading comic books). Presumably you would accept the money and engage in the counterattitudinal advocacy. You might experience some small amount of dissonance (from saying one thing and believing another), but the million dollars is an important element that is *consonant* with your having performed the action, and hence overall there is little dissonance experienced.

But if the incentive had been smaller (less money offered), then the amount of dissonance experienced would have been greater. The greatest possible dissonance would occur if the incentive were only just enough to induce compliance (if the incentive were the minimum needed to get you to comply). Suppose (to continue the example) that you wouldn't have agreed to engage in the counterattitudinal advocacy for anything less than $100. In that case, an offer of exactly $100 — the minimum needed to induce compliance — would have produced the maximum possible dissonance. Any incentive larger than that minimum would only have reduced the amount of dissonance experienced.

Notice that when some substantial dissonance is created through forced compliance, pressure is created to reduce that dissonance. And one easy route to dissonance reduction is to bring one's private beliefs into line with one's behavior. Thus, for example, if you had declared that you liked reading comic books when offered only $100 (your minimum price) for doing so, you would have experienced considerable dissonance, and could easily reduce it by deciding that in fact you think reading comic books isn't quite as bad as you might have thought.

What happens if the incentive offered is insufficient to induce compliance? That is, what are the consequences if a person is offered some incentive for engaging in a counterattitudinal action, and the person doesn't comply? To continue the example, suppose that you had been offered only $10 to say that you like to read comic books. You would decline the offer, thereby losing the possibility of getting the $10 — and hence you would experience some dissonance over that ("I could have had that $10"). But you wouldn't experience very much dissonance, and certainly not as much as if you had turned down an offer of $90. That is, you would experience more dissonance if you decline a $90 offer than if you decline a $10 offer. And how might the dissonance of turning down $90 be reduced? One natural avenue is to strengthen one's initial negative attitude ("I was right to turn down that $90, because reading comic books really is pretty bad").

So the relationship between the amount of incentive offered and the amount of dissonance experienced is depicted (by dissonance theory) as being something like an inverted V. With increasing incentive, there is increasing dissonance — up to the point at which compliance occurs (up to the point at which the incentive is sufficiently large to induce compliance). But beyond that point, increasing incentive produces decreasing dissonance, such that with very large incentives there is little or no dissonance experienced from engaging in the counterattitudinal action. Thus so long as the amount of incentive is sufficient to induce compliance, additional incentive will make it less likely that the person will come to have more favorable attitudes toward the position being advocated.[4]

In a classic experiment, Festinger and Carlsmith (1959) obtained striking evidence for this analysis. In this study, participants performed an exceedingly dull and tedious task. At the conclusion of the task, they were asked to tell a student who was waiting to participate in the experiment (actually, the student was a confederate of the experimenter) that the task was enjoyable and interesting. As incentive for performing this counterattitudinal behavior, participants were offered money; half were offered $1 (low incentive) and half were offered $20 (high incentive). After engaging in the counterattitudinal advocacy, participants' attitudes toward the task were assessed.

Consistent with dissonance theory's predictions, Festinger and Carlsmith found that those receiving $1 came to think that the task was significantly more enjoyable than did those who complied for $20. Those who complied under the influence of a large incentive ($20) presumably experienced less dissonance from engaging in the counterattitudinal act (because they had the $20 that was consonant with performing the act) — and so had little need for attitude change. By contrast, participants receiving the small incentive ($1) presumably experienced more dissonance, and hence had more motivation to change their attitudes so as to reduce dissonance; they reduced their dissonance by coming to have a more favorable attitude toward the dull task.

Subsequent investigations provided additional confirming evidence (for a collection of papers on forced compliance, see Elms, 1969). For instance, in one study (A. R. Cohen, 1962) participants were offered incentives of 50 cents, $1.00, $5.00, or $10.00 for writing a counterattitudinal essay; participants who were offered the smaller incentives came to have more favorable attitudes about the position advocated than did those offered larger incentives. As another example, Aronson and Carlsmith (1963) found that children prohibited from playing with an attractive toy by a mild threat (of punishment for disobedience) subsequently found the toy less attractive than did children prohibited by a severe threat; that is, those who engaged in the counterattitudinal action of avoiding the toy when given only mild incentive to do so apparently experienced greater dissonance (than did those who avoided the toy when given strong incentives to do so), and hence displayed greater underlying attitude change. There have been relatively fewer studies of circumstances in which the incentives offered are insufficient to induce compliance, but this evidence is also generally consistent with dissonance theory predictions. For instance, Darley and Cooper (1972) found that persons who were offered insufficient incentives (to engage in counterattitudinal advocacy) were inclined to strengthen their initial attitudes, and — as expected from dissonance theory — greater strengthening occurred with larger incentives.

THE "LOW, LOW PRICE OFFER" An interesting example of forced-compliance processes is provided by the familiar marketing ploy of the "low, low price offer." Sometimes this offer is cast as a straightforward lower price ("50 cents off"), sometimes as "two for the price of one" (or "three for the price of two"), but in any case the central idea is that a lower price is offered to the consumer. Presumably, the lower price will make purchase more likely.

Now imagine a situation in which a particular consumer is faced with a number of competing brands of (say) soap. This consumer doesn't have an especially positive impression of Brand A — it's not the consumer's usual brand — but Brand A is running a really good low-price special ("three bars for the price of one"). From a dissonance theory point of view, this lower price represents an increased incentive for the consumer to purchase Brand A (increased incentive to engage in the counterattitudinal behavior of buying Brand A). As the "deal" gets better and better — that is, as the price gets lower and lower — there is more and more incentive to comply (incentive to purchase); for example, there is more incentive to comply when the deal is "three for the price of one" than when the deal is "two for the price of one."

The key insight offered by dissonance theory here is this: The greater the incentive to comply, the less dissonance created by the purchase — and hence the smaller the chance for favorable attitude change toward the brand. This consumer might buy Brand A this time (because the price is so low), but the consumer's underlying unfavorable attitude toward Brand A isn't likely to change — precisely because the incentive to comply was so great. That is to say, the "low, low price offer" might boost sales for a while, but it can also undermine the development of more positive attitudes toward the brand.

An illustration of these processes is offered by Doob, Carlsmith, Freedman, Landauer, and Tom (1969), who conducted five field experiments concerning the effects of low introductory selling prices. Using various stores in a chain of discount houses, Doob et al. introduced house brands of a number of common household products (e.g., aluminum foil, toothpaste, light bulbs). In some of the stores the brands were introduced at the regular price, whereas at other stores the brands were introduced with a "low, low introductory price offer" for a short period of time (before having the price increase to the regular price). As one might expect, when the low-price offer was in effect, sales were higher at the stores offering the lower prices. But when prices returned to normal, the subsequent sales were greater at the stores that had the initial higher prices. That is, introducing these products at low introductory prices proved to be harmful to long-run sales, presumably because there was relatively little brand loyalty established by the low introductory selling price. Thus the greater incentive created by the lower price apparently prevented the development of sufficiently positive attitudes toward the brand.

One should not conclude from this that the low-price offer is a foolish marketing stratagem that should never be used. The point is that this marketing technique sets in motion forces opposed to the development of positive attitudes toward the brand, and that these forces are greater as the incentive becomes greater (as the deal gets better). But notice that some low-price offers are better than others (from the point of view of creating favorable attitude change): A low-price offer that is only just barely good enough to induce purchase — an offer that provides just enough incentive to induce compliance — will create the maximum possible dissonance (and so, a marketer might hope, maximum favorable attitude change toward the product). Notice, too, that low-price offers may be useful as strategies for introducing new brands; the marketer's plan would be that the low price would induce initial purchase, and that this exposure to the brand's intrinsic positive characteristics will create a positive attitude toward the brand (thereby enhancing long-term sales). Of course, if the brand doesn't have sufficiently great intrinsic appeal (as was likely with the house brands studied by Doob et al., 1969), then using low introductory prices to induce trial won't successfully create underlying positive attitudes toward the brand. Finally, sometimes marketers are interested only in immediate sales, not in underlying favorable attitude change. For example, when there is a large inventory on hand and the costs of storage are becoming troublesome, or when the purchase in question is likely to be a one-time-only affair (not a matter of repeated purchase), low-price offers might justifiably be very attractive to marketers.

A LIMITING CONDITION   Researchers have not always obtained the forced-compliance effects predicted by dissonance theory. Indeed, with the accumulation of more and more such instances (instances of failure to reproduce the dissonance effects), investigators began to search for the factors that would determine whether one would obtain the expected results. A number of different hypotheses were proposed and discarded (for examples and discussion, see Carlsmith, Collins, & Helmreich, 1966; Elms, 1969; C. A. Kiesler, Collins, & Miller, 1969, pp. 213-214; Rosenberg, 1965).

But one important limiting condition has been successfully identified: In general, one finds the predicted dissonance effects only when the participants feel they had a *choice* about whether to comply (e.g., about whether to perform the advocacy). That is, freedom of choice seems to be a necessary condition for the appearance of dissonance effects in forced-compliance situations (the classic work on this subject is Linder, Cooper, & Jones, 1967). Thus one can expect that inducing counterattitudinal action with minimal incentive will produce substantial dissonance (and corresponding favorable attitude change) only when the person freely chooses to engage in the counterattitudinal behavior.[5]

ALTERNATIVE EXPLANATIONS   There have been a number of alternative explanations or interpretations offered of the forced-compliance research results; of these, two have been especially prominent. One is a self-perception explanation (e.g., Bem, 1972), which suggests that the observed attitude-change effects reflect not underlying dissonance processes, but self-perception and self-attribution processes. Expressed briefly, the idea is that counterattitudinal advocates infer what their attitudes are from seeing themselves engage in the advocacy with a given level of incentive (much as one might infer what another person's attitude is from seeing that person engage in some advocacy under some incentive). The other prominent alternative is an impression-management explanation (e.g., Tedeschi, Schlenker, & Bonoma, 1971). This view argues that the attitude change observed in forced-compliance studies is insincere (not genuine). According to this explanation, participants don't want to appear as though they are "selling out" for a small amount of money, and so attempt to mislead the experimenter into thinking their advocacy was actually consistent with their true beliefs.

There has been extensive (and complex) research bearing on the status of these alternative explanations, and the details of the arguments cannot be reproduced here (for references and useful discussion, see J. Cooper & Fazio, 1984; Wicklund & Brehm, 1976). In the end, however, the evidence suggests that dissonance is in fact a genuine and distinctive phenomenon. To be sure, self-attribution processes operate when dissonance is present (e.g., J. Cooper, Zanna, & Taves, 1978; Zanna & Cooper, 1974), and impression-management concerns do influence the amount of attitude change displayed in experimental research (e.g., Paulhus, 1982). But it is also clear that forced-compliance situations produce sincere attitude changes that can't be accounted for by impression-management processes (e.g., Stults, Messe, & Kerr, 1984); and there is physiological evidence of dissonance arousal that is inconsistent with self-perception analyses (e.g., Croyle & Cooper, 1983). Thus the evidence to date is commonly taken as suggesting not that dissonance theory is seriously flawed, but instead as indicating that both dissonance and self-attribution processes are at work (e.g., Zanna & Cooper, 1976) or that both dissonance and impression-management processes are at work (e.g., Paulhus, 1982).

SUMMARY Dissonance theory's expectations about the effects of incentive for counterattitudinal action on attitude change can, in the end, be said to have been confirmed in broad outline — though not without the discovery of a host of unanticipated processes bearing on the results. When persons freely choose to engage in counterattitudinal action, increasing incentive for such action leads to lessened pressure for making one's beliefs and attitudes consistent with the counterattitudinal act. Hence a persuader seeking long-term behavioral change (by means of underlying attitude change) ought not to create intense pressure to engage in the counterattitudinal behavior; rather, the persuader should seek to offer only just barely enough incentive to induce compliance, and let dissonance-reduction processes encourage subsequent attitude change.

Consider, for example, some social influence tasks commonly faced by parents. In hoping to encourage the young child not to play with the expensive stereo equipment, parents ought to provide only just enough punishment to induce compliance; excessive punishment might produce short-term obedience but not underlying change (e.g., when the parents are present, the child won't play with the equipment — but the child will still *want* to, and when the parents' backs are turned . . .). Or in trying to encourage children to do their homework, parents ought not offer extremely large rewards for compliance; such rewards can undermine the development of positive attitudes toward homework (whereas a minimal reward can induce immediate compliance while also promoting the development of positive attitudes). In short, smaller incentives for freely chosen counterattitudinal behavior are more likely (than larger incentives) to produce underlying favorable attitudes toward that behavior.

CONCLUSION

Dissonance theory does not offer a systematic theory of persuasion (and was not intended to). But dissonance theory has served as a fruitful source of ideas bearing on social influence processes, and has stimulated substantial relevant research. To be sure, the theory's expectations have sometimes received only weak confirmation (as in studies of selective exposure), and unanticipated findings have emerged (as in the discovery of limiting conditions on forced-compliance effects). Nevertheless, cognitive dissonance theory has yielded a number of useful and interesting findings bearing on processes of persuasion.

NOTES

1. This "follows from" is, obviously, a matter of psychological implication, not logical implication. What matters is whether I *think* one belief follows from another—not whether it logically does so follow.

2. This paragraph reproduces the conventional wisdom concerning the history of mass communication effects research. For discussion and correctives, see Bineham (1988), Chaffee and Hochheimer (1985), Delia (1987), and Wartella and Reeves (1985).

3. Some have suggested treating counterattitudinal advocacy as a distinctive sort of persuasion paradigm, one involving the persuadee's active participation as opposed to passive message reception (e.g., G. R. Miller & Burgoon, 1973). Though it is possible to proceed in this way, the dearth of obvious counterattitudinal advocacy circumstances (outside the laboratory) might be taken to recommend the present broader focus on the larger question of the consequences of induced counterattitudinal behavior. In any case, whatever is true of forced compliance generally will presumably also hold for the special case of counterattitudinal advocacy (though the reverse won't hold, of course).

4. Notice that this might be taken to be opposed to a commonsense "reinforcement" idea. One might reason that the more you pay someone to advocate a counterattitudinal view, the greater the reinforcement for holding that view—and hence with increasing incentive (reinforcement) one should find increasing favorable attitude change. But dissonance theory makes exactly the opposite prediction: The greater the reinforcement (incentive), the less likely there is to be favorable attitude change.

5. Those familiar with the standard social psychological treatment of forced-compliance research will have noticed the absence of a second commonly mentioned limiting condition: the occurrence of "aversive consequences" arising from the action. In fact the evidence is rather good that one requirement for the appearance of dissonance effects in counterattitudinal advocacy situations is that advocates believe that some foreseeable, irrevocable aversive event will result from their advocacy (for a review, see J. Cooper & Fazio, 1984). But remember that counterattitudinal advocacy is only a special case of forced compliance (albeit the case that has received the most research attention), and it is not clear that this aversive-consequences limiting condition in fact applies to forced compliance generally (as opposed to counterattitudinal advocacy specifically). Indeed, it is arguable that there are cases of forced compliance that (a) aren't cases of counterattitudinal advocacy, (b) do yield results interpretable using dissonance-theoretic analyses of forced compliance, (c) do seem to require free choice for the appearance of dissonance effects, and

yet (d) appear *not* to involve aversive consequences of the sort usually contemplated. For example, the research (discussed in Chapter 8) concerning the differential effectiveness of liked and disliked communicators seems to satisfy these requirements (e.g., Jones & Brehm, 1967). It may be that the purposes of social psychologists have been well served by the progressive narrowing of dissonance theory to the point that the theory is taken to be a theory of counterattitudinal advocacy (e.g., J. Cooper & Fazio, 1984; for commentary, see Eagly & Chaiken, 1984, p. 340, n. 10), but students of persuasion can profit from a wider view.

5

Theory of Reasoned Action

THE THEORY OF REASONED ACTION is a general account of the determinants of volitional behavior that has been developed by Martin Fishbein and Icek Ajzen (Ajzen & Fishbein, 1980; Fishbein & Ajzen, 1975). The potential relevance of such an account to persuasion should be plain: If one has a general model of what influences (determines) behavior, then one also has a natural list of targets for persuasion. In what follows, the theory itself is described, the current state of research on the theory is reviewed, and the theory's implications for persuasive messages are considered.

THE THEORY OF REASONED ACTION

The theory of reasoned action is based on the idea that the most immediate determinant of a person's behavior is the person's behavioral intention — what the person intends to do.[1] Influencing behavior, then, is to be accomplished through influencing persons' intentions: For example, getting voters to vote for a given political candidate will involve (at a minimum) getting the voters to *intend* to vote for the candidate. The question that naturally arises, then, is, What determines intentions?

THE DETERMINANTS OF INTENTION

The theory of reasoned action proposes that the intention to perform or not perform a given behavior is a function of two factors: the individual's attitude toward the behavior in question and the individual's "subjective norm," which represents his or her general perception of whether important others desire the performance or nonperformance of the behavior. That is, intentions are influenced both by personal attitudinal judgments (my personal evaluation of the action) and by social-normative considerations (what I think other people think I should do).

It is recognized that these two factors will not always contribute equally to the formation of intentions. In some circumstances, one's intentions may be determined largely by one's attitude toward the behavior, and normative considerations may play little or no role; for other circumstances, the normative factor may carry a great deal of weight, while personal attitudes are put aside. That is, the attitudinal and normative factors may carry varying weights in influencing intention.

The theory of reasoned action expresses this algebraically, as follows:

$$BI = (A_B)w_1 + (SN)w_2$$

where BI refers to behavioral intentions, A_B represents attitude toward the behavior, SN represents subjective norm, and w_1 and w_2 represent the weights for each factor. An individual's behavioral intentions are thus a joint function of an attitudinal component and a normative component, each appropriately weighted.

The procedures for assessing the various elements of this model are reasonably well established (for details, see Ajzen & Fishbein, 1980). In assessing behavioral intention, a questionnaire item such as the following is commonly employed:

I intend to smoke cigarettes.

likely _____ _____ _____ _____ _____ _____ _____ unlikely

To measure the attitude toward the behavior (A_B), several evaluative semantic differential scales can be used.

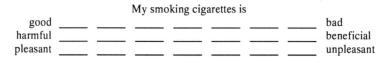

My smoking cigarettes is

good	____	____	____	____	____	____	____	bad
harmful	____	____	____	____	____	____	____	beneficial
pleasant	____	____	____	____	____	____	____	unpleasant

To obtain an index of the subjective norm (SN), an item such as the following is commonly employed:

Most people who are important to me think

I should ____ ____ ____ ____ ____ ____ ____ I should not
smoke cigarettes.

The relative weights of the attitudinal and normative components are determined empirically. These weights are not readily determinable for any single person; that is, there is no very satisfactory way to assess the relative weights of the components for Pat Smith's intention to smoke cigarettes. However, one can assess the relative weights of the components (for a given behavior) across a group of respondents; for example, for a group of nonsmoking adolescent males, it is possible to estimate the relative influence of attitudinal and normative considerations on smoking intentions.[2]

THE DETERMINANTS OF EACH COMPONENT

The attitudinal (A_B) and normative (SN) components of the model are themselves seen to have distinct sets of determinants.

THE DETERMINANTS OF THE ATTITUDINAL COMPONENT. An individual's attitude toward a particular behavior is taken to be a function of his or her salient beliefs about the act (which commonly are beliefs concerning outcomes of the behavior). More specifically, the proposal is that the evaluation of each belief (e_i) and the strength with which each belief is held (b_i) jointly influence the individual's attitude toward the behavior, as represented in the following equation:

$$A_B = \Sigma b_i e_i$$

This is the same summative conception of attitude discussed in Chapter 3. The assessment procedures are identical; the same sorts of belief-strength scales (e.g., probable-improbable, true-false) and belief-evaluation scales (e.g., good-bad, desirable-undesirable) are employed. For instance, the following items assess the respondent's belief strength (b_i) concerning a particular outcome of cigarette smoking:

My smoking cigarettes will increase my risk of cancer.

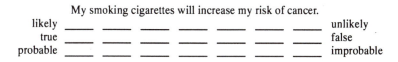

likely	____	____	____	____	____	____	____	unlikely
true	____	____	____	____	____	____	____	false
probable	____	____	____	____	____	____	____	improbable

And the evaluation of that outcome (e_i) can be assessed with items such as the following:

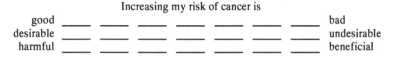

THE DETERMINANTS OF THE NORMATIVE COMPONENT   An individual's subjective norm is taken to be based on his or her judgment of the normative expectations of specific salient others (what I think my parents want me to do, what I think my best friend wants me to do, and so on). The subjective norm is also based on the individual's motivation to comply with each of those referents (how much I want to do what my parents think I should, and so on). Specifically, then, a person's subjective norm is suggested to be a joint function of the normative beliefs that person ascribes to particular salient others (NB_i) and his or her motivation to comply with those others (MC_i). Expressed algebraically:

$$SN = \Sigma NB_i MC_i$$

An individual's normative beliefs are commonly obtained through a set of items in which the normative expectation of each different referent is assessed. For example:

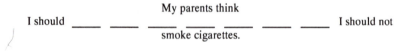

The motivation to comply with each referent is typically assessed through a question such as this:

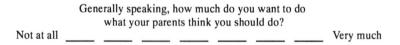

If I believe that my parents, my best friend, my physician, and others who are important to me all think that I should not smoke cigarettes, and I'm motivated to comply with each referent's expectations, then I will surely have a negative subjective norm regarding cigarette smoking (I'm likely to think that, in general, most people who are important to me think I shouldn't smoke cigarettes).

THE INTENTION-BEHAVIOR RELATIONSHIP

Obviously, the prediction of behavioral intention is of interest because intentions are taken to be importantly related to conduct. Although the theory of reasoned action claims that intentions are important determinants of conduct, it does not claim that measures of intention and measures of behavior will always be closely related (a point unappreciated by Sarver, 1983).

In particular, the theory recognizes three circumstances under which measures of intention are not likely to predict behavior very successfully (see Ajzen & Fishbein, 1974; Fishbein & Ajzen, 1976). First, poor prediction is likely if the measures of intention and behavior do not correspond to one another. For instance, my intention to buy to diet cola at the grocery tonight may well predict whether I do buy diet cola at the grocery tonight — but it won't be so useful in predicting whether I will buy Diet Coke (specifically) at the grocery tonight, or whether I will buy diet cola at the cafeteria tomorrow. That is, a given intention is likely to be associated closely with the corresponding behavior; but as the degree of correspondence between the two measures weakens, the intention becomes a poorer predictor of the behavior.

Second, poor prediction is likely if the intention changes in the period between the assessment of intention and the assessment of behavior. Thus, for example, the time interval between the measure of intention and the observation of behavior may importantly influence the strength of association between measures of intention and behavior: The longer the interval, the poorer the correlation between the two, because of the greater chance that intention will change over time (as new information is received). For predicting November election results, voters' intentions in September will be better guides than their intentions in August — and their intentions the day before the election will be better guides than their intentions a week earlier.

Third, poor prediction is likely to the extent that the behavior is not under volitional control. That is, behavior not under volitional control is poorly predicted by intention. For example, whether George marries Martha probably won't be entirely well predicted by George's intention to marry her (since whether they get married depends not just on George's intention but on Martha's as well); on the other hand, whether George *asks* Martha to marry him might be effectively predicted by George's intention to ask — because the asking is largely under George's control.

RESEARCH CONCERNING THE THEORY OF REASONED ACTION

The theory of reasoned action has spawned a great deal of empirical research.[3] In the following sections, research evidence is reviewed concerning the determinants of intention, the determinants of each of the model's components, and the relationship between intention and behavior.

RESEARCH ON THE DETERMINANTS OF INTENTION

GENERAL EVIDENCE Behavioral intentions have proved to be rather predictable from A_B and SN, across an exceptionally wide variety of behaviors, including voting (Bowman & Fishbein, 1978; Fishbein & Ajzen, 1981a; Fishbein, Ajzen, & Hinkle, 1980), consumer purchases (Fishbein & Ajzen, 1980; Warshaw, 1980), family planning (Fishbein, Jaccard, Davidson, Ajzen, & Loken, 1980), seat belt use (Budd, North, & Spencer, 1984), eating in fast-food restaurants (Brinberg & Durand, 1983), conserving energy in the home (Seligman, Hall, & Finegan, 1983), seeking dental care (Hoogstraten, de Haan, & ter Horst, 1985), using credit union services (Gur-Arie, Durand, & Bearden, 1979), jogging (Riddle, 1980), women's occupational orientations (Sperber, Fishbein, & Ajzen, 1980), and consumer complaining (Bearden & Crockett, 1981). The multiple correlations (obtained using A_B and SN to predict BI) in these applications are roughly in the range of .60 to .90. Some investigations have obtained somewhat weaker effects (e.g., in the Zuckerman & Reis, 1978, study of blood donation, the multiple correlation was .50), but for the most part the research findings have been quite supportive (see Sheppard, Hartwick, & Warshaw, 1988, for a review).

Notably, in most applications of the model, the attitudinal component is more strongly correlated with intention than is the normative component—and this effect obtains across a wide variety of behaviors, including most of those just mentioned. Even when both components are significantly weighted (that is, even when SN makes a statistically significant contribution to the prediction of intention), A_B is still commonly the better predictor.[4] Generally speaking, then, it seems that the attitudinal component typically exerts more influence on intention than does the normative component. To be sure, this generalization may be of limited utility: It is always an open question whether a specific intention will be predicted by attitude, norm, or both; and for any given intention, it might turn out that normative considerations are more influential than attitudinal ones. But it appears that, in the absence of any information to the contrary, one should probably assume that the attitude toward the behavior will be a more powerful influence on intention than will the subjective norm.

Although research has produced encouraging results for the theory of reasoned action, it has also given rise to two main questions about the theory's treatment of the determinants of intention. One concerns the relationship of the attitudinal and normative components; the other concerns the sufficiency of the two-component model.

THE RELATION OF THE TWO COMPONENTS Several investigators have suggested that the attitudinal and normative components are not actually distinct, either conceptually or empirically (e.g., Miniard & Cohen, 1979, 1981; Ryan, 1982; Smetana & Adler, 1980). Miniard and Cohen (1981), for instance, found that a manipulation designed to affect SN also influenced A_B, and that a manipulation aimed at influencing A_B also affected SN; on these and other grounds, they argue that the model could not distinguish personal and social influences on behavioral intention.

Indeed, when researchers report the correlation between the model's attitudinal and normative components, the correlation is commonly a significantly positive one (e.g., Bearden & Crockett, 1981; Miniard & Cohen, 1981; Ryan, 1982; Shepherd & D. J. O'Keefe, 1984; Warshaw, 1980): Persons with negative subjective norms are likely to also have relatively unfavorable attitudes toward the behavior (and vice versa); as the attitude toward the behavior becomes more positive, so does the subjective norm (and vice versa); and so on. Even when the intercorrelation is not reported, it can often be deduced from other information reported; typically, the components turn out to be positively correlated — often substantially so. For example, for the studies compiled in Ajzen and Fishbein (1980), the smallest intercorrelation is over .40 (Fishbein, Jaccard, et al., 1980, p. 123), the largest is over .70 (Fishbein, Ajzen, & Hinkle, 1980, p. 181), and the remainder are between .50 and .70 (Fishbein & Ajzen, 1980, p. 170; Fishbein, Ajzen, & McArdle, 1980, p. 233; Fishbein, Bowman, Thomas, Jaccard, & Ajzen, 1980, p. 210; Sperber et al., 1980, p. 123), with most of these between .60 and .70.

But there is evidence suggesting that the two components are in fact different. For example, there is some indication that different persons may display different attitude-intention and norm-intention relationship patterns (Gur-Arie et al., 1979; L. E. Miller & Grush, 1986). And some experimental manipulations appear to have distinct effects on the two components (see Fishbein & Ajzen, 1981b). Research evidence such as this suggests that it is worthwhile to distinguish the two components — that is, to treat attitudinal and normative considerations as distinct influences on intention. Even so, these distinct components are often positively correlated; although the components may be distinct conceptually, they are often related empirically.

Thus the relevant question now seems to be this: Just *when* will the attitudinal and normative components be substantially positively correlated, and when will they be largely unrelated (or perhaps even negatively related)? There is not much good evidence bearing on this question, and hence it is not yet possible to specify the factors that influence the magnitude of the intercorrelation (for some discussion, see Oliver & Bearden, 1985; Shepherd, 1987; Shimp & Kavas, 1984). As a general rule, it seems, one should expect at least moderately positive correlations between the components; this seems to be the overwhelmingly most common finding in the research literature. Indeed, it is difficult to locate instances where intercorrelations below .30 have been reported (for an example, see Zuckerman & Reis, 1978).[5]

THE SUFFICIENCY OF THE TWO COMPONENTS   The other major issue that has been raised concerning the theory of reasoned action's depiction of the determinants of intention focuses on the *sufficiency* of the two-component model. The theory of reasoned action proposes that A_B and SN are the only significant influences on intention; any additional factors that might be related to intention will have their effects indirectly, via A_B and SN, not directly. The question at issue is whether there are any significant direct influences on intention other than A_B and SN. Put somewhat differently: Is there some additional component that might be added to the model that will improve the prediction of intention (over and above the predictability afforded by the attitudinal and normative components)?

A number of possible additions to the theory's two components have been suggested, including personal norms or moral obligations (e.g., Ajzen &

Fishbein, 1969, 1970; Prestholdt, Lane, & Mathews, 1987; Zuckerman & Reis, 1978), social structure (R. A. Davis, 1985; A. E. Liska, 1984), the degree of perceived control over the behavior (e.g., Ajzen & Madden, 1986), and beliefs about the behaviors of others (Grube, Morgan, & McGree, 1986). For the most part, there is only a smattering of evidence to suggest that any of these additions will generally improve the predictability of intention.

The suggestion that enjoys the best empirical support concerns prior behavior (that is, prior performance of the behavior in question). Several studies have found that prior behavior has a direct influence on intention – that is, an effect not mediated through the attitudinal and normative components – such that persons who have performed the action in the past are more likely to intend to perform the action in the future (Bentler & Speckart, 1979, 1981; Budd et al., 1984; Crosby & Muehling, 1983; Fredricks & Dossett, 1983). It may be that these findings reflect a genuine role for past behavior in influencing intention ("I intend to do it, because I've done it before"), or it may be that the findings are a consequence of respondents' use of past behavior as a basis for the prediction of their own future behavior ("I've done it before, so I guess it's likely I'll do it again"; see Warshaw & Davis, 1985); in any case, the role of prior behavior in influencing intention awaits some clarification. Taken at face value, however, these findings should emphasize for persuaders the difficulty of inducing behavioral change: Persons' intentions (and so future conduct) are influenced not only by attitudinal and normative considerations (both of which persuaders might change) but also by past behavior (which persuaders can't change); the inertia of established behaviors apparently has effects on intentions, over and above the effects of attitudes and norms.

On the whole, specific alternatives to the theory of reasoned action are not yet sufficiently well formulated or extensively studied to permit one to suggest their general superiority to the original theory.[6] It may yet be that some alternative model for predicting intentions will come to have the broad base of research support enjoyed by the theory of reasoned action. At present, however, there is no competitor with such extensive evidence of utility.

RESEARCH ON THE DETERMINANTS OF EACH COMPONENT

THE DETERMINANTS OF THE ATTITUDINAL COMPONENT The theory's claims about the determinants of one's attitude toward the act have not engendered much direct debate (but see Bagozzi, 1988). Reasonably strong correlations (roughly .65 and above) between $\Sigma b_i e_i$ and A_B have been observed in a number of investigations (e.g., Bagozzi, 1982; Fishbein, Ajzen, & Hinkle, 1980; Jaccard & Davidson, 1972; G. W. King, 1975; McCarty, Morrison, & Mills, 1983; Riddle, 1980).[7]

THE DETERMINANTS OF THE NORMATIVE COMPONENT The theory's claims about the determinants of the subjective norm have been more controversial. Correlations between $\Sigma NB_i MC_i$ and SN have typically been roughly in the range of .50 to .70 (e.g., Fishbein & Ajzen, 1981a; Fishbein, Jaccard, et al., 1980; Hoogstraten et al., 1985; Riddle, 1980; Seligman et al., 1983). Nevertheless, a variety of concerns have been raised about the normative component's determinants. Two particular issues can serve here as instructive examples of the complexity of the questions involved.

One issue concerns the level of specificity at which the motivation-to-comply (MC) component is assessed. Commonly, MC questions are phrased as general questions about the respondent's desire to comply with a particular referent's beliefs ("In general, how much do you want to do what your best friend thinks you should do?"). But it might plausibly be supposed that a better understanding of the influences of particular referents on the specific intention to be predicted could be obtained by asking an act-specific MC question — that is, a question that asks not about the referent's views generally, but about the referent's views concerning performance of the specific act in question (e.g., "When it comes to voting for George Bush, how much do you want to do what your best friend thinks you should do?"). Or, as a third alternative, the MC question might be of intermediate specificity, focused on the referent's prescriptions about the general topic area or behavioral domain (e.g., "When it comes to politics, how much . . . ").

A second issue concerning determinants of the subjective norm focuses on the scoring procedures to be used. The scales for each determinant (NB and MC) might be scored in either a bipolar (e.g., -3 to $+3$) or unipolar (e.g., 1 to 7) fashion; different scoring procedures can yield different results (e.g., different correlations between $\Sigma NB_i MC_i$ and SN). Some investigations have employed bipolar scoring for both (e.g., Ajzen, 1971; G. W. King, 1975), some have used unipolar scoring for both (e.g., Vinokur-Kaplan, 1978), and still others have used bipolar scoring for one and unipolar scoring for the other (e.g., Smetana & Adler, 1980).[8]

Unfortunately, there is relatively little empirical evidence that offers guidance with respect to the questions of how to phrase the MC item and how to score the NB and MC items — and the evidence that does exist is not uncontroversial (see Fishbein & Ajzen, 1981b; Kantola, Syme, & Campbell, 1982; Miniard & Cohen, 1981, esp. p. 332, n. 9). That is, it is not clear what the most appropriate phrasings and scorings might be.

Moreover, there are yet other complexities and confusions surrounding the normative component. For example, ΣNB_i has sometimes been found to be a better predictor of SN than $\Sigma NB_i MC_i$ (that is, deleting the motivation-to-comply element improves the prediction of SN; Budd et al., 1984; Kantola et al., 1982; Miniard & Page, 1984). And, correspondingly, a number of studies have found that intentions are more predictable from A_B and ΣNB_i than they are from A_B and $\Sigma NB_i MC_i$, even with varied scoring procedures and different levels of MC specificity (Budd & Spencer, 1984b; Chassin et al., 1981; DeVries & Ajzen, 1971; McCarty, 1981; Saltzer, 1981; Schlegel, Crawford, & Sanborn, 1977).

What all this may suggest is that perhaps the theory of reasoned action does not adequately capture the role of normative influences. These difficulties have been acknowledged for some time (see Ajzen & Fishbein, 1980, pp. 246-247), and there has been some preliminary exploration of alternative means of assessing the subjective norm and its determinants (Ajzen & Madden, 1986; Bhagat, Raju, & Sheth, 1979; Burnkrant & Page, 1988; Fredricks & Dossett, 1983). To date, however, not much progress seems to have been made.

RESEARCH ON THE INTENTION-BEHAVIOR RELATIONSHIP

A number of investigations have revealed reasonably strong relationships between assessments of intentions and assessments of behavior in a number of behavioral domains (e.g., Ajzen, 1971; Fishbein, Ajzen, & Hinkle, 1980; Fishbein, Ajzen, & McArdle, 1980; Grube et al., 1986; G. W. King, 1975; Riddle, 1980; Smetana & Adler, 1980); correlations of .65 and greater are not unusual (compare, e.g., Beck, 1981; Brinberg & Durand, 1983). Additionally, what evidence there is bearing directly on the theory's claims about factors influencing the intention-behavior relationship seems largely supportive. That is to say, stronger intention-behavior correlations are to be expected when the measures of intention and behavior correspond, when the intention is stable in the time period between the assessment of intention and the assessment of behavior, and when the behavior is under volitional control (see, e.g., Davidson & Jaccard, 1979).

The central question that has been raised concerning the theory of reasoned action's depiction of the intention-behavior relationship concerns whether intention is sufficient to predict behavior. The theory of reasoned action proposes that intention is the only significant influence on (volitional) behavior; any additional factors that might be related to behavior are claimed to have their effect indirectly, via intention (or via the determinants of intention). The question at issue thus is this: Are there factors that have effects on behavior that aren't mediated through intention? Alternatively put: Are there additional factors that might improve the prediction of behavior (over and above the predictability afforded by intention)?

Several studies have indicated that the prediction of behavior is improved by taking into account prior behavior (e.g., Bentler & Speckart, 1979; Fredricks & Dossett, 1983; Wittenbraker, Gibbs, & Kahle, 1983; compare Brinberg & Durand, 1983). That is, persons who had performed the action in the past were more likely to perform it in the future — over and above the effects of intention on future performance. It may be that this effect underscores the theory's focus on conduct that is under volitional control. One would expect that prior behavior would significantly predict future behavior (beyond the prediction afforded by intention) precisely when the behavior became habitual and routine (and so no longer fully intentional). For persuaders, of course, these findings serve as a reminder of the persuasive difficulties created by entrenched behavioral patterns; past behavior may exert an influence on conduct that is not mediated by intention, and hence securing changes in intention may not be sufficient to yield changes in behavior.[9]

IMPLICATIONS FOR PERSUASION

The theory of reasoned action rather straightforwardly identifies three conditions under which a person's intention to perform a given behavior may change: if the attitudinal component changes (and is significantly weighted), if the normative component changes (and is significantly weighted), or if the relative weighting of the two components changes.

It is presumably apparent why inducing change by altering the attitudinal or normative component requires that the component be significantly weighted. The theory of reasoned action underscores the futility of attempts to change, say, the normative component in circumstances where only the attitudinal component is significantly related to intention. Perhaps not surprisingly, there is empirical evidence indicating that changing a component will lead to a change in intentions only when the component is significantly associated with intention (Ajzen, 1971; Ajzen & Fishbein, 1972; McCarty, 1981).

CHANGING THE ATTITUDINAL COMPONENT

One focus for social influence would be the induction of change in the attitudinal component — influencing the receiver's attitude toward the behavior. According to the theory of reasoned action, A_B is a function of the belief strength (b_i) and evaluation (e_i) of salient beliefs about the action. There are thus a number of possible avenues to changing A_B. For example, in attempting to induce an unfavorable attitude toward a given behavior (e.g., smoking), one might attempt to lead the receiver to add a new salient negative belief about the act ("Maybe you didn't realize that smoking leaves a bad odor on your clothes"). A second possibility is to attempt to increase the unfavorability of an existing negative belief ("You probably already know that smoking can lead to blood circulation problems — but you may not realize just how *serious* such problems are. Impaired circulation is *very* undesirable, even dangerous, . . . "). Third, a persuader might attempt to increase the belief strength (likelihood) of an existing negative belief ("You probably already realize that smoking *can* lead to health problems. But maybe you don't realize just how *likely* it is to do so. You really are at risk . . . "). Fourth, one might try to decrease the favorability of an existing positive belief ("Maybe smoking does give you something to do with your hands, but that's a pretty trivial thing"). Fifth, one might attempt to decrease the belief strength (likelihood) associated with an existing positive belief ("Actually, smoking *won't* help you keep your weight down"). Finally, the attitude toward the act could be changed without adding any new beliefs and without changing the belief strength or evaluation of any existing beliefs, but simply by shuffling the current beliefs around in such a way that a different set of beliefs is salient; since the attitude toward the act is based on salient beliefs about the act, changing the relative salience of currently held beliefs can presumably influence attitudes ("Have you forgotten just how expensive cigarettes are nowadays?"). Obviously, these are not mutually exclusive possibilities; a persuader might well offer arguments designed to implement all these different strategies.

CHANGING THE NORMATIVE COMPONENT

The normative component is a second possible focus for influence attempts. According to the theory of reasoned action, one would influence SN by influencing NB_i and MC_i, in ways precisely parallel to the ways in which A_B is influenced through b_i and e_i. For example, one might attempt to add a new salient referent (one for whom the NB and MC would be appropriately arranged): "Have you considered what your *mother* would think about your doing this?" Or one might attempt to change the normative belief attributed to a current referent: "Oh, no, you're wrong—I talked to George, and he thinks you *should* go ahead and do this." Or one might try to change the motivation to comply with a current referent: "You really shouldn't worry about what *he* thinks—he's a jerk when it comes to things like this."

But here the uncertainties in the research literature concerning the nature and determinants of the subjective norm come home to roost. For example, suppose one is trying to influence a receiver's motivation to comply (MC) with a particular referent. Should one attempt to change the receiver's MC (with that referent) generally? Or the receiver's MC (with that referent) concerning the general behavioral domain? Or the receiver's MC (with that referent) regarding the specific behavior at hand? Perhaps one shouldn't even bother trying to influence MC. After all, it appears that changing MC may not affect SN: Recall the research evidence that SN has been better predicted by ΣNB_i than by $\Sigma NB_i MC_i$, evidence suggesting that the motivation-to-comply component may not affect the subjective norm in the ways predicted by the theory of reasoned action. Given all of this, perhaps it is not surprising that some investigators have found it difficult to manipulate the normative component through persuasive messages (McCarty, 1981)—nor surprising that some treatments of the persuasive applications of the theory of reasoned action have omitted discussion of influencing the subjective norm (Hoogstraten et al., 1985; Stutman & Newell, 1984).

If there is any consolation for persuaders here, perhaps it is to be found in the generalization that the attitudinal component typically (though not always) carries more weight in influencing intention than does the normative component. In the absence of any information to the contrary, persuaders might well elect to focus their efforts on the attitudinal component, thus bypassing the difficulties and complexities of the normative component.

CHANGING THE RELATIVE WEIGHTS OF THE COMPONENTS

The final possible avenue of influence suggested by the theory of reasoned action is that of changing the relative weights of the attitudinal and normative components. For instance, suppose a person has a positive attitude toward the act of attending law school, but has a negative subjective norm (thinks that important others think that she should not go to law school)—and because at present the person places greater emphasis on normative than on attitudinal considerations in making this behavioral decision, she intends not to go to law school. A persuader who wanted to encourage the person's attending law school might try to emphasize that, insofar as a decision like this is concerned, one's personal feelings ought to be more important than what others think ("It's *your* career choice, *your* life, not theirs; in situations like this, you need to do what's right for you—you're the one who has to live with the consequences, not them—and that means basing your choice on what you want, not what somebody else wants," and so on). That is, the persuader might attempt to have the receiver place more emphasis on attitudinal than normative considerations in forming the relevant intention.

But this strategy will be likely to succeed in changing intention only when the attitudinal and normative components incline the receiver in opposite directions. If a persuader wishes to encourage a receiver to attend law school, and the receiver has both a negative attitude toward the act and a negative subjective norm, then changing the relative weights of the two components will not create a positive intention. In this connection, it is important to recall the generally positive correlations that have been observed between the two components. As a rule, it is unlikely that the attitudinal and normative components will pull a person in opposite directions.[10] Consequently, this strategy of influencing intention by influencing the relative weights of the two components is not likely to find wide application.

THE INTENTION-BEHAVIOR RELATIONSHIP

What have just been discussed are three strategies for influencing behavioral intentions (changing the attitude toward the behavior, changing the subjective norm, or changing the relative weights of the components). The point of influencing intention, of course, is eventually to influence behavior. But one should not assume that intentions will unproblematically be reflected in actions, and hence an important question for persuaders to consider is, When will influencing intentions *not* yield corresponding influences on behavior?

As discussed previously, the theory of reasoned action identifies several circumstances under which measures of intention and behavior are not likely to be highly correlated. For example, when the measures of intention and behavior don't correspond, the correlation will be lowered. For persuaders, this underscores the importance of having persuasive aims clearly in mind. A persuader who lacks a clear conception of the particular behavior to be influenced is not in a good position to decide which behavioral intention to attempt to affect. And, given a particular behavioral target, it is important that the corresponding behavioral intention be the focus of persuasive appeals: If one hopes to encourage receivers to buy Windex, then attempting to get them to intend to buy a glass cleaner is not likely to be the most efficient persuasive approach.

As another example, relatively weak intention-behavior correlations are expected when intentions might change subsequently. Hence the time interval between the assessment of intention and the assessment of behavior is important: With longer intervals between the two assessments, one finds lower correlations (presumably because there is a greater chance for intentions to change over time). This suggests the importance of placing persuasive efforts temporally close to the point of decision or action. If persuasion takes place too early, one might change intention in the desired fashion, only to see the intention subsequently change back during the interval preceding the action.

The general point to be noted is that a persuader's focus on changing receivers' intentions — a focus suggested by the theory of reasoned action — should not obscure the importance for persuaders of the connection between intention and action. Intentions will not always be straightforwardly reflected in behavior, and thus persuaders need to be attentive to factors influencing the intention-behavior relationship.

CONCLUSION

The theory of reasoned action is in fact only one example of an attempt to model the determinants of behavior; quite a number of alternative models have been proposed (e.g., Bagozzi, 1988; Bentler & Speckart, 1979; Rosenstock, 1974; Triandis, 1980). However, for the most part these alternatives have not undergone extensive empirical examination, and none of them has been so influential or successful as the theory of reasoned action. Indeed, it is notable that the theory of reasoned action is the theory to which other models of behavioral determinants are commonly compared in empirical tests (see, e.g., Beck, 1981; Fredricks & Dossett, 1983; Seibold & Roper, 1979; Valois, Desharnais, & Godin, 1988) — that is, it is the standard against which others are assessed, and justifiably so. As this chapter has suggested, there is substantial evidence of the theory's empirical success across a wide range of behaviors, with manifestly useful applications to problems of persuasion.

NOTES

1. More carefully put, the theory claims that intentions are the most immediate determinants of at least some (though not all) behaviors; these intention-influenced actions are the ones of concern to the theory. The theory's appeal for those interested in persuasion is thus understandable, since the behaviors of interest to persuaders are ordinarily behaviors largely under volitional control — that is, behaviors for which intentions are indeed likely to be the immediate determinants.

2. The procedure that is usually followed obtains the weights through examination of the beta weights from a multiple-regression analysis. Briefly put: In such an analysis, the attitudinal and normative components are used simultaneously to predict intention; the relative size of the correlation of each component with intention (in conjunction with other information, particularly the correlation between the two components) will yield an indication of the relative weight of each component. (For instance, if the attitudinal component is very strongly correlated with intention, and the normative component is not, the attitudinal component will receive a larger weight — reflecting its greater influence on intention.) This procedure — rather than simply asking people directly how important the attitudinal and normative considerations are to them — is used because there is reason to think that self-reports are not sufficiently accurate (Fishbein & Ajzen, 1975, pp. 159-160). The inadequacy of such self-reports is what has prevented satisfactory estimation of the weights for a given individual's intention to perform a given behavior (but see Budd & Spencer, 1984a).

3. For several reasons, at least some of the research generated by the theory is not very satisfactory for assessing the theory. First, the theory has undergone some development and clarification since its introduction; naturally, some of the early investigations tested earlier versions of the theory, not the current model. For instance, in earlier versions of the model, the social-normative component was not the present general subjective norm, but instead was represented by what are now taken to be the determinants of an individual's subjective norm (i.e., his or her normative beliefs about particular others and motivation to comply with those others). Thus a large number of studies have tested the following model:

$$BI = (A_B)w_1 + (\Sigma NB_i MC_i)w_2$$

Such research efforts confound claims about the determinants of intention with claims about determinants of the subjective norm. Poor results might result from weaknesses in the theory's claims about the determinants of the normative component, rather than weaknesses in claims about the immediate determinants of intentions, and hence such research is not an entirely reliable guide to the status of the current theory. Second, some investigators have not employed appropriate methods for assessing the theory. For example, in research on the determinants of each component, Fishbein and Ajzen have emphasized the importance of assessing respondents' *salient* beliefs and referents, and have described procedures for identifying the modal salient beliefs about the act and the modal salient referents for a given population of respondents (Ajzen & Fishbein, 1980, pp. 68-76). But these careful procedures are not always followed by other investigators.

4. Studies that have predicted intentions using the determinants of A_B or SN (i.e., $\Sigma b_i e_i$ or $\Sigma NB_i MC_i$) in place of A_B or SN have also typically found attitudinal considerations to outweigh normative ones as influences on intention, though the size of the difference between the weights is smaller than when the normative component is assessed through SN and the attitudinal component assessed through A_B (Farley, Lehmann, & Ryan, 1981).

5. The two correlations of A_B and SN with intention constrain the possible values for the correlation between A_B and SN. For example, if the correlations of A_B and SN with intention are .6 and .4, then it is mathematically impossible that the correlation between A_B and SN be (for instance) −.5; if the correlations are .8 and .6, it is impossible for A_B and SN to be negatively correlated at all; if the correlations are .8 and .8, the correlation between A_B and SN must be at least +.28; and so on. The general point is that there are lower limits on the correlation between A_B and SN that are established by the individual correlations of the components with intention, with the lower limit rising as the individual correlations increase. So it may be that whenever the model is quite successful in predicting intention from both A_B and SN individually, A_B and SN will likely be at least moderately positively correlated.

6. Ajzen's (1985) "theory of planned behavior" can serve as a useful example of the unsettled state of these efforts. In several studies, Ajzen has proposed a third influence on intention, namely, perceived behavioral control (that is, the degree to which the person thinks performance of the behavior is likely to be easy or difficult); this research thus uses three predictors of intention: attitude, norm, and perceived control (see, e.g., Ajzen & Madden, 1986; Schifter & Ajzen, 1985). But the most careful theoretical statement of the theory of planned behavior (Ajzen, 1985) claims that perceived control does *not* influence intention (or behavior, for that matter) either directly or indirectly (compare Ajzen, 1989, pp. 250-253). That is, there is some disjuncture between the theoretical formulation and the putative empirical tests of the theory. Moreover, the measures of "perceived control" often seem to be confounded with assessments of attitude or intention or norm. Consider, for instance, that the difference between voting for one candidate and voting for another is a relatively simple matter of which lever to pull (or which computer-card hole to punch); concretely speaking, voting for one candidate is about as easy as voting for another. But imagine having asked about voting intentions in the 1988 presidential election using perceived-control questions of the sort used by Ajzen and Timko (1986): When asked of a lifelong Democrat, the question "How easy/difficult would it be for you to vote for George Bush for president?" might well have received a "very difficult" response, whereas the parallel question "How easy/difficult would

it be for you to vote for Michael Dukakis for president?" could easily have gotten a "very easy" response—even though presumably the degree of control over the two behaviors was exactly the same. What this example suggests is that some measures of perceived control may not be assessing perceived control so much as something closer to (or contaminated by) attitude or intention or norm. The general point is that alternatives to the theory of reasoned action (such as the theory of planned behavior) are not yet developed to a point that makes their superiority to the original theory apparent.

7. However, the issues that have arisen in the context of information-integration models of attitude (see Chapter 3) can naturally arise here as well, since the same summative model of attitude is involved (e.g., Valiquette, Valois, Desharnais, & Godin, 1988).

8. These two issues are related. For example, one might reasonably suppose that general MC questions should be scored in a unipolar fashion (since it is unlikely that a respondent would want to "do the opposite" of what a referent prescribes in *all* circumstances), but that intermediate or act-specific MC questions should be scored as bipolar (since "doing the opposite" is more plausible for such questions)—and indeed this is Fishbein and Ajzen's (1981b) suggestion. However, Fishbein and Ajzen's (1981b, p. 345) view is that an act-specific MC question is less preferable than the alternative, because it amounts to an alternative measure of intention (and so doesn't contribute to an understanding of the determinants of intention).

9. Direct effects of A_B on behavior (that is, effects not mediated through intention) have also been observed in several studies (Bentler & Speckart, 1979; Manstead, Proffitt, & Smart, 1983; Zuckerman & Reis, 1978), though such effects are not dependable (e.g., Bagozzi, 1982; Bentler & Speckart, 1981; Fredricks & Dossett, 1983; Shimp & Kavas, 1984). That is, it appears that (in some instances at least) conduct is shaped in part by evaluative considerations that aren't indexed by assessments of intention, but are tapped by measures of attitude toward the behavior. However theoretically curious this effect may seem, for persuaders such results suggest the importance of focusing persuasive efforts on A_B (since A_B can apparently sometimes have both direct and indirect effects on behavior).

10. To be careful here: A positive correlation between the two components does not necessarily mean that if one component is positive, the other will be as well; it means only that the two components vary directly (so that as one becomes more positive, so does the other). Imagine, for example, that in a group of respondents, each respondent has a positive attitude toward the behavior and a negative subjective norm. But those with very strongly positive attitudes have only slightly negative subjective norms, while those with only slightly positive attitudes have very strongly negative norms. There would be a positive correlation between the two components (as the attitude becomes more positive, the norm also becomes more positive—that is, less negative), even though for each individual one component is positive and the other is negative. But insofar as the persuasive strategy of altering the weights is concerned, the implication is (generally speaking) the same: Altering the weights of the components is not likely to be a broadly successful way of changing intention (because of the unusual requirements for the strategy's working—e.g., a very dramatic change in the weights may be necessary).

6

Elaboration Likelihood Model

THE ELABORATION LIKELIHOOD MODEL (ELM) of persuasion is an approach developed by Richard Petty, John Cacioppo, and their associates (the single most comprehensive treatment of the ELM is provided by Petty & Cacioppo, 1986a; for a briefer summary, see Petty & Cacioppo, 1986b). The ELM suggests that important variations in the nature of persuasion are a function of the likelihood that receivers will engage in "elaboration" of information relevant to the persuasive issue. With variations in the degree of elaboration, different factors influence persuasive outcomes (and there are differences in the character of the persuasive outcomes). Thus in the sections that follow, the natures of variations in the degree of elaboration are described; factors influencing the degree of elaboration are discussed; the different influences on persuasive effects, given relatively high or low elaboration, are treated; and the trade-offs and consequences of elaboration variations are considered.

It should be noted that this treatment of the ELM is cast at a fairly general level, and consequently bypasses a number of the intricacies and subtleties of the model. There are two reasons for this. First, the ELM is still in the process of development and elaboration. Thus, for example, somewhat different descriptions of the ELM have been given in different works by Petty and Cacioppo (1981a, 1983, 1986a, 1986b) and by Cacioppo, Petty, and Stoltenberg (1985). Second, the extant descriptions of the ELM are sometimes not as lucid as one might want, and consequently there is room for some uncertainty about just how the model is to be taken.[1] But the general outlines of the model seem clear enough, hence the correspondingly general treatment of this discussion.

VARIATIONS IN THE DEGREE OF ELABORATION: CENTRAL VERSUS PERIPHERAL ROUTES TO PERSUASION

THE NATURE OF ELABORATION

The elaboration likelihood model is based on the idea that, under different conditions, receivers will vary in the degree to which they are likely to engage in "elaboration" of information relevant to the persuasive issue. By "elaboration" is meant (roughly) engaging in issue-relevant thinking. Thus sometimes receivers will engage in extensive issue-relevant thinking: They will attend closely to a presented message, carefully scrutinize the arguments it contains, reflect on other issue-relevant considerations (e.g., other arguments recalled from memory, or arguments they devise), and so on. But sometimes receivers won't undertake so much issue-relevant thinking; no one can engage in such effort for every persuasive topic or message, and hence sometimes receivers will display relatively little elaboration.[2]

A number of different means have been developed for assessing variations in the degree of elaboration that occurs in a given circumstance (for discussion, see Petty & Cacioppo, 1986a, pp. 35-47). Perhaps the most straightforward of these is the "thought-listing" technique: Immediately following the receipt of a persuasive message, receivers are simply asked to list the thoughts that occurred to them during the communication (for a more detailed description, see Cacioppo, Harkins, & Petty, 1981, pp. 38-47). Presumably the number of issue-relevant thoughts reported is at least a rough index of the amount of issue-relevant thinking going on.[3] Of course, the reported thoughts can also be classified in any number of ways (e.g., according to their substantive content, or according to what appeared to provoke them); one classification obviously relevant to the illumination of persuasive effects is one that categorizes thoughts according to their favorability to the position being advocated by the message. That is, it is possible to see whether a given message appears to evoke predominantly favorable or predominantly unfavorable thoughts about the advocated position.

As is probably already apparent, the degree to which receivers engage in issue-relevant thinking forms a continuum, from cases of extremely high elaboration to cases of little or no elaboration. One might be tempted to think that in circumstances where little or no elaboration occurs, little or no persuasion will occur (after all, the receiver hasn't really engaged the message, and hasn't undertaken much issue-relevant thinking). But the ELM suggests that persuasion can take place at any point along the elaboration continuum — though the nature of the persuasion processes will be very different as the degree of elaboration varies. To bring out the differences in these persuasion processes, the ELM offers a broad distinction between two different "routes to persuasion": a "central" and a "peripheral" route.

CENTRAL AND PERIPHERAL ROUTES TO PERSUASION

The "central route" to persuasion represents the persuasion processes involved when elaboration likelihood is relatively high. Where persuasion is achieved through the central route, it commonly comes about through extensive issue-relevant thinking: careful examination of the information contained in the message, close scrutiny of the message's arguments, consideration of other issue-relevant material (e.g., arguments recalled from memory, arguments devised by the receiver), and so on. In short, persuasion through the central route is achieved through the receiver's thoughtful examination of issue-relevant considerations.

The "peripheral route" represents the persuasion processes involved when elaboration likelihood is relatively low. Where persuasion is achieved through peripheral routes, it commonly comes about because the receiver employs some simple decision rule (some heuristic principle) to evaluate the advocated position. For example, receivers might be guided by whether they like the communicator, or by whether they find the communicator credible. That is, receivers may rely upon various cues (such as communicator credibility) as guides to attitude and belief, rather than engaging in extensive issue-relevant thinking.

Notice, thus: As elaboration likelihood decreases, peripheral cues presumably become progressively more important determinants of persuasive effects; but as elaboration likelihood increases, peripheral cues should have relatively smaller effects on persuasive outcomes. Indeed, one indirect marker of the amount of elaboration (in a given circumstance) is precisely the extent to which observed persuasive effects are a function of available peripheral cues as opposed to (for example) the quality of the message's arguments. If, in a given experimental condition, variations in peripheral cues have more influence on persuasive outcomes than do variations in the strength of the message's arguments, then presumably relatively little elaboration occurred; that is, the persuasive outcomes were presumably achieved through a peripheral, not a central, route to persuasion.

This distinction between the "two routes to persuasion" should not be permitted to obscure the underlying elaboration continuum. The central and peripheral routes to persuasion are not two exhaustive and mutually exclusive categories or kinds of persuasion (compare Stiff, 1986); they simply represent prototypical extremes on the high-to-low elaboration likelihood continuum (for an illuminating discussion, see Petty, Cacioppo, Kasmer, & Haugtvedt, 1987; Petty, Kasmer, Haugtvedt, & Cacioppo, 1987; Stiff & Boster, 1987). The ELM recognizes, for example, that at moderate levels of elaboration likelihood, the persuasion processes involved likely represent a complex admixture of central-route and peripheral-route processes, with correspondingly complex patterns of effects (see, e.g., Petty & Cacioppo, 1986a, pp. 206-207). Thus, in considering the differing character of persuasion achieved through central and peripheral routes, it is important to bear in mind that these routes are offered as convenient, idealized cases representing different points on the elaboration continuum.

A useful illustration of the distinction between central and peripheral routes to persuasion is provided by Petty, Cacioppo, and Goldman's (1981) study of the effects of argument strength and communicator expertise on persuasive effectiveness. In this investigation, the receivers' degree of involvement with the message topic was varied, such that some receivers were relatively involved personally with the issue (and so presumably disposed to engage in high elaboration) whereas for other receivers the topic was relatively uninvolving (and hence these receivers would presumably be less likely to engage in elaboration). The design also varied the quality of the message's arguments (strong versus weak arguments) and the expertise of the communicator (high versus low).

High-involvement receivers were significantly affected by the quality of the arguments contained in the message (being more persuaded by strong arguments than by weak arguments), but were not significantly influenced by the communicator's degree of expertise. By contrast, low-involvement receivers were affected more by expertise variations (being more persuaded by the high expertise source than by the low) than by variations in argument quality. Notice, thus, that where receivers were inclined (by virtue of high involvement) to engage in extensive elaboration, the results of their examination of the message's arguments were much more influential than was the peripheral cue of the communicator's expertise. But where receivers were not inclined to invest the cognitive effort in argument scrutiny, the peripheral cue of expertise had more influence.

As this investigation indicates, persuasion can be obtained either through a central route (involving relatively high elaboration) or through a peripheral route (where little elaboration occurs). But the factors influencing persuasive success are different in the two cases, as illustrated by this study; and, as will be seen, the consequences of persuasion are not identical for the two routes. It thus becomes important to consider what factors influence the degree of elaboration that receivers are likely to undertake, because with variations in elaboration likelihood, different sorts of persuasion processes are engaged.

FACTORS AFFECTING
THE DEGREE OF ELABORATION

There are two broad classes of factors influencing the degree of elaboration that a receiver will likely undertake in any given circumstance. One of these classes concerns the receiver's *motivation* for engaging in elaboration, the other the receiver's *ability* to engage in such elaboration. Notice that in order for extensive elaboration to occur, both ability and motivation must be present. High elaboration will not occur if the receiver is motivated to undertake issue-relevant thinking but unable to do so, nor will it occur if the receiver is able to engage in elaboration but unmotivated to do so.

FACTORS AFFECTING ELABORATION MOTIVATION

A variety of different factors have received at least a smattering of research attention as influences on receivers' motivation to engage in issue-relevant thinking. Three particular influences have been more extensively investigated, however: receiver involvement, the presence of multiple sources, and the receiver's degree of "need for cognition."

RECEIVER INVOLVEMENT The most studied influence on the receiver's motivation for engaging in issue-relevant thinking is the receiver's degree of involvement in the issue, where involvement is understood as the personal relevance of the topic to the receiver. As a given issue becomes increasingly personally relevant to a receiver, the receiver's motivation for engaging in thoughtful consideration of that issue presumably increases—and indeed a number of investigations have reported findings confirming this expectation (e.g., Petty & Cacioppo, 1979b, 1981b, 1984; Petty, Cacioppo, & Goldman, 1981; Petty, Cacioppo, & Schumann, 1983).[4]

It is worth noting that the ELM's research evidence on this matter has employed a clever methodological innovation (introduced by Apsler & Sears, 1968) in the study of receiver involvement. In many earlier studies of the effect of involvement variations on persuasive processes, researchers commonly employed two persuasive topics, one presumably involving to the population from which receivers were drawn, and one not so involving. This obviously creates difficulties in interpreting experimental results, since any observed differences between high- and low-involvement conditions might be due not to the involvement differences, but to some factor connected to the topic differences (e.g., the necessarily different arguments used in the messages on the two topics).

The procedure followed by ELM researchers is exemplified in a study by Petty and Cacioppo (1979b). Receivers in this investigation were college undergraduates; the persuasive messages advocated the adoption of senior comprehensive examinations as a graduation requirement — either at the receivers' college (the high-involvement condition) or at a different, distant college (the low-involvement condition). With this form of involvement manipulation, receivers in parallel high- and low-involvement conditions could hear messages identical in every respect (e.g., with the very same arguments and evidence) save for the name of the college involved, thus simplifying interpretation of experimental findings.

MULTIPLE SOURCES WITH MULTIPLE ARGUMENTS A second factor that has been shown to influence elaboration motivation is the presence of multiple communication sources presenting multiple arguments. When multiple arguments are presented by multiple sources, elaboration motivation increases (Harkins & Petty, 1981a, 1981b, 1987; Moore & Reardon, 1987). For example, when three arguments are presented by three different communicators (each presenting a different argument), those arguments are scrutinized more closely than when the three arguments are all presented by a single source — and more closely than when three different sources present what is basically the same argument with different wording. That is, it is the conjunction of multiple sources and multiple arguments that enhances elaboration motivation.

It has become clear that this elaboration-enhancing effect of multiple sources with multiple arguments derives from the presumed informational independence of the different sources. For example, if the different sources are perceived as representing very similar perspectives or as having worked together in generating the arguments, the elaboration-enhancing effect is diminished (see Harkins & Petty, 1987). Thus when the sources are taken to be informationally independent, engaging in issue-relevant thinking about the sources' arguments is presumably considered worth the effort; but when the sources are not informationally independent, the motivation for carefully considering each communicator's argument is reduced.

NEED FOR COGNITION A third factor influencing elaboration motivation is the receiver's level of need for cognition. "Need for cognition" refers to "the tendency for an individual to engage in and enjoy thinking" (Cacioppo & Petty, 1982, p. 116). This tendency presumably varies among persons; that is, some people are generally disposed to enjoy and engage in effortful cognitive undertakings, whereas others are not. Cacioppo and Petty (1982) developed a need-for-cognition scale as an instrument to assess this individual difference (for follow-up work on this scale, see Cacioppo, Petty, & Kao, 1984; Osberg, 1987; Tanaka, Panter, & Winborne, 1988). Persons high in need for cognition tend to agree with statements such as "I really enjoy a task that involves coming up with new solutions to problems" and "I like to have the responsibility of handling a situation that requires a lot of thinking." Individuals low in need for cognition, by contrast, are more likely to agree with statements such as "I like tasks that require little thought once I've learned them" and "I only think as hard as I have to."

As one might suppose, several investigations have suggested that the need for cognition influences elaboration likelihood. In particular, it appears that persons low in need for cognition are relatively more influenced by peripheral persuasion cues than are those high in need for cognition; and, correspondingly, those high in need for cognition appear to be more influenced by the quality of the message's arguments than are those low in need for cognition (Axsom, Yates, & Chaiken, 1987; Cacioppo, Petty, Kao, & Rodriguez, 1986; Cacioppo, Petty, & Morris, 1983; Haugtvedt, Petty, Cacioppo, & Steidley, 1988). Such findings, of course, are consistent with the supposition that persons high in need for cognition have generally greater motivation for engaging in issue-relevant thinking than do persons low in need for cognition.[5]

FACTORS AFFECTING ELABORATION ABILITY

A number of possible influences on receivers' ability to engage in issue-relevant thinking have been investigated. Two particular factors with relatively more extensive research support are discussed here: the presence of distraction in the persuasive setting, and the receiver's prior knowledge about the persuasive topic.

DISTRACTION   In this context, "distraction" refers to the presence of some distracting stimulus or task accompanying a persuasive message. Research concerning the effects of such distractions have used a variety of forms of distraction, including having an audio message be accompanied by static or beep sounds, or having receivers monitor a bank of flashing lights, copy a list of two-digit numbers, or record the location of an X flashing from time to time on a screen in front of them (for a general discussion of such manipulations, see Petty & Brock, 1981).

The theoretical importance of distraction effects to the ELM should be plain. Under conditions that would otherwise produce relatively high elaboration, distraction should interfere with such issue-relevant thinking. Such interference should enhance persuasion in some circumstances and reduce it in others. Specifically, if a receiver would ordinarily be inclined to engage in favorable elaboration (that is, to have, predominantly, thoughts favoring the advocated position), then distraction, by interfering with such elaboration, would presumably reduce persuasive effectiveness; but if a receiver would ordinarily be inclined to have, predominantly, thoughts unfavorable to the position advocated, then distraction should presumably enhance the success of the message (by interfering with the receiver's having those unfavorable thoughts).[6]

There is quite a bit of research concerning distraction's effects on persuasion, though regrettably little of it is completely suitable for assessing the predictions of the ELM (for some general discussions of this literature, see Baron, Baron, & Miller, 1973; Buller, 1986; Petty & Brock, 1981). But what relevant evidence there is does seem largely compatible with the ELM. For example, studies reporting that distraction enhances persuasive effects have commonly relied upon circumstances in which elaboration likelihood was high and predominantly unfavorable thoughts would be expected (see Petty & Brock, 1981, p. 65). More direct tests of the ELM's predictions have also been generally supportive (for a review, see Petty & Cacioppo, 1986a, pp. 61-68). For instance, Petty, Wells, and Brock (1976, Experiment 1) found that increasing distraction increased the effectiveness of a counterattitudinal message containing weak arguments, but decreased the effectiveness of a counterattitudinal message containing strong arguments. The weak-argument message ordinarily evoked predominantly unfavorable thoughts, and hence distraction — by interfering with such thoughts — enhanced persuasion for that message; but the strong-argument message ordinarily evoked predominantly favorable thoughts, and thus distraction inhibited persuasion for that message.[7]

PRIOR KNOWLEDGE A second factor influencing elaboration ability is the receiver's prior knowledge about the persuasive topic: The more extensive such prior knowledge, the better able the receiver is to engage in issue-relevant thinking. A series of studies by Wood and her associates have indicated that as the extent of receivers' prior knowledge increases, more issue-relevant thoughts occur, the influence of argument strength on persuasive effects increases, and the influence of peripheral cues (such as source likability and message length) decreases (Wood, 1982; Wood & Kallgren, 1988; Wood, Kallgren, & Preisler, 1985; for related work, see Cacioppo, Petty, & Sidera, 1982). As one might expect, this suggests that when receivers with extensive prior knowledge encounter a counterattitudinal message, such receivers are better able to generate counterarguments (i.e., arguments opposing the message's advocated position) and hence in general are less likely to be persuaded (by comparison to receivers with less extensive topic knowledge). But receivers with extensive prior knowledge are also more affected by variations in message argument strength; hence increasing the strength of a counterattitudinal message's arguments will enhance persuasion for receivers with extensive knowledge but will presumably have little effect on receivers with less extensive knowledge.[8]

OTHER INFLUENCES ON ELABORATION ABILITY Various other influences on elaboration ability have received some research attention, but the evidence bearing on these is not very extensive. There is, for example, some research concerning the impact on elaboration ability of message repetition (Cacioppo & Petty, 1985) and the receiver's body posture (Petty, Wells, Heesacker, Brock, & Cacioppo, 1983). For the most part, these studies serve more as demonstrations that such factors can influence elaboration ability than they do as bases for sound generalizations about how and when these factors play such a role.

SUMMARY

As should be apparent, a variety of factors can influence the likelihood of elaboration in a given circumstance, by affecting the motivation or the ability to engage in issue-relevant thinking. With variations in elaboration likelihood, of course, different sorts of persuasion processes are engaged: As elaboration likelihood increases, peripheral cues have diminished effects on persuasive outcomes and central-route processes play correspondingly greater roles. But the factors influencing persuasive effects are different, depending on whether central or peripheral routes to persuasion are followed. Thus the next two sections consider what factors influence persuasive outcomes when elaboration likelihood is relatively high and when it is relatively low.

INFLUENCES ON PERSUASIVE EFFECTS UNDER CONDITIONS OF HIGH ELABORATION: CENTRAL ROUTES TO PERSUASION

THE CRITICAL ROLE OF ELABORATION DIRECTION

Under conditions of relatively high elaboration, the outcomes of persuasive efforts will largely depend on the outcomes of the receiver's thoughtful consideration of issue-relevant arguments (as opposed to largely depending on the operation of simple decision principles activated by peripheral cues). Broadly put, when elaboration is high, persuasive effects will depend upon the predominant valence of the receiver's issue-relevant thoughts: To the extent that the receiver is led to have predominantly favorable thoughts about the advocated position, the message will presumably be relatively successful in eliciting attitude change in the desired direction; but if the receiver has predominantly unfavorable thoughts, then the message will presumably be relatively unsuccessful. Thus the question becomes, Given relatively high elaboration, what influences the direction (the valence) of elaboration?

INFLUENCES ON ELABORATION DIRECTION

There are surely quite a number of different influences on the direction of receivers' issue-relevant thinking, but two particular factors merit attention here: whether the message's advocated position is proattitudinal or counterattitudinal, and the strength (quality) of the message's arguments.

PROATTITUDINAL VERSUS COUNTERATTITUDINAL MESSAGES The receiver's initial attitude and the message's advocated position, considered jointly, will surely influence the direction of elaboration. When the advocated position is one toward which the receiver is already favorably inclined—that is, when the message advocates a "proattitudinal" position—the receiver will presumably ordinarily be inclined to have favorable thoughts about the position advocated. By contrast, when the message advocates a counterattitudinal position, receivers will ordinarily be inclined to have unfavorable thoughts about the point of view being advocated. That is to say, everything else being equal, one expects proattitudinal messages to evoke predominantly favorable thoughts, and counterattitudinal messages to evoke predominantly unfavorable thoughts.

But of course this cannot be the whole story — otherwise nobody would ever be persuaded by a counterattitudinal message. At least sometimes, people are persuaded by the arguments contained in counterattitudinal communications, and hence the ELM suggests that a second influence on elaboration direction is the strength of the message's arguments.

ARGUMENT STRENGTH Recall that under conditions of high elaboration, receivers are motivated (and able) to engage in extensive issue-relevant thinking, including careful examination of the message's arguments. Presumably, then, the direction of receivers' elaboration will depend (at least in part) on the results of such scrutiny: The more favorable the reactions evoked by that scrutiny of message material, the more effective the message should be. If a receiver's examination of the message's arguments reveals shoddy arguments and bad evidence, one presumably expects little persuasion; but a very different outcome would be expected if the message contains powerful arguments, sound reasoning, good evidence, and the like.

That is to say, under conditions of high elaboration the strength (the quality) of the message's arguments should influence the direction of elaboration (and hence should influence persuasive success). And, indeed, quite a number of investigations have reported results indicating just such effects (e.g., Heesacker, Petty, & Cacioppo, 1983; Petty & Cacioppo, 1979b, 1984; Petty, Cacioppo, & Goldman, 1981; Petty, Cacioppo, & Schumann, 1983).

Unhappily, this research evidence is not as illuminating as one might suppose, because of the way in which "argument strength" is operationally defined. To obtain experimental messages containing "strong" or "weak" arguments, ELM researchers pretest various messages: A "strong-argument" message is defined as "one containing arguments such that when subjects are *instructed* to think about the message, the thoughts that they generate are predominantly favorable," and a "weak-argument" message is defined as one in which the arguments "are such that when subjects are instructed to think about them, the thoughts that they generate are predominantly unfavorable." That is to say, ELM research has "postponed the question of what specific qualities make arguments persuasive by defining argument quality in an empirical manner" (Petty & Cacioppo, 1986a, p. 32).

The consequence of this research practice is that it is not possible to say just what made these "strong-argument" messages effective under conditions of high elaboration. (It's not that the messages contained strong arguments — if the messages hadn't been effective under conditions of close scrutiny, they wouldn't have been labeled "strong-argument" messages in the first place.) Hence it is not yet possible to provide much direction to persuaders about just how to compose effective messages under conditions of high elaboration likelihood. One can say "use strong arguments," but that amounts to saying "use arguments that will be effective." It remains to be seen just what sorts of particular characteristics will make messages effective when elaboration likelihood is high.

OTHER INFLUENCES ON ELABORATION DIRECTION Although argument strength is the most studied influence on the direction of elaboration, there have been a few studies bearing on other possible influences on elaboration direction. For example, there is some evidence that when elaboration likelihood is high, forewarning receivers of an impending counterattitudinal message encourages them to have more unfavorable thoughts about the advocated position than they otherwise would have (Petty & Cacioppo, 1977, 1979a). But the focus of ELM research concerning influences on elaboration direction has been the role played by variations in "argument strength," and consequently the greatest amount of research evidence concerns that factor.

SUMMARY: CENTRAL ROUTES TO PERSUASION

Under conditions of high elaboration (e.g., high receiver involvement), the outcome of persuasive efforts depends upon the direction of receivers' elaboration: Where a persuasive message leads receivers to have predominantly favorable thoughts about the position being advocated, persuasive success is likely. And the direction of receivers' elaboration will depend (at least in part) on the character of the message's arguments.

It is worth noting the contrast here between social judgment theory (Chapter 2) and the ELM concerning the role played in persuasion by variations in receiver involvement. Social judgment theory appears to suggest that, in general, as the receiver's level of involvement increases, counterattitudinal messages will inevitably become less effective (because, for example, the receiver's latitude of rejection presumably grows larger as involvement increases). The ELM, by contrast, suggests that as involvement increases, elaboration likelihood increases—and this, in turn, might mean either greater persuasion or lessened persuasion, depending on the direction of the elaboration. As involvement increases, counterattitudinal messages with strong arguments should become more effective, while those with weak arguments should become less effective; indeed, just such patterns of effects have been obtained (e.g., Petty & Cacioppo, 1979b).[9]

INFLUENCES ON PERSUASIVE EFFECTS UNDER CONDITIONS OF LOW ELABORATION: PERIPHERAL ROUTES TO PERSUASION

THE CRITICAL ROLE OF HEURISTIC PRINCIPLES

The ELM suggests that under conditions of relatively low elaboration, the outcomes of persuasive efforts will not generally turn on the results of the receiver's thoughtful consideration of the message's arguments or other issue-relevant information. Instead, persuasive effects will be influenced much more by the receiver's use of simple decision rules or "heuristic principles."[10] These

heuristic principles (or "heuristics," for short) represent simple decision procedures requiring little information processing. The principles are activated by
peripheral cues, that is, by extrinsic features of the communication situation
such as the characteristics of the communicator (e.g., credibility). So, for
example, in a circumstance in which elaboration likelihood is low, receivers
may display agreement with a liked communicator because a simplifying
decision rule ("If I like the source, I'll agree") has been invoked. Heuristic
principles have ordinarily not been studied in a completely direct fashion, and
for good reason. One wouldn't expect (for instance) that self-report indices of
heuristic use would be very valuable; presumably these heuristics are used in a
tacit, nonconscious way, and thus receivers may well not be in a good position
to report on their use of such principles (Chaiken, 1987, p. 24; Petty &
Cacioppo, 1986a, p. 35). Instead, the operation of heuristic principles has been
inferred from the observable influence of peripheral cues on persuasive outcomes. Notice that the ELM expects particular patterns of cue effects on
persuasion: The influence of peripheral cues should be greater under conditions
of relatively low elaboration likelihood (e.g., lower receiver involvement) or
under conditions in which the cue is relatively more salient. The primary
evidence for the operation of heuristic principles consists of research results
conforming to just such patterns of effect.

VARIETIES OF HEURISTIC PRINCIPLES

Although a number of different heuristic principles have been suggested,
three particular heuristics have received relatively more extensive research
attention: the credibility, liking, and consensus heuristics.[11]

CREDIBILITY HEURISTIC One heuristic principle is based on the apparent
credibility of the communicator, and amounts to a belief that "statements by
credible sources can be trusted" (for alternative expressions of related ideas, see
Chaiken, 1987, p. 4; Cialdini, 1987, p. 175). As discussed in Chapter 8, a
number of studies have indicated that as the receiver's involvement in the issue
increases, the effects of communicator credibility diminish (e.g., Johnson &
Scileppi, 1969; Petty, Cacioppo, & Goldman, 1981; Rhine & Severance, 1970).
Similar results have been obtained when elaboration likelihood has been varied
in other ways (e.g., S. B. Kiesler & Mathog, 1968; Ratneshwar & Chaiken,
1986). Thus, consistent with ELM expectations, the peripheral cue of credibility
has been found to have greater impact on persuasive outcomes when elaboration likelihood is relatively low. Moreover, some research suggests that variations in the salience of credibility cues lead to corresponding variations in
credibility's effects (Andreoli & Worchel, 1978; Worchel, Andreoli, & Eason,
1975). All told, there looks to be good evidence for the existence of a credibility
heuristic in persuasion.

LIKING HEURISTIC A second heuristic principle is based on how well the
receiver likes the communicator, and might be expressed by beliefs such as
"people should agree with people they like" or "people I like usually have

correct opinions" (for alternative formulations of this heuristic, see Chaiken, 1987, p. 4; Cialdini, 1987, p. 178). Where this heuristic is invoked, liked sources should prove more persuasive than disliked sources. As discussed in more detail in Chapter 8, the research evidence does suggest that the ordinary advantage of liked communicators over disliked communicators diminishes as the receiver's involvement with the issue increases (e.g., Chaiken, 1980, Experiment 1; Petty, Cacioppo, & Schumann, 1983). Confirming findings have been obtained in studies in which elaboration likelihood varied in other ways (e.g., Wood & Kallgren, 1988) and in studies varying the salience of liking cues (e.g., Chaiken & Eagly, 1983): As elaboration likelihood declines or cue salience increases, the impact of liking cues on persuasion increases. Taken together, then, these studies point to the operation of a liking heuristic that can influence persuasive effects.

CONSENSUS HEURISTIC A third heuristic principle is based on the reactions of other people to the message, and could be expressed as a belief that "if other people believe it, then it's probably true" (for variant phrasings of such a heuristic, see Chaiken, 1987, p. 4; Cialdini, 1987, p. 174). When this heuristic is employed, the approving reactions of others should enhance message effectiveness (and disapproving reactions should impair effectiveness). There are now a number of studies indicating the operation of such a consensus heuristic in persuasion (for a more careful review, see Axsom et al., 1987). For example, several investigations have found that receivers are less persuaded when they overhear an audience expressing disapproval (versus approval) of the communicator's message (e.g., Hylton, 1971; Landy, 1972; Silverthorne & Mazmanian, 1975; for a related study, see Hocking, Margreiter, & Hylton, 1977; for complexities, see Beatty & Kruger, 1978).[12]

OTHER HEURISTICS Various other principles have been suggested as heuristics that receivers may employ in reacting to persuasive messages. For example, it may be that the number of arguments in the message (Chaiken, 1980, Experiment 2; Petty & Cacioppo, 1984) or the sheer length of the message (Wood et al., 1985) can serve as cues that engage corresponding heuristic principles ("the more arguments, the better" or "the longer the message, the better its position must be"). But for the most part there is relatively little research evidence concerning such heuristics, and hence confident conclusions are perhaps premature.

SUMMARY: PERIPHERAL ROUTES TO PERSUASION

Under conditions of low elaboration likelihood, the outcome of persuasive efforts depends less upon the direction of receivers' issue-relevant thinking than upon the operation of heuristic principles, simple decision rules activated by peripheral cues in the persuasion setting. Where receivers are unable or unmotivated to engage in extensive issue-relevant thinking, their reactions to persuasive communications will be guided by simpler principles such as the credibility, liking, and consensus heuristics.[13]

VARIATIONS IN THE DEGREE OF ELABORATION:
TRADE-OFFS AND CONSEQUENCES

As the extensiveness of elaboration varies, different routes to persuasion are engaged: the central route for high elaboration, the peripheral for low. But what is crucial is not the (useful but too simple) distinction between the two persuasion routes, but rather the underlying elaboration likelihood continuum. Thus it is important to bear in mind that, in considering the effects on persuasive outcomes, there is something of a trade-off between peripheral cues and elaboration (issue-relevant thinking): As elaboration likelihood increases, the impact of peripheral cues declines, and the impact of the receiver's issue-relevant thinking increases. For example, as variations in argument strength make more and more difference in outcomes, variations in communicator expertise make less and less (e.g., Petty, Cacioppo, & Goldman, 1981). The ELM does not claim that (for instance) variations in argument strength will make no difference when elaboration likelihood is low, or that variations in communicator credibility will make no difference when elaboration likelihood is high. Rather, the suggestion is that, broadly speaking, the relative impact of elaboration and peripheral cues will vary as elaboration likelihood varies. With greater elaboration likelihood, persuasive effects come to depend more and more on the direction of elaboration (and less and less on peripheral cues); as elaboration likelihood decreases, the impact of peripheral cues increases (and that of elaboration declines).

Although persuasion can be accomplished at any point along the elaboration continuum, this does not mean that the nature of the persuasive effects obtained will be identical. As is already clear, different factors influence persuasive success under different elaboration conditions. But additionally the ELM suggests that, with variations in the amount of elaboration (i.e., variations in the route to persuasion), there are corresponding variations in the character of the persuasive outcomes effected. Specifically, the ELM suggests that attitudes shaped through central-route processes will (compared to attitudes shaped through peripheral-route processes) display greater temporal persistence, be more predictive of subsequent behavior, and be more resistant to counterpersuasion. For each of these claims, there is at least some previous research that can be interpreted as suggesting such effects, but only a smattering of direct research evidence. (For review and discussion of relevant work, see Petty & Cacioppo, 1986a, pp. 173-195.) Thus one might aptly conclude that these are plausible and suggestive hypotheses that deserve more extensive direct empirical scrutiny.

COMMENTARY

The ELM has stimulated a great deal of research over the last decade, impressively summarized by Petty and Cacioppo (1986a). It is obvious that the ELM provides a framework that offers the prospect of reconciling apparently competing findings about the role played in persuasion by various factors. For example: Why is it that the receiver's liking for the communicator sometimes exerts a large influence on persuasive outcomes, and sometimes very little? Because as elaboration likelihood varies, so will the impact of a simple decision rule such as the liking heuristic. Indeed, the ELM's capacity to account for conflicting findings from earlier research makes it an especially important theoretical framework, and unquestionably the most promising recent theoretical development in persuasion research. Even so, there are several facets of ELM theory and research that require some commentary.[14]

LIMITED NUMBER OF TOPICS

One worrisome aspect of ELM research is the relatively small number of message topics used (especially given the large number of studies undertaken). For example, ELM research has repeatedly employed the topic of senior comprehensive exams. This topic has been used in studies by Burnkrant and Howard (1984), Cacioppo and Petty (1985), Cacioppo et al. (1983, Experiment 1), Harkins and Petty (1981a, Experiment 1, Experiment 3, 1981b, 1987), Heesacker et al. (1983), Petty and Cacioppo (1977, Experiment 1, 1979a, 1979b, Experiment 2, 1984), Petty, Cacioppo, and Goldman (1981), Petty, Cacioppo, and Heesacker (1981), Petty, Wells, et al. (1983, Experiment 2), Swasy and Munch (1985) — and this is not an exhaustive list of ELM studies using this one topic. Indeed, the reader of Petty and Cacioppo (1986a) who keeps a running tally will find that of the ELM studies discussed, there look to be roughly twice as many studies on two particular topics (senior comprehensive exams and tuition charges) than on all other topics combined.

What is worrisome about this, of course, is that the ELM purports to be a theory of persuasion generally, not a theory of persuasion about comprehensive exams and tuition charges. One would naturally have reservations about a theory of persuasion resting on evidence from just a few human respondents, and one should similarly have reservations about a theory that rests on evidence from just a few message topics. Theories of persuasion commonly aim to generalize across both persons and topics, and investigators should seek corresponding diversity and breadth in the message topics used in research.[15]

To be sure, the use of a highly restricted set of topics might have seemed attractive in the early days of ELM research; the pretesting necessary for the argument-strength manipulation, for example, might be taken to recommend the initial use of a small set of topics. But once the model's general plausibility has been established — as surely it has been — continued reliance on those topics should become progressively less attractive. At some point the benefits of convenience should be surpassed by the desire to display the model's robustness and generality.

It is probably too much to hope that no future ELM research will employ (for example) the comprehensive examination topic. Still, if the model is truly a general one, then abandoning that topic can only strengthen the model's claims; and if the use of diverse additional topics yields disconfirming results, then we will be on the track of useful information about the ELM's limitations. No matter the outcome, there is much to be gained by diversifying the ELM's evidentiary base.[16]

ARGUMENT STRENGTH

It is important to be clear about the nature of ELM research concerning argument strength (argument quality), lest misleading conclusions be drawn. Argument strength, it will be recalled, is operationally defined by argument effects under conditions of high elaboration: A "strong-argument" message is defined as "one containing arguments such that when subjects are instructed to think about the message, the thoughts that they generate are predominantly favorable," and a "weak-argument" message is defined as one in which the arguments "are such that when subjects are instructed to think about them, the thoughts that they generate are predominantly unfavorable" (Petty & Cacioppo, 1986a, p. 32).

Hence if, in a given investigation, an argument-strength manipulation did *not* influence persuasive effects under conditions of high elaboration (i.e., the message that was thought to contain the stronger arguments did not lead to greater persuasion under such conditions), the conclusion would *not* be "This result disconfirms the ELM's prediction," but instead "The manipulations were somehow defective; either the study didn't effectively manipulate argument strength, or it didn't effectively manipulate elaboration likelihood conditions, because *by definition* stronger arguments lead to greater persuasion under conditions of higher elaboration."

Notice, thus: To say that "under conditions of high elaboration, strong arguments have been found to be more effective than weak arguments" is rather like saying "Bachelors have been found to be unmarried." We didn't need empirical research to find these things out (and indeed there would be something wrong with any empirical research that seemed to disconfirm these claims). And so one ought not be misled by statements such as "Subjects led to believe that the message topic (e.g. comprehensive exams) will (vs. won't) impact on their own lives have also been shown to be less persuaded by weak messages but more persuaded by strong ones" (Chaiken & Stangor, 1987, p. 594). Despite the statement's appearance, this is not a discovery; it is not an empirical result or finding, it is not something that research "shows" to be true, it is not something that could have been otherwise (given the effect of involvement on elaboration). The described relationship is true by definition, given the definition of argument strength used in ELM research.[17]

It is important to grasp this point clearly, because it is important to understand what is and isn't known. It is not yet known what it is about the "strong arguments" (used in ELM research) that makes them persuasive under conditions of high elaboration. One can easily be misled into thinking that an explanation is already in hand—"Obviously, what makes them persuasive is that they're strong arguments"—but (as should be plain) this provides no explanation at all. And, regrettably, inspection of sample ELM messages (e.g., Petty & Cacioppo, 1986a, pp. 54-59) suggests that the strong-versus-weak-argument contrast is formed through confounding a number of different message features (e.g., the desirability of claimed benefits of the advocated position, the relevance of evidence to proffered conclusions, the apparent self-interest of cited evidence sources, the likelihood that claimed outcomes of the policy would affect the receiver, and so on). It will plainly take some time to sort out just what it is about those strong-argument messages that makes them more persuasive (for an initial effort, see Areni & Lutz, 1988).[18]

INVOLVEMENT

The concept of involvement has often appeared in persuasion research as a device for indexing what are taken to be important variations in the sort of relationship that message recipients have to the topic of advocacy, and ELM research is no exception. For the ELM, the concept of "involvement" amounts to the direct personal relevance of the topic to the receiver. Hence the common ELM involvement manipulation on the senior comprehensive examination topic: The comprehensive examination requirement is to be instituted at the receiver's school (thus affecting the receiver personally) or at another, distant school (and so presumably is of little personal relevance to the receiver).

The point to be emphasized here — and it is a point that might have been appreciated from a consideration of social judgment theory — is that (at least as used in the research literature) the concept of involvement is multifaceted, and personal relevance is only one of these facets.[19] "Involvement" might also be taken to refer to the person's judgment of the importance of the issue, or the degree to which the person is strongly committed to a stand on the issue, or the extent to which the person's sense of self is connected to the stand taken, and so on.

These distinctions are important, because these other facets of involvement may not have the same effects as does personal relevance (Chaiken & Stangor, 1987, pp. 594-596; for an example, see Howard-Pitney, Borgida, & Omoto, 1986). For example, the effects on message scrutiny (that is, close attention to the message's contents) may not be the same for increasing personal relevance and for increasing commitment to a position. As personal relevance increases, message scrutiny increases; but as position commitment increases, one can imagine message scrutiny either increasing or decreasing (e.g., increasing where there are cues that message scrutiny will yield position-bolstering material, but decreasing where scrutiny looks to yield position-threatening material).

The implication of these considerations is that the ELM's "involvement" manipulations should be clearly understood specifically as inducing variation in the personal relevance of the topic, not to be confused with variation in other aspects of receiver involvement. The various distinguishable facets of involvement require correspondingly different research treatments if we are to ferret out the effects of receiver involvement (broadly understood) on persuasion.

CONCLUSION

If there is a single key insight about persuasion contributed by the elabora-tion likelihood model, it is the recognition of the variable character of topic-related thinking engaged in by message recipients. Because the extensiveness of topic-relevant thinking varies (from person to person, from situation to situation, and so on), the central factors influencing persuasive success vary: Simple heuristic principles may prevail where little elaboration occurs, but where extensive elaboration is undertaken, the character of the message's contents takes on greater importance. This central idea offers the prospect of reconciling apparently conflicting findings in the research literature concerning the role played by various factors in influencing persuasive effects, and marks the ELM as an important step forward in the understanding of persuasion.

NOTES

1. Consider, for example, the key concept of "elaboration." Petty and Cacioppo (1986a) write that "by elaboration, we mean the extent to which a person carefully thinks about issue-relevant information" (p. 7). In the circumstance in which a persuasive message is received, the conception is more particular: "In a persuasion context, elaboration refers to the extent to which a person scrutinizes the issue-relevant arguments contained in the persuasive communication" (p. 7). But a subsequent discussion of persuasion-context elaboration puts matters somewhat differently: "Recall that by elaboration we mean the process of relating the to-be-evaluated recommendation and arguments [in a message] to other issue-relevant information in memory" (p. 14). To bring out the confusion here, consider the circumstance in which a receiver is provoked by a message to engage in extensive thought about issue-relevant information, but not to scrutinize the arguments in the message carefully; the receiver instead is thinking about other arguments (perhaps self-generated arguments, perhaps previously heard arguments that are recalled). Is this receiver engaged in relatively high elaboration? Yes, if elaboration means thinking about issue-relevant information (e.g., "relating the message's recommendation to other issue-relevant information in memory"). No, if elaboration means "scrutinizing the issue-relevant arguments contained in the message." And matters are not made any clearer by Petty and Cacioppo's apparently (but not certainly) synonymous usage of "elaboration," "message elaboration," "argument elaboration," "issue-relevant elabora-tion" (as if there might be some other kind of elaboration), "message processing," "message scrutiny," "argument processing," and "argument scrutiny." One might have thought that a concept so central to the ELM as the concept of elaboration would have received more careful treatment than this. In any event, these and similar unclarities have motivated the present general description of the ELM.

2. Some recent general presentations of the ELM have included a distinction between two sorts of elaboration: "objective elaboration" and "biased elaboration" (e.g., Petty & Cacioppo, 1986a, pp. 18-19). "Objective elaboration" is intended to refer to a circumstance in which the receiver impartially scrutinizes the message's arguments (and hence the receiver's thoughts are guided by the character of those arguments), and "biased elaboration" is meant to refer to a circumstance in which the receiver does not scrutinize the message's arguments impartially (but instead generates issue-relevant thoughts that are either predominantly favorable or unfavorable to the position advocated, never mind the message's arguments).

The status of this distinction is not entirely clear. At least sometimes this appears to be intended as describing the poles of a continuum for describing two types of relatively high elaboration: When persons engage in high elaboration, they might engage in comparatively objective or comparatively biased elaboration (see, e.g., Petty & Cacioppo, 1986a, p. 18); these two poles are thus distinguished not by the amount of elaboration involved, but by whether the elaboration is objective or biased.

But – depending on the definition of "elaboration" used – objective elaboration and biased elaboration might well be taken to represent different amounts of elaboration (i.e., two different locations on the high-to-low elaboration continuum), with objective elaboration reflecting a greater degree of elaboration than does biased elaboration. If "elaboration" refers to the degree to which the receiver gives careful scrutiny to the message's arguments (as at p. 7 of Petty & Cacioppo, 1986a), then "biased elaboration" represents less elaboration than does "objective elaboration," because biased elaboration reflects less careful consideration of the message's arguments. On the other hand, if "elaboration" refers simply to the amount of issue-relevant thinking, then "biased elaboration" and "objective elaboration" ought to be construed as representing equal amounts of elaboration. Such confusions can be avoided – and a perfectly satisfactory (if general) description of the ELM provided – by passing over the distinction between biased and objective elaboration, and hence that course has been pursued here.

3. Notice that the unclarities surrounding the concept of elaboration (as in note 1) make for corresponding unclarities in the assessment of elaboration. For example, if elaboration is defined as issue-relevant thinking, then greater elaboration should be reflected in greater issue-relevant thinking (e.g., a larger number of issue-relevant thoughts). But compare the suggestion of Cacioppo et al. (1985): "The term *elaboration likelihood* refers to the likelihood that one engages in issue-relevant thinking with the aim of determining the merits of the arguments for a position rather than the total amount of thinking per se in which a person engages. It follows, therefore, that the profile rather than the total number of issue-relevant thoughts should change predictably as the elaboration likelihood regarding a given recommendation increases" (p. 229; for a nearly identical statement, see Cacioppo & Petty, 1984, p. 674). This suggestion – that the total number of issue-relevant thoughts is not a proper index of the degree of elaboration – arises because the definition of elaboration has changed: Rather than elaboration being defined as issue-relevant thinking, it is defined as issue-relevant thinking undertaken with a particular motivation (namely, the motivation of [impartially] determining the merits of the arguments bearing on a given position – or perhaps even more specifically the motivation of impartially determining the merits of the specific arguments that are contained in the message [as opposed to the merits of other issue-relevant arguments]). This same definitional shift gives rise to uncertainties (discussed in note 2) about whether "objective elaboration" and "biased elaboration" are claimed by the ELM to represent equal amounts of elaboration (presumably they do, if "elaboration" refers to issue-relevant thinking generally; but presumably they do not, if "elaboration" refers only to issue-relevant thinking undertaken with the motivations said to be associated with "objective elaboration"). The present description of the ELM treats elaboration as issue-relevant thinking simpliciter, and hence corresponding treatment is given to the question of the assessment of elaboration. It should not pass unnoticed that most of the procedures Petty and Cacioppo (1986a, pp. 35-47) discuss for the assessment of elaboration appear to be more straightforwardly described as amount-of-cognitive-activity indices rather than as amount-of-cognitive-activity-undertaken-with-a-particular-motivation indices.

4. This research support, it should be noted, largely consists of evidence showing that as personal relevance increases, the effects of message-argument quality increase and the effects of peripheral cues decrease.

5. In fact, as pointed out by Chaiken (1987, pp. 16-17), it is not yet entirely clear whether the effects of need for cognition on elaboration likelihood should be ascribed to differences in elaboration motivation or differences in elaboration ability, as need for cognition indices are positively correlated (roughly in the range of .15 to .40) with measures of verbal reasoning skills, ACT scores, and the like (e.g., Cacioppo & Petty, 1982; Cacioppo, Petty, Kao, & Rodriguez, 1986; Cacioppo et al., 1983; K. Olson, Camp, & Fuller, 1984). What little direct evidence there is favors a motivational-difference rather than an ability-difference explanation (Cacioppo, Petty, Kao, & Rodriguez, 1986, Study 1). Either way, of course, need for cognition remains an influence on elaboration likelihood.

6. Actually, the ELM's analysis of distraction effects is a bit more complex than this. For instance, the ELM acknowledges that where the distraction is so intense as to become the focus of

attention, thus interfering with even minimal message reception, one doesn't expect to find the predicted distraction effects. For a more careful discussion, see Petty and Cacioppo (1986a, pp. 61-68).

7. Buller (1986) concludes that the ELM-related "dominant-thought-disruption" hypothesis concerning distraction effects (Petty et al., 1976) seems not supported by the evidence. But Buller's interpretation would appear to have the ELM predict that distraction will enhance the effectiveness of counterattitudinal messages and reduce the effectiveness of proattitudinal messages (see Buller, 1986, pp. 110-111). This interpretation differs from the ELM's analysis of distraction effects in two notable ways. First, the ELM does not predict that distraction will have substantial effects on persuasion in every circumstance, but rather only under conditions of relatively high elaboration likelihood (Petty & Cacioppo, 1986a, p. 68). Since distraction's effects putatively come through interference with elaboration, if elaboration likelihood is already low then presumably distraction will not have large effects. Thus, for example, even if distraction is found to have generally little effect on persuasive outcomes in the research literature, such a finding is not necessarily inconsistent with the ELM (which predicts effects only under certain conditions, namely, high elaboration likelihood). Second, since distraction's effects are taken to come about through interfering with elaboration, the ELM's prediction is that distraction will enhance the effectiveness of messages that (in the absence of distraction) engender predominantly unfavorable elaboration, and will reduce the effectiveness of messages that (without distraction) engender predominantly favorable elaboration. This is not the same as predicting that distraction will enhance counterattitudinal message effectiveness and reduce proattitudinal message effectiveness; not all counterattitudinal messages evoke predominantly unfavorable elaboration, and not all proattitudinal messages evoke predominantly favorable elaboration. The point here is that Buller's negative conclusion about the dominant-thought-disruption hypothesis in fact does not indicate a weakness in the research evidence concerning the ELM's claims about distraction effects.

8. The studies by Wood (1982), Wood and Kallgren (1988), and Wood et al. (1985) all use the same message topic with (it appears) very similar messages, which means that this research evidence does not underwrite generalizations as confident as one might prefer.

9. But this apparent contrast between social judgment theory and the ELM (a contrast emphasized by Petty & Cacioppo, 1979b) may be only apparent, because the conceptions of "involvement" are different for the two theories. For the ELM, involvement is direct personal relevance of the issue; for social judgment theory (as discussed in Chapter 2), the conception of involvement is fuzzier, but (as the phrase "ego-involvement" suggests) commonly is seen to involve the idea that the person's self-concept or identity is connected to the stand taken. Though it can be appealing to run these together under some general concept of "involvement" (or "issue involvement"), these are distinguishable facets of involvement. An issue might be personally relevant to me ("involving," in ELM terms) without my sense of self being bound up in it; the issue of parking fees on my campus, for instance, is personally very relevant, but my sense of myself as a person — my identity — isn't connected to my views on that issue.

10. In fact, the ELM suggests that there are other peripheral-route processes besides heuristic principles — specifically, "simple affective processes" (Petty & Cacioppo, 1986a, p. 8) in which attitudes change "as a result of rather primitive affective and associational processes" (p. 9) such as classical conditioning. Indeed, this additional element appears to be the primary difference between the ELM and Chaiken's (1987) systematic-heuristic model of persuasion. Chaiken's "systematic processing" mode corresponds to the ELM's central route, and her "heuristic mode" refers specifically to the use of heuristic principles of the sort discussed here.

Although the ELM's "peripheral route" is thus a broader term than is Chaiken's "heuristic mode," here the peripheral route is treated in a way that makes it look very like the heuristic mode; that is, the present treatment focuses on the simple rules/inferences (the heuristic principles) rather than on the primitive affective processes that are purported also to represent peripheral routes to persuasion. There are several reasons for this. First, the nonheuristic peripheral-route processes have frankly not gotten much attention in ELM research. Second, at least some of the putative nonheuristic peripheral processes — in particular, those concerning attitude conditioning — are arguably dubious (e.g., Brewer, 1974). But the ELM could abandon a belief in (say) the classical conditioning of attitude with little consequence for the model, which suggests that the ELM's commitment to such processes is nonessential to the model. Third, it may be possible to translate some apparently nonheuristic peripheral processes into heuristic-principle form (e.g., mood effects might reflect a tacit heuristic such as "If it makes me feel good, it must be right"). Fourth, at least to some extent the inclusion of the various nonheuristic peripheral processes in the ELM seems motivated less by substantive considerations than by a desire to use the ELM in a metatheoretical way, permitting the classification of earlier viewpoints as concerning fundamentally central or peripheral routes to persuasion (see, e.g., Petty & Cacioppo, 1981a). But if one's interest is in the ELM as a substantive theory of persuasion (and not primarily as a metatheoretical housing), the motivation for including certain nonheuristic peripheral processes weakens.

11. As Chaiken (1987, p. 5, n. 1) points out, a number of heuristic principles appear to be represented in the various "compliance principles" identified by Cialdini (1984; for a briefer treatment, see Cialdini, 1987).

12. In what might be taken to reflect the operation of a consensus heuristic, Reingen (1982) found that people were more likely to donate to a charity or to agree to donate blood if shown a list of prior donors — and the longer the list, the greater the likelihood of compliance.

13. As a complexity here, notice that something that can function as a peripheral cue may also (or instead) serve to influence elaboration likelihood (see Petty & Cacioppo, 1986a, pp. 204-215). For example, the length of printed messages — suggested by Wood et al. (1985) to be a peripheral cue — might in some circumstances influence elaboration motivation. At least in some settings, a long message may be taken as a sign that enhanced attention to the message's contents can pay dividends — and so as message length increases (up to a point, anyway) so would elaboration motivation. For some interesting evidence on this possibility, see Soley (1986).

14. As note readers will already have noticed, some conceptual difficulties encountered by the ELM have been discussed previously (see notes 1-3, above).

15. In fact, the problem is perhaps a bit worse than portrayed here. It is not just that a small number of topics have been used repeatedly; in a number of cases, the messages used have been quite similar, even identical. The repeated use of messages in persuasion research is discussed in more detail in Chapter 7, but for the moment it is enough to note that such research practices make the ELM's supporting evidence rather less impressive than it might otherwise seem.

16. The heavy reliance on a few topics affects some ELM claims more than others. For example, there is more topical diversity in the research evidence concerning the effects of involvement on elaboration likelihood than in the research evidence concerning, say, the persuasive effects of using rhetorical questions in messages. On this latter topic, for some time the extant ELM-relevant studies all used not only the same topic but (apparently) virtually identical messages (Burnkrant & Howard, 1984; Petty, Cacioppo, & Heesacker, 1981; Swasy & Munch, 1985), and only recently has work using a different topic appeared (Munch & Swasy, 1988).

17. Another example: "A message with strong arguments should tend to produce more agreement when it is scrutinized carefully than when scrutiny is low, but a message with weak arguments should tend to produce less overall agreement when scrutiny is high rather than low. The joint operation of these processes would result in people showing greater attitudinal differentiation of strong from weak arguments when processing is high than when it is low" (Petty & Cacioppo, 1986a, p. 44). Appearances to the contrary, these are not empirical predictions; these are not expectations that might be disconfirmed by empirical results. If a message doesn't produce more agreement when scrutinized carefully than when scrutiny is low, then (definitionally) it cannot possibly be a message with strong arguments.

18. Consumers of the research literature will want to notice that other researchers' "argument-strength" manipulations — that is, the manipulations that others label "argument strength" — do not always match the operationalization common in ELM research (e.g., Hunt, Smith, & Kernan, 1985). Thus in considering argument-strength research — as indeed any research area — close attention to the details of operationalization will be required if misunderstandings are to be avoided.

19. What is of primary concern in the present discussion is what is sometimes called "issue involvement," as opposed to "response involvement" (Zimbardo, 1960). In response involvement, the topic is not particularly important or personally relevant (on intrinsic grounds) to the person, but

exhibiting the right sort of attitude (making the right sort of response) is. Thus where issue involvement leads to the person's engagement with the message on intrinsic grounds (e.g., the issue's importance or personal relevance), response involvement leads to the person's engagement with the message for extrinsic reasons (most commonly, because the recipient's response to the message will be available for public scrutiny, and hence the receiver's impression-management concerns make for a desire to express views of certain sorts rather than others). Issue involvement and response involvement might well be expected to have different effects on persuasion (see Leippe & Elkin, 1987).

Part III

Factors Influencing Persuasive Effects

This section reviews research concerning the effects various factors have on the effectiveness of persuasive messages. The discussion is organized around four groupings of influencing factors: source factors (Chapter 8), message factors (Chapter 9), receiver and context factors (Chapter 10), and the relationship between attitudes and actions (Chapter 11). As will be seen, persuasive outcomes are often dependent on the interplay among these various classes of factors. An introductory chapter provides some background information concerning the study of persuasive effects.

7

The Study of Persuasive Effects

THE RESEARCH TO BE DISCUSSED in the next four chapters is, overwhelmingly, experimental research that systematically investigates the influence that various factors (communicator characteristics, message variations, and so on) have on persuasive outcomes. This chapter first provides some general background on the underlying logic of such experimental research, and then discusses some problems that arise in the study of persuasive effects.

EXPERIMENTAL DESIGN AND CAUSAL INFERENCE

There are various sorts of experimental arrangements used in persuasion effects research, but these can usefully be thought of as variations on a basic design.

THE BASIC DESIGN

The simplest sort of research design employed in the work to be discussed is an experimental design in which the researcher manipulates a single factor (the "independent variable") so as to see its effects on persuasive outcomes (the "dependent variable," so labeled because it presumably depends upon the independent variable).

For instance, an investigator who wishes to investigate the effects of explicit conclusion drawing on attitude change might design a laboratory investigation of the following sort. The researcher would prepare two persuasive messages identical in every respect, except that in one message the persuader's conclusion is drawn explicitly at the end of the message (the "explicit-conclusion message") while in the other message the persuader's conclusion is left implicit (the "implicit-conclusion message"). When participants in this experiment arrive at the laboratory, their attitudes on the persuasive topic are assessed, and then they receive one of the two messages; which message a given participant receives is a matter of chance, perhaps determined by flipping a coin. Thus there will be one set of participants who receive the explicit-conclusion message, and a second set who receive the implicit-conclusion message. After exposure to the persuasive message, receivers' attitudes are assessed again so as to ascertain the degree of attitude change produced by the message.

Suppose that (following conventional statistical procedures) the results indicate reliably greater attitude change for those receiving the explicit-conclusion message than for those receiving the implicit-conclusion message. How might such a result be explained? One can rule out systematic bias in assigning participants to hear one or the other of the messages, because participants were randomly assigned to hear messages; thus, for instance, one can confidently say that it is quite unlikely that those hearing the explicit-conclusion message were just generally more easily persuaded than those hearing the implicit-conclusion message (that is, one can rule out this explanation because people who were easily persuaded were randomly distributed across the two messages).

The obvious explanation for the obtained results, of course, is precisely the presence or absence of an explicit conclusion. Indeed, because this is the *only* factor that varies between the two messages, it presumably *must* be the locus of the observed differences. And this is the general logic of experimental designs such as this: These designs are intended to permit unambiguous causal attribution precisely by virtue of experimental control over factors other than the independent variable.

VARIATIONS ON THE BASIC DESIGN

There are innumerable ways in which this basic experimental arrangement might be varied. For example, one might dispense with the initial attitude assessment (reasoning that the random assignment of participants to the two experimental conditions would likely ensure that the two groups would have roughly comparable initial attitudes); this is commonly called a "posttest-only" design (since there would be only a postmessage assessment of attitude). As another example of variation, an investigator might create an independent variable with more than two conditions (more than two levels). For instance, one might compare the persuasive effects of communicators who were high, moderate, or low in credibility.

The most common and important variation, however, is the inclusion of more than one independent variable in a single experiment. Thus (for instance) rather than doing one experiment to study implicit versus explicit conclusions and a second study to study high versus moderate versus low credibility, a researcher could design a single investigation to study these two variables simultaneously. This would involve creating all six possible combinations of conclusion type and credibility level (3 credibility conditions × 2 conclusion-type conditions = 6 combinations).

Experimental designs with more than one independent variable permit the detection of "interaction effects" involving those variables. An interaction effect is said to occur if the effect of one independent variable depends upon the level of another independent variable; conversely, if the effect of one variable does *not* depend on the level of another variable, then no interaction effect exists. Thus, for example, if the effect of having an implicit or explicit conclusion is *constant*, no matter what the credibility of the source, then no interaction effect would exist between credibility and conclusion type. But if the effect of having an implicit or explicit conclusion *varies* depending on the credibility of the source (say, if high-credibility sources are most effective with explicit conclusions, and low-credibility sources are most effective with implicit conclusions), then an interaction effect (involving credibility and conclusion type) would exist; the effect of one variable (conclusion type) would depend on the level of another (credibility).

TWO GENERAL PROBLEMS
IN STUDYING PERSUASIVE EFFECTS

There are two noteworthy general problems that arise in investigating factors influencing the effectiveness of persuasive messages. One of these concerns the difficulty in making reliable generalizations about the effects of message types; the other concerns the task of defining independent variables in studies of persuasive effects.

GENERALIZING ABOUT MESSAGES

The earlier description of experimental design might make it seem easy to arrive at generalizations about factors influencing persuasive effects. To compare the persuasive effects of (for example) explicit and implicit conclusions, one simply does an experiment of the sort previously described: Create two versions of a given message (one of each conclusion type), and see whether there is any difference in persuasive effect. And indeed this is overwhelmingly the most common sort of experimental design used in studies of persuasive effects.

But this sort of experimental design in fact has important weaknesses, at least if one is interested in arriving at dependable generalizations about the persuasive effects of variations in message features (such as implicit versus explicit conclusions). This design uses a single message to represent each general category (level, type) of the message variable. That is, one particular instance of an explicit-conclusion message and one particular instance of an implicit-conclusion message are compared. And, as Jackson and Jacobs (1983) have pointed out, such "single-message" designs create two important barriers to generalization: One is that the design does not permit unambiguous causal attribution; the other is that the design is blind to the possibility that the effects of a given message factor may not be constant (uniform) across different messages.

AMBIGUOUS CAUSAL ATTRIBUTION Although the logic of experimental research is designed to permit clear and unambiguous causal attribution, "single-message" experimental designs inevitably create some ambiguity concerning what the cause is of any observed differences. This ambiguity arises from the fact that manipulating the variable of interest (say, implicit versus explicit conclusion) inevitably means also concomitantly manipulating *other* variables that aren't of interest.

For example, suppose a researcher created the two messages (implicit conclusion and explicit conclusion) in the following way. First, the explicit-conclusion message was written. Then, to create the implicit-conclusion message, the researcher simply eliminated the final paragraph (which contained the explicit conclusion). These two messages differ in conclusion type, but that's not the only thing that distinguishes the two messages. For one thing, the explicit-conclusion message is now *longer* than the implicit-conclusion message.

It is probably apparent what difficulty this poses, so far as arriving at generalizations is concerned. If the persuasiveness of the two messages differs, how should that difference be explained? One's initial inclination might well be to interpret the difference as resulting from the type of conclusion used. But one could equally well suppose (given the evidence) that it was message length, not conclusion type, that created the difference. And—what's worse—these aren't the only two possibilities. The explicit-conclusion message might be more repetitive than the implicit-conclusion message, or it might seem more insulting (because it says the obvious), or it might be more coherent or better organized, and so on and so on. And the problem is that one doesn't know whether it is conclusion type or some other variable that leads to the observed difference in persuasiveness.

There is another way of expressing this same problem (concerning the ambiguities of causal attribution in single-message designs). To put it most generally: In a single-message design, the manipulation of a given message variable can be described in any number of ways; consequently, problems of causal attribution and generalization arise.

Consider, for example, the following experimental manipulation. Two persuasive messages are prepared arguing in favor of making the sale of cigarettes illegal. Both messages emphasize the harmful physical consequences of smoking, and indeed are generally quite similar, except for the following sort of variation. Where message A reads "There can be no doubt that cigarette

smoking produces harmful physical effects," message B reads "Only an igno-
rant person would doubt that cigarette smoking produces harmful physical
effects"; the statement in message A, "It is therefore readily apparent that the
country should pass legislation to make the sale of cigarettes illegal," is
replaced in message B by the statement "Only the stupid or morally corrupt
would oppose passage of legislation to make the sale of cigarettes illegal"; and
so forth (with a total of four such alterations in the messages).

What is the independent variable under investigation here? That is, how shall
we describe this experimental manipulation? Framing some causal generalization will require that the difference between the two messages be expressed
somehow, but exactly how?

As may already be apparent, there are many possible ways to capture the
difference between message A and message B — and in fact different researchers
have described this very manipulation in quite different ways. The original
investigators (G. R. Miller & Baseheart, 1969) describe this manipulation as a
matter of "opinionated language" as opposed to "nonopinionated language,"
where the difference is that opinionated language, in addition to giving the
source's views on the topic, also conveys the source's views concerning those
who agree or disagree with the source. But Bradac, Bowers, and Courtright
(1980) characterize this manipulation as varying "language intensity," which
they define as the characteristic of language that indicates the degree to which
the speaker's attitude toward a concept deviates from neutrality (pp. 200-201).
Abelson (1986) cites this same manipulation as concerning the effects of having
a "confident style in debating" (p. 227). McGuire (1985) treats this experimental manipulation under the general headings of "forcefulness of delivery" and
"intensity of presentation," and describes the experimental manipulation as
comparing a "more dynamic style" with a "subdued style" (p. 270). And of
course not even these exhaust the possibilities. For instance, one could describe
this as a contrast between extreme and mild (or nonexistent) denigration of
those holding opposing views.

These different descriptions of the experimental manipulation could all be
correct, but of course they are not identical. The phrases "confident debating
style" and "extreme denigration of those holding opposing views" don't mean
the same thing. Unfortunately, if one wishes to frame a causal generalization
from research using this concrete experimental manipulation, one must choose
some particular description. But which one? Given this single-message design,
all the various interpretations are equally good — which is to say, we cannot
make the sorts of unambiguous causal attributions we wished to achieve.

NONUNIFORM EFFECTS OF MESSAGE VARIABLES There is a second barrier to generalization created by single-message designs, one that arises from
the possibility (or probability) that the effect of a given message variable will
not be uniform (constant) across all messages.

Consider again the example of a single-message study examining the effects
of having implicit versus explicit conclusions. Suppose that this study found the

explicit-conclusion message to be significantly more persuasive than the implicit-conclusion message (and let's overlook the problem of deciding that it was conclusion type, not some other factor, that was responsible for the difference). Should we conclude that having explicit conclusions will *always* improve the effectiveness of a message? Not necessarily. After all, there might have been something peculiar about the particular message that was studied (remember that only one message was used). Perhaps there was something (unnoticed by the researchers) that made that particular message especially hospitable to having an explicit conclusion — maybe the topic, maybe the way the rest of the message was organized, maybe the nature of the arguments that were made. Other messages might not be so hospitable to explicit conclusions.

To put the point more abstractly: The effect of a given message variable may not be uniform across messages. Some messages might be helped a lot by having an explicit conclusion, some helped only a little, some even hurt by it. But if that's true, then (obviously) looking at the effects of conclusion type on a *single* message doesn't really provide a very good basis for drawing a general conclusion. So, once again, the typical single-message design used in persuasion effects research creates an obstacle to dependable message generalization, because it overlooks the possibility of nonuniform effects across messages.

DESIGNING FUTURE PERSUASION RESEARCH It has probably already occurred to the reader that there is a pretty straightforward way of dealing with these two obstacles to dependable message generalization. Because those two obstacles arise from the use of a single message to represent an entire category of messages, the straightforward solution is to use multiple messages to represent each category (Jackson & Jacobs, 1983; see also Bradac, 1983; Hewes, 1983). Thus, for example, a study of implicit versus explicit conclusions would want to have many instances of each message type (multiple instances of explicit-conclusion messages, and corresponding multiple instances of implicit-conclusion messages), with as much variation within a category as one can achieve (variation in topic, organization, length, and so on).

With such a multiple-message design, the possibility of nonuniform effects across messages is acknowledged. There is no presumption that the effect of conclusion type will be constant across messages; on the contrary, the design may permit one to detect variation in the effect that conclusion type has across messages. And the chances for unambiguous causal attribution are improved by such a design: Given the variation within the set of messages for a given conclusion type, the researcher can rule out alternative explanations and be more confident in attributing observed differences to the sort of conclusion used.[1]

Beyond the desirability of using multiple-message designs, the generalization problems associated with single-message designs also have implications for how experimental messages are constructed in persuasion research. A number of complex considerations bear on the question of how to construct (or obtain) experimental messages, and the discussion here does not attempt to be a complete one (for more extensive treatments, see Bradac, 1986; Jackson &

Jacobs, 1983). But a sense of the relevant implications can be obtained by focusing on one particular research practice: the practice of repeatedly using the same experimental messages.

The problem of generalizing about message types from individual messages would be serious enough if each investigation of persuasive message effects used only one message to represent each message type (category), but with a different concrete message used in each different study (so that, e.g., every investigation of implicit versus explicit conclusions used only one instance of each type, but every investigation created a *new* instance of each type). But in fact the problem is worse, because it is all too common for the *same* messages to be used again and again in persuasion research (consider, e.g., Pratkanis, Greenwald, Ronis, Leippe, & Baumgardner, 1986).

This practice is readily understandable. First, the task of creating satisfactory experimental materials is difficult and time-consuming, and if existing messages already represent the variables of interest then it can be awfully tempting to employ those materials. Second, in a continuing line of research, a desire for tight experimental control may suggest the reuse of earlier messages. For instance, if a researcher wishes to do a follow-up experiment that investigates the effect of adding some new independent variable to an earlier research design, then the researcher may well want to maximize the comparability of the two investigations. As a means of ensuring such comparability (and thus – in keeping with the general idea behind experimental research – ensuring unambiguous causal inference), the researcher will naturally be led to use the same messages as a means of ruling out one possible source of influence on the results.

But this way of proceeding is, in the end, unsatisfactory, precisely because it complicates, rather than eases, the task of obtaining sound causal generalizations. It complicates this task because single-message instantiations are an unsatisfactory basis for generalizations about message types.[2] What's worse, research experience shows that reusing a message may well not provide the hoped-for gain in inferential ability. More than one investigator has reused a set of messages only to find that even under conditions quite comparable (if not apparently virtually identical) to those in the earlier studies, the messages do *not* produce the same effects (compare, e.g., Experiments 2 and 3 in M. Burgoon, Jones, & Stewart, 1975, or Experiments 1 and 2 in Shepherd & B. J. O'Keefe, 1984). Findings of this sort certainly underscore just how complicated an affair persuasive communication is, but they also suggest that the experimental control gained by reusing messages may be less substantial than one might have thought.

INTERPRETING PAST PERSUASION RESEARCH Employing multiple message designs (and avoiding reusing experimental messages) may help future researchers avoid the message generalization problems created by single-message designs, but a great deal of earlier persuasion effects research relied on single-message designs. How should such research be interpreted?

Obviously, any individual single-message study should be interpreted very cautiously. The interpretive difficulties created by single-message designs are such that one cannot confidently make broad generalizations from a single study using such a design.

But if there are several single-message studies addressing the same research question, then some greater confidence may be warranted. If there are ten investigations comparing explicit and implicit conclusions, and each one has a different single example of each message category, a review that considers the body of studies taken as a whole can transcend this limitation of the individual investigations and provide a sounder basis for generalization.

The recent development of statistical techniques for meta-analysis is particularly noteworthy here (for a general introduction, see Rosenthal, 1984). Broadly, meta-analysis is the use of various quantitative techniques for summarizing the results obtained in a number of separate research studies. Using meta-analytic techniques, a reviewer can systematically examine the different effects obtained in separate investigations, combine these separate studies to yield a picture of the overall results obtained, look for variations among the results of different studies, and so on. Obviously, meta-analysis offers the possibility of overcoming some of the limitations of existing persuasion research using single-message designs. Meta-analysis is not easy to do, and there are disagreements over the desirability, legitimacy, and appropriateness of certain meta-analytic procedures (for discussion, see Hedges & Olkin, 1985). Nevertheless, meta-analytic techniques provide an especially attractive—if underutilized—way of summarizing existing persuasion effects research.

BEYOND MESSAGE VARIABLES This discussion has focused on the message generalizing problems associated with single-message designs. These problems are especially salient for persuasion researchers, because (despite widespread interest in generalizing across messages) single-message designs have been the norm for studies of persuasive effects. Of course, the very same general considerations apply not just to message factors, but to anything; dependable generalizations about a collection of things (messages, people, tables, and so on) commonly require multiple instances of the class. There is, that is to say, nothing unique about these problems of message generalization (as noted by Bradac, 1983). But some focused attention to matters of message generalization is important, if only because single-message designs have so frequently been employed in the search for generalizations about persuasive effects.

VARIABLE DEFINITION

The other noteworthy problem that arises in studying persuasive effects might be labeled the "variable definition" problem, for it concerns how independent variables are defined in research practice. Since this problem arises most clearly in the context of defining message variables (that is, message variations or message types), the following discussion focuses on such variables; as will be seen, however, the difficulties that arise are not limited to message variables.

MESSAGE FEATURES VERSUS RECIPIENT RESPONSES Broadly put, a "message variable" can be defined in one of two ways: in terms of intrinsic message features or in terms of recipient responses. Most message variables have been defined in terms of message features (as one might expect), but occasionally investigators have defined message types not in terms of message features but rather in terms of engendered recipient responses. Because these two ways of defining message variations are consequentially different, the distinction is an important one.

A useful example is provided by the extensive research on "fear appeals" in persuasive messages. A "fear appeal" is a particular type of persuasive message, but exactly *what* type? Some investigators define a "fear appeal" as a message that contains certain sorts of message content (e.g., graphic depictions of consequences of not following the communicator's recommendations, as in gruesome films of traffic accidents used in driver education classes). For other investigators, a "fear appeal" message is one that arouses fear or anxiety in message recipients (that is, "fear appeal" is defined in terms of the responses of message receivers).

Obviously, these two definitions will not necessarily correspond. That is, a message that contains gruesome content (a "fear appeal" by the first definition) might not arouse fear or anxiety in message recipients (i.e., might not be a "fear appeal" by the second definition); similarly, a message might succeed in arousing fear without containing graphic message content. Neither of these two ways of defining "fear appeal" is the correct way. There is no "correct" way to define "fear appeal" (or any other message variation). One can define message types however one likes, so long as one is clear. But it *is* important to be clear about the distinction.

THE IMPORTANCE OF THE DISTINCTION The reason it is important to be clear about the different ways of defining message variables (by reference to message features or by reference to recipient responses) is that the distinction makes a difference — indeed, it makes several differences.

First, generalizations about message types can only cautiously lump together investigations that employ different ways of defining a given variable. Two studies might both call themselves studies of "fear appeals," but if one defines fear appeal in terms of message content while the other defines it in terms of recipient response, it may be difficult to draw reliable generalizations that encompass the two studies.

Second, the different ways of defining message types raise different evidentiary issues concerning the soundness of experimental manipulations. Consider: An investigator who defines "fear appeal" in terms of the presence of certain sorts of message contents, in order to construct defensible examples of fear appeal messages for use in research, need only ensure that the messages do in fact contain the requisite sort of content. By contrast, an investigator who defines "fear appeal" in terms of the engendered audience response, in order to have satisfactory instances of fear appeal messages, must show that the messages in fact engender the required responses.

Third, the different ways of defining message types make for differential immediate utility of research findings for persuaders. Research using message-variation definitions that are based on message features can give obvious direct advice for persuaders concerning the construction of persuasive messages ("Put features X, Y, and Z in your message"), whereas definitions based on recipient responses are likely to be much less helpful ("Do something that engenders such and such a response"). This does not mean that definitions based on message features are necessarily to be preferred, however. For example, it will be seen (in Chapter 9) that at least in the case of fear appeals, a satisfactory picture of the processes involved requires attending both to message features and to induced recipient responses.

BEYOND MESSAGE VARIABLES The extended example in this discussion of the problem of variable definition has been that of a particular message variable (fear appeals), though other message variables — most notably the variable of "argument strength" that figures prominently in elaboration likelihood model research (discussed in Chapter 6) — could have served as well. But in fact these issues of variable definition are not limited to message factors.

Consider, for instance, Cronkhite and Liska's (1976) discussion of communicator credibility. They express astonishment at research results purporting to find variations in source credibility without corresponding variations in effectiveness, or variations in source effectiveness without corresponding variations in source credibility. They ask (rhetorically): "How can a source be more 'credible' but produce no more opinion change; how can a source produce more opinion change without being more credible?" (p. 105). Cronkhite and Liska ask these questions because they define credibility as "the capability of a source to produce changes in receivers' opinions, policies, and overt behaviors" (p. 105), whereas the more common approach (in the research literature) is to define credibility in terms of receivers' impressions of the source's believability, expertise, honesty, or the like (see Chapter 8).

That is to say, Cronkhite and Liska's astonishment derives not from some genuinely baffling research results, but from differences in the way in which communicator credibility is defined. To express the parallel with fear appeals research: A researcher who defines fear appeals in terms of receivers' responses (aroused fear) will be astonished by claims that sometimes fear appeals don't arouse fear; but such a claim makes perfectly good sense to investigators who define fear appeals in terms of message characteristics rather than in terms of receiver responses.

SUMMARY The task of defining independent variables in studies of persuasive effects thus raises matters of some delicacy. If an independent variable is defined in terms of the effects it has (attitude-change effects, fear-arousal effects, and so on), then it becomes necessarily true that that variable has those effects; a failure of an experimental instantiation of the variable to produce the effects can be interpreted only as a failure to manipulate the variable in question successfully. But if an independent variable is defined in ways that make it conceptually independent of its effects, then a failure to produce expected effects is to be interpreted differently. Neither way of defining independent variables is intrinsically better, but noticing the difference between them (and grasping the implications of the difference) is important.

NOTES

1. Actually, it's not enough just to have multiple messages; an appropriate statistical analysis is also required. For a general treatment of these matters, see Jackson and Jacobs (1983); for additional discussion, see Jackson, O'Keefe, and Jacobs (1988), Morley (1988a, 1988b), and D. J. O'Keefe, Jackson, and Jacobs (1988). For discussion of such issues in other research contexts, see H. H. Clark (1973), Fontenelle, Phillips, and Lane (1985), and Richter and Seay (1987).

2. It is important to note that meta-analytic techniques (discussed shortly) are of little help (as a means of coping with message-generalization problems) when the same message is used repeatedly as the instantiation of a message type. Instead of being able to accumulate research results across a large number of different versions of the message type in question, a meta-analyst could accumulate research results only across the same concrete messages; the problems of message generalization would remain.

8

Source Factors

PERSUASION RESEARCHERS have quite naturally focused considerable research attention on the question of how various characteristics of the communicator influence the outcomes of the communicator's persuasive efforts. This chapter's review of such research is focused on two particular communicator characteristics — the communicator's credibility and likability — but concludes with a discussion of other source factors, including the communicator's similarity to the audience.

COMMUNICATOR CREDIBILITY

THE DIMENSIONS OF CREDIBILITY

"Credibility" (or, more carefully expressed, "perceived credibility") refers to the judgments made by a perceiver (e.g., a message recipient) concerning the believability of a communicator. Communicator credibility is thus not an intrinsic property of a communicator; a message source may be thought highly credible by one perceiver and not at all credible by another. But this general notion of credibility has been given a somewhat more careful specification in a number of investigations aimed at identifying the basic underlying dimensions of credibility.

FACTOR-ANALYTIC RESEARCH There have been quite a few factor-analytic studies of the dimensions underlying credibility judgments (e.g., Andersen, 1961; Applbaum & Anatol, 1972, 1973; Baudhuin & Davis, 1972; Berlo, Lemert, & Mertz, 1969; Bowers & Phillips, 1967; Falcione, 1974; Markham, 1968; McCroskey, 1966; Schweitzer & Ginsburg, 1966). In the most common research design in these investigations, respondents rate a number of communication sources on a large number of scales. In a few investigations these scales represent the most frequently mentioned characteristics appearing in previously collected free-response descriptions given of high- and low-credibility communicators (e.g., Berlo et al., 1969; Schweitzer & Ginsburg, 1966), but more commonly the set of scales used is composed of previously employed items with perhaps some new scales included as well (e.g., Baudhuin & Davis, 1972; Falcione, 1974). The ratings given of the sources are then submitted to factor analysis, a statistical procedure that (broadly put) groups the scales on the basis of their intercorrelations: Scales that are comparatively highly intercorrelated will be grouped together as indicating some underlying "factor" or dimension.

There has been a good deal of critical discussion of this factor-analytic research on credibility (see, e.g., Cronkhite & Liska, 1976; Delia, 1976b; Hensley, 1974; Infante, 1980; Lewis, 1974; J. Liska, 1978; McCroskey & Young, 1981; M. L. McLaughlin, 1975; Steinfatt, 1974; Tucker, 1971). Criticism has focused especially on the procedures for initially selecting scales, the frequent absence of a context within which communicators are to be rated by respondents, the problems of rater-scale and concept-scale interactions, and the criteria for identifying and labeling transsituationally stable factors.

Indeed, the general assumption that there *is* some meaningful general set of dimensions of communicator credibility has sometimes been called into question. The general line of argument has been that the communicator characteristics that are functional (useful, relevant) for message recipients to assess may vary a great deal from one circumstance to another, and hence (the argument runs) it is misleading to suppose that there are any truly general (in the sense of transsituationally relevant) dimensions of communicator assessment employed by receivers. Instead, according to this "functional" analysis of credibility, "listeners use different criteria and use their criteria differently depending upon the functions a source is expected to perform in a specific topic-situation" (Cronkhite & Liska, 1976, p. 105; see also Cronkhite & Liska, 1980; S. W. King, 1976).

It certainly is the case that there is substantial variation in the sorts of factor structures that have emerged in factor-analytic investigations of credibility (compare, e.g., Berlo et al., 1969, with Schweitzer & Ginsburg, 1966). At the same time, when there are differences in the sets of initial scales used, the sets of sources rated, the instructions given to raters, and the particular factor-analytic procedures followed (e.g., orthogonal versus oblique solutions sought) — and all these differences do appear in the literature — then perhaps one should not be surprised that differing factor structures have been found.

COMPETENCE AND TRUSTWORTHINESS AS DIMENSIONS OF CREDIBILITY
Without overlooking the problems with this factor-analytic work or the variations in obtained factor structures, one may nevertheless say that with some frequency two very broad (and sensible) dimensions have in fact commonly emerged in factor-analytic investigations of communicator credibility. These are variously labeled in the literature, but two useful terms are "competence" and "trustworthiness."

The competence dimension (sometimes called "expertise," "expertness," "authoritativeness," or "qualification") is commonly represented by scales such as experienced-inexperienced, informed-uninformed, trained-untrained, qualified-unqualified, skilled-unskilled, intelligent-unintelligent, and expert-not expert. These items all seem directed at the assessment of (roughly) whether the communicator is in a position to know the truth, to know what's right or correct. Three or more of these scales are reported as loading on a common factor in investigations by Applbaum and Anatol (1972, Studies 1A, 1B, 2, 3; 1973, Studies 1, 2, 3, 4), Baudhuin and Davis (1972, for similar source, dissimilar source, Nixon, and Manson), Beatty and Behnke (1980), Beatty and Kruger (1978), Berlo et al. (1969, MSU and Lansing studies), Bowers and Phillips (1967), Falcione (1974), Hickson, Powell, Hill, Holt, and Flick (1979), McCroskey (1966), Miles and Leathers (1984), Pearce and Brommel (1972), Schweitzer and Ginsburg (1966, low-credibility study), and Tuppen (1974). And (as these factor-analytic results would indicate) measures of perceived competence that are composed of several such items commonly exhibit high internal reliability (for example, reliability coefficients of .85 or greater have been reported by Beatty & Behnke, 1980; Bell, Zahn, & Hopper, 1984; McCroskey, 1966).

The trustworthiness dimension (sometimes called "character," "safety," or "personal integrity") is commonly represented by scales such as honest-dishonest, trustworthy-untrustworthy, open-minded-closed-minded, just-unjust, fair-unfair, and unselfish-selfish. These items all appear to be related to the assessment of (roughly) whether the communicator will likely be inclined to tell the truth as he or she sees it. Three or more of these scales are reported as loading on a common factor in investigations by Applbaum and Anatol (1972, Studies 1A, 1B, 2, 3; 1973, Studies 2, 3, 4), Baudhuin and Davis (1972, Nixon study), Berlo et al. (1969, MSU study), Falcione (1974), Schweitzer and Ginsburg (1966, low-credibility study), Tuppen (1974), and Whitehead (1968); correspondingly, indices of perceived trustworthiness that are composed of several such items have displayed high internal reliability (for example, reliabilities of .80 or better have been reported by Bradley, 1981; and Tuppen, 1974).[1]

These two dimensions parallel what Eagly, Wood, and Chaiken (1978) have described as the two types of communicator bias that message recipients might infer: knowledge bias and reporting bias. "Knowledge bias refers to a recipient's belief that a communicator's knowledge about external reality is nonveridical, and reporting bias refers to the belief that a communicator's willingness to convey an accurate version of external reality is compromised" (p. 424). A communicator perceived as having a knowledge bias will presumably be viewed as relatively less competent; a communicator viewed as having a reporting bias will presumably be seen as comparatively less trustworthy.

Perhaps it is not surprising that both competence and trustworthiness emerge as basic dimensions of credibility, since as a rule only the conjunction of competence and trustworthiness makes for reliable communications. A communicator who knows what's correct (is competent) but who nevertheless misleads the audience (is untrustworthy, has a reporting bias) produces messages that are unreliable guides to belief and action, just as does the sincere (trustworthy) but uninformed (incompetent, knowledge-biased) communicator. Hence even if one wishes to adopt a "functional" outlook in considering the judgments that message recipients make about "communicant acceptability" (Cronkhite & Liska, 1980), it makes a good deal of sense that judgments about a source's competence and trustworthiness will often be ones functionally relevant to message receivers (see Infante, Parker, Clarke, Wilson, & Nathu, 1983). In law, for example, competence and trustworthiness "correspond to the most common legal reasons for seeking to impeach witnesses. In most cases, impeachment can be based on the witness's incompetence to testify about issues (competence) or possible self-interest and bias on the part of the witness (trustworthiness)" (G. R. Miller & Burgoon, 1982, p. 170).

It should be emphasized, however, that these two dimensions of communicator credibility represent only the most general sorts of communication-relevant judgments made by recipients about communicators. As a number of researchers have indicated, the particular dimensions relevant to the assessment of message sources are likely to vary from circumstance to circumstance, as will the emphasis placed on one or another dimension of judgment (e.g., see S. W. King, 1976; J. Liska, 1978).

FACTORS INFLUENCING CREDIBILITY JUDGMENTS

Judgments of a communicator's competence and trustworthiness are surely influenced by a great many different factors, and it is fair to say that research to date leaves us rather far from a very comprehensive picture of the determinants of these judgments. For the most part, as will be seen, researchers have focused on the effects that message or delivery characteristics have on credibility judgments (as opposed to the effect of, say, information about the communicator's training), perhaps because these characteristics are more nearly under the immediate control of the communicator.

EDUCATION, OCCUPATION, AND EXPERIENCE Although there has been very little systematic research investigating exactly how credibility judgments are influenced by information about the communicator's training, experience, and occupation, precisely these characteristics are the ones most frequently manipulated by investigators in experimental studies of the effects of variations in communicator credibility. That is, a researcher who wishes to compare the effects of a high-credibility source with those of a low-credibility source will most commonly manipulate the receiver's perception of the communicator's credibility by varying the information given about the communicator's education, occupation, experience, and the like. For instance, Haiman (1949) attributed a message concerning health insurance to the surgeon general of the United States or the secretary-general of the Communist party in America. Hewgill and Miller's (1965) study of messages about fallout shelters described the high-credibility communicator as "a professor of nuclear research, recognized as a national authority on the biological effects of radioactivity," while the low-credibility introduction described the source as "a high school sophomore, whose information was based on a term paper prepared for a social studies class" (p. 96).

Similar manipulations are commonplace, and researchers commonly confirm the success of these manipulations by assessing respondents' judgments of the communicators' competence and trustworthiness. As one might expect, such high-credibility introductions do indeed generally lead receivers to perceive the source as more trustworthy and (particularly) more competent than do low-credibility introductions. And what systematic research exists on this matter is (perhaps not surprisingly) quite consistent with these effects. Receiver judgments of communicator trustworthiness and (especially) competence have been found to be significantly influenced by information concerning the communicator's occupation, training, amount of experience, and the like (e.g., Ostermeier, 1967; Swenson, Nash, & Roos, 1984).

NONFLUENCIES IN DELIVERY There have been a number of investigations of how variations in delivery can influence the credibility judgments made of a speaker. Unfortunately, several of these studies have investigated conceptions of delivery that embrace a number of different behavioral features (e.g., Pearce, 1971; Pearce & Brommel, 1972; Pearce & Conklin, 1971). Bowers (1965), for example, compared two speaking styles: One (the "extroverted" delivery style) used rapid, highly fluent speech with negligible pauses, appropriate vocal emphasis, and varied voice quality; the other ("introverted" delivery style) was less rapid, contained pauses and disfluencies, emphasized inappropriate words, and had little vocal variety. Obviously, when a construct (such as "introverted versus extroverted delivery style") is operationally defined as a complex of behavioral features, one cannot easily determine just which feature (or set of features) is responsible for any observed effects.[2]

But one delivery characteristic that has been studied in isolation is the occurrence of nonfluencies in the delivery of oral communications. Nonfluencies include vocalized pauses ("uh, uh"), the superfluous repetition of words or sounds, corrections of slips of the tongue, articulation difficulties, and the like. Several investigations have found that with increasing numbers of nonfluencies, speakers are rated significantly lower on competence, with judgments of trustworthiness typically unaffected (McCroskey & Mehrley, 1969; G. R. Miller & Hewgill, 1964; Schliesser, 1968; Sereno & Hawkins, 1967).

SPEAKING RATE Another delivery characteristic whose effect on credibility perceptions has been investigated is speaking rate. There is a substantial range of possible "normal" speaking rates, and the research question that has arisen is how variations within this range might influence judgments of the communicator's credibility (notice that this is different from asking about the effect of abnormally fast or abnormally slow speaking rates). In two investigations, N. Miller, Maruyama, Beaber, and Valone (1976) found that increasing speaking rates led to significantly greater perceived knowledgeability, intelligence, and objectivity, but this finding is unusual; most other investigators have reported that judgments of competence and trustworthiness are not significantly affected by speaking rate (Addington, 1971; Gundersen & Hopper, 1976, Study 1; Woodall & Burgoon, 1983). Indeed, not even the direction of effect is consistent across these investigations (for instance, faster speech was found to be nonsignificantly associated with lower perceived competence and trustworthiness by Addington, 1971). Whatever effects speaking rate has on credibility, then, those effects are not straightforward.

The speaking-rate investigations discussed thus far have all manipulated speaking rate by natural means—having a speaker record a message several times, varying the rate. With natural speech, as speaking rate increases, there are commonly also changes in other vocal characteristics as well (such as pitch, intonation, and fluency). Using mechanical means called "time compression," however, it is possible to alter rate without these other changes. Results of time-compression studies are of interest both theoretically (since they offer the prospect of examining the effects of varied rate independent of other factors) and practically (since mechanical alteration of speech, though obviously not useful in face-to-face persuasion settings, could be employed in, for example, radio advertising). As with the work on naturally induced rate variations, however, there is some inconsistency in the research findings concerning the effects of time compression on credibility judgments; the safest conclusion seems to be that time compression does not reliably yield enhanced judgments of competence or trustworthiness, and indeed under some circumstances may even significantly reduce perceived competence and trustworthiness (MacLachlan, 1982; Wheeless, 1971; see also Hausknecht & Moore, 1986; Lautman & Dean, 1983).[3]

CITATION OF EVIDENCE SOURCES Persuaders very commonly include evidence in their persuasive messages—that is, relevant facts, opinions, information, and the like, intended to support the persuader's claims. Several investigations have studied the effects on perceived communicator credibility of citing the *sources* of such evidence, as opposed to providing only vague documentation ("Studies show that . . . ") or no documentation at all. On the whole, a communicator's citation of the sources of evidence appears to enhance perceptions of the communicator's competence and trustworthiness, though these effects are sometimes small (Fleshler, Ilardo, & Demoretcky, 1974; McCroskey, 1967, 1969, 1970; McCroskey, Young, & Scott, 1972; Ostermeier, 1967; Whitehead, 1971; for discussion, see Reinard, 1988). McCroskey (1969) has reported that these effects are more commonly found with communicators who are initially low or moderate in credibility than with communicators initially high in credibility, but this may reflect a ceiling effect: A communicator already perceived as highly competent and trustworthy may not be able to improve perceptions of those qualities very much.

These investigations, it should be noted, employed relevant supporting materials that were attributed (when source citations were provided) to high-credibility sources. One should not expect enhanced communicator credibility to result from citations to low-credibility evidence sources or from citations for poor or irrelevant evidence (Luchok & McCroskey, 1978; Warren, 1969).

These findings thus suggest that a communicator's perceived competence and trustworthiness can be influenced by the citation of competent and trust-worthy sources of evidence in the message; the high credibility of the cited sources seems to rub off on the communicator. Some indication of the import of this effect may have been provided by Cantor, Alfonso, and Zillmann (1976), who compared the persuasive success of experts (medical student or nurse) and nonexperts (music student or teacher) using messages concerning intrauterine birth control devices (IUDs); they found that this expertise manipulation did not influence the persuasiveness of the messages. Any number of explanations are possible for this result, but in the present context it is notable that the messages contained references to relevant medical research findings; these were pre-sented by the experts as based on their personal knowledge of the research literature, and were presented by the nonexperts as coming from more tradition-ally recognized experts (their doctors). As Cantor et al. note, this citation of evidence sources by the "nonexpert" communicators may have minimized differences in the perceived expertise of the expert and nonexpert communica-tors, to the point that the expertise manipulation made no difference in persua-sive outcome.

POSITION ADVOCATED The nature of the position the communicator advo-cates on the persuasive issue can influence perceptions of the communicator's competence and trustworthiness. Specifically, a communicator is likely to be perceived as more competent and more trustworthy if the position advocated disconfirms the audience's expectations about the communicator's views (where such expectations derive from knowledge of the source's characteristics or circumstances), though certain sorts of trustworthiness judgments (concern-ing objectivity, open-mindedness, and unbiasedness) appear to be affected more than others (such as sincerity and honesty).

The most straightforward examples of this phenomenon are communicators who argue for positions that are apparently opposed to their own self-interest. Ordinarily, of course, one expects persons to take positions that forward their own interests; sources who support views opposed to their interests thus disconfirm our expectations. And if we wonder why it is that a source is taking this (apparently unusual) position, we may well be led to conclude that the communicator must be especially competent and trustworthy: The source must really know the truth and must really be willing to tell the truth, otherwise why would the source be advocating that position? Thus the chemical engineer who testifies that her company's plant was not safely designed, the military officer who argues that defense appropriations should be reduced—these are communicators who, by virtue of the positions they advocate, may be perceived as especially competent and trustworthy.

An empirical demonstration of this phenomenon was provided in several studies by Walster, Aronson, and Abrahams (1966). Receivers were presented with messages arguing for either more or less power for courts and prosecutors; these messages were depicted as coming from either a prosecutor or a convicted criminal. Obviously, some of these source-message combinations represent sources arguing for positions that are in their own interest (e.g., the criminal arguing that court power should be restricted) while other combinations represent communicators apparently arguing against their own interests (e.g., prosecutors suggesting that prosecutorial powers be reduced). Those communicators arguing for positions opposed to their own interests were perceived as more competent and trustworthy than when they advocated views that favored their self-interests.

Of course, receivers' expectations about the position a communicator will express can derive from sources other than the ordinary presumption that people will favor viewpoints that are in their own interest. A general analysis of the bases of premessage expectancies (and their effects on perceived credibility and persuasive outcomes) has been provided by Eagly, Wood, and Chaiken (1981), who have collaborated on a series of investigations of this topic. As briefly mentioned earlier, Eagly et al. (1981) distinguish two sorts of communicator bias that receivers can recognize and can use to form premessage expectancies about the communicator's position. One is "knowledge bias," which refers to the receiver's belief that the communicator's knowledge of relevant information is somehow biased (perhaps because of the source's background or experience) and thus that the source's message will not accurately reflect reality. The other is "reporting bias," which refers to the receiver's belief that a communicator may not be willing to convey relevant information accurately (for instance, because there are situational pressures that might lead the source to withhold or distort information). A receiver's perception of either sort of communicator bias will lead the receiver to have certain expectations about the position a communicator holds on the issue (and, correspondingly, will provide the receiver with an explanation of *why* the communicator adopts that position).

Thus, for example, we naturally expect that a lifelong Democrat will speak in favor of a Democratic political candidate (because of knowledge bias), or that a speaker speaking about gun control legislation to a meeting of the National Rifle Association will likely oppose such legislation (because of reporting bias); and when such expectations are confirmed, we have ready explanations for why the communicators acted as they did.

But what happens when a communicator advocates a position that violates an expectancy based on knowledge or reporting bias? The receiver now faces the task of explaining why the communicator is defending the advocated position—why the lifelong Democrat is speaking in support of a Republican candidate, or why the speaker addressing the NRA is urging stricter gun control legislation. And at least sometimes the most plausible explanation will be that the facts of the matter were so compelling that the communicator was led to override those personal or situational pressures (that had generated the receiver's expectations) and thus defend the advocated position. Correspondingly, receivers may be led to perceive the communicator as especially competent and trustworthy, precisely because the communicator's expressed position violates the receivers' expectations. And indeed there have been several investigations conducted, the results of which are consistent with this analysis (Eagly & Chaiken, 1975; Eagly et al., 1978; Wood & Eagly, 1981; see also L. Anderson, 1970).

A related expectancy-disconfirmation effect has been observed in studies of advertisements for consumer products. Ordinarily, consumers expect advertisements to tout the advertised product or brand as being "the best" on *every* feature or characteristic that is mentioned. Thus (to use an example from R. E. Smith & Hunt, 1978) an advertisement for exterior house paint that claimed that the product was superior to its competitors on only three mentioned product features (durability, number of coats needed, ease of clean-up) while being equal on two others (number of colors available, nonspill lip on container) would disconfirm receivers' expectations about the message's contents (particularly by contrast to an advertisement claiming that the product was superior on each one of these five features). There have been several experimental comparisons of these two types of advertisements—a "nonvaried-claim" advertisement suggesting superiority for all features of the product, as opposed to a "varied-claim" advertisement suggesting superiority for most (but not all) product features. As one might suppose, varied-claim advertisements are indeed often perceived as more persuasive and truthful than the nonvaried-claim ads (e.g., Hunt & Kernan, 1984; Settle & Golden, 1974; R. E. Smith & Hunt, 1978; compare Hunt, Smith, & Kernan, 1985).

One final point concerning the effects of expectancy disconfirmation on perceived credibility: Though expectancy disconfirmation can enhance perceptions of the communicator's competence and trustworthiness, the communicator likely to be perceived as the most competent and trustworthy may be a qualified source about whom the audience has no expectations so far as message position is concerned. This is suggested by Arnold and McCroskey's

(1967) study of the effects of biased, reluctant, and unbiased testimony on source credibility. In this investigation, receivers heard either a pro-labor or an anti-labor message (on the topic of whether labor unions make a significant contribution to inflation) attributed to one of three sources: a labor leader, a management leader, or a university professor of economics. Though pre-message expectancies were not assessed in this investigation, one is surely on safe ground thinking that (for instance) the labor leader would be expected to offer a pro-labor message (arguing that unions don't significantly increase inflation). Thus receivers heard either "biased testimony" (the labor leader with the pro-labor message or the management leader with the anti-labor message), "reluctant testimony" (the labor leader with the anti-labor message or the management leader with the pro-labor message), or "unbiased testimony" (the economics professor with either message). As one might suppose, the results indicated that there was a tendency for perceptions of competence and trustworthiness to be greater under conditions of reluctant testimony (the expectancy-disconfirmation conditions) than under conditions of biased testimony (the expectancy-confirmation conditions). But the circumstance that seemed to lead to the greatest perceived competence and trustworthiness was the "unbiased testimony" condition, in which presumably the audience had no more than minimal premessage expectancies about the position to be advocated. Thus, in a given circumstance, the communicator most likely to be perceived as most competent and trustworthy may be the well-qualified source about whom the audience has few expectations so far as message position is concerned.[4]

LIKING FOR THE COMMUNICATOR There is indirect evidence indicating that the receiver's liking for the communicator can influence judgments of the communicator's trustworthiness, though not judgments of the communicator's competence. This evidence, derived from factor-analytic investigations of credibility judgments, is the finding that various general evaluation items often load on the same factor as do trustworthiness scales. Thus, for example, items such as friendly-unfriendly, pleasant-unpleasant, nice-not nice, and valuable-worthless have been reported as loading on a common factor with such trustworthiness items as honest-dishonest, trustworthy-untrustworthy, unselfish-selfish, and just-unjust (see, e.g., Applbaum & Anatol, 1972; Bowers & Phillips, 1967; Falcione, 1974; McCroskey, 1966; Pearce & Brommel, 1972). This suggests that liking and trustworthiness judgments are probably more likely to covary than are liking and competence judgments. Such a pattern of results surely makes good sense: One's general liking for a communicator is much more likely to influence one's judgments about the communicator's dispositional trustworthiness (the communicator's general honesty, fairness, open-mindedness, and the like) than it is to influence one's judgments about the communicator's competence (experience, training, expertise, and so on) on some particular topic or subject matter.

HUMOR Including humor in persuasive messages has been found to have rather varied effects on perceptions of the communicator. Where positive effects of humor are found, they tend to most directly involve enhancement of the audience's liking for the communicator — and thus occasionally the trustworthiness of the communicator (since liking and trustworthiness are associated) — but rarely judgments of competence (Chang & Gruner, 1981; Gruner, 1967, 1970; Gruner & Lampton, 1972; Tamborini & Zillmann, 1981). However, the use of humor can also *decrease* the audience's liking for the communicator, the perceived trustworthiness of the communicator, and even the perceived competence of the source (Bryant, Brown, Silberberg, & Elliott, 1981; Munn & Gruner, 1981; P. M. Taylor, 1974); these negative effects seem most likely to obtain when the humor is perceived as excessive or inappropriate for the context. Small amounts of appropriate humor thus may have small enhancing effects on perceived trustworthiness, but are unlikely to affect assessments of the communicator's competence.

EFFECTS OF CREDIBILITY

What effects do variations in communicator credibility have on persuasive outcomes? It might be thought that the answer to this question is pretty simple: As one's credibility increases, so will one's effectiveness. But in fact the answer turns out to be much more complicated.

TWO INITIAL CLARIFICATIONS   There are two preliminary clarifications to be made concerning the research on the effects of communicator credibility. The first is that, in this research, the two primary dimensions of credibility (competence and trustworthiness) are usually not separately manipulated. That is, the research compares a source that is relatively high in both competence and trustworthiness (the "high-credibility" source) with a source that is relatively low in both (the "low-credibility" source).

Obviously, since competence and trustworthiness are conceptually distinct aspects of credibility, it would be possible to manipulate these separately and so examine their separate effects on persuasive outcomes. One could, for instance, compare the effectiveness of a source high in competence but low in trustworthiness with that of a source low in competence but high in trustworthiness.

Overwhelmingly, however, competence and trustworthiness have not been independently manipulated in investigations of credibility's effects. There have been a few efforts at disentangling the effects of competence and trustworthiness (e.g., McGinnies & Ward, 1980; Mowen, Wiener, & Joag, 1987; Wiener & Mowen, 1986), but to date no very clear generalizations seem possible. The point, thus, of this first clarification is to emphasize the limits of current research on credibility's effects: This research concerns credibility generally, rather than the different dimensions of credibility individually.

The second preliminary clarification concerns the nature of the "low-credibility" sources in this research: The low-credibility sources are not low in absolute terms, but are simply *relatively* low in credibility. In absolute terms, the low-credibility communicators are probably accurately described as no better than moderate in credibility.[5] In fact, several researchers have remarked that it is difficult to create believable experimental manipulations that will consistently yield credibility ratings that are low in absolute terms (Greenberg & Miller, 1966; Sternthal, Dholakia, & Leavitt, 1978).[6] Thus although this discussion (like most in the literature) will be cast as a matter of the differential persuasive effectiveness of high- as opposed to low-credibility communicators, it should be remembered that the comparison made in the relevant research is nearly always between a relatively higher-credibility communicator and a relatively lower one, not necessarily between two sources that are in absolute terms high and low in credibility.

With these preliminaries out of the way, we can now turn to a consideration of just how variations in communicator credibility influence persuasive effectiveness. The effects that credibility has on persuasive outcomes are not completely straightforward, but depend centrally on other factors. These factors can be usefully divided into two general categories: factors that influence the *magnitude* of credibility's effects, and factors that influence the *direction* of credibility's effects.

INFLUENCES ON THE MAGNITUDE OF EFFECT The size of the effect that communicator credibility has on persuasive outcomes is not constant, but varies from one circumstance to another. Researchers have identified two important factors that affect just how consequential a role communicator credibility plays in persuasion.

The first of these factors is the receiver's level of involvement with the issue (that is, the degree of direct personal relevance that the issue has for the receiver). As the issue becomes more involving for the receiver, variations in the source's credibility make less difference; thus under conditions of low receiver involvement, the communicator's credibility may make a great deal of difference to the outcome, whereas with highly involved receivers the source's credibility may have little impact (see, e.g., Johnson & Scileppi, 1969; Petty, Cacioppo, & Goldman, 1981; Rhine & Severance, 1970).

In some ways it may seem paradoxical that as an issue becomes more important to a receiver, the source's competence and trustworthiness become *less* important. But this relationship may be more understandable when viewed from the perspective of the elaboration likelihood model (see Chapter 6). For issues of little personal relevance, receivers may be content to let their opinions be shaped by the communicator's apparent credibility; for such issues, it is not worth the effort to follow the details of the arguments. But for highly involving topics, receivers will be more likely to attend closely to the details of the message, to scrutinize the communicator's arguments and evidence, to invest the effort involved in thinking closely about the contents of the message — and that comparatively greater importance of the message contents means that the communicator's credibility will play a smaller role than it otherwise might have.

The second factor influencing the magnitude of credibility's impact is the timing of the identification of the communicator. Often, of course, the communicator's identity is known before the message is received by the audience (e.g., because the source is well known and can be seen by the audience, or because another person introduces the communicator). But in some circumstances, it can be possible to delay identification of the source until after the audience has been exposed to the message (e.g., in television advertisements, where the source's identity may be withheld until the end of the ad; or even in multipage magazine articles, where information about the writer may not appear on the first page of the article, but instead appears only at the very end of the essay). And the timing of the identification of the source does make a substantial difference in the role that source credibility plays in persuasion.

Specifically, the impact of communicator credibility appears to be minimized when the identity of the source is withheld from the audience until after the message has been presented (Greenberg & Miller, 1966; Greenberg & Tannenbaum, 1961; Husek, 1965; Mills & Harvey, 1972; Sternthal et al., 1978; Ward & McGinnies, 1974; for a review, see D. J. O'Keefe, 1987). When the communicator's identity is delayed until after the audience has received the message, the message is apparently heard more nearly on its own terms, without the influence of the communicator's credibility.

It might be thought that this finding implies that high-credibility communicators should not delay their identification (but instead should be sure to identify themselves before the message), whereas low-credibility communicators should strive, where circumstances permit, to have their messages received before the audience is given information about their credibility. But that is a mistaken conclusion, for it is based on the unsound (though natural) assumption that the direction of credibility's effect is constant, with higher credibility always yielding greater persuasion. As we shall see, sometimes lower-credibility communicators are more successful persuaders than higher-credibility sources.

INFLUENCES ON THE DIRECTION OF EFFECT One might plausibly suppose that the direction of credibility's effect would be constant—specifically, that increases in credibility would yield only increases in persuasive effectiveness. Perhaps sometimes only small increases would occur, and sometimes (e.g., under conditions of very high involvement) no increase at all, but at least whenever credibility had an effect it would be in a constant direction, with high-credibility sources being more effective than low-credibility sources.

However plausible such a picture may seem, it is not consistent with the empirical evidence. The direction of credibility's effect is not constant: Several investigations have found that, at least sometimes, low-credibility communicators are significantly more effective than high-credibility communicators (e.g., Bock & Saine, 1975; Dholakia, 1987; Harmon & Coney, 1982; Sternthal et al., 1978). This finding is not easily impeached, as these results have been obtained by different investigators, using various topics, with different subject populations, and with good evidence for the success of the credibility manipulations employed.

The critical factor determining the direction of credibility's effects (that is, determining when a low-credibility source will be more effective than a high-credibility communicator, as opposed to when the high-credibility source will have the advantage) appears to be the nature of the position advocated by the message — specifically, whether the message advocates a position initially opposed by the receiver (a counterattitudinal message) or a position toward which the receiver initially feels at least somewhat favorable (a proattitudinal message). With a counterattitudinal message, the high-credibility communicator will tend to have a persuasive advantage over the low-credibility source; with a proattitudinal message, however, the low-credibility communicator appears to enjoy greater persuasive success than the high-credibility source.

The most direct evidence of this relationship comes from investigations that have varied the counter- or proattitudinal stance of the message (under conditions of low receiver involvement, and with communicators identified prior to messages). Under these conditions, high-credibility communicators are more effective than low-credibility communicators with counterattitudinal messages, but this advantage diminishes as the advocated position gets closer and closer to the receiver's position, to the point that with proattitudinal messages the low-credibility communicator is often more effective than the high-credibility source (Bergin, 1962; Bochner & Insko, 1966; Harmon & Coney, 1982; McGinnies, 1973; Sternthal et al., 1978, Study 2).

Perhaps one way of understanding this effect is to consider the degree to which the receiver might be stimulated to think about arguments and evidence supporting the advocated view. When receivers hear their views defended by a high-credibility source, they may well be inclined to presume that the communicator will do a perfectly good job of advocacy, will defend the viewpoint adequately, will present the best arguments, and so forth — and so they sit back and let the source do the work. But when the source is low in credibility, receivers might be more inclined to "help out" the communicator in defending their common viewpoint, and hence they might be led to think more extensively about supporting arguments — thereby ending up being more persuaded than if they had listened to a higher-credibility source (for some evidence consistent with this account, see Sternthal et al., 1978).

Notice, however, that greater success of low- (as opposed to high-) credibility communicators should not be expected in every case of proattitudinal messages, nor should one expect that high-credibility communicators will have an edge whenever counterattitudinal messages are employed. Rather, one should find such effects only when the conditions promote credibility's having a substantial effect (i.e., only when receiver involvement is low and the communicator is identified prior to the message). That is to say, it is important to consider jointly (simultaneously) the factors influencing the magnitude of credibility's effect and the factors influencing the direction of credibility's effect.

JOINT CONSIDERATION OF THE MAGNITUDE AND DIRECTION OF CREDI-BILITY EFFECTS Taken together, the factors identified as influencing the magnitude of credibility's effects (receiver involvement and timing of communicator identification) and the direction of credibility's effects (whether the message is proattitudinal or counterattitudinal for the receiver) appear capable of encompassing the bulk of research findings concerning the effects of source credibility on persuasive outcomes.

In investigations that have manipulated one of the crucial factors, the research findings are largely consistent with this analysis. For example, with a proattitudinal message on a low-involvement topic, a low-credibility source has been found to be more effective than a high-credibility source when both were identified before the message, but this difference was minimized when the communicators were not identified until after the message (Sternthal et al., 1978, Study 1). As another example, several studies have compared the effectiveness of high- and low-credibility communicators using counterattitudinal messages (with the source identified prior to the message) under varying conditions of involvement; these investigations find that the persuasive advantage enjoyed by the high-credibility communicator (over the low-credibility source) on low-involvement topics diminishes as receiver involvement increases (Johnson & Scileppi, 1969; Petty, Cacioppo, & Goldman, 1981; Rhine & Severance, 1970).

However, most studies comparing high- and low-credibility communicators have not varied receiver involvement, timing of source identification, or the counter- versus proattitudinal character of the message (and hence do not contain the contrasting conditions that are most relevant). Nevertheless, an examination of such investigations finds results that are consistent with this analysis.

For example, those investigations that have found high-credibility communicators to be significantly more effective than low-credibility communicators have typically (a) identified the source prior to the message, (b) employed relatively low-involvement topics, and (c) not used messages advocating positions favored by the receivers (for a general review of such studies, see Andersen & Clevenger, 1963). Indeed, when one finds that an investigation has *not* found high-credibility communicators to enjoy an advantage over low-credibility sources, usually one or more of these conditions has not obtained. Thus, for instance, some investigations that did not find persuasive advantages for higher-credibility sources (even with a counterattitudinal message and with the communicator identified prior to the message) apparently used high-involvement topics (e.g., Benoit, 1987; McGarry & Hendrick, 1974; Plax & Rosenfeld, 1980; Stainback & Rogers, 1983). And other investigations that found lower-credibility sources to enjoy greater persuasive success than high-credibility communicators (with the source identified prior to the message and a low-involvement topic) have used proattitudinal messages (as in Sternthal et al., 1978, Study 1).

The general point to be emphasized is that understanding the effects of communicator credibility requires attending simultaneously to factors influencing the *magnitude* of credibility's effects and to considerations that bear on the *direction* of credibility's effects. Just what difference communicator credibility might make in a given persuasive effort can vary a great deal, depending on the particulars of the circumstance; with variations in the relationship between the receiver's initial position and the position advocated by the message, or with variations in the receiver's level of involvement in the issue, or with variations in the timing of communicator identification, quite different patterns of effect are possible.

LIKING

THE GENERAL RULE

Perhaps it comes as no surprise that a number of investigations have found support for the general principle that, on the whole, liked communicators are more effective influence agents than are disliked communicators (e.g., Eagly & Chaiken, 1975; Giffen & Ehrlich, 1963; Sampson & Insko, 1964). But the general principle that liked persuaders are more successful can be misleading. There are a number of important exceptions and limiting conditions on that principle, discussed in the following section.

SOME EXCEPTIONS AND LIMITING CONDITIONS

Extant research evidence suggests three important caveats concerning the effects of liking for the communicator on persuasive outcomes: The effects of liking can apparently be overridden by credibility; the superiority of liked over disliked communicators appears to obtain only under conditions of low receiver involvement in the issue; and, at least sometimes, disliked communicators can be significantly more effective persuaders than can liked communicators.

LIKING AND CREDIBILITY The effects of liking on persuasive outcomes appear to be weaker than the effects of credibility (Simons, Berkowitz, & Moyer, 1970); thus when the receiver's judgment of the source's credibility conflicts with the receiver's liking for the source, the effects of liking may be overridden by the effects of credibility. This, at least, is implied by the results of Wachtler and Counselman's (1981) research. In this investigation, subjects were asked to make a judgment about the size of the monetary award to be given in a personal injury damage suit. Each participant heard a persuasive message from a source who advocated either a relatively small monetary award or a relatively large one; the source was portrayed either as cold and stingy or as warm and generous. Even though the warm, generous source was liked better than was the cold, stingy communicator, the stingy source was nevertheless sometimes a more effective persuader — namely, when the stingy source was arguing for a relatively large award. Indeed, of the four different source-message combinations, the two most effective ones were the stingy source arguing for a large award and the generous source arguing for a small award. Both these combinations, of course, represent sources who are (given their personalities) advocating an unexpected position and who thus may well have been perceived as relatively higher in credibility. What is particularly of interest is that the communicator who was disliked and (presumably) high in credibility (the stingy source advocating the large award) was significantly more effective than the communicator who was liked and (presumably) low in credibility (the generous source advocating the large award), thus suggesting that the effects of liking for the communicator are weaker than the effects of communicator credibility.

LIKING AND INVOLVEMENT The effects of liking are minimized under conditions of increased receiver involvement. On an issue important to the receiver, when the matter is especially consequential for the receiver, when the issue is personally relevant to the receiver — in short, when the receiver is involved in the issue — the effects of liking on persuasive outcomes are minimized (Chaiken, 1980).

This result is, of course, quite compatible with the distinction between central and peripheral routes to persuasion (discussed in Chapter 6). Where receiver involvement is high, receivers are more likely to engage in systematic active processing of message contents, and to minimize reliance on peripheral cues such as whether they happen to like the communication source. But where receiver involvement is low, receivers are more likely to rely on simplifying heuristics emphasizing noncontent cues such as liking ("I like this person, so I'll agree").

GREATER EFFECTIVENESS OF DISLIKED COMMUNICATORS At least sometimes, *disliked* communicators can be more effective persuaders than liked communicators — even when the communicators are comparable in other characteristics (such as credibility). A demonstration of this possibility has been provided by Zimbardo, Weisenberg, Firestone, and Levy (1965). Participants in this investigation were induced to eat fried grasshoppers. In one condition, the communicator acted snobbish, cold, bossy, tactless, and hostile (the disliked communicator); the liked communicator displayed none of these characteristics. The two communicators were roughly equally successful in inducing participants to eat the fried grasshoppers, but that is not the result of interest. What is of interest is how, among those who did eat the grasshoppers, attitudes toward eating grasshoppers changed. As one might predict from dissonance-theoretic considerations, among those who ate the grasshoppers, the disliked communicator was much more effective in changing attitudes in the desired direction than was the liked communicator: The person who ate the grasshoppers under the influence of the disliked communicator presumably experienced more dissonance — and thus exhibited more attitude change — than did the person induced to eat by the liked source.

This, of course, is the familiar forced-compliance counterattitudinal-action circumstance. But similar results have been obtained in straightforward persuasive-communication situations (J. Cooper, Darley, & Henderson, 1974; Himmelfarb & Arazi, 1974; Jones & Brehm, 1967; compare Eagly & Chaiken, 1975). A notable clarification of this effect was provided by Jones and Brehm (1967), who manipulated both the receiver's liking for the communicator and the recipient's choice about listening to the communication; in the high-choice condition, receivers volunteered to listen to the message, whereas in the no-choice condition receivers were seemingly accidentally exposed to the message (by hearing it playing in an adjacent room). When receivers had not chosen to listen to the communication, the liked communicator was more effective than the disliked communicator; but when receivers had freely chosen to listen to the message, the disliked communicator was more effective than the liked communicator.

Indeed, when other investigations have found disliked communicators to be more successful persuaders than liked communicators, the circumstances appear consistently to have involved the receivers' having freely chosen to listen to the message (J. Cooper et al., 1974; Himmelfarb & Arazi, 1974). For example, in J. Cooper et al.'s (1974) investigation, suburban householders received a counterattitudinal communication (i.e., one opposed to the receiver's views) from either a deviant-appearing communicator (a long-haired hippie) or a conventional-appearing communicator; the deviant-appearing communicator was significantly more effective than the conventionally dressed communicator in persuading these suburbanites, but the message recipients all had freely chosen to receive the communication (and indeed had had two opportunities to decline receiving the communication).

Remembering that one expects to find dissonance effects in forced-compliance circumstances only when the person has freedom of choice about engaging in the discrepant action, the finding that disliked communicators can be more successful than liked communicators only under conditions of choice is perhaps not surprising. Receivers who freely choose to listen to (what turns out to be) an unlikable communicator presumably face a dissonance-reduction task that is not faced by receivers who find themselves (through no fault of their own) listening to an unlikable source. Hence the greater success of disliked (as opposed to liked) communicators is, as the research evidence suggests, obtained only when the receiver has chosen to listen to the message.[7]

OTHER SOURCE FACTORS

Beyond credibility and liking, a large number of other source factors have received at least some research attention as possible influences on persuasive outcomes. This section focuses on two particular additional source factors—similarity and physical attractiveness—but concludes with a more general discussion of other source characteristics.

It is possible, however, to say something comprehensive about the role that all these other factors play in persuasion: As a rule, these other source characteristics appear to influence persuasive outcomes not directly, but indirectly, by influencing the recipient's liking for the communicator or the recipient's judgments of the communicator's credibility (competence or trustworthiness). That is, in each case, the factor's effects on persuasive outcomes seem to be best understood as results of the factor's effects on credibility and liking, rather than as results of some immediate influence that the factor has on persuasive effects.

SIMILARITY

It seems common and natural to assume that, to the degree that receivers perceive similarities between themselves and a persuader, the persuader's effectiveness will be enhanced. The belief that "greater similarity means greater effectiveness" is an attractive one, and is commonly reflected in recommendations that persuaders emphasize commonalities between themselves and the audience.

But, as Simons et al. (1970) have made clear, the relationship of similarity to persuasive effectiveness is much more complex than this common assumption would indicate. Indeed, the research evidence suggests that this common assumption is misleading in important ways; to be sure, there are research findings indicating that persuasive effectiveness can be enhanced by similarity (e.g., Brock, 1965; Woodside & Davenport, 1974), but there are also findings indicating that persuasive effectiveness can be *reduced* by similarity (e.g., Infante, 1978; S. W. King & Sereno, 1973; Leavitt & Kaigler-Evans, 1975), and there are additional findings indicating that similarity has no effect on persuasive outcomes (e.g., Klock & Traylor, 1983; Wagner, 1984).

Two initial clarifications will be helpful in untangling these complexities. First, there are "an infinite number of possible dimensions" of similarity-dissimilarity (Simons et al., 1970, p. 3). One might perceive oneself to be similar or dissimilar to another person in age, occupation, attitudes, physique, income, education, speech dialect, personality, ethnicity, political affiliation, interpersonal style, clothing preferences, and on and on and on. Thus there is not likely to be any truly general relationship between "similarity" and persuasive effectiveness, or indeed between "similarity" and *any* other variable. Different particular similarities or dissimilarities will have different effects, making impossible any sound generalization about "similarity."

Second, as emphasized by Simons et al. (1970) and Hass (1981), similarities most likely do not influence persuasive effectiveness *directly*. Rather, similarities influence persuasive outcomes only *indirectly*, by affecting the receiver's liking for the communicator and the receiver's perception of the communicator's credibility (competence and trustworthiness). And since the effects of similarities may not be identical for liking, perceived competence, and perceived trustworthiness, the relationship of similarities to each of these needs separate attention.

SIMILARITY AND LIKING Given the infinite varieties of possible similarities, there is not likely to be any general relationship between "perceived similarity" and liking for another person. That is to say, "there is no singular 'similarity' effect" on liking, but rather "a multiplicity of effects that depend on both content and context" (Huston & Levinger, 1978, p. 126).

However, the effect on liking of one particular sort of similarity — attitudinal similarity — has received a good deal of empirical attention. What is meant by "attitudinal similarity" is having similar attitudes (similar evaluations of attitude objects) — as opposed to, say, having similar traits, or similar abilities, or similar occupations, or similar backgrounds, or whatever.

There is now a fair amount of evidence that, as a general rule, perceived attitudinal similarity engenders greater liking (for reviews, see Berscheid, 1985; Byrne, 1969). Thus to the extent that message recipients perceive that the communicator has attitudes (on matters other than the topic of the influence attempt) that are similar to theirs, those recipients are likely to come to like the communicator more. Hence, even when not especially relevant to the topic of the influence attempt, perceived attitudinal similarities (between source and audience) can enhance the audience's liking of the source, and so can potentially influence persuasive effectiveness.

A receiver may come to perceive attitudinal similarities through various routes, of course. The communicator might directly express attitudes similar to the attitudes of the audience, or a third party might indicate the presence of attitudinal similarities. But one basis on which a receiver might infer attitudinal similarities would be the presence of *other* kinds of observed similarities (such as similarities in background, personality, occupation, and the like); these other similarities thus may indirectly influence the receiver's liking for a communicator.

The hypothesis that attitudinal similarities can influence persuasive effectiveness by influencing the receiver's liking for the communicator is bolstered by the results of investigations that have varied both communicator credibility (specifically, competence) and communicator-receiver attitudinal similarity. As discussed previously, the effects of liking on persuasive effectiveness appear to be weaker than the effects of credibility; thus if attitudinal similarities influence persuasive effects by influencing liking for the communicator, then the effect of attitudinal similarities on persuasive effectiveness should be smaller than the effect of credibility. And indeed Wagner (1984) and Woodside and Davenport (1974) have found persuasive success to be more influenced by the communicator's expertise than by the communicator's attitudinal similarity.

But it is worth remembering here that enhanced liking of a communicator will not always mean enhanced persuasive effectiveness; as discussed earlier, greater liking for a communicator may enhance, reduce, or have no effect on persuasive effectiveness. Correspondingly, greater perceived attitudinal similarities may (through their influence on the receiver's liking for the communicator) enhance, reduce, or have no influence on persuasive effectiveness. Thus one should not assume that with greater perceived attitudinal similarity comes greater persuasive effectiveness. Rather, with greater perceived attitudinal similarity comes greater liking, which may or may not mean greater persuasive effectiveness.

SIMILARITY AND CREDIBILITY: COMPETENCE JUDGMENTS It is unquestionably the case that perceived similarities (or dissimilarities) between source and audience can influence the audience's judgment of the source's competence (expertise). But there are two noteworthy features of this relationship.

First, the similarity/dissimilarity must be *relevant* to the influence attempt if it is likely to influence judgments of competence. For example, a communicator seeking to influence a receiver's judgment of the president's budget policy will probably not obtain enhanced competence judgments by pointing out that the communicator and recipient are wearing the same color shirt. Correspondingly, Swartz's (1984) manipulation of the communicator's occupational similarity (student versus nonstudent, for an audience of students) in three advertisements for different consumer products found that receivers' judgments of the source's expertise were unrelated to judgments of perceived similarity; presumably, the variations in similarity were not relevant to the persuasive issues involved. The general point to be noticed is that only relevant similarities (or dissimilarities) are likely to influence judgments of the communicator's competence.

The second noteworthy feature is that not all relevant similarities will enhance perceived competence, and not all relevant dissimilarities will damage perceived competence. Different sorts of relevant similarities will have different effects on perceived competence, depending on the circumstance, and hence it is impossible to give a simple generalization about the effects of relevant similarities on perceptions of competence.

For example, a perceived similarity in relevant training and experience may reduce the perceived competence of a communicator (since the receiver may be thinking, "I know as much about this topic as the speaker does"). A perceived dissimilarity in relevant training and experience, on the other hand, might either enhance or damage perceived competence, depending on the direction of the dissimilarity: If the receiver thinks the communicator is dissimilar because the communicator has *better* training and experience, then, presumably, enhanced judgments of the communicator's competence will be likely; but if the receiver thinks the communicator is dissimilar because the communicator has *poorer* training and experience, then most likely the communicator's perceived competence will suffer.

A demonstration of this sort of complexity was provided by Delia's (1975) study of speech dialect similarity. Persons who spoke a general American dialect heard one of two versions of a message from a speaker using either a general American dialect or a southern dialect; the message concerned Governor George Wallace of Alabama, with one version being a pro-Wallace message and the other an anti-Wallace message. Regardless of the position advocated, the speaker with the southern (dissimilar) speech dialect was perceived as more competent than the speaker with the general American (similar) dialect, presumably because the southern speaker could be assumed to have better access to relevant information than would the general American speaker (for related investigations, see Houck & Bowers, 1969; Schenck-Hamlin, 1978).

Notice, thus: Similarities should have varying effects on perceived competence, depending on the particulars of the circumstances. One should not be surprised that the research literature indicates that similar others are sometimes seen as more competent than dissimilar others (e.g., Mills & Kimble, 1973), sometimes as less competent (e.g., Delia, 1975), and sometimes as not differing in competence (e.g., Atkinson, Winzelberg, & Holland, 1985; Swartz, 1984). The effects of perceived similarities and dissimilarities on judgments of communicator competence depend upon whether, and how, the receiver perceives these as relevant to the issue at hand.

SIMILARITY AND CREDIBILITY: TRUSTWORTHINESS JUDGMENTS The relationship between similarities and judgments of the communicator's trustworthiness appears to be complex as well. As we have seen, certain sorts of similarities — specifically, perceived attitudinal similarities — can influence the receiver's liking for the communicator, and enhanced liking for the communicator is commonly accompanied by enhanced judgments of the communicator's trustworthiness. Thus one would expect that perceived attitudinal similarities might (through their influence on liking) exert some effect on perceptions of the communicator's trustworthiness.

But this cannot be the whole story. Delia's (1975) speech dialect investigation, described above, also included assessments of the communicator's trustworthiness. Greater trustworthiness was ascribed to the pro-Wallace speaker using the similar (general American) dialect and to the anti-Wallace speaker using the dissimilar (southern) dialect. This effect is, of course, readily understandable: The southern speaker arguing against Wallace's racism and the northern speaker supporting it could each have been seen as offering views that ran against the tide of regional opinion — and hence seen as speakers who must be especially sincere and honest in their expressions of their opinions.[8]

But notice the complexity of these results so far as similarity is concerned: Sometimes similarity enhanced perceptions of trustworthiness, but sometimes it diminished such perceptions, depending on the position advocated. And (to round things out) other investigators have found that sometimes similarities will have no effect on trustworthiness judgments. Atkinson et al. (1985), for example, found that ethnic similarity-dissimilarity did not influence the perceived trustworthiness of pregnancy counselors for Mexican American or for Anglo clients.

SUMMARY: THE EFFECTS OF SIMILARITY Perhaps it is now clear just how inadequate is a generalization such as "Greater similarity leads to greater persuasive effectiveness." The effects of similarity on persuasive outcomes are complex and indirect, and no single easy generalization will encompass those varied effects. Indeed, there are several instances in which, in a single investigation, similarities have been found to enhance persuasive effectiveness under some conditions but to inhibit persuasive effectiveness under other circumstances (e.g., Goethals & Nelson, 1973; S. W. King & Sereno, 1973; Mills & Kimble, 1973).

Thus if there is a general conclusion to be drawn about source-receiver similarities in persuasion, it surely is that simple generalizations will not do: To say, for example, that "individuals are more likely to be influenced by a persuasive message to the extent that they perceive it as coming from a source similar to themselves" (Hass, 1981, p. 151) is to overlook the complexities of the effects that similarities have on persuasive outcomes.

PHYSICAL ATTRACTIVENESS

The effects of physical attractiveness on persuasive outcomes—like the effects of similarity—are rather varied. For the most part, "existing research does indicate that heightened physical attractiveness generally enhances one's effectiveness as a social influence agent" (Chaiken, 1986, p. 150). But a close look at the research evidence and a consideration of the mechanisms underlying this general effect will underscore the dangers of unqualified reliance on this generalization.

THE RESEARCH EVIDENCE A number of investigations have found that physically attractive communicators are more effective persuaders than their less attractive counterparts (e.g., Horai, Naccari, & Fatoullah, 1974; Snyder & Rothbart, 1971; Widgery & Ruch, 1981; for a review, see Chaiken, 1986). For example, Chaiken's (1979) field study of messages concerning university dining hall menus found that attractive persuaders induced significantly greater persuasion (on both verbal and behavioral indexes of persuasion) than did unattractive persuaders. But attractive communicators do not always enjoy greater persuasive success; for instance, Maddux and Rogers (1980) found that the persuasiveness of a message arguing that people need only four hours of sleep a night was not influenced by the communicator's physical attractiveness (see also Mills & Aronson, 1965). And in some circumstances attractive communicators have been found to be significantly *less* effective persuaders than their unattractive counterparts (J. Cooper et al., 1974).

AN EXPLANATORY MECHANISM What accounts for the observed effects of physical attractiveness on persuasive success? A plausible starting point for an explanation is that the communicator's physical attractiveness influences the recipient's liking for the communicator, which in turn influences persuasive success (see Chaiken, 1986, for a careful elaboration of this idea). After all—and not surprisingly—greater physical attractiveness tends to lead to greater liking (for a review, see Berscheid & Walster, 1974); and, as discussed previously, there is good evidence for the general proposition that, on the whole, liked communicators will be more effective persuaders than will disliked communicators.

This explanation is also consistent with the results of investigations that have examined the effects of communicator physical attractiveness on both liking for the communicator and persuasive effect. If physical attractiveness influences persuasive outcomes indirectly, through an effect on liking, then (a) whenever physical attractiveness influences persuasive outcomes it should also influence liking, and (b) the (presumably immediate) effect of physical attractiveness on liking should be larger than the (presumably mediated) effect of physical attractiveness on persuasive outcomes. These are just the sorts of results commonly observed (e.g., Horai et al., 1974; Snyder & Rothbart, 1971).

But notice: If communicator physical attractiveness influences persuasion through its effect on liking for the communicator, then (at least in principle) it should be possible to find empirical results for physical attractiveness that parallel the observed effects of liking. Thus, in addition to the generally positive effect of communicator physical attractiveness on persuasive outcomes (paralleling the generally positive effect of liking on persuasion), one should also find that (a) credibility can be a more important determinant of persuasion than physical attractiveness, (b) the effects of physical attractiveness on persuasion are largely limited to low-involvement topics, and (c) at least sometimes physically unattractive communicators will be more effective than physically attractive persuaders.

The research evidence relevant to these expectations is not extensive, but it is at least largely supportive. Maddux and Rogers (1980), for instance, found source expertise to be a more powerful determinant of persuasion than was communicator physical attractiveness. Although research on the effects of communicator physical attractiveness has generally not systematically varied the receivers' involvement with the issue, it is nevertheless noteworthy that (as Chaiken, 1986, has emphasized) studies that have found significant effects of communicator physical attractiveness on persuasion overwhelmingly have used what appear to be low-involvement topics. And, as discussed earlier, researchers have found that at least under some circumstances a deviant-appearing communicator will be a more successful persuader than a conventional-appearing source (J. Cooper et al., 1974).

All told, then, an attractive case can be made for supposing that the effects of communicator physical attractiveness on persuasive outcomes can best be explained by the hypothesis that "physical attractiveness affects social influence via its more direct impact on liking for the social influence agent" (Chaiken, 1986, p. 151).

But what of the possibility that communicator physical attractiveness might influence persuasion by influencing perceptions of the communicator's credibility? This alternative has some merit, but the pattern of empirical results suggests that this is not in fact a competitor to (but instead a natural companion of) the explanation that emphasizes effects of attractiveness on liking. To bring this out, however, requires separate consideration of the competence and trustworthiness dimensions of credibility.

Consider first the possibility that judgments of the communicator's competence mediate the effects of communicator physical attractiveness. Investigations that have found physically attractive persuaders to be more successful than unattractive persuaders have typically *not* found the attractive communicators to be rated higher in competence (e.g., Chaiken, 1979; Horai et al., 1974; Snyder & Rothbart, 1971; see also Norman, 1976; Widgery, 1974; compare Patzer, 1983). Thus it is not plausible to suppose that differential judgments of the communicator's competence generally mediate the effect of communicator physical attractiveness on persuasive outcomes.[9]

But physical attractiveness may (at least indirectly) influence judgments of the communicator's trustworthiness. As noted earlier, physical attractiveness influences liking for the communicator; and, also as discussed earlier, there is at least some indirect evidence that the receiver's liking for the communicator can influence the receiver's judgment of communicator trustworthiness. But this roundabout path of influence is likely to mean that physical attractiveness will have only weak effects on trustworthiness judgments: If the effect of communicator physical attractiveness on trustworthiness judgments is mediated by the receiver's liking for the communicator, then (given that liking for the communicator can be influenced by so many other things besides physical attractiveness) one should expect that the effect of attractiveness on trustworthiness will be less strong than the effect of attractiveness on liking (as in fact was found by Patzer, 1983) and indeed will typically be comparatively small, even negligible. Maddux and Rogers (1980), for example, found that physically attractive persuaders were indeed better liked but were not rated as significantly more sincere or honest than were their physically unattractive counterparts (for related results, see Snyder & Rothbart, 1971).

In any event, an understanding of the role that communicator physical attractiveness plays in influencing persuasive outcomes seems to require that central emphasis be given the influence of physical attractiveness on liking. Physical attractiveness appears not to affect persuasive outcomes directly, but rather does so indirectly by means of its influence on the receiver's liking for the communicator.

ABOUT ADDITIONAL SOURCE CHARACTERISTICS

We have seen that the effects of communicator-receiver similarity and communicator physical attractiveness on persuasive outcomes appear to be best explained by the hypothesis that these factors do not influence persuasion directly, but do so only indirectly through their effects on credibility and liking. What this may indicate is that the source characteristics that are most central to persuasive effects (in the sense of most directly influencing persuasive outcomes) are credibility (competence and trustworthiness) and liking. This, in turn, suggests that, in thinking about the effects of any given additional source characteristic on persuasion, the most promising avenue to a clear understanding of that characteristic's effects will be a consideration of how that characteristic might influence credibility or liking.

So consider a source characteristic such as ethnicity (as might be examined in an investigation comparing Hispanic and Anglo communicators; e.g., Ramirez, 1977). It is not likely to prove possible to arrive at very useful generalizations about the effect of ethnicity on persuasive outcomes, precisely because (a) ethnicity's effects on persuasive outcomes will be mediated by its effects on credibility and liking, and (b) ethnicity's effects on credibility and liking will vary substantially from circumstance to circumstance. Consider, for instance, the question of the comparative success of a Hispanic communicator and an Anglo communicator in influencing Hispanic and Anglo message recipients. The answer to this question almost certainly varies from case to case, depending on the particulars involved. With one topic, the Hispanic communicator may be perceived (by Hispanic and Anglo receivers alike) to be more credible than the Anglo communicator; with a different topic, the Anglo communicator may be perceived as more credible (by both Hispanic and Anglo receivers); with yet another topic, there may be no credibility differences associated with the ethnicity of the communicator; or the credibility judgments may depend not just on the topic addressed, but also on the position advocated (as, for example, trustworthiness judgments did in Delia's 1975 study of speech dialect). But (to add to the complexity here) these credibility judgments may not influence persuasive outcomes substantially, since variations in credibility are not always associated with variations in effects; and even when variations in these credibility judgments *are* associated with variations in outcomes, sometimes the lower-credibility communicator will be more effective than the higher-credibility source. So when one adds the complex relationship between ethnicity and credibility to the complex relationship between credibility and persuasive outcomes, the result is a rococo set of possibilities for the relationship between ethnicity and persuasive effects. (And notice: The discussion of this example has focused only on the direct ethnicity-credibility relationship; the picture of ethnicity's effects becomes even more complex when one considers also the ethnicity-liking relationship or the role of perceived ethnic similarity.)

The general point to be underscored is this: The source factors with the most immediate (if complex) effects on persuasive outcomes are credibility and liking. Other source characteristics appear most likely to play a role in persuasion only through influencing credibility and liking. Thus, in considering how any additional source characteristic is likely to influence persuasion, the sensible guiding question to ask is, How is this characteristic likely to be related to liking and credibility?

For many source characteristics, a general answer to this question may not be possible; as just discussed, for instance, there does not seem to be any basis for supposing there are sound generalizations about the effect of communicator ethnicity on persuasive outcomes. But even where broad generalizations are not possible, pursuing this question may nevertheless provide a clearer understanding of the role played by a given communicator characteristic in some specific circumstance. Thus, even though one may not be able to construct sensible generalizations about the persuasive effect of (say) communicator ethnicity, it may still prove possible to trace out likely effects of ethnicity in some particular communicative setting: Given a particular topic, a given position to be advocated, a specified audience, and so forth, insight into the possible effects of the source's ethnicity will most likely be obtained by focusing on the question of how (in that particular concrete circumstance) ethnicity is likely to influence judgments of credibility and liking.

NOTES

1. Not all of the factors that in the research literature have been labeled "trustworthiness" (or "character," "safety," or the like) in fact contain many of the items that here are identified as assessing trustworthiness (e.g., McCroskey, 1966). An important source of confusion is the apparent empirical association between a receiver's liking for a communicator and the receiver's judgment

of the communicator's trustworthiness; this covariation is reflected in factor analyses that have found items such as honest-dishonest, trustworthy-untrustworthy, and fair-unfair to load on the same factor with items such as friendly-unfriendly, pleasant-unpleasant, nice-not nice, and valuable-worthless (see, e.g., Applbaum & Anatol, 1972; Bowers & Phillips, 1967; Falcione, 1974; McCroskey, 1966; Pearce & Brommel, 1972). As suggested later in the text, this pattern can plausibly be interpreted as reflecting the effects of liking on trustworthiness judgments (receivers being inclined to ascribe greater trustworthiness to persons they like). But such empirical association should not obscure the conceptual distinction between trustworthiness and liking (especially because the empirical association is imperfect; see Delia's, 1976b, pp. 374-375, discussion of Whitehead's 1968 results, or consider the stereotypical used-car salesman who is likable but untrustworthy). In this chapter, investigations are treated as bearing on judgments of trustworthiness only when it appears that in fact trustworthiness (and not liking) has been assessed.

2. This doesn't mean that researchers should never investigate the effect of a complex of behavioral features. Quite to the contrary, such studies can be very useful in the early stages of research (when one is casting one's research net widely) or in the later stages of research (when one already knows the effects of individual behavioral features studied in isolation, and now wishes to see the effects of combinations of factors). But such studies obviously cannot provide all the information necessary for understanding the effects of individual behavioral features.

3. A number of investigations that are commonly cited as indicating significant effects of speaking rate on credibility judgments in fact do not involve judgments of competence (Is the communicator informed, trained, qualified, intelligent, expert?) or trustworthiness (Is the communicator honest, trustworthy, open-minded, fair?), but judgments of other characteristics (e.g., Apple, Streeter, & Krauss, 1979; Brown, Strong, & Rencher, 1973, 1974; B. L. Smith, Brown, Strong, & Rencher, 1975; Street & Brady, 1982). For example, what B. L. Smith et al. (1975) labeled as a "competence" judgment consisted of judgments of whether the speaker was strong, active, ambitious, intelligent, good-looking, and confident; what was labeled a "benevolence" dimension consisted of judgments of whether the speaker was polite, just, religious, kind, sincere, happy, likable, dependable, and sociable. It would not be prudent to assume that these straightforwardly correspond to the sorts of competence and trustworthiness judgments of interest here.

4. A similar effect on persuasive outcomes was observed by Weinberger and Dillon (1980). Consumers were provided with unfavorable information about a product, attributed to one of three sources: a trade and professional association (whose self-interest would presumably run counter to disclosure of the negative information), a local consumer panel, or an independent testing agency. The unfavorable information had more impact on purchase intentions when it came from unbiased sources (the consumer panel or testing agency) than when it was presumably "reluctant" testimony from the trade association.

5. For example, in Sternthal et al.'s (1978) investigation, the credibility index (6 summed credibility items) could range from 6 to 42, with a midpoint of 24; the low-credibility communicator's mean rating was 20.57 (not significantly different from the scale midpoint) and the high-credibility communicator's was 28.86. For the 12-item credibility index employed by Ward and McGinnies (1974), overall scores could range from 12 to 60 with a midpoint of 36; the mean rating for the low-credibility communicator was 34.95, while that for the high-credibility communicator was 41.58. Such results are common (e.g., Bochner & Insko, 1966; Greenberg & Miller, 1966, Experiment 1; Johnson & Scileppi, 1969; Neimeyer, Guy, & Metzler, 1989).

6. This difficulty is consistent with studies of the ratings given to "ideal" high- and low-credibility communicators, which have found that when respondents are asked to indicate where a perfectly credible and a perfectly noncredible communicator would be rated on competence and trustworthiness scales, the ratings are not at the absolute extremes (R. A. Clark, Stewart, & Marston, 1972; see also J. K. Burgoon, 1976).

7. It should be noted that the apparent necessity of free choice for the appearance of this effect (the effect of a disliked communicator being more successful than a liked communicator) is consistent not only with a dissonance-based explanation of this phenomenon, but also with attributional accounts (see J. Cooper et al., 1974).

8. Although Delia's (1975) research did not involve assessment of the relevant expectancies, an explanation of these effects could obviously be constructed from Eagly et al.'s (1981) expectancy-disconfirmation ideas (discussed previously).

9. In certain specific circumstances, the communicator's physical attractiveness might influence judgments of competence — namely, when the topic of influence is related to physical attractiveness in relevant ways. For example, physically attractive sources might enjoy greater perceived competence in the realm of beauty products. But generally speaking, the effect of the source's physical attractiveness on persuasive outcomes appears not to be achieved through enhanced perceptions of the source's competence.

9

Message Factors

THIS CHAPTER REVIEWS research concerning the effects that selected message variations have on persuasion. The message factors discussed are grouped into three broad categories: message structure, message content, and sequential-request strategies.

MESSAGE STRUCTURE

Two structural features of persuasive messages have been investigated for their possible effects on persuasive outcomes. One concerns the order of arguments in the message; the other concerns the nature of the message's conclusion.

CLIMAX VERSUS ANTICLIMAX ORDER OF ARGUMENTS

Where should a persuader put the message's most important arguments? One possibility is to save them for last, thereby building to a strong finish; but another possibility is to put the most important arguments first, to be sure they aren't missed. There have been several studies of the relative effectiveness of these two ways of ordering arguments in a message – the climax order (most important arguments last) and the anticlimax order (most important arguments first). In these investigations, the relative importance of different arguments was assessed in pretests (by obtaining ratings of argument importance), and the experimental messages devoted relatively more time or space to the more important arguments than to less important ones.

As it turns out, the choice between these two ways of arranging the arguments in a message seems to be of little consequence; varying the order makes very little difference indeed to overall persuasive effectiveness (Gilkinson, Paulson, & Sikkink, 1954; Gulley & Berlo, 1956; Sikkink, 1956; Sponberg, 1946; for a related study, see Cromwell, 1950, Experiment 2). In the one report of a statistically significant difference between the two orders (Gilkinson et al. 1954, Experiment 2), the climax order was more persuasive; and where nonsignificant differences have been found the direction of effect has generally (but not always) favored the climax order, but in every case the observed differences are quite small. Perhaps the most sensible conclusion to draw is that there might, on average, be some extremely small benefit to be obtained from arranging arguments in a climax order, but this benefit is so small as to be negligible.

It will be useful to bear in mind, however, that the particulars of a persuasive circumstance may suggest that one or another way of arranging arguments will be greatly superior. Consider, for example, appellate oral argument in U.S. courts (e.g., the Supreme Court). An attorney will commonly have a specified amount of time (perhaps 20 or 30 minutes) in which to present arguments. However, the judges are free to break in at any time with questions and counterarguments, and experienced attorneys know that they are not likely to be able to make an uninterrupted presentation. As should be plain, an attorney who plans on saving the most important arguments for last may never get the chance to present those arguments. In this setting, then, an advocate should employ an anticlimax order – placing the most important arguments at the beginning of the presentation – rather than a climax order.

EXPLICIT CONCLUSIONS AND RECOMMENDATIONS

Obviously, persuasive messages have some point – some opinion or belief that the communicator hopes the audience will accept, some recommended course of action that the communicator wishes to have adopted. Should the message explicitly make that point – explicitly state the conclusion or recommendation – or should the message leave the point implicit, and let the receivers figure the conclusion out themselves?

Intuitively, there look to be good reasons for each alternative. For instance, one might think making the conclusion explicit would be superior, because receivers would then be less likely to misunderstand the point of the message. On the other hand, it might be that if the communicator simply supplies the premises, and the audience reasons its own way to the conclusion, then perhaps the audience will be more persuaded than if the communicator had presented the desired conclusion (more persuaded, because they reached the conclusion on their own).

There have been a number of investigations of this question, where an explicit conclusion/recommendation is either included in the message or omitted from it. The overwhelmingly predominant finding is that messages that include explicit conclusions or recommendations are more persuasive than messages without such elements (Biddle, 1966; Cope & Richardson, 1972; Fine, 1957; Hovland & Mandell, 1952; Leventhal, Watts, & Pagano, 1967; Tubbs, 1968; Weiss & Steenbock, 1965; see also E. Cooper & Dinerman, 1951; Feingold & Knapp, 1977; Geller, 1975; Irwin & Brockhaus, 1963). In one other investigation, explicit conclusions led to significantly greater comprehension of the communicator's point, but not to significantly greater attitude change (Thistlethwaite, de Haan, & Kamenetzky, 1955). Notably, however, among receivers with equally good comprehension, there were no significant differences in attitude change as a function of the type of conclusion; that is, conclusions deduced independently by the audience were no more persuasive than conclusions explicitly drawn out by the communicator.

There has often been speculation that the apparent advantage of explicit conclusions/recommendations may be moderated by such factors as audience education, intelligence, familiarity with the topic, and topic complexity (e.g., Hovland & Mandell, 1952). For instance, it is sometimes suggested that as the audience becomes more intelligent or better educated, the advantage of explicit conclusions will be smaller (since such audiences will be able to infer the message's point correctly even though the message leaves the conclusion unstated), and indeed may disappear entirely, with implicit conclusions becoming the preferred technique (since — the speculation goes — the intelligent, educated audience could be insulted by the communicator drawing the conclusion for them). Despite the plausibility of such suggestions, there is scant evidence in any of these studies to show that such factors actually do influence the persuasive advantage of explicit conclusions.[1]

It is worth noting that in several extant studies, the audience was comparatively intelligent and well educated (college students), and even so there was a significant advantage for messages with explicit recommendations or conclusions (e.g., Fine, 1957; Hovland & Mandell, 1952). Obviously, these studies don't show that intelligence or education makes no difference to the amount of persuasive advantage enjoyed by explicit conclusions (it might still be true that the advantage of explicit recommendations would be even larger if the audience were not so well educated). But these studies do indicate that even if increases in receiver education and intelligence are associated with a smaller advantage for explicit conclusions, that advantage is nevertheless sufficiently great to recommend the use of explicit conclusions even with an intelligent, well-educated audience.

What all of this suggests is that persuaders commonly have little to gain (and much to lose) by leaving the message's conclusion implicit. Ordinarily, messages containing explicit statements of the conclusion or desired action will be more effective than messages that omit such statements.[2]

MESSAGE CONTENT

This section reviews research concerning the persuasive effects of certain variations in the contents of messages. Literally dozens of different content variables have received at least some empirical attention, but for the most part this attention consists of an isolated study or two. This review mainly focuses on selected message content factors for which the empirical evidence is somewhat more extensive.

HANDLING OPPOSING ARGUMENTS: ONE-SIDED VERSUS TWO-SIDED MESSAGES

How should a persuader handle opposing arguments? In most circumstances, a persuader will at least be aware of some possible arguments supporting the opposing point of view. What should a persuader do about these, so far as the persuader's own message is concerned?

IGNORING VERSUS REFUTING OPPOSING ARGUMENTS One possibility, of course, is simply to ignore the opposing arguments, and not mention them at all. The persuader would offer only constructive (supporting) arguments, that is, arguments supporting the persuader's position. Alternatively, the persuader might (in addition to providing supporting arguments) attempt to refute those opposing arguments — attack them directly, expose their weaknesses and defects, and so on. Substantial research has compared the persuasive effectiveness of these two message types — a "one-sided" message (that simply offers arguments supporting the advocated position) and a "two-sided" message (that, in addition to making supporting arguments, refutes opposing arguments).[3]

Perhaps not surprisingly, two-sided persuasive messages are, as a rule, more effective than one-sided messages (for a review, see Jackson & Allen, 1987). Persuaders ordinarily gain some advantage if, in addition to providing constructive arguments supporting their views, they also attack opposing considerations directly.

There has often been speculation that this advantage of two-sided messages might depend upon other factors; commonly suggested possible factors include the audience's educational level, the audience's familiarity with the issue, and the audience's initial opinion on the topic (whether the audience is initially favorable or unfavorable to the position advocated). In fact, the only one of these that appears to influence the size of the two-sided advantage is the audience's familiarity with the issue. For both familiar and unfamiliar persuasive topics, two-sided messages are more effective than one-sided messages, but the advantage is greater for familiar issues than for unfamiliar ones (Jackson & Allen, 1987). Thus it appears that persuaders are well advised to employ two-sided messages rather generally (even on issues unfamiliar to the audience).

Researchers have also varied the ways in which the two-sided message is organized. There are three basic organizational patterns possible for two-sided messages. The message can first present the supporting arguments, and then undertake the refutation of opposing arguments (support-then-refute); the message can first refute the opposing considerations, and then introduce the supporting arguments (refute-then-support); or the supportive and refutational materials can be interspersed (interwoven). There is some evidence suggesting that the support-then-refute order and the interwoven order are more effective than the refute-then-support order (Jackson & Allen, 1987).

THE IMPORTANCE OF ADDRESSING RELEVANT OBSTACLES Of course, refuting possible objections is likely to enhance persuasion only when the objections that are refuted are objections actually relevant for the audience. A persuader who refutes objections not held by the audience isn't likely to find enhanced effectiveness from the use of a two-sided message. A useful example here is provided by studies of messages aimed at persuading people to make contributions to a particular charitable cause or organization (e.g., the American Cancer Society).

There are (at least) two potential obstacles to successful persuasion in this circumstance. One is that people don't contribute at all (and hence getting people to give *something* is a possible aim for the persuader); the other is that people who do give may not give very much (and so getting those who donate to give a larger amount may be the persuader's aim). And these two obstacles can be addressed separately; a persuader could do some things designed to boost the percentage of people donating, and other things to try to boost the average donation per donor.[4]

Several studies have examined the effectiveness of one particular strategy designed to improve charitable solicitation: the "even a penny helps" (EAPH) technique (Cialdini & Schroeder, 1976). In the typical research design, communicators engage in face-to-face (e.g., door-to-door) solicitation for a particular charitable organization. In the control condition, the standard solicitation is given. In the experimental (EAPH) condition, the communicator simply adds the sentence "Even a penny will help."

Obviously, the EAPH technique is aimed at addressing the obstacle of people not donating at all. That is, it is primarily designed to increase the percentage of people who donate, by legitimizing small contributions. In a sense, it risks getting a lower average donation per donor in the hopes of boosting the percentage donating so much as to yield an overall gain (in average donation per contact).

But what if the disinclination to donate isn't a genuine obstacle? That is, what if people are already inclined to make a donation (e.g., the standard request already induces a high percentage of donations)? Obviously, in such a situation the EAPH technique probably won't be helpful – it is addressing an obstacle that isn't relevant – and might even backfire (by worsening the obstacle that *is* there, the obstacle of donors not giving very much). It could end up inducing smaller contributions per donor, without substantially increasing the percentage of donors.

In fact, sometimes the EAPH technique increases solicitation effectiveness (as assessed by average donation per contact), but sometimes it doesn't (indeed, sometimes it decreases effectiveness). Where the standard message is already relatively successful in inducing people to make donations, the EAPH technique has led to decreased persuasive effectiveness (Mark & Shotland, 1983); by comparison, when the percentage of people donating in the control condition is relatively low, the technique commonly enhances effectiveness (e.g., Reeves, Macolini, & Martin, 1987).

The general point to be noticed is the importance of addressing *relevant* obstacles to persuasion. The tactic of legitimizing small contributions (EAPH) appears to enhance effectiveness only when persons are initially not inclined to give anything – that is, only when the tactic addresses a relevant obstacle to persuasion. And similarly for the persuasive advantage of two-sided messages: Such advantage is likely to be obtained only when relevant opposing considerations are refuted.

DISCREPANCY

In many circumstances, persuaders have some latitude in just how much opinion change they seek. A persuader might advocate a position only slightly discrepant from (different from) the receiver's point of view, or might advocate a highly discrepant position (or, of course, might advocate some moderately discrepant view). So, for example, if a given audience believes a 5% increase in state taxes is desirable, a persuader seeking a still larger increase might advocate a 7% increase, a 15% increase, or a 30% increase – with these various positions representing views successively more and more discrepant with the audience's initial position.

A number of investigations have examined the question of how such variations in discrepancy – discrepancy between the receiver's position and the position advocated by the message – influence persuasive outcomes. In a way, this research question can be seen as a matter of the relationship between the amount of change *sought* by the message (with greater discrepancy, more change is asked of the audience) and the amount of change *obtained* by the message.[5]

At a minimum, one can confidently say that the relationship between discrepancy and persuasive effectiveness is not simple. Some investigations have found that – at least under some conditions – greater discrepancies are associated with greater effectiveness (i.e., a positive relationship between discrepancy and attitude change; e.g., A. R. Cohen, 1959; Hovland & Pritzker, 1957). But other studies have reported that, at least in some circumstances, with increasing discrepancy, persuasive effectiveness is reduced (a negative relationship; e.g., A. R. Cohen, 1959; Hovland, Harvey, & Sherif, 1957).

The most plausible general image of the relationship of discrepancy and effectiveness is that of an inverted-U-shaped curve, such that relatively little change is obtained with extremely small or extremely large discrepancies, and maximum effectiveness is to be found with moderate levels of discrepancy (for a general discussion of this view, see Whittaker, 1967; for findings of such curvilinearity—at least under some conditions—see, e.g., Aronson, Turner, & Carlsmith, 1963; Freedman, 1964; Sakaki, 1980; M. J. Smith, 1978; Whittaker, 1963, 1965). That is, with increasing discrepancy, there is increasing attitude change—up to a point (the peak of the curve); beyond that point, increases in discrepancy are associated with decreases in attitude change. This general curvilinear model can accommodate otherwise inconsistent findings of positive and negative relationships. For instance, if a given experiment has only relatively small levels of discrepancy, the results might well seem to suggest that increasing discrepancy leads to increasing attitude change (because there wasn't a sufficiently large discrepancy used in the research). Similarly, an experiment using only relatively large discrepancies might yield results indicating that increases in discrepancy lead to lessened effectiveness.

But even this curvilinear conception of the discrepancy-effectiveness relationship requires some complications. It is not likely that there is just *one* curve that describes the relationship; rather, it's likely that there is a *family* of curves—all having the same general inverted-U shape, but with the point of inflection in the curve (the peak, the point at which the curve turns back down) coming at different discrepancies. In some circumstances, that is to say, the point of maximum effectiveness may come at a relatively small discrepancy, but in another situation the point of maximum effectiveness may be at some larger discrepancy.

From this point of view, then, it is not enough to know that the general shape of the discrepancy-effectiveness relationship is that of an inverted U. What is crucial is knowing what factors influence the location of the point of inflection in that curve—knowing the circumstances under which the point of maximum effectiveness occurs at relatively small discrepancies, and those under which it occurs at relatively large ones.

There look to be (at least) two main factors influencing the point of inflection in the discrepancy-effectiveness curve. One is communicator credibility. The peak of the curve appears to occur at smaller discrepancies for low-credibility communicators than it does for high-credibility communicators (see, e.g., Aronson et al., 1963; Bergin, 1962; Bochner & Insko, 1966). That is, the optimal level of discrepancy is likely to be somewhat greater for a high-credibility communicator than for a low-credibility communicator; high-credibility sources can safely advocate somewhat more discrepant positions than can low-credibility sources.

The second is the receiver's degree of involvement with the issue. The research evidence suggests that for relatively high-involvement issues the peak of the curve occurs at lower levels of discrepancy, whereas on relatively uninvolving issues, the curve peaks at some larger discrepancy (see, e.g., Freedman, 1964; Sakaki, 1980). In a sense, then, as the issue becomes more and more personally relevant to the receiver, discrepancy becomes less and less tolerable. This effect of involvement was anticipated by social judgment theory (see Chapter 2). As receivers become more and more involved in an issue, their latitudes of rejection become larger, thus making the range of "objectionable" discrepant positions larger. For low-involvement receivers, a persuader may be able to advocate a quite discrepant view without encountering the (small) latitude of rejection; but for high-involvement receivers, a highly discrepant view is likely to fall in the (large) latitude of rejection.

FEAR APPEALS

The use of fear as a persuasive technique is an altogether common one. "If you don't do what I recommend," the communicator suggests, "then these terrible, fearful consequences will befall you." So, for example, high school driver education programs may show films depicting gruesome traffic accidents in an effort to discourage dangerous driving practices (such as drinking and driving); stop-smoking messages may display the horrors of lung cancer; dental hygiene messages may depict the ravages of gum disease; and so on.

The effectiveness of such "fear appeal" messages has been studied extensively. The central question that researchers have addressed concerns just how strong the fear appeal should be: Are stronger fear appeals more effective than weaker ones, or vice versa, or is there perhaps no general difference between them?

DEFINING FEAR APPEAL VARIATIONS In thinking about this research question, it is crucial to be clear about how "strong" and "weak" (or "high" and "low") fear appeals are to be defined. Unfortunately, there are two fundamentally different — and easily confused — ways of conceiving of the variation in fear appeals. One way of defining variations in the strength of fear appeals is by reference to the properties of the communication. That is, a "high fear appeal message" is one containing explicit, vivid depictions of negative consequences, and a "low fear appeal message" is a tamer, toned-down version. Notice, however, that this way of defining fear appeal variations makes no reference to the actual arousal of fear in the audience. By this definition, a "high fear appeal message" and a "low fear appeal message" might evoke the same degree of fear.

The second way of defining fear appeal variations is by reference to the degree of fear aroused in the audience. In this conception, a "high fear appeal message" is a message that evokes comparatively greater fear or anxiety in receivers, and a "low fear appeal message" is one that elicits relatively less fear.

This way of defining fear appeal variations makes no reference to the intrinsic characteristics of the message, but instead uses the degree of aroused fear as the index for fear appeal variations.

Obviously, these two ways of conceiving of "high versus low" fear appeals are quite different. A message might be a "high fear appeal" by the first definition (because it has lots of gruesome content) but not by the second (if it fails actually to arouse fear). And, equally obviously, there's a potential for great confusion in thinking about a research question such as "Are high fear appeals more effective than low fear appeals?" This question might be interpreted either as "Are messages with more gruesome contents more effective than those with less gruesome contents?" or as "Are messages that arouse greater fear more effective than those arousing less fear?" As it turns out, the research evidence clearly indicates the importance of distinguishing these questions.

THE RESEARCH EVIDENCE The research concerning fear appeals suggests two general conclusions. The first is that message material that is *intended* to induce a high level of fear or anxiety in receivers may or may not do so. Boster and Mongeau's (1984) review of fear appeal research found that message manipulations aimed at inducing different levels of fear just weren't very effective at doing so (across 40 studies, the average correlation between fear manipulations and perceived fear was only .36). That is to say, it's not easy to manipulate the level of fear experienced by an audience. Even experienced researchers working with carefully controlled experimental materials have found it difficult to induce the intended degrees of fear dependably. Notice, then: One can compose a message that is very carefully designed to arouse fear and anxiety — a message containing all sorts of material intended to create fear — and yet that message may fail to do so.

The second conclusion is that message material that *does* induce greater fear or anxiety will, as a rule, enhance the effectiveness of the message. Two meta-analytic reviews of fear appeal research have concluded that higher levels of induced fear are associated with greater persuasive effectiveness (Boster & Mongeau, 1984; Sutton, 1982; for an earlier review, see Higbee, 1969); that is, receivers who report greater fear/anxiety following the persuasive message are also more persuaded by the message.

Taken together, these two general conclusions should make it clear that a message offering explicit, vivid depictions of undesirable possible outcomes might or might not be especially effective in persuading. If such a message fails to arouse much fear, then the message may not have much impact. Persuaders should not assume that a message with intense, gruesome contents will automatically generate substantial fear in the audience. On the contrary, the research evidence indicates that it's quite difficult to manipulate fear dependably through persuasive messages. But messages that do successfully arouse relatively greater fear are likely to be more persuasive than those that arouse less fear.

A CURVILINEAR RELATIONSHIP? Earlier summaries of fear appeal research sometimes suggested that the relationship of fear appeal level to persuasive effectiveness is a curvilinear one, with the greatest effectiveness coming at some moderate level of fear appeal (e.g., Janis, 1967). And intuitively, this might seem to have some appeal; after all, one might think, can't a persuader "go too far" in using fear appeals, and thereby experience reduced effectiveness?

But it is important to be clear about what might be meant by "going too far" in using fear appeals. If by "going too far" is meant "arousing too much fear," then the answer suggested by the research evidence is that it's not likely that a persuader can arouse too much fear. As discussed above, increases in reported fear are reliably associated with increases in persuasive effectiveness. The evidence to date gives scant support for the idea that persuasive effectiveness diminishes at high levels of aroused fear (for general reviews of the relevant work, see Boster & Mongeau, 1984; Sutton, 1982; for a useful critical discussion of the curvilinear hypothesis, see Leventhal, 1970, pp. 160-168).

But if by "going too far" in using fear appeals is meant using message material that is too graphic, too explicit, too gory, then perhaps a persuader *can* overdo it. But notice that this is entirely consistent with the finding that increases in aroused fear are associated with increases in effectiveness. After all, a message that is too gruesome may end up not arousing very much fear (perhaps because the audience doesn't pay much attention). In such a case, the persuader might need to *tone down* the message material in order to *increase* the level of fear produced (and thereby increase the message's effectiveness). Remember: The research evidence indicates that it's not easy to manipulate the level of fear experienced by receivers; we should not be surprised if it should turn out that in some cases a great deal of graphic content doesn't arouse all that much fear.

EXPLAINING FEAR APPEAL EFFECTS   Why is greater aroused fear associated with greater persuasive effectiveness? That is, what is the explanation for this observed effect? At present there are a number of competing explanations, and it's not clear which is the best (for discussion of some of the alternatives, see Beck & Frankel, 1981; Leventhal, Safer, & Panagis, 1983; Sutton, 1982).

But it should not be assumed that an explanation of these findings must give a central causal role to fear (that is, to the emotional reaction evoked by the message); instead, an explanation might emphasize cognitive reactions to the message. For instance, a given message might induce more fear and anxiety in receivers—but it may also lead receivers to believe that the fearful consequences are more severe (more harmful, more noxious, more disadvantageous) than they had previously believed. And it might be that the real force at work behind the message's effectiveness is the change in those beliefs, not the arousal of fear. Fear might arise as a *by-product* of the persuasion process ("I now believe the consequences of poor dental hygiene are much more severe than I did before, and this makes me more anxious about this than I was before"), but the cognitive changes—not the emotional ones—might actually explain the message's effectiveness. From this point of view, then, greater aroused fear will be associated with greater persuasive effectiveness — not because greater fear causes greater effectiveness, but because both fear and effectiveness are caused by the same underlying factor (namely, the cognitive reactions to the message).

In fact, one central way in which the various fear appeal explanations differ is precisely whether the key factor at work is taken to be an emotional reaction (fear) or a cognitive reaction (e.g., a judgment of the seriousness of the problem being depicted). Some theoretical accounts emphasize the causal role of fear (e.g., Hovland, Janis, & Kelley, 1953), whereas others place much greater emphasis on cognitive processes (e.g., Beck & Frankel, 1981; Rogers, 1975; Sutton, 1982). In sorting out these various explanations, one important general question is whether fear has some effect on persuasive outcomes over and above the effects of accompanying cognitive changes. If fear does have such effects, then presumably a good explanation will need to give some causal role to the emotional reaction; if fear does not have such effects, then a purely cognitive explanation might be sufficient. On this issue, research evidence is only beginning to be acquired (see, e.g., Sutton & Eiser, 1984; Sutton & Hallett, 1988, 1989), and hence conclusions are probably premature. In any case, one ought not assume that the observed covariation between induced fear and effectiveness means that induced fear causes effectiveness.

EXAMPLES VERSUS STATISTICAL SUMMARIES

The research question here concerns the relative persuasive impact of two different forms of information: the example (or case history), which describes some event or object in detail, and the statistical summary, which provides a numerical summary of a large number of events or objects (in the form of averages, percentages, and so on). What is often compared, then, is information about the experience of one (or a very few) individuals and equivalent, summarized statistical information about the experiences of many individuals.

For example, Koballa (1986) provided preservice high school teachers with favorable information about a particular type of science curriculum. In one condition the information was presented as the report of a single teacher who had used the curriculum; the teacher discussed how much more interested the students were, how much more the students learned, and how student performance improved in related areas (such as math and writing). In the other condition, the very same points were made (about students being more interested, learning more, improving in related areas), but the information was presented as a statistical summary of the findings of a dozen or so different uses of this curriculum.

Koballa (1986) found that the case study report was much more persuasive than the statistical summary report (even though, obviously, the statistical summary was based on the experience of many different teachers, not just one). And indeed this is the general finding in this line of research: Examples or case histories are more influential than statistical information or other data summaries (for a review, see S. E. Taylor & Thompson, 1982).

One demonstration of this effect can be seen in variations in inquiries at breast cancer detection clinics. For a number of years there has been widespread dissemination of the relevant statistical information concerning the importance of early detection, the cure rates associated with early detection, the desirability of regular mammograms, and the like. However (as noticed by Nisbett, Borgida, Crandall, & Reed, 1976), it takes the occurrence of well-publicized individual cases demonstrating the importance of early detection (e.g., Betty Ford, Nancy Reagan) for inquiries at detection clinics to be increased substantially.

Examples seem to have particularly robust effects on persuasion. Bridges and Reinard (1974), for instance, found that, of various types of argument, argument by example proved the least vulnerable to subsequent refutation; Koballa (1986) found that attitudes induced by case history information were less susceptible to decay (were more stable over time) than were attitudes induced by data summary information; and it seems that case history information can have a substantial impact even if receivers are told that the example is an atypical, unrepresentative one (Hamill, Wilson, & Nisbett, 1980). In short, the example seems to be a particularly powerful form of information, especially when compared to information in statistical summary form.

SEQUENTIAL-REQUEST STRATEGIES

Substantial research has been conducted concerning the effectiveness of two sequential-request influence strategies, the "foot-in-the-door" strategy and the "door-in-the-face" strategy. In each strategy, the request that the communicator is primarily interested in (commonly termed the "critical" request) is preceded by some other request; the question of interest is how compliance with the critical request is affected by the presence of the preceding request.

FOOT-IN-THE-DOOR

THE STRATEGY The foot-in-the-door (FITD) strategy consists of initially making a small request of the receiver, which the receiver grants, and then making the (larger) critical request. The hope is that, having gotten one's foot in the door, the second (critical) request will be looked on more favorably by the receiver. The question is, then: Will receivers be more likely to grant a second request if they've already granted an initial, smaller request? And if so, under what conditions will this occur?

THE RESEARCH EVIDENCE The research evidence suggests that this FITD strategy will, at least sometimes, enhance compliance with the second (critical) request. For example, in Freedman and Fraser's (1966, Experiment 2) FITD condition, homeowners were initially approached by a member of the "Community Committee for Traffic Safety" or the "Keep California Beautiful Committee." The requester either asked that the receiver display a very small sign in his or her front window ("Be a safe driver" or "Keep California beautiful") or asked that the receiver sign a petition supporting appropriate legislation (legislation that would promote either safer driving or keeping California beautiful). Two weeks later, a different requester (from "Citizens for Safe Driving") approached the receiver, asking if the receiver would be willing to have a large, unattractive "Drive Carefully" sign installed in the front yard for a week. In the control condition, where receivers heard only the large request, fewer than 20% agreed to put the sign in the yard. But in the FITD conditions, over 55% agreed.[6] This effect was obtained no matter whether the same topic area was involved in the two requests (safe driving or beautification), and no matter whether the same sort of action was involved (displaying a sign or signing a petition): Even receivers who initially signed the "keep California beautiful" petition were more likely to agree to display the large safe-driving yard sign. As these results suggest, the FITD strategy can have very powerful effects.

However, subsequent research has identified several factors that influence just how effective the strategy is (i.e., the size of the effect that the strategy has). First, if the FITD strategy is to be successful, there must be no obvious external justification for complying with the initial request (Dillard, Hunter, & Burgoon, 1984). For example, if receivers are given some financial reward in exchange for complying with the first request, then the FITD strategy isn't very successful. Second, the larger the first request (presuming it is agreed to by the receiver), the more successful the FITD strategy (Fern, Monroe, & Avila, 1986). Third, the FITD strategy appears to be more successful if the receiver actually performs the action requested in the initial request, as opposed to simply agreeing to perform the action (Beaman, Cole, Preston, Klentz, & Steblay, 1983; Fern et al., 1986; compare Dillard et al., 1984). Fourth, the FITD strategy is more effective when the requests come from institutions that might provide some benefit to the community at large (e.g., civic or environmental groups) as opposed to profit-seeking organizations (Dillard et al., 1984).

Notably, there are several factors that apparently do *not* affect the success of the FITD strategy. The time interval between the two requests appears not to make a difference (Beaman et al., 1983; Dillard et al., 1984; Fern et al., 1986); for example, Cann, Sherman, and Elkes (1975) obtained equivalent FITD effects with no delay between the two requests and with a delay of 7-10 days. Similarly, it doesn't appear to matter whether the same person makes the two requests (Fern et al., 1986).

EXPLAINING FITD EFFECTS The most popular explanation for FITD effects is based on self-perception processes (for a brief statement, see Freedman & Fraser, 1966; a more extensive discussion is provided by DeJong, 1979). Briefly, the explanation is that compliance with the first request leads receivers to make inferences about themselves; in particular, initial compliance is taken to enhance receivers' conceptions of their helpfulness, cooperativeness, and the like. These enhanced self-perceptions, in turn, are thought to increase the probability that the second request will be agreed to.

In some ways, the observed limiting conditions (on the FITD effect) are quite consistent with this self-perception explanation. For example, the presence of an external justification for initial compliance obviously undermines enhancement of the relevant self-perceptions: If you're being paid money in exchange for agreeing to the initial request, it's more difficult to conclude that you're especially cooperative and helpful just because you agreed. Similarly, the larger the request initially agreed to, the more one's self-perceptions of helpfulness and cooperativeness should be enhanced ("If I'm going along with this big request, without any obvious external justification, then I must really be a pretty nice person, the sort of person who does this sort of thing"). And it's easier to think of oneself as being a helpful, socially minded person when one agrees to requests from civic groups as opposed to marketing firms, or when one actually performs the requested action (as opposed to merely saying one will perform it).

The lack of an effect for the time interval between the requests is sometimes seen as inconsistent with the self-perception explanation (e.g., Dillard et al., 1984). Unfortunately, it's not clear what predictions the self-perception explanation would make here. On the one hand, it might be expected that with increasing delay between the two requests, the FITD effect would weaken (because there would be many opportunities, during the time interval, for other events to undermine the self-attributions of helpfulness and cooperativeness). On the other hand, it might be predicted that with increasing delay between the requests, the FITD effect would become stronger (because it takes time for receivers to reflect on the causes of their behavior, and so to make the required self-attributions). Or (as Beaman et al., 1983, note) it might be that both these processes are at work, and cancel each other out.

To be sure, there are some loose ends for the self-perception explanation of FITD effects. For instance, there have been relatively few efforts at directly assessing receivers' self-perceptions of helpfulness (e.g., Rittle, 1981). At present, however, the self-perception explanation appears to be the best available.

DOOR-IN-THE-FACE

THE STRATEGY The door-in-the-face (DITF) strategy turns the foot-in-the-door strategy on its head. The DITF strategy consists of initially making a large request, which the receiver turns down, and then making the smaller critical request. The question is whether initially having the door closed in one's face will enhance the receiver's compliance with the second request.

THE RESEARCH EVIDENCE The research indicates that the DITF strategy can, at least sometimes, enhance compliance. That is, receivers will be more likely to agree to a second, smaller request if they have initially turned down a larger first request. For example, in a study reported by Cialdini et al. (1975, Experiment 1), individuals on campus sidewalks were approached by a student who indicated he or she represented the county youth counseling program. In the DITF condition, persons were initially asked to volunteer to spend two hours a week for a minimum of two years as an unpaid counselor at a local juvenile detention center; no one agreed to this request. The requester then asked if the person would volunteer to chaperone a group of juveniles from the detention center on a two-hour trip to the zoo. Among those in the control condition, who received only the second request, only 17% agreed to chaperone the zoo trip; but among those in the DITF condition, who initially turned down the large request, 50% agreed.

But the research evidence also suggests that there are some limiting conditions on the success of the DITF strategy. One important limiting condition is the size of the time interval between the requests. For the DITF strategy to be effective, there must be little or no delay between the two requests (Dillard et al., 1984; Fern et al., 1986). For instance, Cann et al. (1975) found that the DITF strategy enhanced compliance when the second request immediately followed the first, but not when there was a delay of 7-10 days between the requests. There are also indications that FITD effects are larger when the same requester makes the two requests (Fern et al., 1986) and when the requests come from community organizations (e.g., civic groups) rather than from for-profit institutions (Dillard et al., 1984).

EXPLAINING DITF EFFECTS   There have been two popular explanations of DITF effects. One is the "reciprocal concessions" explanation (see Cialdini et al., 1975). This explanation proposes that the successive requests make the situation appear to be one involving bargaining or negotiation — that is, a situation in which a concession by one side is supposed to be reciprocated by the other. Hence, this explanation suggests, when the smaller second request is made, it represents a concession by the requester — and the receiver thus reciprocates ("Okay, you gave in a little bit by making a smaller request, so I'll concede and go along with it").

A second explanation is the "perceptual contrast" explanation (see R. L. Miller, Seligman, Clark, & Bush, 1976). This explanation suggests that the second request is perceived as smaller than it actually is, because of the "perceptual contrast" with the larger first request. That is, the second request doesn't seem so burdensome as it otherwise might, because it's compared to the larger initial request.

Notice that, for a persuader, it can be important which of these explanations is superior, because the two explanations suggest different points of emphasis in employing the DITF strategy (as pointed out by R. L. Miller et al., 1976). If the reciprocal concessions explanation is true, the important element in the DITF strategy is the making of a concession. Thus this explanation implies that when using the DITF strategy, the requester should make a point of emphasizing the requester's concession ("Gee, I really wanted to get people for that counseling program. Well, there's this other project — less important to me — that I'm also trying to get volunteers for. Would you be willing to chaperone . . . "); this places emphasis on what is presumably the key element, namely, the making of a concession. But if the perceptual contrast explanation is true, the key process at work is the contrast between the sizes of the two requests. Hence this explanation suggests that a requester using the DITF strategy should emphasize the smaller size (lessened burden or cost to the receiver) of the second request ("Well, look, if you can't afford to volunteer that much time, how about this other project that will take a lot less of your time?").

Unhappily, neither explanation seems entirely satisfactory. For starters, neither explanation can easily accommodate the observed limiting conditions on DITF effects. From a reciprocal concessions point of view, the time interval between requests presumably shouldn't make much difference, but in fact it does; a perceptual contrast explanation would presumably predict that whether the same person makes the requests wouldn't matter, but in fact it does matter; and neither explanation easily encompasses the finding that DITF effects seem largely limited to requests for civic, humanitarian, or similar nonprofit causes. Moreover, what additional evidence there is (beyond the matter of these limiting conditions) doesn't decisively indicate the superiority of either explanation (see, e.g., Cantrill & Seibold, 1986; Goldman, McVeigh, & Richterkessing, 1984).

In short, at present it's not clear just what might explain DITF effects. It's possible that some variation of a reciprocal concessions model or a perceptual contrast model will be successful, or it may be that some other explanatory approach will be needed. But thus far there are not many attractive alternatives (for some possibilities, see Goldman et al., 1984; Tybout, Sternthal, & Calder, 1983).

CONCLUSION

Researchers have investigated a number of different message characteristics as possible influences on persuasive effectiveness. These message factors are quite varied, ranging from the details of internal message organization (climax versus anticlimax argument order) to the sequencing of multiple messages (as in FITD and DITF strategies). Indeed, more message characteristics have been studied than could be discussed here, but those described are the more prominent lines of research.

NOTES

1. Some recent research hints that perhaps receiver involvement may influence the size of the advantage enjoyed by explicit-conclusion messages, such that under conditions of high involvement that advantage disappears (Kardes, 1988) or is even reversed (Sawyer, 1988, pp. 172-174), but there is not yet enough evidence to underwrite confident generalizations.

2. It may be that in social-influence settings such as psychotherapy, or perhaps in very unusual persuasive-message circumstances (see, e.g., Linder & Worchel, 1970), there can be some benefit to letting the audience draw the conclusion, but in ordinary persuasive-message contexts the evidence indicates that such benefits are, as a rule, unlikely to obtain.

3. In fact, the literature on message sidedness has operationalized "two-sided" messages in a variety of ways. In each case, the "two-sided" message both includes supporting arguments and

discusses opposing arguments, but there's substantial variation in just *how* the opposing arguments are discussed. Some studies include the opposing arguments in the message, but don't attempt to undermine or overturn those arguments in any way; they simply *mention* the opposing arguments. Other investigations include the opposing arguments, and do not attack them directly, but present the opposing considerations in such a way as to emphasize that those arguments are, on balance, outweighed by the persuader's constructive arguments; that is, the message attempts to *minimize* the opposing considerations, without directly refuting or attacking them. And still other studies discuss the opposing arguments by undertaking to *refute* them explicitly; it is only this last group that is here reviewed as studies of "two-sided" messages. Notably, the classic and oft-cited message sidedness studies are not uniform in their manipulation of sidedness. For example, Jones and Brehm (1970) and Paulson (1954) have support-plus-mention "two-sided" messages; Etgar and Goodwin (1982) and Hass and Linder (1972) use support-plus-minimize "two-sided" messages; and Chu (1967) and Insko (1962) have support-plus-refute "two-sided" messages. Though a thorough examination of the relevant literature remains to be done, it appears that as one moves from support-plus-refute to support-plus-minimize to support-plus-mention messages, the persuasive advantage (of support-plus messages over support-only messages) becomes progressively smaller, even to the point of disappearing entirely. One exception to this pattern may involve consumer product advertising, where support-plus-mention messages appear to be (at least sometimes) capable of retaining the advantage over support-only messages (see, e.g., Alpert & Golden, 1982 – also reported in Golden & Alpert, 1987; Chebat & Picard, 1985).

4. Notice that these two considerations – how many people give, and how much each gives – make independent contributions to what is surely the most appropriate "bottom line" for such solicitations: average donation per contact. If technique A gets 80% of those contacted to donate with an average of 45 cents per donor, and technique B gets only 30% compliance but obtains an average of $1.20 per donor, each technique will yield $36.00 per 100 contacts (36 cents per contact). Note, too, that if the percentage donating is increased, and the average donation per donor drops, the organization can still come out ahead: Technique C might boost the percentage donating to 50% (an increase over technique B) while reducing the average donation per donor to $1.00 (a decrease from technique B), yielding an average of 50 cents per contact – unquestionably a net improvement.

5. This research question is perhaps more difficult to investigate than one might initially suppose. For instance, if a given experiment uses a single message, and so generates varying degrees of discrepancy by using receivers whose initial positions vary, then the degree of discrepancy is confounded with initial position, creating difficulties in interpreting the experimental results. For a nice (if brief) discussion of subtleties here, see Insko (1967, pp. 69-70).

6. Actually, the reported compliance rate in the FITD conditions (55%) does not represent a "pure" FITD effect, since all participants who heard the first request (regardless of whether they agreed to it) were included as FITD subjects in Freedman and Fraser's (1966) data analysis. But this way of analyzing the data makes it unlikely that any dispositional cooperativeness (any general willingness to accede to requests) among FITD subjects (as opposed to control subjects) explains the higher critical-request compliance rate in FITD conditions, since dispositionally cooperative persons were presumably randomly distributed across FITD and control conditions.

10

Receiver and Context Factors

THIS CHAPTER REVIEWS research concerning the effects that various recipient characteristics and contextual factors have on persuasive outcomes. The discussion is organized around three main topics: enduring receiver characteristics (such as sex and personality traits), induced receiver factors (induced states that may influence persuasive effects), and contextual factors.

ENDURING RECEIVER CHARACTERISTICS

GENERAL PERSUASIBILITY

"Persuasibility" refers to how easily someone is persuaded in general (that is, across topics, sources, settings, other receiver characteristics, and so on). It

is an open question whether there is in fact some general persuasibility difference among persons (whether there really is some such persuasibility factor,
something that makes some people simply more easily persuaded than others,
in general).

There is some indirect evidence indicating the existence of such persuasibility differences. This evidence comes from research designs in which persons
receive multiple persuasive messages on various topics; with such designs, one
can look for evidence of intraindividual consistency in the amount of attitude
change displayed. This evidence does suggest that there may indeed be some
differences between persons in how easily they're persuaded, but these differences appear to be rather small (Janis & Field, 1956; McGuire, 1969, p. 242).
That is to say, even if one person is (in general) more easily persuaded than
another, the difference in ease of persuasion is not very great.

No procedure has yet been devised that permits advance identification of
persuasible persons, and there is no good evidence available about the correlates of general persuasibility. The research concerning a general persuasibility
factor thus remains tantalizingly incomplete.

SEX DIFFERENCES IN PERSUASIBILITY

One much-studied question has been whether there are any reliable sex-
related differences in persuasibility: Are women more easily persuaded than
men (in general, or in specifiable circumstances), or men more easily persuaded
than women? [1]

Several reviewers have concluded that the research literature does contain
dependable sex differences in persuasibility, with females being more easily
persuaded than males (see the reviews of Becker, 1986; Eagly & Carli, 1981).
However, these differences are quite small. Expressed as a correlation coefficient, the association between sex and persuasibility has been estimated as in
the neighborhood of .05 to .08 (Becker, 1986, p. 195; Eagly & Carli, 1981, p. 7).
Moreover, it is not clear whether this observed difference actually reflects some
genuinely general sex difference in persuasibility, as opposed to being a spuri-
ous difference attributable to other factors. Two other factors have been suggested as possibly underlying the observed persuasibility differences.

One such factor concerns the nature of the topics of the persuasive messages
used in research. Broadly put, the suggestion is that topics are sex linked in
important ways; for some topics, males may be more knowledgeable and
interested, whereas for other topics females will be more knowledgeable and
interested. And (this line of reasoning runs) persons will be more likely to let
themselves be influenced on topics about which they are not especially knowledgeable or interested. Hence the apparent greater persuasibility of females
might reflect nothing more than a preponderance of male-related topics among
studies of persuasive messages.

The research evidence does not give very strong support to this explanation.
Eagly and Carli (1981) did find that sex differences in topic interest and
knowledgeability were indeed associated with sex differences in persuasibility:

The topics with greater male interest and knowledgeability were the topics on which females tended to show greater persuasibility (and vice versa). But Eagly and Carli also found that male-oriented topics were *not* overrepresented in the research literature (if anything, the persuasion topics tended to be slightly more interesting to females than to males). Since masculine topics have not predominated in the research literature, the observed sex differences in persuasibility are unlikely to be attributable to a generalized use of male-biased contents.

The other factor that has been proposed as potentially underlying the observed sex difference in persuasibility is the sex of the investigator. Eagly and Carli (1981) report evidence suggesting that whereas female researchers tend to find no sex differences in persuasibility, male researchers tend to find women to be more easily persuaded than men. This evidence is not uncontroversial, and other analyses of the research literature seem not to have confirmed this influence of the researcher's sex on the findings (see Becker, 1986). Perhaps the most that can be said at present is that the investigator's sex may explain the observed sex differences in persuasibility, but the issue is very much an open one.[2]

If the observed sex differences in persuasibility are not largely attributable to artifacts such as the nature of the topic or the sex of the researcher, then some other explanation needs to be found (for a careful discussion of some possibilities, see Eagly & Wood, 1985). Perhaps the most obvious explanations are ones focusing on cultural training and socialization. For example, it might be that whereas males are typically encouraged to be analytical, critical, independent thinkers, females may commonly be encouraged to preserve social harmony and express support for others — thereby creating conditions that foster the appearance of sex differences in persuasibility. If this is the relevant explanation, then to the extent that the relevant socialization patterns change, so will apparent sex differences in persuasibility.

In any event, the size of the sex differences in persuasibility that have been observed offers little comfort to persuaders. Even if entirely nonspurious, the general difference in persuasibility between an all-female audience and an all-male audience will be very small indeed.

PERSONALITY TRAITS

Quite a number of different receiver personality characteristics have been examined for their possible effects on persuasive outcomes. Unhappily, there are few dependable generalizations to be drawn. In part this reflects the fact that the research evidence (on any single personality trait) is commonly not extensive; but more fundamentally it reflects the complex and confused state of the research findings that have been reported.

A representative example may be found in the research concerning the relationship between the receiver's degree of self-esteem (the degree to which the person thinks highly of him- or herself) and persuasive effects. Some investigators have found a positive relationship: As the receiver's self-esteem increases, so does the amount of attitude change displayed following persuasive messages (e.g., Nisbett & Gordon, 1967). Others have reported a negative relationship: With greater self-esteem comes less attitude change (e.g., Janis, 1955). Still others have reported that the greatest attitude change is obtained at moderate levels of self-esteem, suggesting an inverted-U-shaped relationship between self-esteem and attitude change (e.g., D. F. Cox & Bauer, 1964). And yet other investigators have found that attitude change is *minimized* at moderate levels of self-esteem, indicative of a U-shaped relationship (e.g., Silverman, 1964). Obviously, the relationship between receiver self-esteem and persuasion is not a simple or straightforward one (for discussions, see Romer, 1981; Skolnick & Heslin, 1971).

Few other personality traits have been so extensively studied (for their relationships to persuasive effects) as self-esteem, but what research exists does not promise any simpler patterns of effect (for an indication of the complexities, see Eagly, 1981; McGuire, 1968). On the whole, the research concerning the relationship of recipient personality characteristics and persuasive effects is characterized by complex and (apparently) inconsistent results.

Why are the findings concerning personality traits and attitude change so confused? Any number of alternative explanations are possible (including the idea that the notion of stable, global personality traits is somehow defective; see Mischel, 1973), but one intriguing suggestion is that offered by McGuire (1968). Briefly put, the central idea is that any personality trait will simultaneously have effects that enhance persuasion and effects that inhibit persuasion.[3] For example, more intelligent receivers will likely be better able to understand persuasive messages (which presumably should enhance persuasion), but they should also be better able to see weaknesses in the message, to think up counterarguments, and so on (which should inhibit persuasion). Persons low in self-esteem may be less confident in their own judgments (and so be susceptible to persuasion), but low self-esteem can be associated with diminished interest in outside events, making it less likely that messages will be closely attended to (which can mean reduced persuasion). And so on, for other personality traits.

If both persuasion-enhancing and persuasion-inhibiting effects are associated with a given personality characteristic, the question becomes how these simultaneous competing effects balance out in any given case. In one circumstance, the persuasion-enhancing effects may predominate; in another, the persuasion-inhibiting effects may be stronger. And all sorts of *other* factors may influence which effects predominate. Consider, for example, the potential role of message comprehensibility in mediating the effects of receiver intelligence. If the previous analysis of the effect of receiver intelligence is sound, one should expect that with easy-to-understand messages (where high intelligence isn't needed to understand the communication), the persuasion-inhibiting effects of intelligence should predominate, making high-intelligence receivers relatively difficult to persuade. Conversely, with messages that were difficult to counterargue (thereby minimizing the persuasion-inhibiting effects of receiver intelligence), one might expect high-intelligence receivers to be relatively easy to persuade.

As presumably is obvious, this makes for an awfully complicated conception of how recipient personality traits are related to persuasive outcomes. But then, a complicated picture is what the research evidence suggests. The merits of McGuire's (1968) particular analysis aside, the research concerning the persuasive effects of receiver personality characteristics certainly indicates that simple models are unlikely to be satisfactory.

INDUCED RECEIVER FACTORS

The preceding section discussed the role played in persuasion by natural, enduring receiver states or characteristics (such as personality traits); in this section, induced recipient characteristics are considered.

INDUCING RESISTANCE TO PERSUASION: INOCULATION THEORY AND RESEARCH

It's all very well to persuade someone to one's point of view — but once persuaded, the person may be exposed to counterpersuasion, that is, persuasive messages advocating some other viewpoint. How can receivers be made *resistant* to such persuasive efforts? An illuminating line of research concerning this question has been stimulated by William McGuire's "inoculation theory," which focuses on the processes by which persons can be made resistant to persuasion (for a general review, see McGuire, 1964).

THE BIOLOGICAL METAPHOR The fundamental ideas of inoculation theory can be usefully displayed through a biological metaphor. Consider the question: How can one make persons resistant to a disease virus (such as smallpox)? One possibility is what might be called "supportive" treatments — making sure persons get adequate rest, a good diet, sufficient exercise, necessary vitamin supplements, and so on. The hope, obviously, is that this treatment will make it less likely that the disease will be contracted. But another approach to inducing resistance is inoculation (as with smallpox vaccines). An inoculation treatment consists of exposing persons to small doses of the disease virus. The dose is small (so as not to bring on the disease itself), but is sufficient to stimulate the body's defenses so that any later massive attack (e.g., a smallpox epidemic) can be defeated.

These ideas probably already suggest the fundamental approach that inoculation theory suggests for inducing resistance to persuasion (namely, giving people inoculatory treatments involving exposure to "small doses" of the opposing view). But the biological metaphor can be elaborated yet another step, by noticing the sorts of circumstances that commonly make people especially susceptible to disease viruses. Perhaps understandably, infants who are raised in a germ-free environment (an "aseptic" environment) are often quite vulnerable when exposed to large doses of a disease virus. After all, their bodies haven't had the opportunities to develop resistance to the various viruses (having never been exposed to them). So (to consider the parallel) the *beliefs* that should be especially susceptible to attack are beliefs that have been maintained in a "germ-free" *social* environment, not exposed to attack; these beliefs McGuire terms "cultural truisms."

CULTURAL TRUISMS A cultural truism is a belief that (within a given culture, a given social environment) is rarely, if ever, attacked. These beliefs are "truisms" in one's culture — everybody holds these beliefs, and no one criticizes them. Examples of cultural truisms that have been used in research include "It's a good idea to brush after every meal if possible," "Mental illness is not contagious," and "The effects of penicillin have been, almost without exception, beneficial to humanity."

Inoculation theory suggests that cultural truisms are especially vulnerable to attack, for two reasons. First, the believer has no practice in defending the belief. The belief is never attacked, so there's never any opportunity (or need) to defend the belief. Second, the believer is unmotivated to undertake the necessary practice (since the belief is regarded as unassailable). Consider, for example: One can easily imagine that in idle moments one might mentally rehearse arguments that support one's position on a controversial issue such as abortion, but it's unlikely that one would ever mentally rehearse arguments in favor of brushing after every meal. That is, there's no motivation to rehearse arguments in defense of cultural truisms.

Consistent with this analysis, cultural truisms have been found to indeed be especially susceptible to persuasive attack (e.g., McGuire & Papageorgis, 1961). Plausible-sounding attacking messages proved to reduce receivers' beliefs in the truisms substantially. How, then, might one go about making truisms more resistant to persuasion?

SUPPORTIVE AND REFUTATIONAL TREATMENTS McGuire and his associates have compared the effectiveness of various different treatments for inducing resistance to persuasion on cultural truisms. In the general design of this research, receivers are initially exposed to some treatment designed to induce resistance to persuasion on a given truism. Receivers are then exposed to an attack on that truism, to see whether the treatment has made them resistant to the attack.[4]

Following the biological metaphor, two different treatments have been studied. The "supportive" treatment consists of giving receivers arguments supporting the truism; this treatment parallels the "supportive" medical treatment (good diet, adequate rest, and so on). The "refutational" treatment consists of first showing receivers a weak attack on the truism, and then refuting that attack; this refutational treatment is intended as a conceptual parallel to medical inoculation (in that receivers are exposed to weak doses of the opposing view, which are then overturned). For example, on the toothbrushing truism, the refutational treatment might consist of showing receivers a poorly argued message suggesting that excessive brushing will wear away the enamel on one's teeth, and then giving receivers a refutation of that attack.

As one might expect from the biological metaphor, the refutational treatment is much more effective in conferring resistance to persuasion than is the supportive treatment (see, e.g., McGuire, 1961b; McGuire & Papageorgis, 1961). Inoculating the receiver through exposure to refutation of antitruism arguments is a better way of inducing resistance to subsequent antitruism messages than is simply providing protruism (supportive) material.

It is important to note that the refutational treatment does not simply immunize receivers against the one particular antitruism argument that receivers see refuted. Rather, the refutational treatment confers resistance to *other* antitruism arguments as well (e.g., Papageorgis & McGuire, 1961). That is, the refutational treatment doesn't simply convince receivers that "this one antitruism argument is defective," but actually stimulates the receivers' defenses against other antitruism arguments.

The combination of supportive and refutational treatments has also been studied for its effectiveness in conferring resistance. The combination is in fact more effective in inducing resistance than is the refutational treatment alone (e.g., McGuire, 1961a). Why does adding a supportive treatment to the refutational treatment enhance resistance (given that the supportive treatment by itself has little effect on resistance)? By itself, the supportive material may seem to be useless (who needs arguments and evidence in favor of toothbrushing?) — but since the refutational treatment shows the truism to be potentially vulnerable to attack, there's a natural motivation for the bolstering material provided by the supportive treatment.

NONTRUISMS The inoculation research discussed thus far has concerned inducing resistance to persuasion for cultural truisms. Truisms are a theoretically important focus of inoculation research (because the theory suggests that truisms will be especially vulnerable to attack), but it's obviously important to consider the induction of resistance to persuasion for nontruisms (i.e., more controversial beliefs and attitudes).

The research here is rather less systematic than the work on cultural truisms, but several general conclusions seem warranted. First, supportive treatments and refutational treatments are more nearly equally effective in conferring resistance to persuasion on nontruism topics (see, e.g., Adams & Beatty, 1977; M. Burgoon & Chase, 1973; Pryor & Steinfatt, 1978; Szybillo & Heslin, 1973). Because the issue is not a cultural truism, receivers probably don't assume that their belief is invulnerable; hence the refutational treatment is not needed to underscore the usefulness of the supporting materials.

As with cultural truisms, however, the resistance produced by refutational treatments does appear to generalize to novel arguments (e.g., Pryor & Steinfatt, 1978; Szybillo & Heslin, 1973). That is, the refutational treatment not only makes persons resistant to the particular argument that's refuted, but makes them resistant to additional new arguments as well.

Finally, for nontruisms the combination of supportive and refutational treatments appears to confer greater resistance than do supportive treatments alone (for a review, see Jackson & Allen, 1987), just as for truisms. The combination of supportive and refutational treatments, it will be noticed, amounts to creating a "two-sided" persuasive message (as discussed in Chapter 9), that is, a message that gives both arguments supporting the communicator's view and refutations of counterarguments. Thus this last finding can be expressed in terms of message sidedness: Two-sided messages are more effective at conferring resistance to persuasion than are one-sided messages.

WARNING

Inoculation theory suggests that one's awareness that a belief is vulnerable to attack may be sufficient to lead one to bolster one's defense of that belief (and thereby reduce the effectiveness of attacks on it). A natural corollary of this line of thought is that simply warning a person of an impending counterattitudinal message will decrease the effectiveness of the attack once it's presented. And a fair amount of research has been conducted concerning the effects of such warning on resistance to persuasion on nontruism topics.[5]

Two different sorts of warnings have been studied (see Papageorgis, 1968). One type simply warns receivers that they will hear a message intended to persuade them, without providing any information about the topic of the message, the viewpoint to be advocated, and so on; this sort of warning, then, merely warns of the *persuasive intent* of an impending communication. The other type of warning consists of telling receivers of the *topic and position* of the message (that is, the issue the message is about, and the position the message advocates on that issue).

Both sorts of warnings can confer resistance to persuasion, and appear to do so by stimulating counterarguing in the audience (e.g., Petty & Cacioppo, 1977, 1979a). Topic-position warnings, of course, make it possible for receivers to engage in anticipatory counterarguing (that is, counterarguing before the message is received), because the audience knows the issue to be discussed and the view to be advocated. Thus as the time interval between the topic-position warning and the onset of the message increases, there is more opportunity for the audience to engage in counterarguing (and hence greater resistance can be built up). Freedman and Sears (1965b), for example, showed high school students messages arguing that teenagers should not be allowed to drive. Students received a warning of the topic and position of the impending message, but the time interval between the warning and the message varied (no delay between warning and message, a 2-minute delay, or a 10-minute delay). With increasing delay, there was increasing resistance to persuasion.

Persuasive-intent warnings, of course, do not permit anticipatory counterarguing, since the receivers don't know what the message will be about; consequently, variations in the time interval between a persuasive-intent warning and the communication have little effect on resistance (e.g., Hass & Grady, 1975). But persuasive-intent warnings do apparently stimulate greater counterarguing during the persuasive message, thereby reducing receivers' susceptibility to persuasion.

Notably, warnings create greater resistance to persuasion on topics that are personally relevant (highly involving) to the receivers than on topics not so relevant (e.g., Petty & Cacioppo, 1979a). Apparently, the degree to which one's defenses are aroused by being warned of an impending counterattitudinal communication will vary depending on one's degree of involvement with the issue.[6]

CONTEXTUAL FACTORS

This section discusses research concerning the influence that features of the persuasion context have on persuasive outcomes. Three general areas of research are discussed: primacy-recency effects (which involve successive communications on an issue), communication medium effects, and the persistence of persuasive effect.

PRIMACY-RECENCY

Some persuasion contexts involve a debatelike setting, in which two communicators defend different sides of a given issue. A simplified debate setting — in which each communicator gives only one message (with no rebuttals or follow-up speeches) — has been the focus of substantial research aimed at addressing the question of whether there is any advantage associated with either speaking position. Is there some intrinsic advantage to being the first of two speakers in such a setting, or to being the second? If the first communication enjoys some advantage over the second, a "primacy effect" is said to occur; if the second position is more advantageous, a "recency effect" is said to occur.

The research evidence quite clearly shows that there is no *general* advantage to either position (for more detailed reviews of this work, see Insko, 1967, pp. 49-61; Rosnow, 1966; Rosnow & Robinson, 1967). There is, that is to say, no general "primacy effect" or "recency effect." In varying circumstances, both primacy effects (e.g., Lund, 1925) and recency effects (e.g., Cromwell, 1950) have been obtained. There is some indication, however, that primacy effects are more likely to be found with interesting, controversial, and familiar topics; conversely, recency effects are more common with topics that are relatively uninteresting, noncontroversial, or unfamiliar (see Rosnow, 1966). However, the obtained primacy-recency differences appear to be relatively small. Thus, for example, any effects of variation in speaking position can be erased if one side's arguments are stronger: The side with the stronger arguments has the advantage, whichever speaking position it occupies (Rosnow & Robinson, 1967, p. 102).

Thus persuaders who find themselves in the position of choosing whether to speak first or second might well base the choice on the topic of discussion: More controversial, interesting, and familiar topics would appear to recommend choosing the first position. But whatever advantage this confers is very slight indeed — and so persuaders who lose the coin flip need not fear that all is lost.

MEDIUM

Persuasion can be pursued through any number of different communication media: face-to-face interaction, telephone interaction, television, radio, printed/written communication (books, magazines, newspapers, brochures, and such mass media — but also personal letters), and so on. It might very well be supposed that variations in the medium of communication might affect persuasive outcomes.

But there has been surprisingly little research concerning the effects of variations in communication medium on persuasive outcomes. In part, surely, this reflects the difficulties in undertaking useful research in this area.

UNTANGLING THE EFFECTS OF COMMUNICATION MEDIUM A central barrier to understanding medium effects is the very nature of communication media. The common communication media represent bundles of different attributes, and it is not easy to untangle just which attribute (or set of attributes) is responsible for any observed differences between media.

Imagine, for example, that a company finds that its advertising messages are more effective on television than on radio. What might account for this differential effectiveness? One possibility is that television is an audiovisual medium, whereas radio is an audio-only medium, and it might be that this difference in information channel (audio plus visual information, as opposed to only audio information) made the company's advertising more effective. But it's also possible that the television advertising and the radio advertising reached different audiences (i.e., one group of people saw the television advertising, and a different group heard the radio advertising). It could be that this company's target audience was more likely to watch the television programs on which the company's advertising appeared than it was to hear the radio programs on which the company advertised — and so the television advertising was superior.

Or imagine that a business finds that face-to-face communication is more effective (in selling the company's products) than radio advertising. How might this difference be explained? Once again, there is a difference in the information channels involved (audiovisual information in face-to-face interaction, audio only in radio), and that might account for the difference in effectiveness. But radio advertising is a noninteractive medium, whereas face-to-face interaction is an interactive one. Interactive communication media make it possible for participants to adjust moment by moment to the other's reactions, whereas noninteractive media do not. It's possible that the face-to-face messages were more successful than the radio advertising because the company's communicators were skilled at using the interactive resources provided by face-to-face conversation.

It should be plain that unraveling the bases of differences among communication media will involve sorting out a large number of factors that distinguish media (different channels of information, different audiences reached, differences between interactive and noninteractive media, and so on). A great deal of careful work will be required before we can hope to obtain a very clear picture of just how and why variations in communication media influence persuasive outcomes (for a related line of analysis, see Chaffee & Mutz, 1988).

WRITTEN VERSUS AUDIOTAPED VERSUS VIDEOTAPED MESSAGES There is, however, some informative initial research concerning a simplified set of comparisons among written, audiotaped, and videotaped messages. This research does not find there to be any general advantage associated with one or another of these forms; it's not true that messages are typically more persuasive in (say) videotaped form than in written form.

However, there is heightened salience and impact of source characteristics as one moves from written to audiotaped to videotaped messages. For example, credibility variations and likability variations make more of a difference in videotaped messages than they do in written messages (Andreoli & Worchel, 1978; Chaiken & Eagly, 1983; Worchel, Andreoli, & Eason, 1975). As the communicator becomes more "present," more "real," the communicator's characteristics play a greater role in influencing persuasive outcomes.

There is also some evidence that more complex persuasive messages (more complex with respect to sentence structure and vocabulary) are more effective in written form than in audiotaped or videotaped forms (Chaiken & Eagly, 1976). But it is important not to misinterpret the nature of this finding. In this research, those who received written messages could reread portions of the text; but the audiotaped and videotaped messages were played for the receivers (i.e., the receivers did not control the pace of presentation). One might well suppose that the crucial difference here is the degree to which the receiver controls the pace of presentation of the message. When reading text on a page in front of them, receivers can reread material that was initially difficult to grasp; receivers hearing or watching a tape controlled by someone else don't have that option.

Notice, thus, that this differential effectiveness of complex material in written, audiotaped, or videotaped formats is probably *not* due to the information channel involved (audiovisual, audio only, visual only). Indeed, a clever experimenter could probably show that, with the appropriate experimental arrangement, complex messages are *less* effective in written form than in audiotaped or videotaped form. To produce this finding, one might compare written messages where the pace of presentation was not controlled by the receiver (as when written text scrolls across a computer screen, and the receiver can't control the scrolling) with audiotaped or videotaped messages where the receiver did control the presentation (where the receiver, for example, controls the cassette player, and can rewind and so review portions of the message at will).

In any event, this surely underscores the difficulties involved in studying the effects that communication medium has on persuasive outcomes. We are still some distance from having a very satisfactory general understanding of such effects — in good measure because we are some way from having a good grasp of the character of communication media themselves.

THE PERSISTENCE OF PERSUASION

Persuaders are sometimes interested in obtaining success at some specific point of decision or action — getting the voter to cast a favorable ballot on election day, getting a person to make a charitable donation on the spot, and so on. And sometimes there is no specific point in the future at which the persuader desires success; product advertising, for example, hopes to be successful at some indeterminate time in the future (whenever the receiver has occasion to be in a position to make the relevant purchase). In either case, questions of the *persistence* of persuasive effects arise. For instance, depending on how long-lasting a message's effects are, a persuader may be able to forgo subsequent persuasive efforts (e.g., an advertiser may not need to purchase so much advertising time).

THE DECAY OF MESSAGE EFFECTS There is a well-established empirical generalization concerning the persistence of persuasion: On the whole, persuasive effects tend to dissipate over time (for a general review, see Cook & Flay, 1978). Perhaps they decay slowly, perhaps rapidly, and sometimes they may not decay at all. But generally speaking, one should expect that persuasive effects will evaporate as time passes. Old habits and attitudes can return, competing persuasive messages can be received, and hence the impact of a given persuasive effort is likely to diminish over time.

There is, thus, a corresponding rule of thumb concerning the temporal placement of persuasive messages: For maximum effect, persuasive messages should be delivered temporally close to the point of decision or action. So, for example, in political campaigns, candidates should (everything else being equal) buy more advertising time for the period just before election day than for time slots well in advance of the election.[7]

INFLUENCES ON THE DECAY OF EFFECTS Of course, not all persuasive effects will decay at the same rate. Unfortunately, at present there is not a good deal of dependable information about just what factors influence the rate of decay. A tentative list of possible influences might include the following three factors. (a) The number of supporting points (arguments, instances, and the like) in the message appears to affect persistence; with more supporting points, there is greater persistence of persuasive effect (Leventhal & Niles, 1965; compare Calder, Insko, & Yandell, 1974). (b) Communicator credibility (at least in the case of counterattitudinal messages) may influence persistence; there is some evidence that higher credibility is associated with greater persistence (see Cook & Flay, 1978, p. 13). (c) Finally, the receiver's involvement in the issue may play a role; greater involvement may be associated with greater persistence (Cook & Flay, 1978, p. 47). There is scattered evidence concerning other possible influences on persistence—for example, Chaiken and Eagly (1983) found marginally greater persistence with written messages than with audiotaped or videotaped messages—but dependable generalizations seem elusive at present.

There is, however, an emerging attractive general conception of the persistence of persuasion, derived from perspectives such as the elaboration likelihood model (discussed in Chapter 6). The central idea is that persuasion is more persistent when obtained through relatively central routes than when obtained through relatively peripheral routes. When the receiver is led to focus more on the message and to engage in message-relevant thinking, to elaborate message contents, and the like (as when the issue is highly involving), obtained persuasive effects will be more likely to persist. (For more detailed discussion of this approach to understanding the persistence of persuasive effects, see Petty & Cacioppo, 1986a, pp. 173-184.)

THE SLEEPER EFFECT: INCREASES IN EFFECTIVENESS OVER TIME? Will persuasive effects *always* decay over time, or is it possible that some might *increase* with the passage of time? No small effort has been devoted to tracking down the possibility of a "sleeper effect" in persuasion (defined as an increase in persuasive effectiveness over time).[8] There has often been substantial confusion over this question, in good measure because of definitional problems.[9]

However, it is now clear that it *is* possible, under very specific and unusual laboratory circumstances, to find a sleeper effect—to find an increase in the persuasive effectiveness of a message over time. The relevant conditions are these: Receivers notice the important arguments in a message (for example, by being told to underline them); following the message, receivers are given a strong "discounting cue" indicating that the information in the message (or the message's conclusion) is false; and receivers rate the trustworthiness of the source before completing postcommunication attitude assessments (Pratkanis & Greenwald, 1985; Pratkanis, Greenwald, Leippe, & Baumgardner, 1988). Indeed, as Pratkanis and Greenwald (1985) point out, this observed sleeper effect isn't really an exception to the general idea of decay of effect. The relevant experimental situation has two sources of effect—the message and the discounting cue—with differential rates of decay. The discounting cue has a strong initial (negative) effect that dissipates more quickly than does the (positive) effect of the message, thus yielding the observed sleeper effect.

But there is no practical circumstance in which enhanced effectiveness over time is likely to be obtained dependably. (Perhaps more carefully put: There is not yet any good research evidence available that identifies such a circumstance.) Hence the ability of researchers to produce sleeper effects in peculiar laboratory situations should not lead persuaders to abandon the principle that, as a rule, decay of persuasive effects is to be expected.

CONCLUSION

As the research reviewed in this chapter makes plain, persuasive effects are often dependent on receiver characteristics (both enduring and induced) and contextual factors. Though researchers are well along in studying various receiver attributes as influences on persuasion, only a few features of the communication context have gotten much research attention thus far.

NOTES

1. To be clear: The question of interest here concerns not sex differences in influenceability generally, but in persuasibility specifically. Various sorts of influence situations have been examined for possible sex differences in influenceability; it is studies of influence through persuasive messages (as opposed to, say, studies of conformity to group pressure) that are of interest here. The distinction is important, because it appears that the size and nature of sex differences in influenceability varies depending upon the kind of influence situation studied (see, e.g., Eagly & Carli, 1981).

2. Becker's (1986) best fitting model for explaining sex differences in persuasibility did not include the sex of the researcher. However, there are several relevant differences between Becker's (1986) procedure and that of Eagly and Carli (1981). For example, Becker used a more defensible

means of investigating the relationship between authorship and study outcome than did Eagly and Carli (see Becker, 1986, p. 189). But Becker's analysis apparently used percentage of male authors as the predictor of outcome, whereas Eagly and Carli used a dichotomized authorship variable as the predictor (because, they indicated, percentage of male authors was a highly skewed variable). Moreover, Becker's report does not give details on just what her analysis revealed concerning the relevant association (see Becker, 1986, p. 196). The upshot of all this is that one cannot very confidently offer conclusions on this issue.

3. In fact, McGuire's (1968) view is much more detailed and complicated than this. Specifically, McGuire identifies two mediators (reception of the message and yielding to the message) that can be differentially affected by a personality trait. But even if the details of McGuire's two-factor view are not entirely well supported (for a useful discussion, see Eagly, 1981, pp. 183-185), one may nevertheless appreciate the general idea that a personality characteristic can have simultaneous competing effects on persuasive outcomes.

4. Only portions of McGuire's work are discussed here; for example, only passive (not active) treatments are considered. For more detailed reviews, see Insko (1967, pp. 296-329); C. A. Kiesler, Collins, and Miller (1969, pp. 133-142); and McGuire (1964). One matter of some delicacy that is not treated here concerns the definition of "resistance to persuasion," which poses more difficulties than one might initially suppose; a useful (if incomplete) discussion of this topic has been provided by Pryor and Steinfatt (1978, pp. 220-221).

5. For cultural truisms, it appears that warning is even less successful than supportive treatments in conferring resistance to persuasion (e.g., McGuire & Papageorgis, 1962).

6. A number of complexities in the research literature on warning are passed over here. For example, on low-involvement topics, topic-position warnings seem initially to produce opinion change *toward* the to-be-advocated position (e.g., J. Cooper & Jones, 1970), but this change is apparently merely a strategic anticipatory shift toward neutrality (which disappears when the expectation of the impending message is canceled). For further discussion, see Cialdini and Petty (1981).

7. Actually, this generalization (about political campaigns) is too simple, because the time of action (voting) can be very different from the time of decision. Indeed, studies of political campaigns have found it useful to distinguish "early deciders" (who make up their minds well before election day) from "late deciders" (see, e.g., Nimmo, 1970, pp. 24-25). Obviously, for early deciders, advertising that appears just before election day may well come too late to influence their decisions (it may influence whether they implement their decisions, i.e., whether they actually vote, but that's another matter). So if, in a given election campaign, there are a great many late deciders, then a last-minute advertising blitz may well be an appropriate strategy; but as the proportion of early deciders increases (as it well might for, say, high-visibility elections that spark considerable voter interest), then last-minute advertising becomes a less attractive persuasive approach.

8. This is what is sometimes called an "absolute sleeper effect," as distinct from a "relative sleeper effect," which involves only different rates of decay over time under different conditions. For discussion, see Gruder et al. (1978).

9. For a time, the phrase "sleeper effect" was used to refer specifically to "a delayed increase in the persuasive impact of a communication *from a source low in credibility*" (Gillig & Greenwald, 1974, p. 132; emphasis added). Thus defined, there's no reason to think a genuine sleeper effect has ever been demonstrated (Gillig & Greenwald, 1974). But the application of the phrase has shifted with time, such that now it is common to define a sleeper effect as "a delayed increase in the impact of a persuasive message" (Pratkanis et al., 1988, p. 203) — never mind whether the source is low in credibility. Thus the narrower question of whether low-credibility sources specifically might exhibit delayed effectiveness has been replaced by the broader question of delayed effectiveness generally.

11

Attitudes and Actions: The Attitude-Behavior Relationship

THERE IS AN ASSUMPTION common to much of the research considered in this book, and indeed an assumption embedded in the very concept of attitude: the assumption that attitudes are important determinants of action, that attitudes somehow have substantial effects on conduct. Indeed, the assumption of an intimate connection between attitude and action underlies the identification of persuasion with attitude change (e.g., Beisecker & Parson, 1972).

But obviously this assumption deserves closer inspection, particularly by students of persuasion. After all, knowledge of how to change attitudes through persuasive communication would presumably be of little profit if changes in attitude were not somehow connected to changes in behavior.

As it turns out, the attitude-behavior relationship is not a simple one. Instead, a number of factors have been identified that influence just how closely attitudes and behaviors will be related; this chapter discusses the research bearing on several of these factors. From the point of view of a persuader, these factors are important to consider, because they will affect the degree to which attitude change will be reflected in behavioral change; that is to say, in the end these factors can influence persuasive success, just as much as source characteristics or message features do.

THE SPECTER OF
LOW ATTITUDE-BEHAVIOR CORRELATIONS

Are attitudes related to actions? Do persons' attitudes influence their overt conduct? For a time, it appeared as though these questions were to be answered in the negative. That is, it appeared as though assessments of persons' attitudes bore little relation to those persons' behavior. In a well-known 1969 article reviewing research to that date, Wicker concluded that "taken as a whole, these studies suggest that it is considerably more likely that attitudes will be unrelated or only slightly related to overt behaviors than that attitudes will be closely related to actions" (p. 65). In the research Wicker reviewed, the correlations between attitudinal and behavioral measures were rarely larger than .30, and quite commonly were near zero.

An example of such findings is provided by Wicker's (1971) subsequent study of the consistency of religious attitudes and behaviors among a group of church members. Various measures of religious attitudes were used, but these correlated (on the average) only .27 with the frequency of attending church services, .16 with the amount of money contributed to the church, and .11 with holding positions of responsibility in the church (p. 23, Table 1). In short, attitude and actions appeared to be hardly related at all.

The possibility that attitudes and actions are essentially unrelated spawned no little worry. After all, if attitudes and actions are largely uncorrelated, then knowing a person's attitude is little guide to predicting that person's actions — and changing that person's attitude won't necessarily produce changes in that person's conduct.

There were a number of substantive responses to the (apparent) problem of low correlations between assessments of attitude and assessments of behavior. It was suggested, for example, that the problem lay in the need for improved attitude assessment techniques (e.g., G. R. Miller, 1967; Tittle & Hill, 1967), or in the use of attitude as a mentalistic concept (e.g., DeFleur & Westie, 1963; compare Alexander, 1966; Weissberg, 1964). These (and many other) suggestions have for the most part proved to be unhelpful (for collections of papers on the attitude-behavior relationship, see Cushman & McPhee, 1980; A. E. Liska, 1975; Thomas, 1971).

But one general approach to the problem that has yielded useful insights has been the attempt to identify factors moderating the attitude-behavior relationship — that is, factors influencing attitude-behavior consistency. In effect, this approach aims at answering the question, If attitudes and behaviors are not *always* so directly associated as once was presumed, then when will they be strongly related? An answer to this question obviously suggests circumstances under which persuasive messages that induce attitude change will also be likely to engender behavioral change.

The next section reviews research aimed at identifying such moderating factors. As will be seen, this work suggests that the earlier pessimistic conclusions about the attitude-behavior relationship are overdrawn; but it also suggests that the attitude-behavior relationship is far from simple.

THE SEARCH FOR MODERATING FACTORS

Under what conditions will attitudes be strongly correlated with behaviors? A large number of different possible moderating factors have been suggested. In fact, Wicker's (1969) review paper concludes with a long list of possible "other variables" that might influence the attitude-behavior relationship. Plausible suggestions have included the existence of other attitudes, the intensity of the attitude, the confidence with which the attitude is held, the centrality of the attitude, the presence or absence of other persons in the situation, the social norms surrounding the situation, the salience of the attitude, personality variables, the occurrence of unforeseen extraneous events, and the amount of information the person has about the attitude object.

Regrettably, however, the research evidence concerning most of these possibilities has been rather sparse. Much of the work consists of relatively isolated investigations of a given possible moderating variable; as a result, the evidence bearing on the role played by any single factor tends to be scant. There are, however, several particular factors for which relatively more evidence exists; these are reviewed in the following sections.

THE PERCEIVED RELEVANCE OF ATTITUDE TO BEHAVIOR

Whether individuals will act consistently with their attitudes surely depends in part on whether they perceive their attitude as relevant to their behavioral choices. For example, investors who see their antiapartheid attitudes as relevant to their investment decisions will, obviously, make different investments than if they thought those attitudes were not relevant to those actions. In general, "it may be only when individuals explicitly define their attitudes as relevant and appropriate guides to action that they can be expected to turn to their general attitudinal orientations for guidance in making their behavioral choices" (Snyder, 1982, p. 114). That is to say, one factor influencing attitude-behavior consistency is the perceived relevance of the attitude to the action.

But this immediately suggests a possible strategy for influencing attitude-behavior consistency, namely, influencing the perceived relevance of an attitude to a behavior. To the extent that a persuader can induce a receiver to see a given attitude as relevant to a given behavioral choice, the receiver will be more likely to act in a way consistent with that attitude.

As an example: In a study by Snyder and Kendzierski (1982), participants read arguments in an affirmative action court case and rendered individual verdicts in the case. Participants' affirmative action attitudes had been obtained earlier, permitting assessment of attitude-behavior consistency (consistency between their general attitudes toward affirmative action and their judicial decisions in the particular case). The critical experimental manipulation consisted of giving some participants instructions from the judge emphasizing that the case dealt with a contemporary issue (affirmative action) and thus that decisions in this case could have implications not only for the involved parties, but also for affirmative action programs generally (because of the precedent-setting nature of judicial decisions). The judge did not explicitly tell these participants to make their decisions based on their attitudes, but the instructions did offer the opportunity for participants to see the relevance of their attitudes for their decision. The participants who did not receive the instructions exhibited little consistency between their affirmative action attitudes and their decisions (the correlation was .08). But those who received the instructions suggesting the relevance of those attitudes to their decision displayed substantially greater consistency (the correlation was .51).

What this should suggest to persuaders is the desirability (and sometimes necessity) of focusing receivers' attention on the *relevance* of attitudes to action. Indeed, often the task the persuader faces is not that of inducing attitude change, because the desired attitude is already present; instead, the job is that of getting the audience to make the connection between attitude and action, getting the audience to see the relevance of the attitude to the behavioral choice. For example, it's not enough to convince people to have favorable attitudes toward good health (indeed, they probably already have such attitudes); what's needed is to convince people that such attitudes are relevant to the behavioral choices they make concerning exercise, diet, medical care, and the like. Similarly, persons who express positive attitudes toward energy conservation and environmental protection may need to be induced to translate those attitudes into specific activities — to see that those attitudes are relevant to (for example) the choice of a thermostat setting. (These and other examples are nicely discussed by Snyder, 1982.)

It is possible to create conditions under which the perceived relevance of an attitude to an action is heightened (as Snyder & Kendzierski, 1982, did in their affirmative action case study). A second study by Snyder and Kendzierski (1982) offers another illustration. Participants in this investigation were undergraduates known to have attitudes favorable to psychological research; they were asked to volunteer to participate in extra sessions of a psychology experiment. This was an especially demanding request (involving returning on two different days, at inconvenient times, and so on). Indeed, in the control condition — despite the favorable attitudes — only 25% of the participants volunteered.

Before responding to the request, each participant overheard a conversation between two other students (confederates of the experimenters) who were discussing the request. The first student said, "I don't know if I should volunteer or if I shouldn't volunteer. What do you think?" In the control condition, the second student responded, "Beats me — it's up to you." In the experimental condition, the response was, "Well, I guess that whether you do or whether you don't is really a question of how worthwhile you think experiments are." This response was designed to underscore for participants the relevance of their attitudes toward psychological research as guides for decision making in this situation. Whereas only 25% of the control-condition participants agreed to volunteer (i.e., acted consistently with their favorable attitudes), 60% of the experimental-condition participants agreed. That is, there was much greater attitude-behavior consistency among those who heard the conversation suggesting the relevance of their attitudes for their actions.

Obviously, then, when the relevance of an attitude for an action is heightened, behavior is much more likely to be consistent with that attitude — and hence one means of influencing behavior is the strategy of emphasizing the relevance of an existing attitude to a current behavioral choice. There is not yet much systematic research evidence concerning this strategy (see Borgida & Campbell, 1982; Shepherd, 1985; Snyder, 1982; Snyder & Kendzierski, 1982), and so little can be said about limits to the strategy's effectiveness, variations on the strategy, and so on. But as a final bit of testimony to the potential effectiveness of the strategy, consider the thousands of encyclopedias — and, more recently, home computers — purchased by parents who were prodded by sellers asking, "You want your children to have a good education, don't you? To have an edge in school? To get ahead in life?" Fundamentally, these questions attempt to get the parent to see the relevance of existing attitudes to the behavioral decision at hand, and reflect the seller's understanding that the perceived relevance of an attitude to an action can indeed be influenced.

FORMATIVE BASIS OF ATTITUDE

A second factor influencing attitude-behavior consistency is the manner in which the attitude was formed or shaped. A number of studies have shown that attitudes based on direct behavioral experience with the attitude object are more predictive of later behavior toward the object than are attitudes based on indirect experience (for a review, see Fazio & Zanna, 1981).

For example, during a housing shortage at Cornell University — well publicized on campus — some freshmen had to be placed in temporary quarters (thus giving them firsthand experience with the problem); other freshmen were given permanent dormitory rooms (and so knew of the problem less directly). The two groups had equally negative attitudes regarding the housing crisis, but the strength of the attitude-behavior relationship differed. Those whose attitudes were formed on the basis of direct experience exhibited greater consistency between their attitudes and behaviors aimed at alleviating the crisis than did students whose attitudes were based on indirect experience (Regan & Fazio, 1977).

A similar effect was observed by R. E. Smith and Swinyard (1983), who compared attitude-behavior consistency for product attitudes that were based either on a trial experience with a sample of the product (direct experience) or on exposure to advertising messages about the product (indirect experience). Much greater attitude-behavior consistency was observed for those persons who had had the opportunity to try the product than for those who had merely read about it. For example, purchase of the product was more highly correlated with attitudes based on product trial (.57) than with attitudes based on product advertising (.18).

It is important to note that this finding does *not* mean that product-trial influence strategies (providing free samples through the mail, offering grocery store shoppers a taste of a new food product, and the like) will be more effective (in producing sales) than advertising strategies. Attitudes based on direct experience are more predictive of behavior than attitudes based on indirect experience — which means (for example) that persons with *negative* product attitudes based on direct experience are less likely to purchase the product than persons with similarly negative attitudes based on indirect experience. The shopper who has a negative attitude toward a food product because of having read about it might still come to purchase the product; the shopper whose negative attitude is based on tasting the product, however, is much less likely to do so.

In short, attitudes induced by direct experience will be more strongly correlated with behavior than attitudes induced by indirect experience. Two persons may have equally positive attitudes, but may differ in whether they act consistently with those attitudes, because of underlying differences in the ways in which the attitudes were formed.

SELF-MONITORING

The personality variable of "self-monitoring" (Snyder, 1974, 1979) has been found to influence the consistency of attitudes and actions. Low self-monitors guide their behavioral choices primarily on the basis of internal states and personal dispositions; they are inclined to agree with statements such as "My behavior is usually an expression of my true inner feelings, attitudes, and beliefs" and "I would not change my opinions (or the way I do things) in order to please someone else or win their favor." High self-monitors are more inclined to base their behavioral choices on cues to situational appropriateness; they tend to agree with statements such as "I am not always the person I appear to be" and "When I am uncertain how to act in social situations, I look to the behavior of others for cues."

In a number of different studies, low self-monitors have exhibited greater attitude-behavior consistency than high self-monitors. The differences are typically not large and sometimes fail to achieve statistical significance, but the effect is quite consistent (e.g., Ajzen, Timko, & White, 1982; Shepherd, 1985; Snyder & Kendzierski, 1982; Snyder & Swann, 1976; Kline, 1987; Zanna, Olson, & Fazio, 1980; for a general discussion, see Snyder, 1982).

The implication of this finding is that persuasion through attitude change should be more effective in producing behavioral change for some people (low self-monitors) than for others (high self-monitors). Persons whose conduct is generally more influenced by situational specifics than by attitudinal dispositions will naturally be less inclined to act consistently with their attitudes.

CORRESPONDENCE BETWEEN
ATTITUDINAL AND BEHAVIORAL MEASURES

Whether one finds consistency between an attitudinal measure and a behavioral measure depends in part on the nature of the measures involved. There is good evidence indicating that substantial attitude-behavior correlations will be obtained only when the attitudinal measure and the behavioral measure correspond in specificity (Ajzen & Fishbein, 1977). For example, a general attitude will probably not be especially strongly correlated with a highly specific behavior. A general attitude measure corresponds to a general behavioral measure, not to a specific one, and hence general attitude measures should be correlated more strongly with general behavioral measures than with specific ones.

For example, general attitudes toward religion might or might not be especially strongly correlated with performance of the particular act of (say) reading books about religious philosophy. But attitudes toward religion may well be strongly correlated with a general religious-behavior index — that is, an index based on *multiple* behaviors (whether the person reads books about religious philosophy, attends religious services, listens to religious programs on radio or television, owns records of religious music, donates money to religious institutions, consults clergy about personal problems, and so on). No one of these behaviors may be very strongly predicted by religious attitude, but the overall pattern of these behaviors might well be associated with religious attitude. That is, even though the correlation of the general attitude with any one of these behaviors might be relatively small, the correlation of the general attitude with a multiple-act behavioral measure may be much greater.

Several investigations have yielded information about the relative strength of the attitude-behavior association when single-act and multiple-act behavioral measures are used; the number of acts used in the multiple-act measure varied, as did the topics under investigation. In these studies, the average correlation between general attitude and any single-act index of behavior was roughly .30; by contrast, the average correlation between general attitude and a multiple-act behavioral measure was approximately .65 (Babrow & O'Keefe, 1984; Fishbein & Ajzen, 1974; D. J. O'Keefe & Shepherd, 1982; Sjoberg, 1982; Weigel & Newman, 1976).

In a way, this may seem like a technical or methodological point concerning the nature of the behavioral measure. For instance, one might think of this finding as nothing more than an elementary example of a fundamental idea in measurement validity: More good items mean a better measuring instrument (e.g., the larger the number of good questions on an examination, the better the exam as an index of learning); thus with a multiple-item behavioral index, one has a better measure of the relevant behavior. Indeed, the higher attitude-behavior correlations that are obtained with multiple-act behavioral measures may be seen to be a straightforward consequence of the properties of the correlation coefficient (see Dawes & Smith, 1985, pp. 560-561).

But this overlooks the practical import of these results. These results underscore the folly of supposing that a single specific behavior will necessarily or
typically be strongly associated with a receiver's general attitude. Correspondingly, these findings should emphasize to persuaders the importance of carefully considering the focus of one's influence attempts.

For instance, if one hopes to encourage participation in a community recycling program, it might seem quite natural to construct persuasive messages
aimed at inducing favorable attitudes toward protecting the environment. But
in fact this is not likely to be a particularly efficient persuasive strategy. Even
if the messages succeed in producing positive environmental-protection attitudes, those general attitudes may not be especially strongly associated with the
specific behavior that is wanted (recycling program participation). A more
effective focus for persuasive efforts might well be specific attitudes toward
participation in the recycling program, rather than general environmental attitudes.[1]

In sum, attitudinal measures and behavioral measures are likely to be
strongly associated only when there is substantial *correspondence* between the
two measures. General attitudes will commonly be highly correlated only with
general (multiple-act) behavioral indices; specific attitudes will typically be
highly correlated only with correspondingly specific behavioral indices.

SUMMARY

As should be clear, research evidence is beginning to accumulate concerning
influences on attitude-behavior consistency. The four factors discussed here —
perceived attitude relevance, the manner of attitude formation, self-monitoring,
and the degree of correspondence between the attitudinal and behavioral measures — are not the only ones that have been studied, but one can be reasonably
confident in identifying these as important influences on the attitude-behavior
relationship.

TOWARD MODELS OF
THE ATTITUDE-BEHAVIOR RELATIONSHIP

As evidence continues to be gathered that specifies the factors influencing
the strength of the attitude-behavior relationship, the next task to be faced is that
of constructing some suitable general account of *why* all these various factors
influence attitude-behavior consistency. That is, instead of simply having a list
of specific moderating factors, a more abstract theoretical account is wanted —
one that explains how and why each moderating factor plays the role it does (see
Zanna & Fazio, 1982). Investigators are only beginning to explore such general
models of the attitude-behavior relationship, but Snyder's (1982) analysis can
serve as a useful example of what is to be sought.

Snyder (1982) identifies two general principles governing attitude-behavior
consistency. One is the "availability" principle, which holds that a person's
attitude must be *available* to the individual before that attitude can be used as a

guide to action. A person may have a given attitude, but that attitude might not be (so to speak) ready to hand, available to serve as a guide to behavioral choice: The press of situational demands may mean that persons have little cognitive energy to consider their attitudes, and hence little likelihood of acting consistently with them. Snyder's other principle is the "relevance" principle, which suggests that attitude-behavior consistency is likely only when the attitude is taken to be *relevant* to the action at hand. For any number of reasons, persons might not see a given attitude as a germane and appropriate guide to behavior; in such circumstances, substantial attitude-behavior consistency is unlikely.

These two general principles might be used to encompass the various moderating factors discussed previously. The greater attitude-behavior consistency that is obtained when the attitudinal and behavioral measures correspond might be explained as simply an instance of the relevance principle at work: For example, a specific attitude toward a given action is more likely to be deemed relevant to that action than is some general attitude. Similarly, self-monitoring differences in attitude-behavior consistency could be explained by the relevance principle: Low self-monitors are naturally more inclined (than high self-monitors) to see their attitudes as relevant guides to their behavioral decisions, and hence they exhibit greater consistency.[2] And, of course, perceived attitude relevance is a straightforward application of the relevance principle. Finally, the availability principle might be used to explain the effects of direct versus indirect experience. One effect of variations in the nature of attitude formation may be to create variations in how strongly the attitude is associated with the object, thereby making for variations in how available the attitude is as a guide to action; attitudes based on direct experience might be more readily available (more easily accessed) than attitudes based on indirect experience, thereby creating greater attitude-behavior consistency (e.g., Fazio, Chen, McDonel, & Sherman, 1982).

One cannot yet confidently say whether Snyder's particular analysis will prove to be successful, or whether alternative views might not be preferable (for a useful discussion, see Fazio, 1986); general models of the attitude-behavior relationship are in the early stages of development, and broad conclusions are surely premature. But models of this general sort obviously represent the next step in research on the attitude-behavior relationship.

CONCLUSION

As should be apparent, the earlier pessimistic assessments of the strength of the attitude-behavior relationship have given way to a more encouraging (but also more complicated) picture of the relationship. To be sure, one cannot justifiably assume that attitude-action consistency will always be found, nor that attitudes are the only significant influences on conduct — and consequently persuaders ought not assume that attitude change will unproblematically ensure behavioral change. At the same time, however, deeper examinations of the attitude-behavior relationship have revealed that moderate to high attitude-behavior consistency can indeed be obtained under appropriate conditions; and for persuaders these findings reaffirm the potential behavioral benefits of a focus on attitude change as central to persuasive effects.

NOTES

1. This point is sometimes denigrated, with a reaction of the following sort: "Of *course* people's evaluation of specific behaviors will be related to their performance of those specific behaviors. What's really interesting and important is the matter of how and when *general* attitudes are related to specific behaviors" (for some reactions along these lines, see Abelson, 1981; Dawes & Smith, 1985). Without denying the interest and importance of the question of how general attitudes are related to specific behaviors, one may nevertheless say that this reaction should not be allowed to overshadow the very concrete, pragmatic point here: Persuaders interested in influencing a given specific behavior will be well advised to attend to changing the correspondingly specific attitudes, rather than some general attitude whose influence on the behavior of interest is uncertain.

2. The availability principle could also be used to explain self-monitoring differences in attitude-behavior consistency: The attitudes of low self-monitors might commonly be more readily available than the attitudes of high self-monitors.

Part IV

Compliance-Gaining Message Production

The study of persuasion, as represented in the preceding chapters, is a remarkably lopsided enterprise. Substantial effort has been devoted to the questions of how and why persuasive messages have the effects they do, but it is only recently that much research attention has been given to questions of how and why persons produce the social influence efforts they do. Chapter 12 considers the current state of such research.

12

Compliance-Gaining Message Production

AS THE PRECEDING CHAPTERS have surely made clear, extensive theoretical and empirical attention has been devoted to the study of persuasion. But these research efforts have been focused on only one aspect of the process of persuasion, namely, persuasive *effects*. That is, the great bulk of persuasion theory and research has concerned the questions of how and why persuasive messages have the effects they do.

In recent years, however, investigators have given increasing attention to understanding the *production* of persuasive messages — that is, to understanding how and why persons produce the messages they do when seeking to influence others. This chapter discusses research in this developing area of work.

By way of general orientation, two preliminary observations will be helpful. First, the interests of researchers in this area have extended beyond persuasive messages or situations, as commonly conceived, and hence this area is usually referred to as the study of "compliance-gaining" (compliance-gaining messages or situations). For example, some researchers have studied what have been called "regulative" messages (occurring in "regulative" communication situations). Regulative communication situations are those in which the influencing agent enjoys some conventional normative authority over the behavior of the influence target; that is, one party has some conventionalized authority to control (regulate) the behavior of the other party, as in employer-employee relationships, parent-child relationships, and the like. Regulative communication situations differ from straightforward persuasive situations, in that (for instance) the regulative situation offers avenues of influence that are usually not available in exemplary persuasive situations. For instance, an employer might use simple orders or commands as a way of getting the employee to do what the employer wants. But both regulative and persuasive communication involve the communicator seeking the compliance of the target (trying to influence the target in some way), and hence they have commonly been grouped under the broad heading of compliance-gaining.

The second preliminary observation is that the study of compliance-gaining message production has thus far been rather much concerned with several general conceptual and methodological issues, and consequently the substantive yield from this research area is not all that one might hope. Of course, whenever new areas of inquiry are opened up, there is commonly a good deal of preliminary ground-clearing work to be done, methodological issues to be addressed, and so forth — and hence in some ways it is not surprising that such matters have preoccupied researchers in the area.

This chapter's discussion reflects these concerns, and is organized around a series of questions that a researcher will face in undertaking work in this area. The questions discussed here are not, of course, the only ones that an investigator will have to address, but they do serve to highlight central methodological issues that have arisen in the study of compliance-gaining messages. The questions to be considered are as follows:

(1) Which feature of compliance-gaining messages is to be studied?
(2) Should hypothetical scenarios or naturally occurring compliance-gaining situations be studied?
(3) Should compliance-gaining efforts be assessed through checklist questionnaires or through free-response data collection?

Following the discussion of these questions, a concluding section summarizes the current state of compliance-gaining message production research. (For other general discussions of this research area, see G. R. Miller, Boster, Roloff, & Seibold, 1987; Seibold, Cantrill, & Meyers, 1985.)

WHICH MESSAGE FEATURE?

In studying compliance-gaining message production, the substantive questions of interest have (naturally enough) concerned just what factors might influence the sorts of compliance-gaining messages that persons produce. For example, there have been studies of how the intimacy of the relationship between the interactants influences compliance-gaining, how the characteristics of the influencer (individual differences such as personality traits, sex, and the like) are related to compliance-gaining messages, and so on. There are, that is to say, a number of different possible independent variables that can be investigated as possible influences on compliance-gaining.

But there are also a number of different possible *facets* of compliance-gaining messages that might be studied—that is, a number of different possible dependent variables. As a result, one question that requires initial attention concerns which feature of compliance-gaining messages is to be studied. That is, which aspect or facet of compliance-gaining efforts is of interest?

THE IMPORTANCE OF
MESSAGE FEATURE SPECIFICATION

Compliance-gaining messages (like any other behavior) have a number of different features or aspects that can be studied. One might examine the politeness of compliance-gaining messages; one might examine whether the message invokes the communicator's expertise; one might examine the vividness of the language used, or the ratio between adjectives and nouns, or the degree to which the message is adapted to the particular audience addressed, or the extent to which social-normative and relational considerations are adduced as underwriting compliance, and on and on. There is no limit to the number of different aspects of compliance-gaining messages that might be studied.

Correspondingly, an investigator needs to be clear about just which aspect of compliance-gaining messages is under investigation. That is to say, well-formulated research questions about compliance-gaining message production require a specification of the message feature of interest. In the absence of such specification, the research question is inevitably malformed.

Consider, for instance, a research question such as "Does the intimacy of the relationship between the interactants influence the compliance-gaining messages produced?" Though at first glance this may seem like a perfectly sensible question, a closer look will reveal that it is not sufficiently carefully put. After all, compliance-gaining messages in intimate and nonintimate relationships might be very similar in some ways, but very different in others; relational intimacy thus might influence some aspects of compliance-gaining behavior, but be unrelated to other facets.[1] A better-formulated research question might be "Does relational intimacy influence the politeness of compliance-gaining messages?" or "Does relational intimacy influence the listener-adaptedness of compliance-gaining messages?" or "Does relational intimacy influence whether compliance-gaining messages invoke the communicator's expertise?" These questions specify which message feature is of interest, and hence permit meaningful research.

Similarly, "Do situational variations influence compliance-gaining messages?" and "Are compliance-gaining messages similar in persuasive and in regulative situations?" and "Is the communicator's sex related to differences in compliance-gaining messages?" and "Do persons high and low in dogmatism (or cognitive complexity or extroversion or self-monitoring) produce similar compliance-gaining messages?" are all badly formulated research questions. Each of these fails to specify the particular feature of compliance-gaining messages that is to be examined, and consequently does not permit a reasonable answer.

The general point, thus, is this: Well-framed research questions about compliance-gaining message production will be ones that specify the particular *feature* of compliance-gaining messages that is of interest.

ALTERNATIVE MESSAGE CLASSIFICATION SCHEMES

As it happens, quite a number of different facets of compliance-gaining messages have received at least some empirical attention. That is, researchers have described (classified) compliance-gaining messages in a variety of different ways. But one may usefully distinguish two broad and general sorts of classification schemes that have been employed: functional and strategic.

FUNCTIONAL CLASSIFICATION SCHEMES One general sort of message classification involves describing messages in terms of the apparent goals pursued by the message (i.e., the functions or jobs pursued through the message). The communicative ends attendant to compliance-gaining can be distinguished in any number of ways, but a common distinction is that between (broadly) task goals and nontask goals. The task goal represents the manifest communicative function of the circumstance (for compliance-gaining situations, the task goal is obtaining compliance). Nontask goals are additional goals that a communicator might or might not pursue (e.g., the goal of being polite).

For example, R. A. Clark and Delia (1979) distinguished three categories of communicative function: instrumental, interpersonal, and identity. Instrumental objectives are task goals, those related to the immediate problem that defines the task of the communication situation (e.g., obtaining compliance); interpersonal objectives concern the establishment or maintenance of the communicator's relationship with others; and identity objectives concern the communicator's presented image, the creation or maintenance of a particular self-identity. It is easy enough to see that one way in which compliance-gaining efforts can vary is the configuration of the objectives sought by the communicator: in some cases the instrumental objective might be the communicator's only goal, whereas in other cases both instrumental and interpersonal objectives might be in play.

As another example: Dillard, Segrin, and Harden's (1989) goal analysis is based on a distinction between "primary" (i.e., task or instrumental) and "secondary" goals, but differentiates five categories of secondary goals. These are identity goals (related to one's self-concept), interaction goals (concerning social appropriateness and impression management), personal resource goals (reflecting a concern for one's own welfare), relational resource goals (concerning, e.g., relationship maintenance), and arousal management goals (related to one's nervousness or apprehension). As Dillard et al.'s research suggests, different configurations of these goals can be associated with corresponding systematic variations in the character of compliance-gaining efforts.

STRATEGIC CLASSIFICATION SCHEMES Another general sort of message classification involves describing messages in terms of the strategies employed in the message — that is, the means of achieving the message's goals (particularly the central task goal).[2] Quite a number of different strategy classification systems have been offered, but a useful example is provided by Marwell and Schmitt (1967).

Marwell and Schmitt (1967) identified 16 compliance-gaining techniques: promise (if you comply, I'll reward you), threat (if you don't comply, I'll punish you), positive expertise (if you comply, you'll be rewarded because of "the nature of things"), negative expertise (if you don't comply, you'll be punished because of "the nature of things"), liking (I act friendly and helpful to get you in a good frame of mind so that you'll comply), pregiving (I reward you before requesting compliance), aversive stimulation (I continually punish you until you comply), debt (I indicate that you owe me compliance because of my previous favors to you), moral appeal (I indicate that you are immoral if you don't comply), positive self-feeling (I tell you you'll feel better about yourself if you comply), negative self-feeling (I tell you you'll feel worse about yourself if you don't comply), positive altercasting (I tell you that a person with good qualities would comply), negative altercasting (I tell you that only a person with bad qualities would not comply), altruism (I indicate that I need your compliance very badly), positive esteem (I indicate that people you value will think better of you if you comply), and negative esteem (I indicate that people you value will think worse of you if you don't comply).

Marwell and Schmitt's category system is not the only strategy classification system; quite a number of different strategic classification schemes have been suggested (e.g., Dillard & Fitzpatrick, 1985; Falbo, 1977; Kipnis, Schmidt, & Wilkinson, 1980; G. R. Miller, Boster, Roloff, & Seibold, 1977; Nelson, 1988; Rule, Bisanz, & Kohn, 1985; Schenck-Hamlin, Wiseman, & Georgacarakos, 1982). Most of these are, like Marwell and Schmitt's system, intended to be general compliance-gaining strategy schemes. For example, Buss, Gomes, Higgins, and Lauterbach (1987) have marked out six general means of manipulating others: charm (e.g., giving compliments), silent treatment (e.g., ignoring the target person), coercion (e.g., yelling or threatening), reason (e.g., pointing out the advantages of compliance), regression (pouting or sulking), and debasement (lowering oneself to obtain compliance).

Other strategic classification systems are intended to apply to specific sorts of compliance-gaining circumstances (e.g., Cooke & Kipnis, 1986). For instance, Arch (1979) offered a five-category scheme for describing influence strategies in personal selling: similarity influence (based on buyer-seller similarity), expert influence (based on the seller's skills or knowledge), company-reputation influence (based on the attributes of the seller's company), impression-management influence (based on the seller's presentation of self), and ingratiation influence (based on the seller's dispensing favors and flattery to the buyer). As another example, Kearney, Plax, Richmond, and McCroskey (1984) developed a list of 22 "behavior alteration techniques" that might be used by teachers to affect student classroom misconduct, including invoking the student's responsibility to the class and referring to the model behavior of one of the student's peers.

Given the existence of these various strategic classification systems — and particularly the existence of different putatively "general" typologies — the question naturally arises of the relationship among these. Unhappily, it appears that sometimes — too frequently — the assumption has been that there is some single "correct" general strategy classification scheme, some one best general list of strategies. At least some investigators appear to have been trying to locate the one correct (or best, or most nearly correct) compliance-gaining strategy list. That is, sometimes researchers have appeared to want to answer questions such as "How many basic compliance-gaining strategies are there, and what are they?" or "Is this list of strategies more valid than that list?" (For examples, see Cody, McLaughlin, & Jordan, 1980; G. R. Miller et al., 1977; Wiseman & Schenck-Hamlin, 1981.)

But this surely is a misguided venture, as perhaps might be brought out by examining a parallel case. Consider the question "How many types of books are there?" Obviously, the answer cannot be "two" or "five" or "sixteen" — or indeed any single number. How many types of books there are will depend on the dimension(s) used to classify books. If we classify books according to whether they are hardcover or paperback, we will have two categories (two types of books); if we classify books according to the languages in which they are written, then we will have many more categories (equal to the number of languages in which books have been written); if we classify books along some dimension such as fictional-nonfictional, then we will have some number of categories representing different points along the dimension (e.g., the *roman à clef* will presumably fall into some intermediate category), with the number of categories dependent upon the fineness of the distinctions we want to (and are able reliably to) draw; and so on.

But this then raises the question of which dimensions one *should* use for classifying books. The number and types of categories for distinguishing books will vary depending on the classification dimension(s) used, so which dimensions are the right ones? As is probably obvious, there is no one correct dimension (or set of dimensions) for classifying books; we classify books in different ways for different purposes. But the implication of this is that the question "How many types of books are there?" is not a meaningful one. We will have different numbers and types of categories for describing books, depending on the different dimensions of interest.

Similarly, "How many basic compliance-gaining strategies are there?" is not a meaningful question. How many types of compliance-gaining strategies there are will depend on the dimension(s) used to classify them. We might classify (describe) compliance-gaining strategies along any number of different dimensions — the power base implicitly referred to by the strategy (e.g., Wheeless, Barraclough, & Stewart, 1983), the listener-adaptedness of the strategy (e.g., R. A. Clark & Delia, 1976), the politeness of the strategy (e.g., Baxter, 1984), the directness of the strategy (e.g., Falbo & Peplau, 1980), the reward versus punishment orientation of the strategy (G. R. Miller & Parks, 1982), and so on.

But no one of these dimensions is the correct (or best, or most nearly correct) dimension for classifying compliance-gaining strategies, and no combination of dimensions is the correct or best combination. We may classify strategies differently — and so have very different strategy lists — depending on which facet of strategies is of interest. Thus there is no one correct (or best, or most nearly correct) list of compliance-gaining strategies — and hence "How many types of compliance-gaining strategies are there?" is not a meaningful question. Rather, there are many different possible "strategy" classifications, each potentially useful for capturing a different dimension of compliance-gaining strategies.[3]

OTHER CLASSIFICATION SCHEMES There are yet other possible classifications of compliance-gaining messages, classifications not straightforwardly characterizable as functional or strategic in character. For example, there have been several classification schemes specifically aimed at illuminating various aspects of "accounts." An account is a proffered explanation of negatively valued (e.g., untoward, inappropriate, illegal) conduct. M. B. Scott and Lyman (1968), for instance, distinguished two broad categories of accounts: justifications and excuses. A justification accepts responsibility for the act in question, but denies the negative evaluation (e.g., "I did it, but it wasn't wrong"). An excuse accepts the negative evaluation, but denies full responsibility for the act (e.g., "It was wrong, but I was forced to do it — I had no choice"). Schonbach (1980) suggested two additional categories: concessions (e.g., offers of restitution) and refusals (i.e., refusals to give an account). Others have suggested that accounts can be classified by the stability of the causes referred to (Folkes & Morgenstern, 1981) or by the degree to which the account aggravates the degree of tension present as against minimizing (defusing) such tension (Cody & McLaughlin, 1985, 1988).

Indeed, there is no limit to the number of different aspects of compliance-gaining messages that might be studied (and hence no limit to the number of possible classification schemes for such messages). Investigators have examined such diverse facets of social influence messages as syntactic homogeneity (Wallis, 1985), phonemic features (Sherblom & Reinsch, 1981), the "powerfulness" of the language used (O'Barr, 1982, pp. 61-75), the gender-related stereotypicality of the influence attempt (Carli, 1989), and so on.

SUMMARY There is a limitless number of possible classification schemes for compliance-gaining messages, and correspondingly a limitless number of dependent variables that might be considered in studies of compliance-gaining message production. A researcher might ask how a given independent variable—say, the relationship between the interactants—influences the goals pursued in compliance-gaining messages, or how it is related to the "powerfulness" of the language used in compliance-gaining messages, or how it affects the listener-adaptedness of the messages used, and on and on.

THE DANGERS OF
UNPRINCIPLED CLASSIFICATION SCHEMES

The importance of this initial methodological question—"Which message feature is to be studied?"—can perhaps be appreciated by noticing the consequences of failing to specify the message feature under investigation. As it happens, many commonly used compliance-gaining message classification systems do not have a clearly specified message feature (or set of features) that is the focus of analysis. Indeed, many message classification systems that have been used in the study of compliance-gaining message production amount to an unprincipled crazy quilt of categories, with little conceptual coherence. Recall, for example, Marwell and Schmitt's (1967) list of 16 compliance-gaining techniques: promise, threat, positive expertise, negative expertise, liking, pre-giving, aversive stimulation, debt, moral appeal, positive self-feeling, negative self-feeling, positive altercasting, negative altercasting, altruism, positive esteem, and negative esteem.

The consequence of having such a hodgepodge of categories is that research results using such a category system are very nearly uninterpretable. If, for instance, a researcher finds that (in a given circumstance) persons are more likely to choose "promise" than "moral appeal," it's not at all clear just what he or she has found—because it's not clear just what the underlying dimension is supposed to be that might distinguish these. Notice that if one wants to *explain* such a finding, one will presumably have recourse to some characterization of the difference(s) between "promise" and "moral appeal"—but because the category system is not constructed in a way that is designed to illuminate such differences, it is unhelpful in narrowing the range of possible explanations.[4]

This problem can perhaps be brought into relief by noticing that there are other, different crazy-quilt lists of compliance-gaining techniques. Recall, for example, that Buss et al. (1987) have suggested a list of six manipulation tactics (charm, silent treatment, coercion, reason, regression, and debasement). Suppose that a researcher finds that (in a given situation) persons are more likely to use charm than coercion. How is this result to be explained? And how might it be integrated with (say) a finding that in the same situation, persons are more likely to use Marwell and Schmitt's "promise" technique than their "moral appeal" technique? As should be apparent, a message classification system that lacks a clearly specified message feature (or set of features) yields research results that are, in the end, of diminished value. And, unhappily, such unprincipled ad hoc systems continue to proliferate (e.g., Rueda & Smith, 1983; T. E. Smith, 1988; Vecchio & Sussmann, 1989).

This isn't to say that one might not be able to *devise* some dimension that might underlie a given hodgepodge of categories. On the contrary, one *can* array such message categories along some dimension. In fact, one can array such categories in many different ways. But what is crucial is that the categories be arrayed in *some* fashion, and not treated as simply a crazy quilt.

Marwell and Schmitt's list of techniques again provides a convenient example. One could contrast Marwell and Schmitt's various categories on the basis of whether they represent relatively prosocial as opposed to antisocial techniques; or one might differentiate them by the degree to which they emphasize social-normative and relational considerations (as opposed to not emphasizing these) as a basis for compliance; or one might contrast them on the degree to which they emphasize the desirable outcomes of compliance as opposed to the undesirable outcomes of noncompliance; and so on. That is, there are any number of different ways in which these categories can be seen to reflect underlying dimensions of difference.[5]

What is important is that *some* such underlying dimension animate the design and analysis of research projects using this list of techniques. Meaningful interpretation of research results based on Marwell and Schmitt's categories — or any such set of unprincipled categories — depends upon treating the categories as something other than simply a crazy-quilt collection. The focus of attention must be the underlying dimension of interest (e.g., prosocial versus antisocial techniques), not the categories themselves.[6]

SUMMARY

There is a limitless number of possible classification schemes for compliance-gaining messages; any number of different aspects of compliance-gaining messages can be (and have been) studied. Correspondingly, an initial question faced in the study of compliance-gaining message production is this: Just which message feature is to be studied (just which way of classifying messages is to be used)? Well-formulated research questions about compliance-gaining message production require a specification of the message feature of interest — and when there is no such feature specified (as in unprincipled message classification schemes), research progress is unnecessarily impeded.

HYPOTHETICAL SCENARIOS OR NATURAL SETTINGS?

Given that a researcher has identified some particular message feature of interest, the question arises of how to obtain the compliance-gaining messages to be studied. If, for example, one wished to compare men's and women's compliance-gaining messages with respect to their politeness, one would need to somehow obtain samples of men's and women's messages for comparison.

One possibility would be to use naturally occurring influence settings as the sites for data collection. For example, one might arrange to collect the messages produced by customers at the complaint desk of a department store. But naturally occurring situations obviously don't permit much experimental control (over the features of the situation, the nature of the event stimulating the influence attempt, and so on). Moreover, such situations can present difficulties in collecting additional information that might be wanted. For instance, if one is interested in seeing how various personality factors influence compliance-gaining messages, then the relevant personality measures will need to be administered—but this obviously can be awkward in natural settings. To be sure, naturally occurring compliance-gaining situations have obvious strengths as data collection sites (e.g., they are useful for ruling out certain artifactual influences on the results). But especially in the early stages of research, most investigators have found that the disadvantages of natural settings outweigh their advantages.

Consequently, researchers have (to date) overwhelmingly preferred to employ hypothetical scenarios.[7] With this procedure, participants are presented with a description of some hypothetical circumstance in which they are called upon to produce some compliance-gaining message, and their responses to that circumstance are then obtained. Some effort is usually made to use scenarios that will be realistic and natural for the participants. For instance, in one study in which college undergraduates were the participants, the scenario was roughly as follows: "You're failing French, but your roommate is doing well in the course. You'd like your roommate to spend several hours tutoring you, but he/she is very busy studying for exams" (Marwell & Schmitt, 1967). In a study in which young children were the participants, the scenario was "Your birthday is coming up, and you very much want to have a large overnight party," with the mother as the influence target (R. A. Clark & Delia, 1976). The use of hypothetical scenarios provides the investigator a great deal of control over the stimulus situation, but leaves open the question of external validity—the question of whether responses to hypothetical situations mirror the responses to actual compliance-gaining situations.

Either of these options—hypothetical scenarios or natural settings—has benefits and costs; the primary trade-off is between experimental control (maximized by hypothetical scenarios) and external validity (maximized by naturally occurring settings). As mentioned above, researchers thus far have preferred to maximize experimental control.

But in a few cases investigators have used a research arrangement that promises to minimize these trade-offs. In this procedure, the setting is artificially arranged (i.e., not naturally occurring) but has a genuine social-influence task. For example, Applegate (1982) showed a five-dollar bill to participants in a laboratory experiment, and told the participants that each was to try to persuade the other to let him or her have the five dollars (with assurances that participants would in fact receive the money, and with a stipulation that the money couldn't be split); participants were videotaped during an ensuing

10-minute discussion period, and their persuasive messages subsequently analyzed. Other investigators have videotaped laboratory participants discussing
some issue on which they disagree (e.g., Carli, 1989; B. J. O'Keefe & Shepherd,
1987).

This research arrangement exploits the advantages afforded by the laboratory setting (e.g., control over topics, ability to administer questionnaires), but
minimizes the validity threats associated with hypothetical scenarios. Such a
procedure will not be suitable for every research question concerning compliance-gaining message production, but it surely deserves broader use.

CHECKLIST OR FREE-RESPONSE METHODS?

If an investigator elects to use hypothetical scenarios as the arrangement for
data collection, then an additional question arises of how to assess the message
feature of interest. There are two primary means of gathering the relevant
information about message production: free-response methods and checklist
methods.

FREE-RESPONSE METHODS

In free-response methods, following the description of the hypothetical
situation, participants are asked to produce messages. That is, participants are
asked to write out (or speak aloud) their message (e.g., "Write down what you
would say to get your roommate to tutor you"). The participant's response thus
is "free," in the sense that it is relatively unconstrained: Participants may say
whatever they like.

These free-response messages are subsequently analyzed by the investigator
for the feature(s) of interest. One could, for instance, use something like R. A.
Clark and Delia's (1976) scheme to classify the messages according to the
degree of listener-adaptedness exhibited; or, armed with Marwell and Schmitt's
(1967) strategy list, one could classify messages according to which of those
strategies was used by the message; or one could assess the degree to which
powerful (versus powerless) language was employed; or the politeness of the
messages could be assessed; and so on.

CHECKLIST METHODS

In checklist methods, following the description of the hypothetical situation,
participants are given a list of preformulated alternative possibilities and are
asked to rate each one for likelihood of use (say, by checking the relevant point
on a rating scale). The investigator then analyzes the ratings, with an eye to
locating differences (in likelihood of use) among the provided alternatives.

This basic checklist procedure permits any number of variations. The alternatives on the checklist, for instance, might be expressed as abstract descriptions of different message types or as different particular concrete messages.
And various instructions can be used: Rating each alternative for likelihood of
use is the most common procedure, but participants might be asked to check the

one they'd most likely use, to check all the ones they'd be willing to use, to rank order the possibilities by likelihood of use, and so on (for discussion of such alternatives, see Seibold, 1988, p. 154).

COMPARING CHECKLIST
AND FREE-RESPONSE METHODS

In choosing between these methods, considerations of the relative advantages and disadvantages of each method are plainly relevant. But the central criterion should surely be the external validity of each method — that is, the extent to which each method yields accurate information about compliance-gaining efforts.

In considering this question, one must initially take up the matter of whether the two methods yield similar results concerning compliance-gaining. After all, if the two methods produce similar results, then presumably the two methods must be roughly equally accurate (or inaccurate) as indicators of compliance-gaining behavior — and hence the two methods would presumably enjoy roughly equal external validity.

The issue of whether the two methods yield dissimilar conclusions, of course, requires evidence from comparable (related) checklist and free-response methods. That is, the relevant evidence is that drawn from a comparison of a given checklist and its free-response counterpart (i.e., some coding or classification system for the free-response data, where the categories of the coding system correspond to the categories on the checklist). But there are two ways in which this comparison can be performed, and it is important to distinguish the two analyses.

DIRECT COMPARISON OF MEANS One way of comparing the two procedures is by direct comparison (category by category) of the relevant means (means for likelihood of use or means for role-played use). Several such comparisons have found divergences between the results of checklist procedures and the results of free-response methods. Neuliep (1986), for example, obtained likelihood-of-use rankings for 14 persuasive messages (based on the typology of Schenck-Hamlin et al., 1982) in a compliance-gaining situation; participants subsequently role-played that situation, and the free-response messages were coded into the 14 message categories. Neuliep reported poor correspondence between results from the two methods; that is, the likelihood-of-use rankings did not accurately reflect the role-played compliance-gaining efforts. For example, participants high in dogmatism indicated (on the checklist questionnaire) that they would be very unlikely to use threats; in the free-response (role-played) data, however, threat was one of the techniques most commonly used by those participants. (For similar findings of discrepant results from the two methods, see Burke & Clark, 1982; Burleson et al., 1988, Studies 6 and 7; R. A. Clark, 1979; Dillard, 1988; see also Cody, 1982.)

COMPARISON OF INDEPENDENT-VARIABLE EFFECTS Some investigations have compared checklist and free-response methods in a second sort of way, by asking, "Do the independent variables that influence compliance-gaining as assessed by checklist methods show similar effects when compliance-gaining is assessed with free-response methods?" (for examples of such comparisons, see R. A. Clark, 1979; Sorensen, Plax, & Kearney, 1989). That is, the question is whether the factors that appear to influence compliance-gaining efforts as assessed by one method correspond to the factors influencing compliance-gaining as assessed by the other. If, for example, situational variations that make a difference using checklist methods also make a difference using free-response methods, then the conclusion appears to be that the methods can be treated as equivalent (e.g., Sorensen et al., 1989).

But this is an uncareful conclusion. It is possible for a given independent variable to have similar effects on compliance-gaining as assessed through checklist methods and through free-response methods, even though in *other* respects the methods produce dissimilar results.

Suppose, for example, that one has a system of six discrete, unordered categories for classifying compliance-gaining efforts (with ABCDEF representing the six categories). One constructs both a checklist questionnaire (to obtain likelihood-of-use ratings for each of the six alternatives) and a free-response coding system (with six categories, representing each of the alternatives), and obtains data using both methods. The particular message feature of interest is (say) the prosociality of the messages. Categories A, B, and C represent relatively prosocial compliance-gaining efforts, whereas D, E, and F are relatively antisocial. So one obtains a "prosociality of compliance-gaining" index for each method: With the checklist, the index is based on the average likelihood-of-use ratings across the three prosocial categories as opposed to the average across the three antisocial categories; with the free-response data, the index is based on the average frequencies for the three prosocial categories and the three antisocial categories.[8] Suppose that a given independent variable (say, the sex of the communicator) shows similar effects for both indices — for instance, that females are more likely to use prosocial messages than are males. (For a study in which circumstances such as these obtain, see Sorensen et al., 1989.) Should one conclude that the two methods are generally equivalent? No, for two reasons.

First, this similarity of effect could obtain even though there were large differences (between the methods) *within* the prosocial and antisocial categories. For example, by likelihood-of-use ratings, A might appear much more likely than C; but in the free-response data, C could appear much more frequently than A. The analysis of communicator-sex effects on message prosociality collapses the A, B, and C categories together (as it should, given an interest in the underlying prosocial-antisocial dimension), which has the effect of submerging differences among A, B, and C. The point is this: A finding that a given variable has similar influences on some facet of compliance-gaining efforts as assessed through checklist methods and through free-response methods is not evidence that the two methods are generally interchangeable, because differences within collapsed categories may still exist.

Second, the observed similarity of effect could obtain even though *other* ways of treating the underlying dimensions (of the category system) yield dissimilar effects. To continue the example: Suppose categories A, B, and F represent messages that emphasize relational considerations as a basis for compliance (e.g., "You owe it to me"), whereas categories C, D, and E represent messages that emphasize nonrelational considerations (e.g., "It would benefit you in thus-and-so way"). From checklist (likelihood-of-use) data and free-response data, one could construct appropriate indices of the degree to which relationally oriented appeals were made. But the checklist data could indicate that respondents are more likely to use relationally oriented appeals (ABF) than they are to use nonrelationally oriented appeals (CDE)—whereas the free-response data could indicate exactly the opposite. The point here is this: Finding that checklist and free-response methods show similar effects of independent variables for *one* aspect of compliance-gaining efforts (e.g., prosociality) does not provide evidence that the two methods will show similar effects of independent variables for *other* aspects of compliance-gaining (e.g., relationally oriented) appeals.

What has just been suggested is that, when one compares checklist and free-response methods by seeing whether the two methods find similar effects for a given independent variable, a finding of similar effects (e.g., Sorensen et al., 1989) does not warrant a conclusion that the two methods are completely interchangeable. What conclusion is warranted by a finding of *dissimilar* effects (e.g., R. A. Clark, 1979)? Here, too, caution is required. A finding that comparable checklist and free-response procedures produce dissimilar effects shows unequivocally that the two particular procedures (that is, the particular checklist studied and its free-response counterpart) aren't entirely interchangeable; but such a finding does not warrant a conclusion that checklist and free-responses methods are never interchangeable, or will never produce similar results. As the example discussed above shows, even with a given checklist and its free-response counterpart, it is possible to find dissimilar effects for one aspect of compliance-gaining (e.g., the use of relationally oriented appeals) while finding similar effects for another (e.g., prosociality).

Although findings of dissimilarity (between checklist and free-response methods) in observed effects do not warrant the claim that the two methods are never interchangeable, such findings do warrant the claim that the two methods cannot justifiably be *assumed* to be interchangeable. The observed cases of divergence make it plain that, in any given application, the prudent assumption is that the two methods cannot be guaranteed to yield similar results. In the absence of direct evidence of similarity of effects, then, one ought not presume that a given checklist will provide results identical to its free-response counterpart.

SUMMARY In any case, one can say quite confidently that comparable checklist and free-response methods will not always yield similar results (Burke & Clark, 1982; Burleson et al., 1988; R. A. Clark, 1979; Dillard, 1988; Neuliep,

1986). And this, in turn, indicates that the two methods cannot always both be producing accurate information about actual compliance-gaining efforts. That is to say, there is good reason to suppose that in at least some cases, one or another of these methods will enjoy greater external validity. The question, naturally enough, is, Which one?

In this regard, there are two notable differences between the checklist and free-response procedures. First, the free-response task is a more natural and realistic task than is the checklist task. In everyday life, people are called upon to compose messages in a free-response fashion; they don't ordinarily face a menu of preformulated alternatives (see R. A. Clark, 1979, p. 273).[9]

Second, with the checklist method, participants may select (rate as highly likely for them to use) messages they could not have or would not have generated spontaneously. For instance, the alternatives on the checklist might include some message that a participant wouldn't have thought of—but when presented with that message as a possibility, the participant realizes its advantages (e.g., realizes that, compared to the spontaneously thought-of line of action, the proffered message is more likely to be effective, or is more socially acceptable) and so indicates a high likelihood of use. This difficulty is not encountered by free-response methods: Persons can't very well provide spontaneously any messages that they can't provide spontaneously.

Indeed, there are now a number of investigations suggesting that checklist respondents are inclined to choose (give high likelihood-of-use ratings to) messages that are (roughly put) "nicer"—less threatening, more accommodating, with more concern for the target's feelings—than the messages they spontaneously produce with free-response methods (Burleson et al., 1988; R. A. Clark, 1979; Cody, 1982; Neuliep, 1986). Some have even suggested that likelihood-of-use ratings reflect little more than such item-desirability biases (Burleson et al., 1988; for additional discussion of this view, see Boster, 1988; Burleson & Wilson, 1988; Hunter, 1988; Seibold, 1988). Even if one believes this suggestion goes too far, it still remains the case that checklist methods are susceptible to contaminating influences not present in free-response methods.

These two considerations suggest that free-response methods are likely (though not guaranteed) to enjoy greater external validity than would corresponding checklist methods.[10] But there is another relevant difference, not connected to the matter of external validity, between these methods: Free-response methods provide a richer data source than do checklist procedures. Because free-response messages are not made to fit any fixed set of response categories, the investigator is able to analyze *any* message feature that is of interest. Indeed, examination of the free-response messages may lead the investigator to detect some previously unnoticed aspect of messages, and so to refine the initial message analysis system, or indeed to construct a wholly new message analysis system. (For an example of such development of a message analysis system, see Cody & McLaughlin, 1988.) Moreover, the free-response data are available for subsequent reanalysis if some new message feature becomes of interest.

CONCLUSION

These differences all recommend the conclusion that free-response methods are generally preferable to checklist procedures for the study of compliance-gaining message production. The greater naturalness of the free-response task, its imperviousness to certain sorts of response influences encountered by checklist methods, and the greater richness of its data suggest its superiority on grounds of validity and heuristic value.

But it should also be remembered that (practically speaking) the choice between these methods arises only where hypothetical scenarios are the basis for data collection. Where investigators exploit naturally occurring compliance-gaining situations (e.g., Cody & McLaughlin's 1988 study of accounts in traffic court) or create compliance-gaining tasks in more controlled settings (e.g., Applegate's 1982 five-dollar task), free-response methods will naturally be preferred (if not required).[11]

THE STATE OF COMPLIANCE-GAINING
MESSAGE PRODUCTION RESEARCH

In many ways, the current state of research concerning compliance-gaining message production is aptly characterized as murky and unsettled. Indeed, dependable substantive generalizations may well seem premature. The following sections discuss, first, prominent barriers to research progress in this area and, second, the evidentiary requirements for broad conclusions.

BARRIERS TO DEPENDABLE GENERALIZATION

One reason for the elusiveness of dependable generalizations, of course, is the previously mentioned use of unprincipled message category systems. Another is the widespread use of checklist procedures, which creates room for concern about the external validity of the conclusions. But there are other reasons as well.

SINGLE-MESSAGE INSTANTIATIONS Some checklist-method research has used single-message instantiations of message categories, creating barriers to generalization. For example, in a number of studies using Marwell and Schmitt's category system, participants have rated the likelihood of use of each of 16 different messages (or quasi-messages), where each of Marwell and Schmitt's categories is represented by a single message (e.g., Lustig & King, 1980; Sillars, 1980). So, for instance, in the hypothetical scenario in which the respondent is failing French and is trying to get the roommate to tutor the respondent, Marwell and Schmitt's "promise" technique might be represented by an item such as "You tell your roommate that if he/she tutors you, you'll do your roommate's laundry for the next two weeks."

The problem with such a design is that it makes it impossible to distinguish the effects due to the abstract message category (promise) from the effects due to the particular concrete message used (the specific promise of doing the roommate's laundry for the next two weeks).[12] And unhappily (for the purposes of generalization) it has been shown that, in such a design, the likelihood-of-use ratings for Marwell and Schmitt's categories vary substantially depending upon the particular messages used. Jackson and Backus (1982) constructed a number of different lists with single-message instantiations of Marwell and Schmitt's categories; they found that for a given compliance-gaining situation, the average list-to-list correlation of likelihood-of-use ratings was only .49 (for related findings, see Hample & Dallinger, 1987a, 1987b).

The implication of this finding for summarizing research results is notable: One can't justifiably treat one list of concrete instantiations as automatically equivalent to another list of different instantiations (since the different concrete lists can produce substantively very different likelihood-of-use ratings); consequently, one can't treat the *results* from a study using a given concrete message list as comparable to the results from a study using a different concrete message list. So, for example: Suppose one study of a given compliance-gaining situation finds its "debt" message to be significantly more likely to be used than its "pregiving" message, but a second study of the same situation using a different set of 16 messages finds pregiving and debt equally likely to be used; in such a circumstance, one cannot justifiably conclude that there is any inconsistency between the results (no inconsistency attributable to the abstract message categories of "debt" and "pregiving," that is); the apparent inconsistency might as easily be due to the different message lists.

Indeed, a number of the reported effects found in earlier single-message-instantiation checklist studies disappear when multiple examples are used (Jackson & Backus, 1982). That is, instances of claimed effects in the literature are not genuinely attributable to message categories, but are the haphazard outcomes of the particular messages used. The implication of this, obviously enough, is that one ought to resist offering substantive generalizations based on checklist studies using single-message instantiations.[13]

THINLY SPREAD RESEARCH Another obstacle to generalization is the fact that research efforts have been spread rather thin, in the sense that small amounts of research have been done with many different message category systems. Of the large number of different possible message classification schemes, relatively few have seen sustained research use. It is not uncommon for an investigator to devise a new ad hoc message category system for each new research project — and hence the research literature is filled with message classification systems that have been used only once or twice.

This might not be such a drawback (so far as substantive generalizations are concerned) if each classification scheme were animated by a clear underlying dimension (or set of dimensions). All too frequently, however, the category systems are unprincipled ones, making meaningful comparison across studies virtually impossible. Thus the proliferation of unprincipled ad hoc message category systems has inevitably meant that research efforts have been spread more thinly than one might have hoped.

SOME EXAMPLES   The extant barriers to generalization become even more apparent if one turns to examples of the ways in which different investigators have approached a given compliance-gaining circumstance. For instance, there are a number of papers that might be thought potentially relevant to the matter of differences between mothers and fathers in the sorts of child control techniques used. An examination of just three of these (deTurck & Miller, 1983; B. McLaughlin, 1983; T. E. Smith, 1988) reveals substantial methodological variations. Each uses a different way of classifying parental control techniques (e.g., deTurck and Miller use categories from Marwell & Schmitt, 1967, whereas Smith uses a unique seven-category system), different ages of children are involved, and information about the use of various techniques is acquired differently — as perceived by adolescents who respond to a preformulated list of techniques (deTurck & Miller, 1983), as reported by parents in a recollection procedure that yields free-response information subsequently classified into categories (T. E. Smith, 1988), or as determined from videotaping parent-child interactions that are subsequently coded (B. McLaughlin, 1983). Even this far-from-exhaustive set of studies makes apparent the problems of creating a unified substantive account in this research area. And if one then seeks to incorporate, say, Sinha's (1985) hypothetical-scenario research with mothers as respondents — an investigation that uses yet a fourth way of classifying parental control strategies — the difficulties multiply.

Consider, as another example, several papers relevant to the matter of the influence techniques used in intimate relationships. For instance, Belk et al. (1988) asked respondents to indicate their frequency of use (in their close relationship) of each of 13 influence techniques (asking, bargaining, laissez-faire, negative affect, persistence, persuasion, positive affect, reasoning, stating importance, suggesting, talking, telling, and withdrawal — these taken from Falbo & Peplau, 1980). Howard, Blumstein, and Schwartz (1986) asked respondents how often their relational partners use each of 24 different tactics, with these then grouped into six categories (manipulation, supplication, bullying, autocracy, disengagement, and bargaining). Dillard and Fitzpatrick (1985) had married couples role-play two compliance-gaining situations, with the interactions subsequently coded for the frequency of use of each of eight compliance-gaining strategies reflecting three general categories (appeals to values or obligations, invocation of identification or relationship, reference to expectancies or consequences). Again, the variations in the message categories used and in the data collection techniques employed — even in this small subset of relevant papers — make for manifest obstacles to the integration of research results.

THE REQUIREMENTS FOR GENERALIZATION

Although obviously there are significant barriers to confident substantive generalization concerning compliance-gaining message production, it is going too far to say that there are *no* reliable generalizations to be found in this research area; for that reason, this chapter's emphasis on methodological issues (not substantive findings) may seem misplaced. On the other hand, it is surely important to recognize the difficulties that have impeded rapid research progress in this domain. Moreover, one is now in a position to identify the sort of research evidence that will be required to underwrite general substantive claims. Specifically, one will want to have a body of research — something more than a study or two — that (a) is focused on some well-specified message feature, (b) does not use checklist procedures (or at least not exclusively), and — ideally — (c) offers at least some research evidence that goes beyond hypothetical scenarios.

There are few sustained lines of research that satisfy these constraints, and correspondingly few dependable conclusions to be drawn. The most prominent research fitting these requirements is "constructivist" research concerning the development of audience adaptation (listener-adaptedness) in persuasive and regulative messages (for some general discussions of this work, see Burleson, 1989; Delia, O'Keefe, & O'Keefe, 1982). This line of work — relying exclusively on the analysis of free-response messages — has yielded good evidence that increasing age and social-cognitive sophistication are accompanied by a wider range of listener-adaptation strategies and by the use of more effective listener-adaptation strategies. The research evidence includes designs comparing children of different ages (e.g., R. A. Clark & Delia, 1976, 1977; Delia & Clark, 1977; Delia, Kline, & Burleson, 1979) and designs examining age-homogeneous groups of persons who differ in social-cognitive development (e.g., Applegate, 1982; Kline & Ceropski, 1984; B. J. O'Keefe & Delia, 1979). Many of the investigations use hypothetical scenarios, but confirming evidence has also come from naturalistic observation (e.g., Applegate, 1980) and from experimenter-structured conversational situations (e.g., B. J. O'Keefe & Shepherd, 1987). Further evidence of the utility of this general approach has been obtained in the successful extension of this line of work to communicative functions other than compliance-gaining (e.g., Burleson, 1984).

Thus there is now substantial evidence in hand concerning the factors associated with effective adaptation of compliance-gaining messages to their tasks. Much of the recent work in this research line has turned to a consideration of how best to construct explanatory frameworks for this evidence. For example, B. J. O'Keefe and Delia (1982) have suggested that the message coding systems employed in this research are better interpreted as assessing message multifunctionality (the number and types of goals pursued) rather than listener-adaptedness or person-centeredness. Whereas Burleson (1989) treats this research under the umbrella concept of "person-centered communication," B. J. O'Keefe and Delia (1988) argue for abandoning person-centeredness as the organizing framework and employing instead a "rational goals analysis" that views message production as a process of practical reasoning in which messages are derived in the service of goals (e.g., B. J. O'Keefe, 1988).

Notably, this research tradition has from the beginning emphasized the importance of specifying the abstractive dimensions for message analysis and, correlatively, the necessity of building a research program based on such established message-analytic methods (see, e.g., Delia et al., 1982). Even in this research line, however, theoretical reinterpretations of the message analysis systems have been forwarded. But note that advancing theory through reinterpretation of the message analysis systems has been possible because researchers have taken pains to specify message features carefully and apply the corresponding analytic systems to diverse natural message populations produced in response to a wide range of tasks. There is a larger moral here, for the ongoing development of message analysis systems in this well-established research tradition surely underscores the necessity of continuing attention to fundamental conceptual and methodological issues in the study of compliance-gaining message production.

CONCLUSION

Substantive progress in the study of compliance-gaining message production has encountered a number of difficulties. The conjunction of unprincipled category systems, the use of checklist methods (especially with single-message instantiations), and the existence of only small amounts of research with any particular category system makes for a rather unsettled research picture. Very broadly speaking, however, this state of affairs is simply a natural consequence of this research's being in the early stages of development. While fundamental conceptual and methodological issues are being ironed out, one can hardly expect rapid substantive development.

It ought to be noted, however, that in the study of compliance-gaining message production, the main substantive questions pursued to date have largely concerned the ways in which various factors (e.g., situational variations, differences in the interactants' relationship, individual differences of the interactants) are associated with differences in compliance-gaining messages. That is, the question has been "What influences (this or that facet of) compliance-gaining messages?"

But this is not the only sort of question that can be — or has been — asked about the production of social influence attempts. Researchers have begun to investigate such diverse topics as the development and use of means of resisting compliance-gaining attempts (e.g., M. L. McLaughlin, Cody, & Robey, 1980; McQuillen & Higginbotham, 1986), factors affecting persons' beliefs that an influence attempt has been successful (e.g., McCallum & Schopler, 1984), persons' explanations for persuasive success or failure (e.g., Andrews, 1987), and so on. That is to say, quite a number of different questions can be asked about the processes attendant to the production of compliance-gaining messages, and, correspondingly, there remains a good deal of relatively unexplored territory in this research area.

NOTES

1. To be sure, one *could* pursue a research question such as "Does relational intimacy influence compliance-gaining efforts?" but the results would not be illuminating. After all, even in the absence

of any research evidence, we can say that the answer to a question such as "Do compliance-gaining messages in intimate and in nonintimate relationships differ?" is almost certainly yes (if we look long enough, we can almost certainly find *some* way in which such messages differ) – but this is hardly very informative.

2. Occasionally much is made of the distinction between strategies – general, abstract characterizations of means of influence – and tactics – concrete, particular instantiations of strategies (e.g., Berger, 1985, pp. 484-485; G. R. Miller et al., 1987, pp. 94-96; Wheeless et al., 1983, pp. 112-115). But whether something is a "strategy" or a "tactic" depends entirely upon the level at which one's discussion is to be pitched, and hence is not something that can be settled in any general way. "Is threat really a strategy, or is it perhaps just a tactic?" isn't a sensible question, because one can imagine both more abstract categories that encompass threat as one particular case and more concrete categories that exemplify different ways of concretizing threat. No one level of this indefinitely extendable hierarchy is uniquely properly termed the "strategy" level, and hence any reasonably abstract classification of means of influence might usefully be called a classification of "strategies." Thus here "strategic classifications" is used to label any such abstract classification. The strategy-tactic distinction does draw one's attention to the point that a given general category of means of influence (strategy) might be implemented in different particular ways (tactics), but the distinction ought not be invested with any special significance.

3. It should not go unnoticed that the fact that there is no one correct list of compliance-gaining strategies means that certain sorts of research questions are not well formulated. For example, "Are different compliance-gaining strategies preferred in intimate and in nonintimate relationships?" is an ill-formed research question; one might sensibly ask "Are there differences in the power base invoked by preferred compliance-gaining strategies in intimate and in nonintimate relationships?" or "Are there differences in the degree of listener-adaptedness of the strategies preferred in intimate and in nonintimate relationships?" but one cannot meaningfully ask "Do the preferred compliance-gaining strategies differ in intimate and in nonintimate relationships?" Compliance-gaining strategies have many different facets, and meaningful research questions about compliance-gaining strategies require identification of the particular aspect of strategies that is of interest.

4. By way of contrast, consider a message classification system based explicitly on some particular dimension of message variation, such as R. A. Clark and Delia's (1976) system for assessing the listener-adaptedness of persuasive message strategies. Using an elaborated version of this system, Delia et al. (1979) found that older children (compared to younger ones) were more likely to display the capability to employ certain strategies – specifically, those higher-level strategies reflecting greater listener-adaptedness. In considering how to explain this result, one already knows that one relevant difference between the strategy categories is precisely the difference in listener-adaptedness, and so immediately certain explanations (e.g., ones based on age-related developments in social cognition) suggest themselves.

5. The suggestion that Marwell and Schmitt's categories are a conceptual hodgepodge is sometimes reproved with an unusual argument that runs as follows: If, in a checklist procedure using Marwell and Schmitt's categories, one sums (for each respondent) the respondent's likelihood-of-use ratings across the 16 strategies, the resulting index represents a point on a unidimensional scale that is an indicator of a single latent trait (perhaps "verbal aggressiveness," though this isn't entirely clear yet); hence these categories (and indeed the associated checklist procedure with the sum-of-the-ratings scoring) are sensible (the main evidence for this argument is provided by Hunter & Boster, 1987; for examples of this argument, see Boster, Stiff, & Reynolds, 1985, p. 179; G. R. Miller et al., 1987, pp. 97-98). There are two things to notice about this line of argument. First, it transforms the use of likelihood-of-use ratings of Marwell and Schmitt's strategy list – transforms them from being an indicator of compliance-gaining behavior to being the basis of an index of a factor that *influences* compliance-gaining behavior. In a sense, then, these ratings now serve as the basis for an independent (predictor) variable (e.g., verbal aggressiveness) rather than the originally intended dependent (criterion) variable (compliance-gaining behavior). There is nothing wrong with this transformation, but one should not forget that investigators still need some way to assess the criterion variable. Nor should one forget that this new predictor variable is not intrinsically worth investigating as an influence on compliance-gaining efforts; like any other factor, it might influence

some facets of compliance-gaining while not affecting other facets. Second, of *course* it is possible to devise some dimension along which Marwell and Schmitt's categories can be arrayed (as just discussed in the text); this argument suggests "affective impact of the message" as such a dimension (Hunter & Boster, 1987). But this is not the only dimension along which these categories can be sensibly arrayed (keeping in mind that the question "Along what dimensions can these categories be sensibly arrayed?" is different from the question "What sort of scale can we make if we look at summed likelihood-of-use ratings across these categories?"). The point thus remains that if one seeks to use Marwell and Schmitt's categories to describe compliance-gaining conduct, meaningful research will require arraying these categories along *some* dimension (or set of dimensions) — which is to say that, as they stand, Marwell and Schmitt's categories are indeed a hodgepodge.

6. Correspondingly, it should be noted, the data analysis must be conducted in a fashion that acknowledges the underlying dimension(s) of interest. For example, one may need to group or weight the various categories on the basis of the dimension of interest.

7. In a few cases, researchers have followed methodological paths other than natural settings or hypothetical scenarios, such as having participants recall compliance-gaining episodes (e.g., Dillard & Burgoon, 1985; T. E. Smith, 1988) or having participants keep diaries of relevant communication events (see Cody & McLaughlin, 1988, pp. 123-124), but these are relatively rarely used procedures.

8. The description of these indices is purposefully crude and incomplete, as the details of the construction of the relevant indices would depend on (among other things) the details of the research design.

9. It appears that some have thought the checklist task to be defensible (with respect to its realism and naturalism) because it simulates the underlying cognitive machinery of message production. The suggestion is that message production comes about through the communicator's (nonconsciously) selecting one among several alternative messages, and — the argument runs — the checklist procedure simply exteriorizes this underlying process. From this point of view, the checklist procedure *is* a natural one, because communicators do (*ex hypothesi*) face a menu of preformulated alternative messages. But this argument depends upon one's supposing that the underlying machinery of message production *is* such a selection process. But this supposition is (a) at a minimum unrequired, that is, there is nothing that compels such a supposition; (b) not underwritten by any direct evidence, that is, there is nothing that supports making such a supposition; (c) avoidable, that is, there are alternative models of the message production process built on different suppositions (e.g., B. J. O'Keefe, 1988); and (d) arguably quite implausible, that is, there is good reason to want not to make this supposition (for critical discussion of message production models constructed on such an assumption, see Seibold et al., 1985). In short, the putative naturalness and realism of checklist procedures appear to derive from implausible, avoidable, unevidenced, and unrequired presumptions.

10. Now Seibold (1988) has suggested that, insofar as the comparison is to be made between checklist methods and free-response methods where both rely upon hypothetical scenarios, there is little evidence to suggest that either bears much correspondence to actual compliance-gaining message conduct. On this view, there is little reason to favor one methodological avenue over the other, insofar as conclusions about compliance-gaining message production are concerned. Seibold is right, surely, to underscore the desirability of having direct evidence concerning the interpretation of results from one or another approach. At the same time, however, there are — as just discussed — good reasons for supposing that, generally speaking, the results from free-response studies are more likely to bear a resemblance to compliance-gaining message conduct than are the results from checklist studies (see also Burleson & Wilson, 1988, pp. 182-183).

11. A researcher *could*, in such circumstances, use some version of a checklist procedure. For instance, at a department store complaint desk, one could ask complainers to complete a checklist questionnaire describing the strategies they intend to use (or did just use), and ignore the actual messages. But where messages are available, surely these are generally to be preferred as a source of information about compliance-gaining.

12. The solution to this problem, obviously enough, is to use multiple examples of each message category. Thus the researcher would create a number of different promise messages, a

number of different threat messages, and so on. This design problem and its solution are, of course, precisely parallel to the design problem and solution discussed in Chapter 7 concerning single-message designs in the study of persuasive effects.

13. Other variations in checklist procedures have also been found to be consequential for research results. Specifically, Jackson and Backus (1982) found that different likelihood-of-use ratings are obtained for Marwell and Schmitt's (1967) 16 techniques when one gives participants concrete messages to rate and when one gives them abstract descriptions of the techniques. Such a finding again recommends caution in offering generalizations: These different forms of checklist procedures cannot be assumed to yield consistent results.

References

Abelson, R. P. (1981). Psychological status of the script concept. *American Psychologist, 36,* 715-729.

Abelson, R. P. (1986). Beliefs are like possessions. *Journal for the Theory of Social Behavior, 16,* 223-250.

Adams, W. C., & Beatty, M. J. (1977). Dogmatism, need for social approval, and the resistance to persuasion. *Communication Monographs, 44,* 321-325.

Addington, D. W. (1971). The effect of vocal variations on ratings of source credibility. *Speech Monographs, 38,* 242-247.

Ajzen, I. (1971). Attitudinal versus normative messages: An investigation of the differential effects of persuasive communication on behavior. *Sociometry, 34,* 263-280.

Ajzen, I. (1985). From intentions to actions: A theory of planned behavior. In J. Kuhl & J. Beckman (Eds.), *Action control: From cognition to behavior* (pp. 11-39). Berlin: Springer-Verlag.

Ajzen, I. (1989). Attitude structure and behavior. In A. R. Pratkanis, S. J. Breckler, & A. G. Greenwald (Eds.), *Attitude structure and function* (pp. 241-274). Hillsdale, NJ: Lawrence Erlbaum.

Ajzen, I., & Fishbein, M. (1969). The prediction of behavioral intentions in a choice situation. *Journal of Experimental Social Psychology, 5,* 400-416.

Ajzen, I., & Fishbein, M. (1970). The prediction of behavior from attitudinal and normative variables. *Journal of Experimental Social Psychology, 6,* 466-487.

Ajzen, I., & Fishbein, M. (1972). Attitudes and normative beliefs as factors influencing behavioral intentions. *Journal of Personality and Social Psychology, 21,* 1-9.

Ajzen, I., & Fishbein, M. (1974). Factors influencing intentions and the intention-behavior relation. *Human Relations, 27,* 1-15.

Ajzen, I., & Fishbein, M. (1977). Attitude-behavior relations: A theoretical analysis and review of empirical research. *Psychological Bulletin, 84,* 888-918.

Ajzen, I., & Fishbein, M. (1980). *Understanding attitudes and predicting social behavior.* Englewood Cliffs, NJ: Prentice-Hall.

Ajzen, I., & Madden, T. J. (1986). Prediction of goal-directed behavior: Attitudes, intentions, and perceived behavioral control. *Journal of Experimental Social Psychology, 22,* 453-474.

Ajzen, I., & Timko, C. (1986). Correspondence between health attitudes and behavior. *Basic and Applied Social Psychology, 7,* 259-276.

Ajzen, I., Timko, C., & White, J. B. (1982). Self-monitoring and the attitude-behavior relation. *Journal of Personality and Social Psychology, 42*, 426-435.

Alexander, C. N., Jr. (1966). Attitude as a scientific concept. *Social Forces, 45*, 278-281.

Allen, C. T., & Janiszewski, C. A. (1989). Assessing the role of contingency awareness in attitudinal conditioning with implications for advertising research. *Journal of Marketing Research, 26*, 30-43.

Allport, G. W. (1935). Attitudes. In C. Murchison (Ed.), *A handbook of social psychology* (pp. 798-844). Worcester, MA: Clark University Press.

Alpert, M. I., & Golden, L. L. (1982). The impact of education on the relative effectiveness of one-sided and two-sided communications. In B. J. Walker, W. O. Bearden, W. R. Darden, P. E. Murphy, J. R. Nevin, J. C. Olson, & B. A. Weitz (Eds.), *An assessment of marketing thought and practice* (pp. 30-33). Chicago: American Marketing Association.

Andersen, K. E. (1961). *An experimental study of the interaction of artistic and nonartistic ethos in persuasion.* Unpublished doctoral dissertation, University of Wisconsin — Madison.

Andersen, K. E., & Clevenger, T., Jr. (1963). A summary of experimental research in ethos. *Speech Monographs, 30*, 59-78.

Anderson, J. A., & Avery, R. K. (1978). An analysis of changes in voter perception of candidates' positions. *Communication Monographs, 45*, 354-361.

Anderson, L. (1970). An experimental study of reluctant and biased authority-based assertions. *Journal of the American Forensic Association, 7*, 79-84.

Anderson, L. R. (1970). Prediction of negative attitude from congruity, summation, and logarithm formulae for the evaluation of complex stimuli. *Journal of Social Psychology, 81*, 37-48.

Anderson, N. H. (1965). Averaging versus adding as a stimulus-combination rule in impression formation. *Journal of Experimental Psychology, 70*, 394-400.

Anderson, N. H. (1971). Integration theory and attitude change. *Psychological Review, 78*, 171-206.

Anderson, N. H. (1981a). *Foundations of information integration theory.* New York: Academic Press.

Anderson, N. H. (1981b). Integration theory applied to cognitive responses and attitudes. In R. E. Petty, T. M. Ostrom, & T. C. Brock (Eds.), *Cognitive responses in persuasion* (pp. 361-397). Hillsdale, NJ: Lawrence Erlbaum.

Andreoli, V., & Worchel, S. (1978). Effects of media, communicator, and message position on attitude change. *Public Opinion Quarterly, 42*, 59-70.

Andrews, P. H. (1987). Gender differences in persuasive communication and attribution of success and failure. *Human Communication Research, 13*, 372-385.

Applbaum, R. L., & Anatol, K. W. E. (1972). The factor structure of source credibility as a function of the speaking situation. *Speech Monographs, 39*, 216-222.

Applbaum, R. L., & Anatol, K. W. E. (1973). Dimensions of source credibility: A test for reproducibility. *Speech Monographs, 40*, 231-237.

Apple, W., Streeter, L. A., & Krauss, R. M. (1979). Effects of pitch and speech rate on personal attributions. *Journal of Personality and Social Psychology, 37*, 715-727.

Applegate, J. L. (1980). Adaptive communication in educational contexts: A study of teachers' communicative strategies. *Communication Education, 29*, 158-170.

Applegate, J. L. (1982). The impact of construct system development on communication and impression formation in persuasive contexts. *Communication Monographs, 49*, 277-289.

Apsler, R., & Sears, D. O. (1968). Warning, personal involvement, and attitude change. *Journal of Personality and Social Psychology, 9*, 162-166.

Arch, D. C. (1979). The development of influence strategy scales in buyer-seller interactions. In N. Beckwith, M. Houston, R. Mittelstaedt, K. B. Monroe, & S. Ward (Eds.), *1979 educators' conference proceedings* (pp. 440-444). Chicago: American Marketing Association.

Areni, C. S., & Lutz, R. J. (1988). The role of argument quality in the elaboration likelihood model. In M. J. Houston (Ed.), *Advances in consumer research* (Vol. 15, pp. 197-203). Provo, UT: Association for Consumer Research.

Arnold, W. E., & McCroskey, J. C. (1967). The credibility of reluctant testimony. *Central States Speech Journal, 18*, 97-103.

Aronson, E., & Carlsmith, J. M. (1963). Effect of the severity of threat on the devaluation of forbidden behavior. *Journal of Abnormal and Social Psychology, 66,* 584-588.

Aronson, E., Turner, J. A., & Carlsmith, J. M. (1963). Communicator credibility and communication discrepancy as determinants of opinion change. *Journal of Abnormal and Social Psychology, 67,* 31-36.

Atkins, A. L., Deaux, K. K., & Bieri, J. (1967). Latitude of acceptance and attitude change: Empirical evidence for a reformulation. *Journal of Personality and Social Psychology, 6,* 47-54.

Atkinson, D. R., Winzelberg, A., & Holland, A. (1985). Ethnicity, locus of control for family planning, and pregnancy counselor credibility. *Journal of Counseling Psychology, 32,* 417-421.

Audi, R. (1972). On the conception and measurement of attitudes in contemporary Anglo-American psychology. *Journal for the Theory of Social Behavior, 2,* 179-203.

Audi, R. (1974). A cognitive-motivational theory of attitudes. *Southwestern Journal of Philosophy, 5*(1), 77-88.

Axsom, D., Yates, S., & Chaiken, S. (1987). Audience response as a heuristic cue in persuasion. *Journal of Personality and Social Psychology, 53,* 30-40.

Babrow, A. S., & O'Keefe, D. J. (1984). Construct differentiation as a moderator of attitude-behavior consistency: A failure to confirm. *Central States Speech Journal, 35,* 160-165.

Bagozzi, R. P. (1978). The construct validity of the affective, behavioral, and cognitive components of attitude by analysis of covariance structures. *Multivariate Behavioral Research, 13,* 9-31.

Bagozzi, R. P. (1982). A field investigation of causal relations among cognitions, affect, intentions, and behavior. *Journal of Marketing Research, 19,* 562-584.

Bagozzi, R. P. (1984). Expectancy-value attitude models: An analysis of critical measurement issues. *International Journal of Research in Marketing, 1,* 295-310.

Bagozzi, R. P. (1985). Expectancy-value attitude models: An analysis of critical theoretical issues. *International Journal of Research in Marketing, 2,* 43-60.

Bagozzi, R. P. (1988). The rebirth of attitude research in marketing. *Journal of the Market Research Society, 30,* 163-195.

Bagozzi, R. P., Tybout, A. M., Craig, C. S., & Sternthal, B. (1979). The construct validity of the tripartite classification of attitudes. *Journal of Marketing Research, 16,* 88-95.

Baron, R. S., Baron, P. H., & Miller, N. (1973). The relation between distraction and persuasion. *Psychological Bulletin, 80,* 310-323.

Baudhuin, E. S., & Davis, M. K. (1972). Scales for the measurement of ethos: Another attempt. *Speech Monographs, 39,* 296-301.

Baxter, L. A. (1984). An investigation of compliance-gaining as politeness. *Human Communication Research, 10,* 427-456.

Beaman, A. L., Cole, C. M., Preston, M., Klentz, B., & Steblay, N. M. (1983). Fifteen years of foot-in-the-door research: A meta-analysis. *Personality and Social Psychology Bulletin, 9,* 181-196.

Bearden, W. O., & Crockett, M. (1981). Self-monitoring, norms, and attitudes as influences on consumer complaining. *Journal of Business Research, 9,* 255-266.

Beatty, M. J., & Behnke, R. R. (1980). Teacher credibility as a function of verbal content and paralinguistic cues. *Communication Quarterly, 28*(1), 55-59.

Beatty, M. J., & Kruger, M. W. (1978). The effects of heckling on speaker credibility and attitude change. *Communication Quarterly, 26*(2), 46-50.

Beck, K. H. (1981). Driving while under the influence of alcohol: Relationship to attitudes and beliefs in a college population. *American Journal of Drug and Alcohol Abuse, 8,* 377-388.

Beck, K. H., & Frankel, A. (1981). A conceptualization of threat communications and protective health behavior. *Social Psychology Quarterly, 44,* 204-217.

Becker, B. J. (1986). Influence again: An examination of reviews and studies of gender differences in social influence. In J. S. Hyde & M. C. Linn (Eds.), *The psychology of gender: Advances through meta-analysis* (pp. 178-209). Baltimore: Johns Hopkins University Press.

Beisecker, T. D., & Parson, D. W. (1972). Introduction. In T. D. Beisecker & D. W. Parson (Eds.), *The process of social influence* (pp. 1-6). Englewood Cliffs, NJ: Prentice-Hall.

Belch, G. E., & Belch, M. A. (1987). The application of an expectancy value operationalization of function theory to examine attitudes of boycotters and nonboycotters of a consumer product. In

M. Wallendorf & P. F. Anderson (Eds.), *Advances in consumer research* (Vol. 14, pp. 232-236). Provo, UT: Association for Consumer Research.

Belk, S. S., Snell, W. E., Jr., Garcia-Falconi, R., Hernandez-Sanchez, J. E., Hargrove, L., & Holtzman, W. H., Jr. (1988). Power strategy use in the intimate relationships of women and men from Mexico and the United States. *Personality and Social Psychology Bulletin, 14*, 439-447.

Bell, R. A., Zahn, C. J., & Hopper, R. (1984). Disclaiming: A test of two competing views. *Communication Quarterly, 32*, 28-36.

Bem, D. J. (1972). Self-perception theory. In L. Berkowitz (Ed.), *Advances in experimental social psychology* (Vol. 6, pp. 1-62). New York: Academic Press.

Benoit, W. L. (1987). Argumentation and credibility appeals in persuasion. *Southern Speech Communication Journal, 52*, 181-197.

Bentler, P. M., & Speckart, G. (1979). Models of attitude-behavior relations. *Psychological Bulletin, 86*, 452-464.

Bentler, P. M., & Speckart, G. (1981). Attitudes "cause" behaviors: A structural equation analysis. *Journal of Personality and Social Psychology, 40*, 226-238.

Berger, C. R. (1985). Social power and interpersonal communication. In M. L. Knapp & G. R. Miller (Eds.), *Handbook of interpersonal communication* (pp. 439-499). Beverly Hills, CA: Sage.

Bergin, A. E. (1962). The effect of dissonant persuasive communications upon changes in a self-referring attitude. *Journal of Personality, 30*, 423-438.

Berlo, D. K., Lemert, J. B., & Mertz, R. J. (1969). Dimensions for evaluating the acceptability of message sources. *Public Opinion Quarterly, 33*, 563-576.

Berscheid, E. (1985). Interpersonal attraction. In G. Lindzey & E. Aronson (Eds.), *Handbook of social psychology* (3rd ed., Vol. 2, pp. 413-484). New York: Random House.

Berscheid, E., & Walster, E. (1974). Physical attractiveness. In L. Berkowitz (Ed.), *Advances in experimental social psychology* (Vol. 7, pp. 157-215). New York: Academic Press.

Bertrand, J. T. (1979). Selective avoidance on health topics: A field test. *Communication Research, 6*, 271-294.

Bettman, J. R., Capon, N., & Lutz, R. J. (1975). Cognitive algebra in multi-attribute attitude models. *Journal of Marketing Research, 12*, 151-164.

Bhagat, R. S., Raju, P. S., & Sheth, J. N. (1979). Attitudinal theories of consumer choice: A comparative analysis. *European Research, 7*, 51-62.

Biddle, P. R. (1966). *An experimental study of ethos and appeal for overt behavior in persuasion.* Unpublished doctoral dissertation, University of Illinois, Urbana-Champaign.

Bineham, J. L. (1988). A historical account of the hypodermic model in mass communication. *Communication Monographs, 55*, 230-246.

Blumler, J. G., & Gurevitch, M. (1982). The political effects of mass communication. In M. Gurevitch, T. Bennett, J. Curran, & J. Woollacott (Eds.), *Culture, society, and the media* (pp. 236-267). London: Methuen.

Bochner, S., & Insko, C. A. (1966). Communicator discrepancy, source credibility, and opinion change. *Journal of Personality and Social Psychology, 4*, 614-621.

Bock, D. G., & Saine, T. J. (1975). The impact of source credibility, attitude valence, and task sensitivity on trait errors in speech evaluation. *Speech Monographs, 42*, 229-236.

Bolton, G. M. (1974). The lost letter technique as a measure of community attitudes toward a major social issue. *Sociological Quarterly, 15*, 567-570.

Borgida, E., & Campbell, B. (1982). Belief relevance and attitude-behavior consistency: The moderating role of personal experience. *Journal of Personality and Social Psychology, 42*, 239-247.

Boster, F. J. (1988). Comments on the utility of compliance-gaining message selection tasks. *Human Communication Research, 15*, 169-177.

Boster, F. J., & Mongeau, P. (1984). Fear-arousing persuasive messages. In R. N. Bostrom (Ed.), *Communication yearbook 8* (pp. 330-375). Beverly Hills, CA: Sage.

Boster, F. J., Stiff, J. B., & Reynolds, R. A. (1985). Do persons respond differently to inductively-derived and deductively-derived lists of compliance gaining message strategies? A reply to Wiseman and Schenck-Hamlin. *Western Journal of Speech Communication, 49*, 177-187.

Bostrom, R. N. (1982). Theoretical interactions of receivers, sources, and attitude objects: "RSO" theory. In M. Burgoon (Ed.), *Communication yearbook 5* (pp. 833-855). New Brunswick, NJ: Transaction.

Bowers, J. W. (1965). The influence of delivery on attitudes toward concepts and speakers. *Speech Monographs, 32*, 154-158.

Bowers, J. W., & Phillips, W. A. (1967). A note on the generality of source-credibility scales. *Speech Monographs, 34*, 185-186.

Bowman, C. H., & Fishbein, M. (1978). Understanding public reaction to energy proposals: An application of the Fishbein model. *Journal of Applied Social Psychology, 8*, 319-340.

Bradac, J. J. (1983). On generalizing cabbages, messages, kings, and several other things: The virtues of multiplicity. *Human Communication Research, 9*, 181-187.

Bradac, J. J. (1986). Threats to generalization in the use of elicited, purloined, and contrived messages in human communication research. *Communication Quarterly, 34*, 55-65.

Bradac, J. J., Bowers, J. W., & Courtright, J. A. (1980). Lexical variations in intensity, immediacy, and diversity: An axiomatic theory and causal model. In R. N. St. Clair & H. Giles (Eds.), *The social and psychological contexts of language* (pp. 193-223). Hillsdale, NJ: Lawrence Erlbaum.

Bradley, P. H. (1981). The folk-linguistics of women's speech: An empirical examination. *Communication Monographs, 48*, 73-90.

Brent, E., & Granberg, D. (1982). Subjective agreement with the presidential candidates of 1976 and 1980. *Journal of Personality and Social Psychology, 42*, 393-403.

Breckler, S. J. (1984). Empirical validation of affect, behavior, and cognition as distinct components of attitude. *Journal of Personality and Social Psychology, 47*, 1191-1205.

Brehm, J. W. (1956). Postdecision changes in the desirability of alternatives. *Journal of Abnormal and Social Psychology, 52*, 384-389.

Brewer, W. F. (1974). There is no convincing evidence for operant or classical conditioning in adult humans. In W. B. Weimer & D. S. Palermo (Eds.), *Cognition and the symbolic processes* (pp. 1-42). Hillsdale, NJ: Lawrence Erlbaum.

Bridges, D. A., & Reinard, J. C., Jr. (1974). The effects of refutational techniques on attitude change. *Journal of the American Forensic Association, 10*, 203-212.

Brinberg, D., & Durand, J. (1983). Eating at fast-food restaurants: An analysis using two behavioral intention models. *Journal of Applied Social Psychology, 13*, 459-472.

Brock, T. C. (1965). Communicator-recipient similarity and decision change. *Journal of Personality and Social Psychology, 1*, 650-654.

Brown, B. L., Strong, W. J., & Rencher, A. C. (1973). Perceptions of personality from speech: Effects of manipulations of acoustical parameters. *Journal of the Acoustical Society of America, 54*, 29-35.

Brown, B. L., Strong, W. J., & Rencher, A. C. (1974). Fifty-four voices from two: The effects of simultaneous manipulations of rate, mean fundamental frequency, and variance of fundamental frequency on ratings of personality from speech. *Journal of the Acoustical Society of America, 55*, 313-318.

Bryant, J., Brown, D., Silberberg, A. R., & Elliott, S. M. (1981). Effects of humorous illustrations in college textbooks. *Human Communication Research, 8*, 43-57.

Budd, R. J., North, D., & Spencer, C. (1984). Understanding seat-belt use: A test of Bentler and Speckart's extension of the "theory of reasoned action." *European Journal of Social Psychology, 14*, 69-78.

Budd, R. J., & Spencer, C. (1984a). Latitude of rejection, centrality, and certainty: Variables affecting the relationship between attitudes, norms, and behavioural intentions. *British Journal of Social Psychology, 23*, 1-8.

Budd, R. J., & Spencer, C. P. (1984b). Predicting undergraduates' intentions to drink. *Journal of Studies on Alcohol, 45*, 179-183.

Buller, D. B. (1986). Distraction during persuasive communication: A meta-analytic review. *Communication Monographs, 53*, 91-114.

Burgoon, J. K. (1976). The ideal source: A reexamination of source credibility measurement. *Central States Speech Journal, 27*, 200-206.

Burgoon, J. K., Burgoon, M., Miller, G. R., & Sunnafrank, M. (1981). Learning theory approaches to persuasion. *Human Communication Research, 7,* 161-179.

Burgoon, M., & Chase, L. J. (1973). The effects of differential linguistic patterns in messages attempting to induce resistance to persuasion. *Speech Monographs, 40,* 1-7.

Burgoon, M., Jones, S. B., & Stewart, D. (1975). Toward a message-centered theory of persuasion: Three empirical investigations of language intensity. *Human Communication Research, 1,* 240-256.

Burke, J. A., & Clark, R. A. (1982). An assessment of methodological options for investigating the development of persuasive skills across childhood. *Central States Speech Journal, 33,* 437-445.

Burleson, B. R. (1984). Comforting communication. In H. E. Sypher & J. L. Applegate (Eds.), *Communication by children and adults: Social cognitive and strategic processes* (pp. 63-104). Beverly Hills, CA: Sage.

Burleson, B. R. (1989). The constructivist approach to person-centered communication: Analysis of a research exemplar. In B. Dervin, L. Grossberg, B. J. O'Keefe, & E. Wartella (Eds.), *Rethinking communication: Vol. 2. Paradigm exemplars* (pp. 29-46). Newbury Park, CA: Sage.

Burleson, B. R., & Wilson, S. R. (1988). On the continued undesirability of item desirability: A reply to Boster, Hunter, and Seibold. *Human Communication Research, 15,* 178-191.

Burleson, B. R., Wilson, S. R., Waltman, M. S., Goering, E. M., Ely, T. K., & Whaley, B. B. (1988). Item desirability effects in compliance-gaining research: Seven studies documenting artifacts in the strategy selection procedure. *Human Communication Research, 14,* 429-486.

Burnell, P., & Reeve, A. (1984). Persuasion as a political concept. *British Journal of Political Science, 14,* 393-410.

Burnkrant, R. E., & Howard, D. J. (1984). Effects of the use of introductory rhetorical questions versus statements on information processing. *Journal of Personality and Social Psychology, 47,* 1218-1230.

Burnkrant, R. E., & Page, T. J., Jr. (1988). The structure and antecedents of the normative and attitudinal components of Fishbein's theory of reasoned action. *Journal of Experimental Social Psychology, 24,* 66-87.

Buss, D. M., Gomes, M., Higgins, D. S., & Lauterbach, K. (1987). Tactics of manipulation. *Journal of Personality and Social Psychology, 52,* 1219-1229.

Byrne, D. (1969). Attitudes and attraction. In L. Berkowitz (Ed.), *Advances in experimental social psychology* (Vol. 4, pp. 35-89). New York: Academic Press.

Cacioppo, J. T., Harkins, S. G., & Petty, R. E. (1981). The nature of attitudes and cognitive responses and their relationships to behavior. In R. E. Petty, T. M. Ostrom, & T. C. Brock (Eds.), *Cognitive responses in persuasion* (pp. 31-54). Hillsdale, NJ: Lawrence Erlbaum.

Cacioppo, J. T., & Petty, R. E. (1982). The need for cognition. *Journal of Personality and Social Psychology, 42,* 116-131.

Cacioppo, J. T., & Petty, R. E. (1984). The elaboration likelihood model of persuasion. In T. C. Kinnear (Ed.), *Advances in consumer research* (Vol. 11, pp. 673-675). Provo, UT: Association for Consumer Research.

Cacioppo, J. T., & Petty, R. E. (1985). Central and peripheral routes to persuasion: The role of message repetition. In L. F. Alwitt & A. A. Mitchell (Eds.), *Psychological processes and advertising effects: Theory, research, and application* (pp. 91-111). Hillsdale, NJ: Lawrence Erlbaum.

Cacioppo, J. T., Petty, R. E., & Geen, T. R. (1989). Attitude structure and function: From the tripartite to the homeostasis model of attitudes. In A. R. Pratkanis, S. J. Breckler, & A. G. Greenwald (Eds.), *Attitude structure and function* (pp. 275-309). Hillsdale, NJ: Lawrence Erlbaum.

Cacioppo, J. T., Petty, R. E., & Kao, C. F. (1984). The efficient assessment of need for cognition. *Journal of Personality Assessment, 48,* 306-307.

Cacioppo, J. T., Petty, R. E., Kao, C. F., & Rodriguez, R. (1986). Central and peripheral routes to persuasion: An individual difference perspective. *Journal of Personality and Social Psychology, 51,* 1032-1043.

Cacioppo, J. T., Petty, R. E., Losch, M. E., & Kim, H. S. (1986). Electromyographic activity over facial muscle regions can differentiate the valence and intensity of affective reactions. *Journal of Personality and Social Psychology, 50,* 260-268.

Cacioppo, J. T., Petty, R. E., & Morris, K. J. (1983). Effects of need for cognition on message evaluation, recall, and persuasion. *Journal of Personality and Social Psychology, 45,* 805-818.

Cacioppo, J. T., Petty, R. E., & Sidera, J. A. (1982). The effects of a salient self-schema on the evaluation of proattitudinal editorials: Top-down versus bottom-up message processing. *Journal of Experimental Social Psychology, 18,* 324-338.

Cacioppo, J. T., Petty, R. E., & Stoltenberg, C. D. (1985). Processes of social influence: The elaboration likelihood model of persuasion. In P. C. Kendall (Ed.), *Advances in cognitive-behavioral research and therapy* (Vol. 4, pp. 215-274). New York: Academic Press.

Calder, B. J., Insko, C. A., & Yandell, B. (1974). The relation of cognitive and memorial processes to persuasion in a simulated jury trial. *Journal of Applied Social Psychology, 4,* 62-93.

Cann, A., Sherman, S. J., & Elkes, R. (1975). Effects of initial request size and timing of a second request on compliance: The foot in the door and the door in the face. *Journal of Personality and Social Psychology, 32,* 774-782.

Cantor, J. R., Alfonso, H., & Zillmann, D. (1976). The persuasive effectiveness of the peer appeal and a communicator's first-hand experience. *Communication Research, 3,* 293-310.

Cantrill, J. G., & Seibold, D. R. (1986). The perceptual contrast explanation of sequential request strategy effectiveness. *Human Communication Research, 13,* 253-267.

Carli, L. L. (1989). Gender differences in interaction style and influence. *Journal of Personality and Social Psychology, 56,* 565-576.

Carlsmith, J. M., Collins, B. E., & Helmreich, R. L. (1966). Studies in forced compliance I: The effect of pressure for compliance on attitude change produced by face-to-face role playing and anonymous essay writing. *Journal of Personality and Social Psychology, 4,* 1-13.

Carlson, E. R. (1956). Attitude change through modification of attitude structure. *Journal of Abnormal and Social Psychology, 52,* 256-261.

Chaffee, S. H., & Hochheimer, J. L. (1985). The beginnings of political communication research in the United States: Origins of the "limited effects" model. In E. M. Rogers & F. Balle (Eds.), *The media revolution in America and western Europe* (pp. 267-296). Norwood, NJ: Ablex.

Chaffee, S. H., & Miyo, Y. (1983). Selective exposure and the reinforcement hypothesis: An intergenerational panel study of the 1980 presidential campaign. *Communication Research, 10,* 3-36.

Chaffee, S. H., & Mutz, D. C. (1988). Comparing mediated and interpersonal communication data. In R. P. Hawkins, J. M. Wiemann, & S. Pingree (Eds.), *Advancing communication science: Merging mass and interpersonal processes* (pp. 19-43). Newbury Park, CA: Sage.

Chaiken, S. (1979). Communicator physical attractiveness and persuasion. *Journal of Personality and Social Psychology, 37,* 1387-1397.

Chaiken, S. (1980). Heuristic versus systematic information processing and the use of source versus message cues in persuasion. *Journal of Personality and Social Psychology, 39,* 752-766.

Chaiken, S. (1986). Physical appearance and social influence. In C. P. Herman, M. P. Zanna, & E. T. Higgins (Eds.), *Physical appearance, stigma, and social behavior: The Ontario Symposium, vol. 3* (pp. 143-177). Hillsdale, NJ: Lawrence Erlbaum.

Chaiken, S. (1987). The heuristic model of persuasion. In M. P. Zanna, J. M. Olson, & C. P. Herman (Eds.), *Social influence: The Ontario Symposium, vol. 5* (pp. 3-39). Hillsdale, NJ: Lawrence Erlbaum.

Chaiken, S., & Eagly, A. H. (1976). Communication modality as a determinant of message persuasiveness and message comprehensibility. *Journal of Personality and Social Psychology, 34,* 605-614.

Chaiken, S., & Eagly, A. H. (1983). Communication modality as a determinant of persuasion: The role of communicator salience. *Journal of Personality and Social Psychology, 45,* 241-256.

Chaiken, S., & Stangor, C. (1987). Attitudes and attitude change. *Annual Review of Psychology, 38,* 575-630.

Chang, M.-J., & Gruner, C. R. (1981). Audience reaction to self-disparaging humor. *Southern Speech Communication Journal, 46,* 419-426.

Chassin, L., Corty, E., Presson, C. C., Olshavsky, R. W., Bensenberg, M., & Sherman, S. J. (1981). Predicting adolescents' intentions to smoke cigarettes. *Journal of Health and Social Behavior, 22*, 445-455.

Chebat, J.-C., & Picard, J. (1985). The effects of price and message-sidedness on confidence in product and advertisement with personal involvement as a mediator variable. *International Journal of Research in Marketing, 2*, 129-141.

Chomsky, N. (1959). Review of Skinner's *Verbal behavior. Language, 35*, 26-58.

Chu, G. C. (1967). Prior familiarity, perceived bias, and one-sided versus two-sided communications. *Journal of Experimental Social Psychology, 3*, 243-254.

Cialdini, R. B. (1984). *Influence: How and why people agree to things.* New York: William Morrow.

Cialdini, R. B. (1987). Compliance principles of compliance professionals: Psychologists of necessity. In M. P. Zanna, J. M. Olson, & C. P. Herman (Eds.), *Social influence: The Ontario Symposium, vol. 5* (pp. 165-184). Hillsdale, NJ: Lawrence Erlbaum.

Cialdini, R. B., & Petty, R. E. (1981). Anticipatory opinion effects. In R. E. Petty, T. M. Ostrom, & T. C. Brock (Eds.), *Cognitive responses in persuasion* (pp. 217-235). Hillsdale, NJ: Lawrence Erlbaum.

Cialdini, R. B., & Schroeder, D. A. (1976). Increasing compliance by legitimizing paltry contributions: When even a penny helps. *Journal of Personality and Social Psychology, 34*, 599-604.

Cialdini, R. B., Vincent, J. E., Lewis, S. K., Catalan, J., Wheeler, D., & Darby, B. L. (1975). Reciprocal concessions procedure for inducing compliance: The door-in-the-face technique. *Journal of Personality and Social Psychology, 31*, 206-215.

Clark, H. H. (1973). The language-as-fixed-effect fallacy: A critique of language statistics in psychological research. *Journal of Verbal Learning and Verbal Behavior, 12*, 335-359.

Clark, R. A. (1979). The impact of self interest and desire for liking on the selection of communicative strategies. *Communication Monographs, 46*, 257-273.

Clark, R. A., & Delia, J. G. (1976). The development of functional persuasive skills in childhood and early adolescence. *Child Development, 47*, 1008-1014.

Clark, R. A., & Delia, J. G. (1977). Cognitive complexity, social perspective-taking, and functional persuasive skills in second- to ninth-grade children. *Human Communication Research, 3*, 128-134.

Clark, R. A., & Delia, J. G. (1979). Topoi and rhetorical competence. *Quarterly Journal of Speech, 65*, 187-206.

Clark, R. A., & Stewart, R. (1971). Latitude of rejection as a measure of ego involvement. *Speech Monographs, 38*, 228-234.

Clark, R. A., Stewart, R., & Marston, A. (1972). Scale values for highest and lowest levels of credibility. *Central States Speech Journal, 23*, 193-196.

Cody, M. J. (1982). A typology of disengagement strategies and an examination of the role intimacy, reactions to inequity and relational problems play in strategy selection. *Communication Monographs, 49*, 148-170.

Cody, M. J., & McLaughlin, M. L. (1985). Models for the sequential construction of accounting episodes: Situational and interactional constraints on message selection and evaluation. In R. L. Street, Jr., & J. N. Cappella (Eds.), *Sequence and pattern in communicative behaviour* (pp. 50-69). London: Edward Arnold.

Cody, M. J., & McLaughlin, M. L. (1988). Accounts on trial: Oral arguments in traffic court. In C. Antaki (Ed.), *Analyzing everyday explanation: A casebook of methods* (pp. 113-126). Newbury Park, CA: Sage.

Cody, M. J., McLaughlin, M. L., & Jordan, W. L. (1980). A multidimensional scaling of three sets of compliance-gaining strategies. *Communication Quarterly, 28*(3), 34-46.

Cohen, A. R. (1959). Communication discrepancy and attitude change: A dissonance theory approach. *Journal of Personality, 27*, 386-396.

Cohen, A. R. (1962). An experiment on small rewards for discrepant compliance and attitude change. In J. W. Brehm & A. R. Cohen, *Explorations in cognitive dissonance* (pp. 73-78). New York: Wiley.

Cohen, A. R. (1964). *Attitude change and social influence.* New York: Basic Books.

Cohen, J. B., Fishbein, M., & Ahtola, O. T. (1972). The nature and uses of expectancy-value models in consumer attitude research. *Journal of Marketing Research, 9*, 456-460.

Converse, J., Jr., & Cooper, J. (1979). The importance of decisions and free-choice attitude change: A curvilinear finding. *Journal of Experimental Social Psychology, 15*, 48-61.

Cook, T. D., & Flay, B. R. (1978). The persistence of experimentally induced attitude change. In L. Berkowitz (Ed.), *Advances in experimental social psychology* (Vol. 11, pp. 1-57). New York: Academic Press.

Cooke, M., & Kipnis, D. (1986). Influence tactics in psychotherapy. *Journal of Counseling and Clinical Psychology, 54*, 22-26.

Cooper, E., & Dinerman, H. (1951). Analysis of the film "Don't Be a Sucker": A study in communication. *Public Opinion Quarterly, 15*, 243-264.

Cooper, J., Darley, J. M., & Henderson, J. E. (1974). On the effectiveness of deviant- and conventional-appearing communicators: A field experiment. *Journal of Personality and Social Psychology, 29*, 752-757.

Cooper, J., & Fazio, R. H. (1984). A new look at dissonance theory. In L. Berkowitz (Ed.), *Advances in experimental social psychology* (Vol. 17, pp. 229-266). New York: Academic Press.

Cooper, J., & Jones, R. A. (1970). Self-esteem and consistency as determinants of anticipatory opinion shifts. *Journal of Personality and Social Psychology, 14*, 312-320.

Cooper, J., Zanna, M. P., & Taves, P. A. (1978). Arousal as a necessary condition for attitude change following induced compliance. *Journal of Personality and Social Psychology, 36*, 1101-1106.

Cope, F., & Richardson, D. (1972). The effects of reassuring recommendations in a fear-arousing speech. *Speech Monographs, 39*, 148-150.

Cotton, J. L. (1985). Cognitive dissonance in selective exposure. In D. Zillmann & J. Bryant (Eds.), *Selective exposure to communication* (pp. 11-33). Hillsdale, NJ: Lawrence Erlbaum.

Cotton, J. L., & Hieser, R. A. (1980). Selective exposure to information and cognitive dissonance. *Journal of Research in Personality, 14*, 518-527.

Cox, D. F., & Bauer, R. A. (1964). Self-confidence and persuasibility in women. *Public Opinion Quarterly, 28*, 453-466.

Cox, D. S., & Locander, W. B. (1987). Product novelty: Does it moderate the relationship between ad attitudes and brand attitudes? *Journal of Advertising, 16*(3), 39-44.

Crockett, W. H. (1982). Balance, agreement, and positivity in the cognition of small social structures. In L. Berkowitz (Ed.), *Advances in experimental social psychology* (Vol. 15, pp. 1-57). New York: Academic Press.

Cromwell, H. (1950). The relative effect on audience attitude of the first versus the second argumentative speech of a series. *Speech Monographs, 17*, 105-122.

Cronen, V. E., & Conville, R. L. (1975). Fishbein's conception of belief strength: A theoretical, methodological, and experimental critique. *Speech Monographs, 42*, 143-150.

Cronkhite, G., & Liska, J. (1976). A critique of factor analytic approaches to the study of credibility. *Communication Monographs, 43*, 91-107.

Cronkhite, G., & Liska, J. R. (1980). The judgment of communicant acceptability. In M. E. Roloff & G. R. Miller (Eds.), *Persuasion: New directions in theory and research* (pp. 101-139). Beverly Hills, CA: Sage.

Crosby, L. A., & Muehling, D. D. (1983). External variables and the Fishbein model: Mediation, moderation, or direct effects? In R. P. Bagozzi & A. M. Tybout (Eds.), *Advances in consumer research* (Vol. 10, pp. 94-99). Ann Arbor, MI: Association for Consumer Research.

Croyle, R. T., & Cooper, J. (1983). Dissonance arousal: Physiological evidence. *Journal of Personality and Social Psychology, 45*, 782-791.

Cushman, D. P., & McPhee, R. D. (Eds.). (1980). *Message-attitude-behavior relationship: Theory, methodology, and application.* New York: Academic Press.

Darley, S. A., & Cooper, J. (1972). Cognitive consequences of forced noncompliance. *Journal of Personality and Social Psychology, 24*, 321-326.

Davidson, A. R., & Jaccard, J. J. (1979). Variables that moderate the attitude-behavior relation: Results of a longitudinal survey. *Journal of Personality and Social Psychology, 37*, 1364-1376.

Davis, M. H., & Runge, T. E. (1981). Beliefs and attitudes in a gubernatorial primary: Some limitations on the Fishbein model. *Journal of Applied Social Psychology, 11*, 93-113.

Davis, R. A. (1985). Social structure, belief, attitude, intention, and behavior: A partial test of Liska's revisions. *Social Psychology Quarterly, 48,* 89-93.

Dawes, R. M., & Smith, T. L. (1985). Attitude and opinion measurement. In G. Lindzey & E. Aronson (Eds.), *Handbook of social psychology* (3rd ed., Vol. 1, pp. 509-566). New York: Random House.

DeBono, K. G. (1987). Investigating the social-adjustive and value-expressive functions of attitudes: Implications for persuasion processes. *Journal of Personality and Social Psychology, 52,* 279-287.

DeFleur, M. L., & Ball-Rokeach, S. (1982). *Theories of mass communication* (4th ed.). New York: Longman.

DeFleur, M. L., & Westie, F. R. (1963). Attitude as a scientific concept. *Social Forces, 42,* 17-31.

DeJong, W. (1979). An examination of self-perception mediation of the foot-in-the-door effect. *Journal of Personality and Social Psychology, 37,* 2221-2239.

Delia, J. G. (1975). Regional dialect, message acceptance, and perceptions of the speaker. *Central States Speech Journal, 26,* 188-194.

Delia, J. G. (1976a). Change of meaning processes in impression formation. *Communication Monographs, 43,* 142-157.

Delia, J. G. (1976b). A constructivist analysis of the concept of credibility. *Quarterly Journal of Speech, 62,* 361-375.

Delia, J. G. (1987). Communication research: A history. In C. R. Berger & S. H. Chaffee (Eds.), *Handbook of communication science* (pp. 20-98). Newbury Park, CA: Sage.

Delia, J. G., & Clark, R. A. (1977). Cognitive complexity, social perception, and the development of listener-adapted communication in six-, eight-, ten-, and twelve-year-old boys. *Communication Monographs, 44,* 326-345.

Delia, J. G., Crockett, W. H., Press, A. N., & O'Keefe, D. J. (1975). The dependency of interpersonal evaluations on context-relevant beliefs about the other. *Speech Monographs, 42,* 10-19.

Delia, J. G., Kline, S. L., & Burleson, B. R. (1979). The development of persuasive communication strategies in kindergarteners through twelfth-graders. *Communication Monographs, 46,* 241-256.

Delia, J. G., O'Keefe, B. J., & O'Keefe, D. J. (1982). The constructivist approach to communication. In F. E. X. Dance (Ed.), *Human communication theory* (pp. 147-191). New York: Harper & Row.

deTurck, M. A., & Miller, G. R. (1983). Adolescent perceptions of parental persuasive message strategies. *Journal of Marriage and the Family, 45,* 543-552.

DeVries, D. L., & Ajzen, I. (1971). The relationship of attitudes and normative beliefs to cheating in college. *Journal of Social Psychology, 83,* 199-207.

Dholakia, R. R. (1987). Source credibility effects: A test of behavioral persistence. In M. Wallendorf & P. F. Anderson (Eds.), *Advances in consumer research* (Vol. 14, pp. 426-430). Provo, UT: Association for Consumer Research.

Diab, L. N. (1965). Studies in social attitudes: III. Attitude assessment through the semantic differential technique. *Journal of Social Psychology, 67,* 303-314.

Dillard, J. P. (1988). Compliance-gaining message-selection: What is our dependent variable? *Communication Monographs, 55,* 162-183.

Dillard, J. P., & Burgoon, M. (1985). Situational influences on the selection of compliance-gaining messages: Two tests of the predictive utility of the Cody-McLaughlin typology. *Communication Monographs, 52,* 289-304.

Dillard, J. P., & Fitzpatrick, M. A. (1985). Compliance-gaining in marital interaction. *Personality and Social Psychology Bulletin, 11,* 419-433.

Dillard, J. P., Hunter, J. E., & Burgoon, M. (1984). Sequential-request persuasive strategies: Meta-analysis of foot-in-the-door and door-in-the-face. *Human Communication Research, 10,* 461-488.

Dillard, J. P., Segrin, C., & Harden, J. M. (1989). Primary and secondary goals in the production of interpersonal influence messages. *Communication Monographs, 56,* 19-38.

DiVesta, F. J., & Merwin, J. C. (1960). The effects of need-oriented communications on attitude change. *Journal of Abnormal and Social Psychology, 60,* 80-85.

Donnelly, J. H., Jr., & Ivancevich, J. M. (1970). Post-purchase reinforcement and back-out behavior. *Journal of Marketing Research, 7,* 399-400.

Doob, A. N., Carlsmith, J. M., Freedman, J. L., Landauer, T. K., & Tom, S., Jr. (1969). Effect of initial selling price on subsequent sales. *Journal of Personality and Social Psychology, 11,* 345-350.

Dover, P. A., & Olson, J. C. (1977). Dynamic changes in an expectancy-value attitude model as a function of multiple exposures to product information. In B. A. Greenberg & D. N. Bellinger (Eds.), *Contemporary marketing thought: 1977 educators' proceedings* (pp. 455-460). Chicago: American Marketing Association.

Eagly, A. H. (1981). Recipient characteristics as determinants of responses to persuasion. In R. E. Petty, T. M. Ostrom, & T. C. Brock (Eds.), *Cognitive responses in persuasion* (pp. 173-195). Hillsdale, NJ: Lawrence Erlbaum.

Eagly, A. H., & Carli, L. L. (1981). Sex of researchers and sex-typed communications as determinants of sex differences in influenceability: A meta-analysis of social influence studies. *Psychological Bulletin, 90,* 1-20.

Eagly, A. H., & Chaiken, S. (1975). An attribution analysis of the effect of communicator characteristics on opinion change: The case of communicator attractiveness. *Journal of Personality and Social Psychology, 32,* 136-144.

Eagly, A. H., & Chaiken, S. (1984). Cognitive theories of persuasion. In L. Berkowitz (Ed.), *Advances in experimental social psychology* (Vol. 17, pp. 267-359). New York: Academic Press.

Eagly, A. H., & Telaak, K. (1972). Width of the latitude of acceptance as a determinant of attitude change. *Journal of Personality and Social Psychology, 23,* 388-397.

Eagly, A. H., & Wood, W. (1985). Gender and influenceability: Stereotype versus behavior. In V. E. O'Leary, R. K. Unger, & B. S. Wallston (Eds.), *Women, gender, and social psychology* (pp. 225-256). Hillsdale, NJ: Lawrence Erlbaum.

Eagly, A. H., Wood, W., & Chaiken, S. (1978). Causal inferences about communicators and their effect on opinion change. *Journal of Personality and Social Psychology, 36,* 424-435.

Eagly, A. H., Wood, W., & Chaiken, S. (1981). An attribution analysis of persuasion. In J. H. Harvey, W. Ickes, & R. F. Kidd (Eds.), *New directions in attribution research* (Vol. 3, pp. 37-62). Hillsdale, NJ: Lawrence Erlbaum.

Elms, A. C. (Ed.). (1969). *Role playing, reward, and attitude change.* New York: Van Nostrand Reinhold.

Etgar, M., & Goodwin, S. A. (1982). One-sided versus two-sided comparative message appeals for new brand introductions. *Journal of Consumer Research, 8,* 460-465.

Falbo, T. (1977). The multidimensional scaling of power strategies. *Journal of Personality and Social Psychology, 35,* 537-547.

Falbo, T., & Peplau, L. A. (1980). Power strategies in intimate relationships. *Journal of Personality and Social Psychology, 38,* 618-628.

Falcione, R. L. (1974). The factor structure of source credibility scales for immediate superiors in the organizational context. *Central States Speech Journal, 25,* 63-66.

Farley, J. U., Lehmann, D. R., & Ryan, M. J. (1981). Generalizing from "imperfect" replication. *Journal of Business, 54,* 597-610.

Fazio, R. H. (1986). How do attitudes guide behavior? In R. M. Sorrentino & E. T. Higgins (Eds.), *Handbook of motivation and cognition* (pp. 204-243). New York: Guilford.

Fazio, R. H., Chen, J., McDonel, E. C., & Sherman, S. J. (1982). Attitude accessibility, attitude-behavior consistency, and the strength of the object-evaluation association. *Journal of Experimental Social Psychology, 18,* 339-357.

Fazio, R. H., & Zanna, M. P. (1981). Direct experience and attitude-behavior consistency. In L. Berkowitz (Ed.), *Advances in experimental social psychology* (Vol. 14, pp. 161-202). New York: Academic Press.

Feingold, P. C., & Knapp, M. L. (1977). Anti-drug abuse commercials. *Journal of Communication, 27*(1), 20-28.

Fern, E. F., Monroe, K. B., & Avila, R. A. (1986). Effectiveness of multiple request strategies: A synthesis of research results. *Journal of Marketing Research, 23,* 144-152.

Festinger, L. (1957). *A theory of cognitive dissonance*. Stanford, CA: Stanford University Press.

Festinger, L. (Ed.). (1964). *Conflict, decision, and dissonance*. Stanford, CA: Stanford University Press.

Festinger, L., & Carlsmith, J. M. (1959). Cognitive consequences of forced compliance. *Journal of Abnormal and Social Psychology, 58*, 203-210.

Festinger, L., & Walster, E. (1964). Post-decision regret and decision reversal. In L. Festinger (Ed.), *Conflict, decision, and dissonance* (pp. 100-110). Stanford, CA: Stanford University Press.

Fine, B. J. (1957). Conclusion-drawing, communicator credibility, and anxiety as factors in opinion change. *Journal of Abnormal and Social Psychology, 54*, 369-374.

Fishbein, M. (1967a). A behavior theory approach to the relations between beliefs about an object and the attitude toward the object. In M. Fishbein (Ed.), *Readings in attitude theory and measurement* (pp. 389-400). New York: Wiley.

Fishbein, M. (1967b). A consideration of beliefs, and their role in attitude measurement. In M. Fishbein (Ed.), *Readings in attitude theory and measurement* (pp. 257-266). New York: Wiley.

Fishbein, M. (Ed.). (1967c). *Readings in attitude theory and measurement*. New York: Wiley.

Fishbein, M., & Ajzen, I. (1974). Attitudes towards objects as predictors of single and multiple behavioral criteria. *Psychological Review, 81*, 59-74.

Fishbein, M., & Ajzen, I. (1975). *Belief, attitude, intention, and behavior*. Reading, MA: Addison-Wesley.

Fishbein, M., & Ajzen, I. (1976). Misconceptions about the Fishbein model: Reflections on a study by Songer-Nocks. *Journal of Experimental Social Psychology, 12*, 579-584.

Fishbein, M., & Ajzen, I. (1980). Predicting and understanding consumer behavior: Attitude-behavior correspondence. In I. Ajzen & M. Fishbein (Eds.), *Understanding attitudes and predicting social behavior* (pp. 148-172). Englewood Cliffs, NJ: Prentice-Hall.

Fishbein, M., & Ajzen, I. (1981a). Attitudes and voting behaviour: An application of the theory of reasoned action. In G. M. Stephenson & J. M. Davis (Eds.), *Progress in applied social psychology* (Vol. 1, pp. 253-313). New York: Wiley.

Fishbein, M., & Ajzen, I. (1981b). On construct validity: A critique of Miniard and Cohen's paper. *Journal of Experimental Social Psychology, 17*, 340-350.

Fishbein, M., Ajzen, I., & Hinkle, R. (1980). Predicting and understanding voting in American elections: Effects of external variables. In I. Ajzen & M. Fishbein (Eds.), *Understanding attitudes and predicting social behavior* (pp. 173-195). Englewood Cliffs, NJ: Prentice-Hall.

Fishbein, M., Ajzen, I., & McArdle, J. (1980). Changing the behavior of alcoholics: Effects of persuasive communication. In I. Ajzen & M. Fishbein (Eds.), *Understanding attitudes and predicting social behavior* (pp. 217-242). Englewood Cliffs, NJ: Prentice-Hall.

Fishbein, M., Bowman, C. H., Thomas, K., Jaccard, J. J., & Ajzen, I. (1980). Predicting and understanding voting in British elections and American referenda: Illustrations of the theory's generality. In I. Ajzen & M. Fishbein (Eds.), *Understanding attitudes and predicting social behavior* (pp. 196-216). Englewood Cliffs, NJ: Prentice-Hall.

Fishbein, M., & Hunter, R. (1964). Summation versus balance in attitude organization and change. *Journal of Abnormal and Social Psychology, 69*, 505-510.

Fishbein, M., Jaccard, J. J., Davidson, A. R., Ajzen, I., & Loken, B. (1980). Predicting and understanding family planning behaviors: Beliefs, attitudes, and intentions. In I. Ajzen & M. Fishbein (Eds.), *Understanding attitudes and predicting social behavior* (pp. 130-147). Englewood Cliffs, NJ: Prentice-Hall.

Fishbein, M., & Raven, B. H. (1962). The AB scales: An operational definition of belief and attitude. *Human Relations, 15*, 35-44.

Fleming, D. (1967). Attitude: The history of a concept. *Perspectives in American History, 1*, 287-365.

Fleshler, H., Ilardo, J., & Demoretcky, J. (1974). The influence of field dependence, speaker credibility set, and message documentation on evaluations of speaker and message credibility. *Southern Speech Communication Journal, 39*, 389-402.

Folkes, V. S., & Morgenstern, D. (1981). Account-giving and social perception. *Personality and Social Psychology Bulletin, 7*, 451-458.

Fontenelle, G. A., Phillips, A. P., & Lane, D. M. (1985). Generalizing across stimuli as well as subjects: A neglected aspect of external validity. *Journal of Applied Psychology, 70,* 101-107.

Fredricks, A. J., & Dossett, D. L. (1983). Attitude-behavior relations: A comparison of the Fishbein-Ajzen and the Bentler-Speckart models. *Journal of Personality and Social Psychology, 45,* 501-512.

Freedman, J. L. (1964). Involvement, discrepancy, and change. *Journal of Abnormal and Social Psychology, 69,* 290-295.

Freedman, J. L. (1965). Preference for dissonant information. *Journal of Personality and Social Psychology, 2,* 287-289.

Freedman, J. L., & Fraser, S. C. (1966). Compliance without pressure: The foot-in-the-door technique. *Journal of Personality and Social Psychology, 4,* 195-202.

Freedman, J. L., & Sears, D. O. (1965a). Selective exposure. In L. Berkowitz (Ed.), *Advances in experimental social psychology* (Vol. 2, pp. 57-97). New York: Academic Press.

Freedman, J. L., & Sears, D. O. (1965b). Warning, distraction, and resistance to influence. *Journal of Personality and Social Psychology, 1,* 262-266.

Frey, D. (1986). Recent research on selective exposure to information. In L. Berkowitz (Ed.), *Advances in experimental social psychology* (Vol. 19, pp. 41-80). New York: Academic Press.

Gardner, M. P. (1985). Does attitude toward the ad affect brand attitude under a brand evaluation set? *Journal of Marketing Research, 22,* 192-198.

Geller, E. S. (1975). Increasing desired waste disposals with instructions. *Man-Environment Systems, 5,* 125-128.

Giffen, K., & Ehrlich, L. (1963). Attitudinal effects of a group discussion on a proposed change in company policy. *Speech Monographs, 30,* 377-379.

Gilkinson, H., Paulson, S. F., & Sikkink, D. E. (1954). Effects of order and authority in an argumentative speech. *Quarterly Journal of Speech, 40,* 183-192.

Gillig, P. M., & Greenwald, A. G. (1974). Is it time to lay the sleeper effect to rest? *Journal of Personality and Social Psychology, 29,* 132-139.

Glixman, A. F. (1965). Categorizing behavior as a function of meaning domain. *Journal of Personality and Social Psychology, 2,* 370-377.

Goethals, G. R., & Nelson, R. E. (1973). Similarity in the influence process: The belief-value distinction. *Journal of Personality and Social Psychology, 25,* 117-122.

Golden, L. L., & Alpert, M. I. (1987). Comparative analysis of the relative effectiveness of one-sided and two-sided communication for contrasting products. *Journal of Advertising, 16*(1), 18-25.

Goldman, M., McVeigh, J. F., & Richterkessing, J. L. (1984). Door-in-the-face procedure: Reciprocal concession, perceptual contrast, or worthy person. *Journal of Social Psychology, 123,* 245-251.

Granberg, D. (1982). Social judgment theory. In M. Burgoon (Ed.), *Communication yearbook 6* (pp. 304-329). Beverly Hills, CA: Sage.

Granberg, D., & Campbell, K. E. (1977). Effect of communication discrepancy and ambiguity on placement and opinion shift. *European Journal of Social Psychology, 7,* 137-150.

Granberg, D., & Jenks, R. (1977). Assimilation and contrast effects in the 1972 election. *Human Relations, 30,* 623-640.

Granberg, D., Kasmer, J., & Nanneman, T. (1988). An empirical examination of two theories of political perception. *Western Political Quarterly, 41,* 29-46.

Granberg, D., & Steele, L. (1974). Procedural considerations in measuring latitudes of acceptance, rejection, and noncommitment. *Social Forces, 52,* 538-542.

Green, B. F. (1954). Attitude measurement. In G. Lindzey (Ed.), *Handbook of social psychology* (Vol. 1, pp. 335-369). Reading, MA: Addison-Wesley.

Greenberg, B. S., & Miller, G. R. (1966). The effects of low-credible sources on message acceptance. *Speech Monographs, 33,* 127-136.

Greenberg, B. S., & Tannenbaum, P. H. (1961). The effects of bylines on attitude change. *Journalism Quarterly, 38,* 535-537.

Greenwald, A. G. (1968). On defining attitude and attitude theory. In A. G. Greenwald, T. C. Brock, & T. M. Ostrom (Eds.), *Psychological foundations of attitudes* (pp. 361-388). New York: Academic Press.

Greenwald, A. G., & Leavitt, C. (1985). Cognitive theory and audience involvement. In L. F. Alwitt & A. A. Mitchell (Eds.), *Psychological processes and advertising effects* (pp. 221-240). Hillsdale, NJ: Lawrence Erlbaum.

Grube, J. W., Morgan, M., & McGree, S. T. (1986). Attitudes and normative beliefs as predictors of smoking intentions and behaviours: A test of three models. *British Journal of Social Psychology, 25*, 81-93.

Gruder, C. L., Cook, T. D., Hennigan, K. M., Flay, B. R., Alessis, C., & Halamaj, J. (1978). Empirical tests of the absolute sleeper effect predicted from the discounting cue hypothesis. *Journal of Personality and Social Psychology, 36*, 1061-1074.

Gruner, C. R. (1967). Effect of humor on speaker ethos and audience information gain. *Journal of Communication, 17*, 228-233.

Gruner, C. R. (1970). The effect of humor in dull and interesting informative speeches. *Central States Speech Journal, 21*, 160-166.

Gruner, C. R., & Lampton, W. E. (1972). Effects of including humorous material in a persuasive sermon. *Southern Speech Communication Journal, 38*, 188-196.

Gulley, H. E., & Berlo, D. K. (1956). Effect of intercellular and intracellular speech structure on attitude change and learning. *Speech Monographs, 23*, 288-297.

Gundersen, D. F., & Hopper, R. (1976). Relationships between speech delivery and speech effectiveness. *Communication Monographs, 43*, 158-165.

Gur-Arie, O., Durand, R. M., & Bearden, W. O. (1979). Attitudinal and normative dimensions of opinion leaders and nonleaders. *Journal of Psychology, 101*, 305-312.

Hackman, J. R., & Anderson, L. R. (1968). The strength, relevance, and source of beliefs about an object in Fishbein's attitude theory. *Journal of Social Psychology, 76*, 55-67.

Haiman, F. S. (1949). An experimental study of the effects of ethos in public speaking. *Speech Monographs, 16*, 190-202.

Hamill, R., Wilson, T. D., & Nisbett, R. E. (1980). Insensitivity to sample bias: Generalizing from atypical cases. *Journal of Personality and Social Psychology, 39*, 578-589.

Hammond, K. R. (1948). Measuring attitudes by error-choice: An indirect method. *Journal of Abnormal and Social Psychology, 43*, 38-48.

Hample, D., & Dallinger, J. M. (1987a). Individual differences in cognitive editing standards. *Human Communication Research, 14*, 123-144.

Hample, D., & Dallinger, J. M. (1987b). Self-monitoring and the cognitive editing of arguments. *Central States Speech Journal, 38*, 152-165.

Harkins, S. G., & Petty, R. E. (1981a). Effects of source magnification of cognitive effort on attitudes: An information-processing view. *Journal of Personality and Social Psychology, 40*, 401-413.

Harkins, S. G., & Petty, R. E. (1981b). The multiple source effect in persuasion: The effects of distraction. *Personality and Social Psychology Bulletin, 7*, 627-635.

Harkins, S. G., & Petty, R. E. (1987). Information utility and the multiple source effect. *Journal of Personality and Social Psychology, 52*, 260-268.

Harmon, R. R., & Coney, K. A. (1982). The persuasive effects of source credibility in buy and lease situations. *Journal of Marketing Research, 19*, 255-260.

Hartley, E. L. (1967). Attitude research and the jangle fallacy. In C. W. Sherif & M. Sherif (Eds.), *Attitude, ego-involvement, and change* (pp. 88-104). New York: Wiley.

Harvey, O. J., & Rutherford, J. (1958). Gradual and absolute approaches to attitude change. *Sociometry, 21*, 61-68.

Hass, R. G. (1981). Effects of source characteristics on cognitive responses and persuasion. In R. E. Petty, T. M. Ostrom, & T. C. Brock (Eds.), *Cognitive responses in persuasion* (pp. 141-172). Hillsdale, NJ: Lawrence Erlbaum.

Hass, R. G., & Grady, K. (1975). Temporal delay, type of forewarning, and resistance to influence. *Journal of Experimental Social Psychology, 11*, 459-469.

Hass, R. G., & Linder, D. E. (1972). Counterargument availability and the effects of message structure on persuasion. *Journal of Personality and Social Psychology, 23*, 219-233.

Haugtvedt, C., Petty, R. E., Cacioppo, J. T., & Steidley, T. (1988). Personality and ad effectiveness: Exploring the utility of need for cognition. In M. J. Houston (Ed.), *Advances in consumer research* (Vol. 15, pp. 209-212). Provo, UT: Association for Consumer Research.

Hausknecht, D. R., & Moore, D. L. (1986). The effects of time compressed advertising on brand attitude judgments. In R. J. Lutz (Ed.), *Advances in consumer research* (Vol. 13, pp. 105-110). Provo, UT: Association for Consumer Research.

Hedges, L. V., & Olkin, I. (1985). *Statistical methods for meta-analysis.* New York: Academic Press.

Heesacker, M., Petty, R. E., & Cacioppo, J. T. (1983). Field dependence and attitude change: Source credibility can alter persuasion by affecting message-relevant thinking. *Journal of Personality, 51*, 653-666.

Heider, F. (1946). Attitudes and cognitive organization. *Journal of Psychology, 21*, 107-112.

Heider, F. (1958). *The psychology of interpersonal relations.* New York: Wiley.

Hensley, W. E. (1974). A criticism of "Dimensions of source credibility: A test for reproducibility." *Speech Monographs, 41*, 293-294.

Herek, G. M. (1986). The instrumentality of attitudes: Toward a neofunctional theory. *Journal of Social Issues, 42*, 99-114.

Herek, G. M. (1987). Can functions be measured? A new perspective on the functional approach to attitudes. *Social Psychology Quarterly, 50*, 285-303.

Hewes, D. E. (1983). Confessions of a methodological puritan: A response to Jackson and Jacobs. *Human Communication Research, 9*, 187-191.

Hewgill, M. A., & Miller, G. R. (1965). Source credibility and response to fear-arousing communications. *Speech Monographs, 32*, 95-101.

Hewstone, M., & Young, L. (1988). Expectancy-value models of attitude: Measurement and combination of evaluations and beliefs. *Journal of Applied Social Psychology, 18*, 958-971.

Hickson, M., III, Powell, L., Hill, S. R., Jr., Holt, G. B., & Flick, H. (1979). Smoking artifacts as indicators of homophily, attraction, and credibility. *Southern Speech Communication Journal, 44*, 191-200.

Higbee, K. L. (1969). Fifteen years of fear arousal: Research on threat appeals: 1953-1968. *Psychological Bulletin, 72*, 426-444.

Himmelfarb, S., & Arazi, D. (1974). Choice and source attractiveness in exposure to discrepant messages. *Journal of Experimental Social Psychology, 10*, 516-527.

Hines, G. H. (1980). A longitudinal comparative study of nonreactive attitude measurement of controversial topics. *Perceptual and Motor Skills, 51*, 567-574.

Hocking, J., Margreiter, D., & Hylton, C. (1977). Intra-audience effects: A field test. *Human Communication Research, 3*, 243-249.

Holbrook, M. B. (1977). Comparing multiattribute attitude models by optimal scaling. *Journal of Consumer Research, 4*, 165-171.

Holbrook, M. B., & Hulbert, J. M. (1975). Multi-attribute attitude models: A comparative analysis. In M. J. Schlinger (Ed.), *Advances in consumer research* (Vol. 2, pp. 375-388). Ann Arbor, MI: Association for Consumer Research.

Hoogstraten, J., de Haan, W., & ter Horst, G. (1985). Stimulating the demand for dental care: An application of Ajzen and Fishbein's theory of reasoned action. *European Journal of Social Psychology, 15*, 401-414.

Horai, J., Naccari, N., & Fatoullah, E. (1974). The effects of expertise and physical attractiveness upon opinion agreement and liking. *Sociometry, 37*, 601-606.

Houck, C. L., & Bowers, J. W. (1969). Dialect and identification in persuasive messages. *Language and Speech, 12*, 180-186.

Hovland, C. I., Harvey, O. J., & Sherif, M. (1957). Assimilation and contrast effects in reactions to communication and attitude change. *Journal of Abnormal and Social Psychology, 55*, 244-252.

Hovland, C. I., Janis, I. L., & Kelley, H. H. (1953). *Communication and persuasion.* New Haven, CT: Yale University Press.

Hovland, C. I., & Mandell, W. (1952). An experimental comparison of conclusion-drawing by the communicator and by the audience. *Journal of Abnormal and Social Psychology, 47*, 581-588.

Hovland, C. I., & Pritzker, H. A. (1957). Extent of opinion change as a function of amount of change advocated. *Journal of Abnormal and Social Psychology, 54*, 257-261.

Howard, J. A., Blumstein, P., & Schwartz, P. (1986). Sex, power, and influence tactics in intimate relationships. *Journal of Personality and Social Psychology, 51*, 102-109.

Howard-Pitney, B., Borgida, E., & Omoto, A. M. (1986). Personal involvement: An examination of processing differences. *Social Cognition, 4*, 39-57.

Hughes, G. D. (1971). *Attitude measurement for marketing strategies.* Glenview, IL: Scott, Foresman.

Hunt, J. M., & Kernan, J. B. (1984). The role of disconfirmed expectancies in the processing of advertising messages. *Journal of Social Psychology, 124*, 227-236.

Hunt, J. M., Smith, M. F., & Kernan, J. B. (1985). The effects of expectancy disconfirmation and argument strength on message processing level: An application to personal selling. In E. C. Hirschman & M. B. Holbrook (Eds.), *Advances in consumer research* (Vol. 12, pp. 450-454). Provo, UT: Association for Consumer Research.

Hunter, J. E. (1988). Failure of the social desirability response set hypothesis. *Human Communication Research, 15*, 162-168.

Hunter, J. E., & Boster, F. J. (1987). A model of compliance-gaining message selection. *Communication Monographs, 54*, 63-84.

Hurwitz, J. (1986). Issue perception and legislative decision making: An application of social judgment theory. *American Politics Quarterly, 14*, 150-185.

Husek, T. R. (1965). Persuasive impacts of early, late, or no mention of a negative source. *Journal of Personality and Social Psychology, 2*, 125-128.

Huston, T. L., & Levinger, G. (1978). Interpersonal attraction and relationships. *Annual Review of Psychology, 29*, 115-156.

Hylton, C. (1971). Intra-audience effects: Observable audience response. *Journal of Communication, 21*, 253-265.

Infante, D. A. (1971). Predicting attitude from desirability and likelihood ratings of rhetorical propositions. *Speech Monographs, 38*, 321-326.

Infante, D. A. (1972). Cognitive structure as a predictor of post speech attitude and attitude change. *Speech Monographs, 39*, 55-61.

Infante, D. A. (1973). The perceived importance of cognitive structure components: An adaptation of Fishbein's theory. *Speech Monographs, 40*, 8-16.

Infante, D. A. (1975). Differential function of desirable and undesirable consequences in predicting attitude and attitude change toward proposals. *Speech Monographs, 42*, 115-134.

Infante, D. A. (1978). Similarity between advocate and receiver: The role of instrumentality. *Central States Speech Journal, 29*, 187-193.

Infante, D. A. (1980). The construct validity of semantic differential scales for the measurement of source credibility. *Communication Quarterly, 28*(2), 19-26.

Infante, D. A., Parker, K. R., Clarke, C. H., Wilson, L., & Nathu, I. A. (1983). A comparison of factor and functional approaches to source credibility. *Communication Quarterly, 31*, 43-48.

Insko, C. A. (1962). One-sided versus two-sided communications and countercommunications. *Journal of Abnormal and Social Psychology, 65*, 203-206.

Insko, C. A. (1967). *Theories of attitude change.* New York: Appleton-Century-Crofts.

Irwin, J. V., & Brockhaus, H. H. (1963). The "teletalk project": A study of the effectiveness of two public relations speeches. *Speech Monographs, 30*, 359-368.

Jaccard, J. (1981). Toward theories of persuasion and belief change. *Journal of Personality and Social Psychology, 40*, 260-269.

Jaccard, J., Brinberg, D., & Ackerman, L. J. (1986). Assessing attribute importance: A comparison of six methods. *Journal of Consumer Research, 12*, 463-468.

Jaccard, J. J., & Davidson, A. R. (1972). Toward an understanding of family planning behaviors: An initial investigation. *Journal of Applied Social Psychology, 2*, 228-235.

Jaccard, J., & Sheng, D. (1984). A comparison of six methods for assessing the importance of perceived consequences in behavioral decisions: Applications from attitude research. *Journal of Experimental Social Psychology, 20*, 1-28.

Jackson, S., & Allen, M. (1987, May). *Meta-analysis of the effectiveness of one-sided and two-sided argumentation.* Paper presented at the annual meeting of the International Communication Association, Montreal.

Jackson, S., & Backus, D. (1982). Are compliance-gaining strategies dependent on situational variables? *Central States Speech Journal, 33,* 469-479.

Jackson, S., & Jacobs, S. (1983). Generalizing about messages: Suggestions for design and analysis of experiments. *Human Communication Research, 9,* 169-181.

Jackson, S., O'Keefe, D. J., & Jacobs, S. (1988). The search for reliable generalizations about messages: A comparison of research strategies. *Human Communication Research, 15,* 127-142.

Janis, I. L. (1955). Anxiety indices related to susceptibility to persuasion. *Journal of Abnormal and Social Psychology, 51,* 663-667.

Janis, I. L. (1967). Effects of fear arousal on attitude change: Recent developments in theory and experimental research. In L. Berkowitz (Ed.), *Advances in experimental social psychology* (Vol. 3, pp. 166-224). New York: Academic Press.

Janis, I. L., & Field, P. B. (1956). A behavioral assessment of persuasibility: Consistency of individual differences. *Sociometry, 19,* 241-259.

Johnson, H. H., & Scileppi, J. A. (1969). Effects of ego-involvement conditions on attitude change to high and low credibility communicators. *Journal of Personality and Social Psychology, 13,* 31-36.

Jones, R. A., & Brehm, J. W. (1967). Attitudinal effects of communicator attractiveness when one chooses to listen. *Journal of Personality and Social Psychology, 6,* 64-70.

Jones, R. A., & Brehm, J. W. (1970). Persuasiveness of one- and two-sided communications as a function of awareness there are two sides. *Journal of Experimental Social Psychology, 6,* 47-56.

Judd, C. M., Kenny, D. A., & Krosnick, J. A. (1983). Judging the positions of political candidates: Models of assimilation and contrast. *Journal of Personality and Social Psychology, 44,* 952-963.

Kantola, S. J., Syme, G. J., & Campbell, N. A. (1982). The role of individual differences and external variables in a test of the sufficiency of Fishbein's model to explain behavioral intentions to conserve water. *Journal of Applied Social Psychology, 12,* 70-83.

Kardes, F. R. (1988). Spontaneous inference processes in advertising: The effects of conclusion omission and involvement on persuasion. *Journal of Consumer Research, 15,* 225-233.

Katz, D. (1960). The functional approach to the study of attitudes. *Public Opinion Quarterly, 24,* 163-204.

Katz, D. (1989). Foreword. In A. R. Pratkanis, S. J. Breckler, & A. G. Greenwald (Eds.), *Attitude structure and function* (pp. xi-xiv). Hillsdale, NJ: Lawrence Erlbaum.

Kearney, P., Plax, T. G., Richmond, V. P., & McCroskey, J. C. (1984). Power in the classroom IV: Alternatives to discipline. In R. N. Bostrom (Ed.), *Communication yearbook 8* (pp. 724-746). Beverly Hills, CA: Sage.

Kidder, L. H., & Campbell, D. T. (1970). The indirect testing of social attitudes. In G. F. Summers (Ed.), *Attitude measurement* (pp. 333-385). Chicago: Rand McNally.

Kiesler, C. A., Collins, B. E., & Miller, N. (1969). *Attitude change: A critical analysis of theoretical approaches.* New York: Wiley.

Kiesler, S. B., & Mathog, R. B. (1968). Distraction hypothesis in attitude change: Effects of effectiveness. *Psychological Reports, 23,* 1123-1133.

King, G. W. (1975). An analysis of attitudinal and normative variables as predictors of intentions and behavior. *Speech Monographs, 42,* 237-244.

King, M. (1978). Assimilation and contrast of presidential candidates' issue positions, 1972. *Public Opinion Quarterly, 41,* 515-522.

King, S. W. (1976). Reconstructing the concept of source perceptions: Toward a paradigm of source appropriateness. *Western Speech Communication, 40,* 216-225.

King, S. W., & Sereno, K. K. (1973). Attitude change as a function of degree and type of interpersonal similarity and message type. *Western Speech, 37,* 218-232.

Kipnis, D., Schmidt, S. M., & Wilkinson, I. (1980). Intraorganizational influence tactics: Explorations in getting one's way. *Journal of Applied Psychology, 65,* 440-452.

Kline, S. L. (1987). Self-monitoring and attitude-behavior correspondence in cable television subscription. *Journal of Social Psychology, 127,* 605-609.

Kline, S. L., & Ceropski, J. M. (1984). Person-centered communication in medical practice. In G. M. Phillips & J. T. Wood (Eds.), *Emergent issues in human decision making* (pp. 120-141). Carbondale: Southern Illinois University Press.

Klock, S. J., & Traylor, M. B. (1983). Older and younger models in advertising to older consumers: An advertising effectiveness experiment. *Akron Business and Economic Review, 14*(4), 48-52.

Koballa, T. R., Jr. (1986). Persuading teachers to reexamine the innovative elementary science programs of yesterday: The effect of anecdotal versus data-summary communications. *Journal of Research in Science Teaching, 23*, 437-449.

Lalljee, M., Brown, L. B., & Ginsburg, G. P. (1984). Attitudes: Disposition, behaviour, or evaluation? *British Journal of Social Psychology, 23*, 233-244.

Landy, D. (1972). The effects of an overheard audience's reaction and attractiveness on opinion change. *Journal of Experimental Social Psychology, 8*, 276-288.

Larson, C., & Sanders, R. (1975). Faith, mystery, and data: An analysis of "scientific" studies of persuasion. *Quarterly Journal of Speech, 61*, 178-194.

Lautman, M. R., & Dean, K. J. (1983). Time compression of television advertising. In L. Percy & A. G. Woodside (Eds.), *Advertising and consumer psychology* (pp. 219-236). Lexington, MA: Lexington.

Leavitt, C., & Kaigler-Evans, K. (1975). Mere similarity versus information processing: An exploration of source and message interaction. *Communication Research, 2*, 300-306.

Leippe, M. R., & Elkin, R. A. (1987). When motives clash: Issue involvement and response involvement as determinants of persuasion. *Journal of Personality and Social Psychology, 52*, 269-278.

Leventhal, H. (1970). Findings and theory in the study of fear communications. In L. Berkowitz (Ed.), *Advances in experimental social psychology* (Vol. 5, pp. 119-186). New York: Academic Press.

Leventhal, H., & Niles, P. (1965). Persistence of influence for varying durations of exposure to threat stimuli. *Psychological Reports, 16*, 223-233.

Leventhal, H., Safer, M. A., & Panagis, D. M. (1983). The impact of communications on the self-regulation of health beliefs, decisions, and behavior. *Health Education Quarterly, 10*, 3-29.

Leventhal, H., Watts, J. C., & Pagano, F. (1967). Effects of fear and instructions on how to cope with danger. *Journal of Personality and Social Psychology, 6*, 313-321.

Lewis, J. J. (1974). A criticism of "The factor structure of source credibility as a function of the speaking situation." *Speech Monographs, 41*, 287-290.

Likert, R. (1932). A technique for the measurement of attitudes. *Archives of Psychology, 22*(Whole No. 140), 1-55.

Linder, D. E., Cooper, J., & Jones, E. E. (1967). Decision freedom as a determinant of the role of incentive magnitude in attitude change. *Journal of Personality and Social Psychology, 6*, 245-254.

Linder, D. E., & Worchel, S. (1970). Opinion change as a result of effortfully drawing a counterattitudinal conclusion. *Journal of Experimental Social Psychology, 6*, 432-448.

Liska, A. E. (Ed.). (1975). *The consistency controversy: Readings on the impact of attitude on behavior.* Cambridge, MA: Schenkman.

Liska, A. E. (1984). A critical examination of the causal structure of the Fishbein/Ajzen attitude-behavior model. *Social Psychology Quarterly, 47*, 61-74.

Liska, J. (1978). Situational and topical variations in credibility criteria. *Communication Monographs, 45*, 85-92.

Luchok, J. A., & McCroskey, J. C. (1978). The effect of quality of evidence on attitude change and source credibility. *Southern Speech Communication Journal, 43*, 371-383.

Lull, J., & Cappella, J. (1981). Slicing the attitude pie: A new approach to attitude measurement. *Communication Quarterly, 29*, 67-80.

Lund, F. H. (1925). The psychology of belief: A study of its emotional and volitional determinants: III. The determinants of belief and the ideal of rationality. *Journal of Abnormal and Social Psychology, 20*, 174-196.

Lustig, M. W., & King, S. W. (1980). The effect of communication apprehension and situation on communication strategy choices. *Human Communication Research, 7*, 74-82.

Lutz, R. J. (1975a). Changing brand attitudes through modification of cognitive structure. *Journal of Consumer Research, 1*(4), 49-59.

Lutz, R. J. (1975b). First-order and second-order cognitive effects in attitude change. *Communication Research, 2*, 289-299.

Lutz, R. J. (1976). Conceptual and operational issues in the extended Fishbein model. In B. B. Anderson (Ed.), *Advances in consumer research* (Vol. 3, pp. 469-476). Cincinnati, OH: Association for Consumer Research.

Lutz, R. J. (1981). A reconceptualization of the functional approach to attitudes. In J. N. Sheth (Ed.), *Research in marketing* (Vol. 5, pp. 165-210). Greenwich, CT: JAI.

Lutz, R. J., & Bettman, J. R. (1977). Multiattribute models in marketing: A bicentennial review. In A. G. Woodside, J. N. Sheth, & P. D. Bennett (Eds.), *Consumer and industrial buying behavior* (pp. 137-149). New York: North-Holland.

Lutz, R. J., MacKenzie, S. B., & Belch, G. E. (1983). Attitude toward the ad as a mediator of advertising effectiveness: Determinants and consequences. In R. P. Bagozzi & A. M. Tybout (Eds.), *Advances in consumer research* (Vol. 10, pp. 532-539). Ann Arbor, MI: Association for Consumer Research.

Machleit, K. A., & Wilson, R. D. (1988). Emotional feelings and attitude toward the advertisement: The roles of brand familiarity and repetition. *Journal of Advertising, 17*(3), 27-35.

MacKenzie, S. B., Lutz, R. J., & Belch, G. E. (1986). The role of attitude toward the ad as a mediator of advertising effectiveness: A test of competing explanations. *Journal of Marketing Research, 23*, 130-143.

MacLachlan, J. (1982). Listener perception of time-compressed spokespersons. *Journal of Advertising Research, 22*(2), 47-51.

Maddux, J. E., & Rogers, R. W. (1980). Effects of source expertness, physical attractiveness, and supporting arguments on persuasion: A case of brains over beauty. *Journal of Personality and Social Psychology, 39*, 235-244.

Makdah, S. J., & Diab, L. N. (1976). Categorization as a function of attitude and ego-involvement. *Journal of Social Psychology, 98*, 9-18.

Manis, M. (1960). The interpretation of opinion statements as a function of recipient attitude. *Journal of Abnormal and Social Psychology, 60*, 340-344.

Manstead, A. S. R., Proffitt, C., & Smart, J. L. (1983). Predicting and understanding mothers' infant-feeding intentions and behavior: Testing the theory of reasoned action. *Journal of Personality and Social Psychology, 44*, 657-671.

Mark, M. M., & Shotland, R. L. (1983). Increasing charitable contributions: An experimental evaluation of the American Cancer Society's recommended solicitation procedures. *Journal of Voluntary Action Research, 12*(2), 8-21.

Markham, D. (1968). The dimensions of source credibility of television newscasters. *Journal of Communication, 18*, 57-64.

Markley, O. W. (1971). Latitude of rejection: An artifact of own position. *Psychological Bulletin, 75*, 357-359.

Marwell, G., & Schmitt, D. R. (1967). Dimensions of compliance-gaining behavior: An empirical analysis. *Sociometry, 30*, 350-364.

Maze, J. R. (1973). The concept of attitude. *Inquiry, 16*, 168-205.

Mazis, M. B., Ahtola, O. T., & Klippel, R. E. (1975). A comparison of four multi-attribute models in the prediction of consumer attitudes. *Journal of Consumer Research, 2*, 38-52.

McCallum, D. M., & Schopler, J. (1984). Agent and observer attributions of influence: The effects of target response. *Personality and Social Psychology Bulletin, 10*, 410-418.

McCarty, D. (1981). Changing contraceptive usage intentions: A test of the Fishbein model of intention. *Journal of Applied Social Psychology, 11*, 192-211.

McCarty, D., Morrison, S., & Mills, K. C. (1983). Attitudes, beliefs, and alcohol use: An analysis of relationships. *Journal of Studies on Alcohol, 44*, 328-341.

McCroskey, J. C. (1966). Scales for the measurement of ethos. *Speech Monographs, 33*, 65-72.

McCroskey, J. C. (1967). The effects of evidence in persuasive communication. *Western Speech, 31*, 189-199.

McCroskey, J. C. (1969). A summary of experimental research on the effects of evidence in persuasive communication. *Quarterly Journal of Speech, 55*, 169-176.

McCroskey, J. C. (1970). The effects of evidence as an inhibitor of counterpersuasion. *Speech Monographs, 37*, 188-194.

McCroskey, J. C., & Burgoon, M. (1974). Establishing predictors of latitude of acceptance-rejection and attitudinal intensity: A comparison of assumptions of social judgment and authoritarian personality theories. *Speech Monographs, 41*, 421-426.

McCroskey, J. C., & Mehrley, R. S. (1969). The effects of disorganization and nonfluency on attitude change and source credibility. *Speech Monographs, 36*, 13-21.

McCroskey, J. C., & Young, T. J. (1981). Ethos and credibility: The construct and its measurement after three decades. *Central States Speech Journal, 32*, 24-34.

McCroskey, J. C., Young, T. J., & Scott, M. D. (1972). The effects of message sidedness and evidence on inoculation against counterpersuasion in small group communication. *Speech Monographs, 39*, 205-212.

McGarry, J., & Hendrick, C. (1974). Communicator credibility and persuasion. *Memory and Cognition, 2*, 82-86.

McGinnies, E. (1973). Initial attitude, source credibility, and involvement as factors in persuasion. *Journal of Experimental Social Psychology, 9*, 285-296.

McGinnies, E., & Ward, C. D. (1980). Better liked than right: Trustworthiness and expertise as factors in credibility. *Personality and Social Psychology Bulletin, 6*, 467-472.

McGuire, W. J. (1961a). The effectiveness of supportive and refutational defenses in immunizing and restoring beliefs against persuasion. *Sociometry, 24*, 184-197.

McGuire, W. J. (1961b). Persistence of the resistance to persuasion induced by various types of prior defenses. *Journal of Abnormal and Social Psychology, 64*, 241-248.

McGuire, W. J. (1964). Inducing resistance to persuasion: Some contemporary approaches. In L. Berkowitz (Ed.), *Advances in experimental social psychology* (Vol. 1, pp. 191-229). New York: Academic Press.

McGuire, W. J. (1968). Personality and susceptibility to social influence. In E. F. Borgatta & W. W. Lambert (Eds.), *Handbook of personality theory and research* (pp. 1130-1187). Chicago: Rand McNally.

McGuire, W. J. (1969). The nature of attitudes and attitude change. In G. Lindzey & E. Aronson (Eds.), *The handbook of social psychology* (2nd ed., Vol. 3, pp. 136-314). Reading, MA: Addison-Wesley.

McGuire, W. J. (1985). Attitudes and attitude change. In G. Lindzey & E. Aronson (Eds.), *The handbook of social psychology* (3rd ed., Vol. 2, pp. 233-346). New York: Random House.

McGuire, W. J., & Papageorgis, D. (1961). The relative efficacy of various types of prior belief-defense in producing immunity against persuasion. *Journal of Abnormal and Social Psychology, 62*, 327-337.

McGuire, W. J., & Papageorgis, D. (1962). Effectiveness of forewarning in developing resistance to persuasion. *Public Opinion Quarterly, 26*, 24-34.

McLaughlin, B. (1983). Child compliance to parental control techniques. *Developmental Psychology, 19*, 667-673.

McLaughlin, M. L. (1975). Recovering the structure of credibility judgments: An alternative to factor analysis. *Speech Monographs, 42*, 221-228.

McLaughlin, M. L., Cody, M. J., & Robey, C. S. (1980). Situational influences on the selection of strategies to resist compliance-gaining attempts. *Human Communication Research, 7*, 14-36.

McQuillen, J. S., & Higginbotham, D. C. (1986). Children's reasoning about compliance-resisting behaviors. In M. L. McLaughlin (Ed.), *Communication yearbook 9* (pp. 673-690). Beverly Hills, CA: Sage.

McSweeney, F. K., & Bierley, C. (1984). Recent developments in classical conditioning. *Journal of Consumer Research, 11*, 619-631.

Miles, E. W., & Leathers, D. G. (1984). The impact of aesthetic and professionally-related objects on credibility in the office setting. *Southern Speech Communication Journal, 49*, 361-379.

Milgram, S., Mann, L., & Harter, S. (1965). The lost-letter technique: A tool of social research. *Public Opinion Quarterly, 29*, 437-438.

Miller, G. R. (1967). A crucial problem in attitude research. *Quarterly Journal of Speech, 53,* 235-240.

Miller, G. R. (1980). On being persuaded: Some basic distinctions. In M. E. Roloff & G. R. Miller (Eds.), *Persuasion: New directions in theory and research* (pp. 11-28). Beverly Hills, CA: Sage.

Miller, G. R., & Baseheart, J. (1969). Source trustworthiness, opinionated statements, and response to persuasive communication. *Speech Monographs, 36,* 1-7.

Miller, G. R., Boster, F., Roloff, M., & Seibold, D. (1977). Compliance-gaining message strategies: A typology and some findings concerning effects of situational differences. *Communication Monographs, 44,* 37-51.

Miller, G. R., Boster, F. J., Roloff, M. E., & Seibold, D. R. (1987). MBRS rekindled: Some thoughts on compliance gaining in interpersonal settings. In M. E. Roloff & G. R. Miller (Eds.), *Interpersonal processes: New directions in communication research* (pp. 89-116). Newbury Park, CA: Sage.

Miller, G. R., & Burgoon, J. K. (1982). Factors affecting assessments of witness credibility. In N. L. Kerr & R. M. Bray (Eds.), *Psychology of the courtroom* (pp. 169-194). New York: Academic Press.

Miller, G. R., & Burgoon, M. (1973). *New techniques of persuasion.* New York: Harper & Row.

Miller, G. R., Burgoon, M., & Burgoon, J. K. (1984). The functions of human communication in changing attitudes and gaining compliance. In C. C. Arnold & J. W. Bowers (Eds.), *Handbook of rhetorical and communication theory* (pp. 400-474). Boston: Allyn & Bacon.

Miller, G. R., & Hewgill, M. A. (1964). The effect of variations in nonfluency on audience ratings of source credibility. *Quarterly Journal of Speech, 50,* 36-44.

Miller, G. R., & Parks, M. R. (1982). Communication in dissolving relationships. In S. W. Duck (Ed.), *Personal relationships 4: Dissolving personal relationships* (pp. 127-154). New York: Academic Press.

Miller, L. E., & Grush, J. E. (1986). Individual differences in attitudinal versus normative determination of behavior. *Journal of Experimental Social Psychology, 22,* 190-202.

Miller, N., Maruyama, G., Beaber, R. J., & Valone, K. (1976). Speed of speech and persuasion. *Journal of Personality and Social Psychology, 34,* 615-624.

Miller, R. L., Seligman, C., Clark, N. T., & Bush, M. (1976). Perceptual contrast versus reciprocal concession as mediators of induced compliance. *Canadian Journal of Behavioral Science, 8,* 401-409.

Mills, J., & Aronson, E. (1965). Opinion change as a function of the communicator's attractiveness and desire to influence. *Journal of Personality and Social Psychology, 1,* 173-177.

Mills, J., & Harvey, J. (1972). Opinion change as a function of when information about the communicator is received and whether he is attractive or expert. *Journal of Personality and Social Psychology, 21,* 52-55.

Mills, J., & Kimble, C. E. (1973). Opinion change as a function of perceived similarity of the communicator and subjectivity of the issue. *Bulletin of the Psychonomic Society, 2,* 35-36.

Milord, J. T., & Perry, R. P. (1976). Salient attitudes: A test of Fishbein's linear model. *Journal of Social Psychology, 99,* 297-298.

Miniard, P. W., & Cohen, J. B. (1979). Isolating attitudinal and normative influences in behavioral intentions models. *Journal of Marketing Research, 16,* 102-110.

Miniard, P. W., & Cohen, J. B. (1981). An examination of the Fishbein-Ajzen behavioral-intentions model's concepts and measures. *Journal of Experimental Social Psychology, 17,* 309-339.

Miniard, P. W., & Page, T. J., Jr. (1984). Causal relationships in the Fishbein behavioral intention model. In T. C. Kinnear (Ed.), *Advances in consumer research* (Vol. 11, pp. 137-142). Provo, UT: Association for Consumer Research.

Mischel, W. (1973). Toward a cognitive social learning reconceptualization of personality. *Psychological Review, 80,* 252-283.

Mitchell, A. A. (1986). The effect of verbal and visual components of advertisements on brand attitudes and attitude toward the advertisement. *Journal of Consumer Research, 13,* 12-24.

Mitchell, A. A., & Olson, J. C. (1981). Are product attribute beliefs the only mediator of advertising effects on brand attitude? *Journal of Marketing Research, 18,* 318-332.

Moore, D. J., & Reardon, R. (1987). Source magnification: The role of multiple sources in the processing of advertising appeals. *Journal of Marketing Research, 24,* 412-417.

Morley, D. D. (1988a). Meta-analytic techniques: When generalizing to message populations is not possible. *Human Communication Research, 15,* 112-126.

Morley, D. D. (1988b). Reply to Jackson, O'Keefe, and Jacobs. *Human Communication Research, 15,* 143-147.

Mowen, J. C., Wiener, J. L., & Joag, S. (1987). An information integration analysis of how trust and expertise combine to influence source credibility and persuasion. In M. Wallendorf & P. F. Anderson (Eds.), *Advances in consumer research* (Vol. 14, p. 564). Provo, UT: Association for Consumer Research.

Muehling, D. D., & Laczniak, R. N. (1988). Advertising's immediate and delayed influence on brand attitudes: Considerations across message-involvement levels. *Journal of Advertising, 17*(4), 23-34.

Mueller, D. J. (1970). Physiological techniques of attitude measurement. In G. F. Summers (Ed.), *Attitude measurement* (pp. 534-552). Chicago: Rand McNally.

Munch, J. M., & Swasy, J. L. (1988). Rhetorical question, summarization frequency, and argument strength effects on recall. *Journal of Consumer Research, 15,* 69-76.

Munn, W. C., & Gruner, C. R. (1981). "Sick" jokes, speaker sex, and informative speech. *Southern Speech Communication Journal, 46,* 411-418.

Nakanishi, M., & Bettman, J. R. (1974). Attitude models revisited: An individual level analysis. *Journal of Consumer Research, 1,* 16-21.

Neimeyer, G. J., Guy, J., & Metzler, A. (1989). Changing attitudes regarding the treatment of disordered eating: An application of the elaboration likelihood model. *Journal of Social and Clinical Psychology, 8,* 70-86.

Nelson, M. C. (1988). The resolution of conflict in joint purchase decisions by husbands and wives: A review and empirical test. In M. J. Houston (Ed.), *Advances in consumer research* (Vol. 15, pp. 436-441). Provo, UT: Association for Consumer Research.

Neuliep, J. W. (1986). Self-report vs. actual use of persuasive messages by high and low dogmatics. *Journal of Social Behavior and Personality, 1,* 213-222.

Nimmo, D. (1970). *The political persuaders: The techniques of modern election campaigns.* Englewood Cliffs, NJ: Prentice-Hall.

Nisbett, R. E., Borgida, E., Crandall, R., & Reed, H. (1976). Popular induction: Information is not necessarily informative. In J. S. Carroll & J. W. Payne (Eds.), *Cognition and social behavior* (pp. 113-133). Hillsdale, NJ: Lawrence Erlbaum.

Nisbett, R. E., & Gordon, A. (1967). Self-esteem and susceptibility to social influence. *Journal of Personality and Social Psychology, 5,* 268-276.

Norman, R. (1976). When what is said is important: A comparison of expert and attractive sources. *Journal of Experimental Social Psychology, 12,* 294-300.

O'Barr, W. M. (1982). *Linguistic evidence: Language, power, and strategy in the courtroom.* New York: Academic Press.

O'Keefe, B. J. (1988). The logic of message design: Individual differences in reasoning about communication. *Communication Monographs, 55,* 80-103.

O'Keefe, B. J., & Delia, J. G. (1979). Construct comprehensiveness and cognitive complexity as predictors of the number and strategic adaptation of arguments and appeals in a persuasive message. *Communication Monographs, 46,* 231-240.

O'Keefe, B. J., & Delia, J. G. (1982). Impression formation and message production. In M. E. Roloff & C. R. Berger (Eds.), *Social cognition and communication* (pp. 33-72). Beverly Hills, CA: Sage.

O'Keefe, B. J., & Delia, J. G. (1988). Communicative tasks and communicative practices: The development of audience-centered message production. In B. A. Rafoth & D. L. Rubin (Eds.), *The social construction of written communication* (pp. 70-98). Norwood, NJ: Ablex.

O'Keefe, B. J., & Shepherd, G. J. (1987). The pursuit of multiple objectives in face-to-face persuasive interactions: Effects of construct differentiation on message organization. *Communication Monographs, 54,* 396-419.

O'Keefe, D. J. (1987). The persuasive effects of delaying identification of high- and low-credibility communicators: A meta-analytic review. *Central States Speech Journal, 38*, 63-72.

O'Keefe, D. J., Jackson, S., & Jacobs, S. (1988). Reply to Morley. *Human Communication Research, 15*, 148-151.

O'Keefe, D. J., & Shepherd, G. J. (1982). Interpersonal construct differentiation, attitudinal confidence, and the attitude-behavior relationship. *Central States Speech Journal, 33*, 416-423.

Oliver, R. L., & Bearden, W. O. (1985). Crossover effects in the theory of reasoned action: A moderating influence attempt. *Journal of Consumer Research, 12*, 324-340.

Olson, J. C., & Dover, P. A. (1978). Attitude maturation: Changes in related belief structures over time. In H. K. Hunt (Ed.), *Advances in consumer research* (Vol. 5, pp. 333-342). Ann Arbor, MI: Association for Consumer Research.

Olson, J. M., & Zanna, M. P. (1979). A new look at selective exposure. *Journal of Experimental Social Psychology, 15*, 1-15.

Olson, K., Camp, C., & Fuller, D. (1984). Curiosity and need for cognition. *Psychological Reports, 54*, 71-74.

Osberg, T. M. (1987). The convergent and discriminant validity of the need for cognition scale. *Journal of Personality Assessment, 51*, 441-450.

Osgood, C. E., Suci, G. J., & Tannenbaum, P. H. (1957). *The measurement of meaning.* Urbana: University of Illinois Press.

Osgood, C. E., & Tannenbaum, P. H. (1955). The principle of congruity in the prediction of attitude change. *Psychological Review, 62*, 42-55.

Ostermeier, T. H. (1967). Effects of type and frequency of reference upon perceived source credibility and attitude change. *Speech Monographs, 34*, 137-144.

Papageorgis, D. (1968). Warning and persuasion. *Psychological Bulletin, 70*, 271-282.

Papageorgis, D., & McGuire, W. J. (1961). The generality of immunity to persuasion produced by pre-exposure to weakened counterarguments. *Journal of Abnormal and Social Psychology, 62*, 475-481.

Park, C. W., & Mittal, B. (1985). A theory of involvement in consumer behavior: Problems and issues. In J. N. Sheth (Ed.), *Research in consumer behavior* (Vol. 1, pp. 201-231). Greenwich, CT: JAI.

Patzer, G. L. (1983). Source credibility as a function of communicator physical attractiveness. *Journal of Business Research, 11*, 229-241.

Paulhus, D. (1982). Individual differences, self-presentation, and cognitive dissonance: Their concurrent operation in forced compliance. *Journal of Personality and Social Psychology, 43*, 838-852.

Paulson, S. F. (1954). The effects of the prestige of the speaker and acknowledgement of opposing arguments on audience retention and shift of opinion. *Speech Monographs, 21*, 267-271.

Peak, H. (1955). Attitude and motivation. In M. R. Jones (Ed.), *Nebraska Symposium on Motivation* (Vol. 3, pp. 149-188). Lincoln: University of Nebraska Press.

Pearce, W. B. (1971). The effect of vocal cues on credibility and attitude change. *Western Speech, 35*, 176-184.

Pearce, W. B., & Brommel, B. J. (1972). Vocalic communication in persuasion. *Quarterly Journal of Speech, 58*, 298-306.

Pearce, W. B., & Conklin, F. (1971). Nonverbal vocalic communication and perceptions of a speaker. *Speech Monographs, 38*, 235-241.

Peay, M. Y. (1980). Changes in attitudes and beliefs in two-person interaction situations. *European Journal of Social Psychology, 10*, 367-377.

Petty, R. E., & Brock, T. C. (1981). Thought disruption and persuasion: Assessing the validity of attitude change experiments. In R. E. Petty, T. M. Ostrom, & T. C. Brock (Eds.), *Cognitive responses in persuasion* (pp. 55-79). Hillsdale, NJ: Lawrence Erlbaum.

Petty, R. E., & Cacioppo, J. T. (1977). Forewarning, cognitive responding, and resistance to persuasion. *Journal of Personality and Social Psychology, 35*, 645-655.

Petty, R. E., & Cacioppo, J. T. (1979a). Effects of forewarning of persuasive intent and involvement on cognitive responses and persuasion. *Personality and Social Psychology Bulletin, 5*, 173-176.

Petty, R. E., & Cacioppo, J. T. (1979b). Issue involvement can increase or decrease persuasion by enhancing message-relevant cognitive responses. *Journal of Personality and Social Psychology, 37*, 1915-1926.

Petty, R. E., & Cacioppo, J. T. (1981a). *Attitudes and persuasion: Classic and contemporary approaches.* Dubuque, IA: Wm. C Brown.

Petty, R. E., & Cacioppo, J. T. (1981b). Issue involvement as a moderator of the effects on attitude of advertising content and context. In K. B. Monroe (Ed.), *Advances in consumer research* (Vol. 8, pp. 20-24). Ann Arbor, MI: Association for Consumer Research.

Petty, R. E., & Cacioppo, J. T. (1983). Central and peripheral routes to persuasion: Application to advertising. In L. Percy & A. G. Woodside (Eds.), *Advertising and consumer psychology* (pp. 3-23). Lexington, MA: D. C. Heath.

Petty, R. E., & Cacioppo, J. T. (1984). The effects of involvement on responses to argument quantity and quality: Central and peripheral routes to persuasion. *Journal of Personality and Social Psychology, 46*, 69-81.

Petty, R. E., & Cacioppo, J. T. (1986a). *Communication and persuasion: Central and peripheral routes to attitude change.* New York: Springer-Verlag.

Petty, R. E., & Cacioppo, J. T. (1986b). The elaboration likelihood model of persuasion. In L. Berkowitz (Ed.), *Advances in experimental social psychology* (Vol. 19, pp. 123-205). New York: Academic Press.

Petty, R. E., Cacioppo, J. T., & Goldman, R. (1981). Personal involvement as a determinant of argument-based persuasion. *Journal of Personality and Social Psychology, 41*, 847-855.

Petty, R. E., Cacioppo, J. T., & Heesacker, M. (1981). Effects of rhetorical questions on persuasion: A cognitive response analysis. *Journal of Personality and Social Psychology, 40*, 432-440.

Petty, R. E., Cacioppo, J. T., Kasmer, J. A., & Haugtvedt, C. P. (1987). A reply to Stiff and Boster. *Communication Monographs, 54*, 257-262.

Petty, R. E., Cacioppo, J. T., & Schumann, D. (1983). Central and peripheral routes to advertising effectiveness: The moderating role of involvement. *Journal of Consumer Research, 10*, 135-146.

Petty, R. E., Kasmer, J. A., Haugtvedt, C. P., & Cacioppo, J. T. (1987). Source and message factors in persuasion: A reply to Stiff's critique of the elaboration likelihood model. *Communication Monographs, 54*, 233-249.

Petty, R. E., Wells, G. L., & Brock, T. C. (1976). Distraction can enhance or reduce yielding to propaganda: Thought disruption versus effort justification. *Journal of Personality and Social Psychology, 34*, 874-884.

Petty, R. E., Wells, G. L., Heesacker, M., Brock, T. C., & Cacioppo, J. T. (1983). The effects of recipient posture on persuasion: A cognitive response analysis. *Personality and Social Psychology Bulletin, 9*, 209-222.

Plax, T. G., & Rosenfeld, L. B. (1980). Individual differences in the credibility and attitude change relationship. *Journal of Social Psychology, 111*, 79-89.

Powell, F. A. (1966). Latitudes of acceptance and rejection and the belief-disbelief dimension: A correlational comparison. *Journal of Personality and Social Psychology, 4*, 453-457.

Powell, L. (1976). The measurement of involvement: A comparison of two techniques. *Communication Quarterly, 24*(3), 27-32.

Pratkanis, A. R., Breckler, S. J., & Greenwald, A. G. (Eds.). (1989). *Attitude structure and function.* Hillsdale, NJ: Lawrence Erlbaum.

Pratkanis, A. R., & Greenwald, A. G. (1985). A reliable sleeper effect in persuasion: Implications for opinion change theory and research. In L. F. Alwitt & A. A. Mitchell (Eds.), *Psychological processes and advertising effects* (pp. 157-173). Hillsdale, NJ: Lawrence Erlbaum.

Pratkanis, A. R., Greenwald, A. G., Leippe, M. R., & Baumgardner, M. H. (1988). In search of reliable persuasion effects: III. The sleeper effect is dead. Long live the sleeper effect. *Journal of Personality and Social Psychology, 54*, 203-218.

Pratkanis, A. R., Greenwald, A. G., Ronis, D. L., Leippe, M. R., & Baumgardner, M. H. (1986). Consumer-product and sociopolitical messages for use in studies of persuasion. *Personality and Social Psychology Bulletin, 12*, 536-538.

Prestholdt, P. H., Lane, I. M., & Mathews, R. C. (1987). Nurse turnover as reasoned action: Development of a process model. *Journal of Applied Psychology, 72*, 221-227.

Pryor, B., & Steinfatt, T. M. (1978). The effects of initial belief level on inoculation theory and its proposed mechanisms. *Human Communication Research, 4*, 217-230.

Ramirez, A. (1977). Social influence and ethnicity of the communicator. *Journal of Social Psychology, 102*, 209-213.

Ratneshwar, S., & Chaiken, S. (1986). When is the expert source more persuasive? A heuristic processing analysis. In T. A. Shimp, S. Sharma, G. John, J. A. Quelch, J. H. Lindgren, Jr., W. Dillon, M. P. Gardner, & R. F. Dyer (Eds.), *1986 AMA educators' proceedings* (p. 86). Chicago: American Marketing Association.

Reeves, R. A., Macolini, R. M., & Martin, R. C. (1987). Legitimizing paltry contributions: On-the-spot vs. mail-in requests. *Journal of Applied Social Psychology, 17*, 731-738.

Regan, D. T., & Fazio, R. (1977). On the consistency between attitudes and behavior: Look to the method of attitude formation. *Journal of Experimental Social Psychology, 13*, 28-45.

Reinard, J. C. (1988). The empirical study of the persuasive effects of evidence: The status after fifty years of research. *Human Communication Research, 15*, 3-59.

Reingen, P. H. (1982). Test of a list procedure for inducing compliance with a request to donate money. *Journal of Applied Psychology, 67*, 110-118.

Rhine, R. J. (1967). Some problems in dissonance theory research on information selectivity. *Psychological Bulletin, 68*, 21-28.

Rhine, R. J., & Severance, L. J. (1970). Ego-involvement, discrepancy, source credibility, and attitude change. *Journal of Personality and Social Psychology, 16*, 175-190.

Richter, M. L., & Seay, M. B. (1987). ANOVA designs with subjects and stimuli as random effects: Applications to prototype effects on recognition memory. *Journal of Personality and Social Psychology, 53*, 470-480.

Riddle, P. K. (1980). Attitudes, beliefs, behavioral intentions, and behaviors of women and men toward regular jogging. *Research Quarterly for Exercise and Sport, 51*, 663-674.

Rittle, R. H. (1981). Changes in helping behavior: Self- versus situational perceptions as mediators of the foot-in-the-door effect. *Personality and Social Psychology Bulletin, 7*, 431-437.

Rogers, R. W. (1975). A protection motivation theory of fear appeals and attitude change. *Journal of Psychology, 91*, 93-114.

Romer, D. (1981). A person-situation causal analysis of self-reports of attitudes. *Journal of Personality and Social Psychology, 41*, 562-576.

Romer, D. (1983). Effects of own attitude on polarization of judgment. *Journal of Personality and Social Psychology, 44*, 273-284.

Rosen, S. (1961). Postdecision affinity for incompatible information. *Journal of Abnormal and Social Psychology, 63*, 188-190.

Rosenberg, M. J. (1956). Cognitive structure and attitudinal affect. *Journal of Abnormal and Social Psychology, 53*, 367-372.

Rosenberg, M. J. (1965). When dissonance fails: On eliminating evaluation apprehension from attitude measurement. *Journal of Personality and Social Psychology, 1*, 28-42.

Rosenstock, I. M. (1974). Historical origins of the Health Belief Model. *Health Education Monographs, 2*, 328-335.

Rosenthal, R. (1984). *Meta-analytic procedures for social research.* Beverly Hills, CA: Sage.

Rosnow, R. L. (1966). Whatever happened to the "law of primacy"? *Journal of Communication, 16*, 10-31.

Rosnow, R. L., & Robinson, E. J. (1967). Primacy-recency. In R. L. Rosnow & E. J. Robinson (Eds.), *Experiments in persuasion* (pp. 99-104). New York: Academic Press.

Rueda, R., & Smith, D. C. (1983). Interpersonal tactics and communicative strategies of Anglo-American and Mexican-American mildly mentally retarded and nonretarded students. *Applied Research in Mental Retardation, 4*, 153-161.

Rule, B. G., Bisanz, G. L., & Kohn, M. (1985). Anatomy of a persuasion schema: Targets, goals, and strategies. *Journal of Personality and Social Psychology, 48*, 1127-1140.

Ryan, M. J. (1982). Behavioral intention formation: The interdependency of attitudinal and social influence variables. *Journal of Consumer Research, 9*, 263-278.

Ryan, M. J., & Bonfield, E. H. (1975). The Fishbein extended model and consumer behavior. *Journal of Consumer Research, 2*, 118-136.

Sakaki, H. (1980). Communication discrepancy and ego involvement as determinants of attitude change. *Journal of the Nihon University College of Industrial Technology, 13*, 1-9.

Saltzer, E. B. (1981). Cognitive moderators of the relationship between behavioral intentions and behavior. *Journal of Personality and Social Psychology, 41*, 260-271.

Sampson, E. E., & Insko, C. A. (1964). Cognitive consistency and performance in the autokinetic situation. *Journal of Abnormal and Social Psychology, 68*, 184-192.

Sarver, V. T., Jr. (1983). Ajzen and Fishbein's "theory of reasoned action": A critical assessment. *Journal for the Theory of Social Behavior, 13*, 155-163.

Sawyer, A. G. (1988). Can there be effective advertising without explicit conclusions? Decide for yourself. In S. Hecker & D. W. Stewart (Eds.), *Nonverbal communication in advertising* (pp. 159-184). Lexington, MA: D. C. Heath.

Schenck-Hamlin, W. J. (1978). The effects of dialectical similarity, stereotyping, and message agreement on interpersonal perceptions. *Human Communication Research, 5*, 15-26.

Schenck-Hamlin, W. J., Wiseman, R. L., & Georgacarakos, G. N. (1982). A model of properties of compliance-gaining strategies. *Communication Quarterly, 30*, 92-100.

Schifter, D. E., & Ajzen, I. (1985). Intention, perceived control, and weight loss: An application of the theory of planned behavior. *Journal of Personality and Social Psychology, 49*, 843-851.

Schlegel, R. P., Crawford, C. A., & Sanborn, M. D. (1977). Correspondence and mediational properties of the Fishbein model: An application to adolescent alcohol use. *Journal of Experimental Social Psychology, 13*, 421-430.

Schliesser, H. F. (1968). Information transmission and ethos of a speaker using normal and defective speech. *Central States Speech Journal, 19*, 169-174.

Schonbach, P. (1980). A category system for account phases. *European Journal of Social Psychology, 10*, 195-200.

Schweitzer, D., & Ginsburg, G. P. (1966). Factors of communicator credibility. In C. W. Backman & P. F. Secord (Eds.), *Problems in social psychology* (pp. 94-102). New York: McGraw-Hill.

Scott, M. B., & Lyman, S. M. (1968). Accounts. *American Sociological Review, 33*, 46-62.

Scott, W. A. (1969). Attitude measurement. In G. Lindzey & E. Aronson (Eds.), *Handbook of social psychology* (2nd ed., Vol. 2, pp. 204-273). Reading, MA: Addison-Wesley.

Searle, J. R. (1969). *Speech acts.* Cambridge: Cambridge University Press.

Sears, D. O. (1965). Biased indoctrination and selectivity of exposure to new information. *Sociometry, 28*, 363-376.

Sears, D. O., & Freedman, J. L. (1967). Selective exposure to information: A critical review. *Public Opinion Quarterly, 31*, 194-213.

Seibold, D. R. (1988). A response to "Item desirability in compliance-gaining research." *Human Communication Research, 15*, 152-161.

Seibold, D. R., Cantrill, J. G., & Meyers, R. A. (1985). Communication and interpersonal influence. In M. L. Knapp & G. R. Miller (Eds.), *Handbook of interpersonal communication* (pp. 551-611). Beverly Hills, CA: Sage.

Seibold, D. R., & Roper, R. E. (1979). Psychosocial determinants of health care intentions: Test of the Triandis and Fishbein models. In D. Nimmo (Ed.), *Communication yearbook 3* (pp. 625-643). New Brunswick, NJ: Transaction.

Seligman, C., Hall, D., & Finegan, J. (1983). Predicting home energy consumption: An application of the Fishbein-Ajzen model. In R. P. Bagozzi & A. M. Tybout (Eds.), *Advances in consumer research* (Vol. 10, pp. 647-651). Ann Arbor, MI: Association for Consumer Research.

Sereno, K. K., & Hawkins, G. J. (1967). The effects of variations in speakers' nonfluency upon audience ratings of attitude toward the speech topic and speakers' credibility. *Speech Monographs, 34*, 58-64.

Settle, R. B., & Golden, L. L. (1974). Attribution theory and advertiser credibility. *Journal of Marketing Research, 11*, 181-185.

Shavitt, S. (1989). Operationalizing functional theories of attitude. In A. R. Pratkanis, S. J. Breckler, & A. G. Greenwald (Eds.), *Attitude structure and function* (pp. 311-337). Hillsdale, NJ: Lawrence Erlbaum.

Shepherd, G. J. (1985). Linking attitudes and behavioral criteria. *Human Communication Research, 12*, 275-284. (Erratum notice: *Human Communication Research, 12*, 358)

Shepherd, G. J. (1987). Individual differences in the relationship between attitudinal and normative determinants of behavioral intent. *Communication Monographs, 54*, 221-231.

Shepherd, G. J., & O'Keefe, B. J. (1984). The relationship between the developmental level of persuasive strategies and their effectiveness. *Central States Speech Journal, 35*, 137-152.

Shepherd, G. J., & O'Keefe, D. J. (1984). Separability of attitudinal and normative influences on behavioral intentions in the Fishbein-Ajzen model. *Journal of Social Psychology, 122*, 287-288.

Sheppard, B. H., Hartwick, J., & Warshaw, P. R. (1988). The theory of reasoned action: A meta-analysis of past research with recommendations for modifications and future research. *Journal of Consumer Research, 15*, 325-343.

Sherblom, J., & Reinsch, N. L., Jr. (1981). Persuasive intent as a determinant of phonemic choice. *Journal of Psycholinguistic Research, 10*, 619-628.

Sherif, C. W. (1980). Social values, attitudes, and involvement of the self. In M. M. Page (Ed.), *Nebraska Symposium on Motivation 1979: Beliefs, attitudes, and values* (pp. 1-64). Lincoln: University of Nebraska Press.

Sherif, C. W., Kelly, M., Rodgers, H. L., Jr., Sarup, G., & Tittler, B. I. (1973). Personal involvement, social judgment and action. *Journal of Personality and Social Psychology, 27*, 311-328.

Sherif, C. W., Sherif, M., & Nebergall, R. E. (1965). *Attitude and attitude change: The social judgment-involvement approach.* Philadelphia: W. B. Saunders.

Sherif, M., & Hovland, C. I. (1961). *Social judgment: Assimilation and contrast effects in communication and attitude change.* New Haven, CT: Yale University Press.

Sheth, J. N., & Talarzyk, W. W. (1972). Perceived instrumentality and value importance as determinants of attitudes. *Journal of Marketing Research, 9*, 6-9.

Shimp, T. A., & Kavas, A. (1984). The theory of reasoned action applied to coupon usage. *Journal of Consumer Research, 11*, 795-809.

Shotland, R. L., Berger, W. G., & Forsythe, R. (1970). A validation of the lost-letter technique. *Public Opinion Quarterly, 34*, 278-281.

Sikkink, D. (1956). An experimental study of the effects on the listener of anticlimax order and authority in an argumentative speech. *Southern Speech Journal, 22*, 73-78.

Sillars, A. L. (1980). The stranger and the spouse as target persons for compliance-gaining strategies: A subjective expected utility model. *Human Communication Research, 6*, 265-279.

Silverman, I. (1964). Differential effects of ego threat upon persuasibility for high and low self-esteem subjects. *Journal of Abnormal and Social Psychology, 69*, 567-572.

Silverthorne, C. P., & Mazmanian, L. (1975). The effects of heckling and media of presentation on the impact of a persuasive communication. *Journal of Social Psychology, 96*, 229-236.

Simons, H. W. (1976). *Persuasion: Understanding, practice, and analysis.* Reading, MA: Addison-Wesley.

Simons, H. W. (1986). *Persuasion: Understanding, practice, and analysis* (2nd ed.). New York: Random House.

Simons, H. W., Berkowitz, N. N., & Moyer, R. J. (1970). Similarity, credibility, and attitude change: A review and a theory. *Psychological Bulletin, 73*, 1-16.

Sinha, S. R. (1985). Maternal strategies for regulating children's behavior. *Journal of Cross-Cultural Psychology, 16*, 27-40.

Sjoberg, L. (1982). Attitude-behavior correlation, social desirability, and perceived diagnostic value. *British Journal of Social Psychology, 21*, 283-292.

Skolnick, P., & Heslin, R. (1971). Quality versus difficulty: Alternative interpretations of the relationship between self-esteem and persuasibility. *Journal of Personality, 39*, 242-251.

Smetana, J. G., & Adler, N. E. (1980). Fishbein's value x expectancy model: An examination of some assumptions. *Personality and Social Psychology Bulletin, 6*, 89-96.

Smith, B. L., Brown, B. L., Strong, W. J., & Rencher, A. C. (1975). Effects of speech rate on personality perception. *Language and Speech, 18*, 145-152.

Smith, M. J. (1978). Discrepancy and the importance of attitudinal freedom. *Human Communication Research, 4*, 308-314.

Smith, R. E., & Hunt, S. D. (1978). Attributional processes and effects in promotional situations. *Journal of Consumer Research, 5*, 149-158.

Smith, R. E., & Swinyard, W. R. (1983). Attitude-behavior consistency: The impact of product trial versus advertising. *Journal of Marketing Research, 20*, 257-267.

Smith, T. E. (1988). Parental control techniques: Relative frequencies and relationships with situational factors. *Journal of Family Issues, 9*, 155-176.

Snyder, M. (1974). Self-monitoring of expressive behavior. *Journal of Personality and Social Psychology, 30*, 526-537.

Snyder, M. (1979). Self-monitoring processes. In L. Berkowitz (Ed.), *Advances in experimental social psychology* (Vol. 12, pp. 85-128). New York: Academic Press.

Snyder, M. (1982). When believing means doing: Creating links between attitudes and behavior. In M. P. Zanna, E. T. Higgins, & C. P. Herman (Eds.), *Consistency in social behavior: The Ontario Symposium, vol. 2* (pp. 105-130). Hillsdale, NJ: Lawrence Erlbaum.

Snyder, M., & DeBono, K. G. (1989). Understanding the functions of attitudes: Lessons from personality and social behavior. In A. R. Pratkanis, S. J. Breckler, & A. G. Greenwald (Eds.), *Attitude structure and function* (pp. 339-359). Hillsdale, NJ: Lawrence Erlbaum.

Snyder, M., & Kendzierski, D. (1982). Acting on one's attitudes: Procedures for linking attitude and behavior. *Journal of Experimental Social Psychology, 18*, 165-183.

Snyder, M., & Rothbart, M. (1971). Communicator attractiveness and opinion change. *Canadian Journal of Behavioral Science, 3*, 377-387.

Snyder, M., & Swann, W. B., Jr. (1976). When actions reflect attitudes: The politics of impression management. *Journal of Personality and Social Psychology, 34*, 1034-1042.

Soley, L. C. (1986). Copy length and industrial advertising readership. *Industrial Marketing Management, 15*, 245-251.

Sorensen, G., Plax, T. G., & Kearney, P. (1989). The strategy selection-construction controversy: A coding scheme for analyzing teacher compliance-gaining message constructions. *Communication Education, 38*, 102-118.

Sperber, B. M., Fishbein, M., & Ajzen, I. (1980). Predicting and understanding women's occupational orientations: Factors underlying choice intentions. In I. Ajzen & M. Fishbein (Eds.), *Understanding attitudes and predicting social behavior* (pp. 113-129). Englewood Cliffs, NJ: Prentice-Hall.

Sponberg, H. (1946). A study of the relative effectiveness of climax and anti-climax order in an argumentative speech. *Speech Monographs, 13*, 35-44.

Staats, A. W., & Staats, C. K. (1958). Attitudes established by classical conditioning. *Journal of Abnormal and Social Psychology, 57*, 37-40.

Stainback, R. D., & Rogers, R. W. (1983). Identifying effective components of alcohol abuse prevention programs: Effects of fear appeals, message style, and source expertise. *International Journal of the Addictions, 18*, 393-405.

Steinfatt, T. M. (1974). A criticism of "Dimensions of source credibility: A test for reproducibility." *Speech Monographs, 41*, 291-292.

Steinfatt, T. M. (1977). Measurement, transformations, and the real world: Do the numbers represent the concept? *Et Cetera, 34*, 277-289.

Sternthal, B., Dholakia, R., & Leavitt, C. (1978). The persuasive effect of source credibility: Tests of cognitive response. *Journal of Consumer Research, 4*, 252-260.

Stiff, J. B. (1986). Cognitive processing of persuasive message cues: A meta-analytic review of the effects of supporting information on attitudes. *Communication Monographs, 53*, 75-89.

Stiff, J. B., & Boster, F. J. (1987). Cognitive processing: Additional thoughts and a reply to Petty, Kasmer, Haugtvedt, and Cacioppo. *Communication Monographs, 54*, 250-256.

Street, R. L., Jr., & Brady, R. M. (1982). Speech rate acceptance ranges as a function of evaluative domain, listener speech rate, and communication context. *Communication Monographs, 49*, 290-308.

Stults, D. M., Messe, L. A., & Kerr, N. L. (1984). Belief discrepant behavior and the bogus pipeline: Impression management or arousal attribution. *Journal of Experimental Social Psychology, 20*, 47-54.

Stutman, R. K., & Newell, S. E. (1984). Beliefs versus values: Salient beliefs in designing a persuasive message. *Western Journal of Speech Communication, 48*, 362-372.

Summers, G. F. (Ed.). (1970). *Attitude measurement.* Chicago: Rand McNally.

Sutton, S. R. (1982). Fear-arousing communications: A critical examination of theory and research. In J. R. Eiser (Ed.), *Social psychology and behavioral medicine* (pp. 303-337). New York: Wiley.

Sutton, S. R., & Eiser, J. R. (1984). The effect of fear-arousing communications on cigarette smoking: An expectancy-value approach. *Journal of Behavioral Medicine, 7*, 13-33.

Sutton, S. R., & Hallett, R. (1988). Understanding the effects of fear-arousing communications: The role of cognitive factors and amount of fear aroused. *Journal of Behavioral Medicine, 11*, 353-360.

Sutton, S. R., & Hallett, R. (1989). The contribution of fear and cognitive factors in mediating the effects of fear-arousing communications. *Social Behavior, 4*, 83-98.

Swanson, D. L. (1976). Information utility: An alternative perspective in political communication. *Central States Speech Journal, 27*, 95-101.

Swartz, T. A. (1984). Relationship between source expertise and source similarity in an advertising context. *Journal of Advertising, 13*(2), 49-55.

Swasy, J. L., & Munch, J. M. (1985). Examining the target of receiver elaborations: Rhetorical question effects on source processing and persuasion. *Journal of Consumer Research, 11*, 877-886.

Swenson, R. A., Nash, D. L., & Roos, D. C. (1984). Source credibility and perceived expertness of testimony in a simulated child-custody case. *Professional Psychology, 15*, 891-898.

Szybillo, G. J., & Heslin, R. (1973). Resistance to persuasion: Inoculation theory in a marketing context. *Journal of Marketing Research, 10*, 396-403.

Tamborini, R., & Zillmann, D. (1981). College students' perceptions of lecturers using humor. *Perceptual and Motor Skills, 52*, 427-432.

Tanaka, J. S., Panter, A. T., & Winborne, W. C. (1988). Dimensions of the need for cognition: Subscales and gender differences. *Multivariate Behavioral Research, 23*, 35-50.

Taylor, P. M. (1974). An experimental study of humor and ethos. *Southern Speech Communication Journal, 39*, 359-366.

Taylor, S. E., & Thompson, S. C. (1982). Stalking the elusive "vividness" effect. *Psychological Review, 89*, 155-181.

Tedeschi, J. T., Schlenker, B. R., & Bonoma, T. V. (1971). Cognitive dissonance: Private ratiocination or public spectacle? *American Psychologist, 26*, 685-695.

Thistlethwaite, D. L., de Haan, H., & Kamenetzky, J. (1955). The effects of "directive" and "nondirective" communication procedures on attitudes. *Journal of Abnormal and Social Psychology, 51*, 107-113.

Thomas, K. (Ed.). (1971). *Attitudes and behavior.* Baltimore: Penguin.

Thurstone, L. L. (1931). The measurement of social attitudes. *Journal of Abnormal and Social Psychology, 26*, 249-269.

Thurstone, L. L., & Chave, E. J. (1929). *The measurement of attitude.* Chicago: University of Chicago Press.

Tittle, C. R., & Hill, R. J. (1967). Attitude measurement and prediction of behavior: An evaluation of conditions and measurement techniques. *Sociometry, 30*, 199-213.

Tognacci, L. N., & Cook, S. W. (1975). Conditioned autonomic responses as bidirectional indicators of racial attitude. *Journal of Personality and Social Psychology, 31*, 137-144.

Triandis, H. C. (1980). Values, attitudes, and interpersonal behavior. In M. M. Page (Ed.), *Nebraska Symposium on Motivation 1979: Beliefs, attitudes, and values* (pp. 195-259). Lincoln: University of Nebraska Press.

Tubbs, S. L. (1968). Explicit versus implicit conclusions and audience commitment. *Speech Monographs, 35*, 14-19.

Tucker, R. K. (1971). On the McCroskey scales for the measurement of ethos. *Central States Speech Journal, 22*, 127-129.

Tuppen, C. J. S. (1974). Dimensions of communicator credibility: An oblique solution. *Speech Monographs, 41,* 253-260.

Tybout, A. M., Sternthal, B., & Calder, B. J. (1983). Information availability as a determinant of multiple request effectiveness. *Journal of Marketing Research, 20,* 280-290.

Valiquette, C. A. M., Valois, P., Desharnais, R., & Godin, G. (1988). An item-analytic investigation of the Fishbein and Ajzen multiplicative scale: The problem of a simultaneous negative evaluation of belief and outcome. *Psychological Reports, 63,* 723-728.

Valois, P., Desharnais, R., & Godin, G. (1988). A comparison of the Fishbein and Ajzen and the Triandis attitudinal models for the prediction of exercise intention and behavior. *Journal of Behavioral Medicine, 11,* 459-472.

Vecchio, R. P., & Sussman, M. (1989). Preferences for forms of supervisory social influence. *Journal of Organizational Behavior, 10,* 135-143.

Vinokur-Kaplan, D. (1978). To have — or not to have — another child: Family planning attitudes, intentions, and behavior. *Journal of Applied Social Psychology, 8,* 29-46.

Wachtler, J., & Counselman, E. (1981). When increased liking for a communicator decreases opinion change: An attribution analysis of attractiveness. *Journal of Experimental Social Psychology, 17,* 386-395.

Wagner, W. (1984). Social comparison of opinions: Similarity, ability, and the value-fact distinction. *Journal of Psychology, 117,* 197-202.

Wallis, D. A. (1985). Linguistic correlates of attitude and intention in persuasive communication. *Journal of Social Psychology, 125,* 347-354.

Walster, E. (1964). The temporal sequence of post-decision processes. In L. Festinger (Ed.), *Conflict, decision, and dissonance* (pp. 112-127). Stanford, CA: Stanford University Press.

Walster, E., Aronson, E., & Abrahams, D. (1966). On increasing the persuasiveness of a low prestige communicator. *Journal of Experimental Social Psychology, 2,* 325-342.

Ward, C. D., & McGinnies, E. (1974). Persuasive effects of early and late mention of credible and noncredible sources. *Journal of Psychology, 86,* 17-23.

Warren, I. D. (1969). The effect of credibility in sources of testimony on audience attitudes toward speaker and message. *Speech Monographs, 36,* 456-458.

Warshaw, P. R. (1980). A new model for predicting behavioral intentions: An alternative to Fishbein. *Journal of Marketing Research, 17,* 153-172.

Warshaw, P. R., & Davis, F. D. (1985). Disentangling behavioral intention and behavioral expectation. *Journal of Experimental Social Psychology, 21,* 213-228.

Wartella, E., & Reeves, B. (1985). Historical trends in research on children and the media: 1900-1960. *Journal of Communication, 35*(2), 118-133.

Weigel, R. H., & Newman, L. S. (1976). Increasing attitude-behavior correspondence by broadening the scope of the behavioral measure. *Journal of Personality and Social Psychology, 33,* 793-802.

Weinberger, M. G., & Dillon, W. R. (1980). The effects of unfavorable product rating information. In J. C. Olson (Ed.), *Advances in consumer research* (Vol. 7, pp. 528-532). Ann Arbor, MI: Association for Consumer Research.

Weiss, W., & Steenbock, S. (1965). The influence on communication effectiveness of explicitly urging action and policy consequences. *Journal of Experimental Social Psychology, 1,* 396-406.

Weissberg, N. C. (1964). Commentary on DeFleur and Westie's "Attitude as a scientific concept." *Social Forces, 43,* 422-425.

Wheeless, L. R. (1971). Some effects of time-compressed speech on persuasion. *Journal of Broadcasting, 15,* 415-420.

Wheeless, L. R., Barraclough, R., & Stewart, R. (1983). Compliance-gaining and power in persuasion. In R. N. Bostrom (Ed.), *Communication yearbook 7* (pp. 105-145). Beverly Hills, CA: Sage.

White, G. L., & Gerard, H. B. (1981). Postdecision evaluation of choice alternatives as a function of valence of alternatives, choice, and expected delay of choice consequences. *Journal of Research in Personality, 15,* 371-382.

Whitehead, J. L., Jr. (1968). Factors of source credibility. *Quarterly Journal of Speech, 54*, 59-63.

Whitehead, J. L., Jr. (1971). Effects of authority-based assertion on attitude and credibility. *Speech Monographs, 38*, 311-315.

Whittaker, J. O. (1963). Opinion change as a function of communication-attitude discrepancy. *Psychological Reports, 13*, 763-772.

Whittaker, J. O. (1965). Attitude change and communication-attitude discrepancy. *Journal of Social Psychology, 65*, 141-147.

Whittaker, J. O. (1967). Resolution of the communication discrepancy issue in attitude change. In C. W. Sherif & M. Sherif (Eds.), *Attitude, ego-involvement, and change* (pp. 159-177). New York: Wiley.

Wicker, A. W. (1969). Attitudes versus actions: The relationship of verbal and overt behavioral responses to attitude objects. *Journal of Social Issues, 25*(4), 41-78.

Wicker, A. W. (1971). An examination of the "other variables" explanation of attitude-behavior inconsistency. *Journal of Personality and Social Psychology, 19*, 18-30.

Wicklund, R. A., & Brehm, J. W. (1976). *Perspectives on cognitive dissonance.* Hillsdale, NJ: Lawrence Erlbaum.

Widgery, R. N. (1974). Sex of receiver and physical attractiveness of source as determinants of initial credibility perception. *Western Speech, 38*, 13-17.

Widgery, R. N., & Ruch, R. S. (1981). Beauty and the Machiavellian. *Communication Quarterly, 29*, 297-301.

Wiener, J. L., & Mowen, J. C. (1986). Source credibility: On the independent effects of trust and expertise. In R. J. Lutz (Ed.), *Advances in consumer research* (Vol. 13, pp. 306-310). Provo, UT: Association for Consumer Research.

Wilmot, W. W. (1971a). Ego-involvement: A confusing variable in speech communication research. *Quarterly Journal of Speech, 57*, 429-436.

Wilmot, W. W. (1971b). A test of the construct and predictive validity of three measures of ego involvement. *Speech Monographs, 38*, 217-227.

Wiseman, R. L., & Schenck-Hamlin, W. (1981). A multidimensional scaling validation of an inductively-derived set of compliance-gaining strategies. *Communication Monographs, 48*, 251-270.

Wittenbraker, J., Gibbs, B. L., & Kahle, L. R. (1983). Seat belt attitudes, habits, and behaviors: An adaptive amendment to the Fishbein model. *Journal of Applied Social Psychology, 13*, 406-421.

Wood, W. (1982). Retrieval of attitude-relevant information from memory: Effects on susceptibility to persuasion and on intrinsic motivation. *Journal of Personality and Social Psychology, 42*, 798-810.

Wood, W., & Eagly, A. H. (1981). Stages in the analysis of persuasive messages: The role of causal attributions and message comprehension. *Journal of Personality and Social Psychology, 40*, 246-259.

Wood, W., & Kallgren, C. A. (1988). Communicator attributes and persuasion: Recipients' access to attitude-relevant information in memory. *Personality and Social Psychology Bulletin, 14*, 172-182.

Wood, W., Kallgren, C. A., & Preisler, R. M. (1985). Access to attitude-relevant information in memory as a determinant of persuasion: The role of message attributes. *Journal of Experimental Social Psychology, 21*, 73-85.

Woodall, W. G., & Burgoon, J. K. (1983). Talking fast and changing attitudes: A critique and clarification. *Journal of Nonverbal Behavior, 8*, 126-142.

Woodmansee, J. J. (1970). The pupil response as a measure of social attitudes. In G. F. Summers (Ed.), *Attitude measurement* (pp. 514-533). Chicago: Rand McNally.

Woodside, A. G., & Davenport, J. W., Jr. (1974). The effect of salesman similarity and expertise on consumer purchasing behavior. *Journal of Marketing Research, 11*, 198-202.

Worchel, S., Andreoli, V., & Eason, J. (1975). Is the medium the message? A study of the effects of media, communicator, and message characteristics on attitude change. *Journal of Applied Social Psychology, 5*, 157-172.

Wyer, R. S., Jr. (1974). *Cognitive organization and change: An information processing approach.* Hillsdale, NJ: Lawrence Erlbaum.

Yamagishi, T., & Hill, C. T. (1981). Adding versus averaging models revisited: A test of a path-analytic integration model. *Journal of Personality and Social Psychology, 41,* 13-25.

Zaichkowsky, J. L. (1985). Measuring the involvement construct. *Journal of Consumer Research, 12,* 341-352.

Zanna, M. P., & Cooper, J. (1974). Dissonance and the pill: An attribution approach to studying the arousal properties of dissonance. *Journal of Personality and Social Psychology, 29,* 703-709.

Zanna, M. P., & Cooper, J. (1976). Dissonance and the attribution process. In J. H. Harvey, W. J. Ickes, & R. F. Kidd (Eds.), *New directions in attribution research* (Vol. 1, pp. 199-217). Hillsdale, NJ: Lawrence Erlbaum.

Zanna, M. P., & Fazio, R. H. (1982). The attitude-behavior relation: Moving toward a third generation of research. In M. P. Zanna, E. T. Higgins, & C. P. Herman (Eds.), *Consistency in social behavior: The Ontario Symposium, vol. 2* (pp. 283-301). Hillsdale, NJ: Lawrence Erlbaum.

Zanna, M. P., Olson, J. M., & Fazio, R. H. (1980). Attitude-behavior consistency: An individual difference perspective. *Journal of Personality and Social Psychology, 38,* 432-440.

Zimbardo, P. G. (1960). Involvement and communication discrepancy as determinants of opinion conformity. *Journal of Abnormal and Social Psychology, 60,* 86-94.

Zimbardo, P. G., Weisenberg, M., Firestone, I., & Levy, B. (1965). Communicator effectiveness in producing public conformity and private attitude change. *Journal of Personality, 33,* 233-255.

Zuckerman, M., & Reis, H. T. (1978). Comparison of three models for predicting altruistic behavior. *Journal of Personality and Social Psychology, 36,* 498-510.

Author Index

256

Subject Index

About the Author

DANIEL J. O'KEEFE is an Associate Professor in the Department of Speech Communication, University of Illinois at Urbana-Champaign. He received his Ph.D. from the University of Illinois, and has taught at the University of Michigan and Pennsylvania State University. His work has received the Speech Communication Association's Charles Woolbert Research Award, the Speech Communication Association's Golden Anniversary Monograph Award, and the American Forensic Association's Outstanding Monograph Award.